Edward Bancroft

Edward Bancroft
Scientist, Author, Spy

THOMAS J. SCHAEPER

Yale

UNIVERSITY PRESS

New Haven & London

Published with assistance from the Annie Burr Lewis Fund.

Yale University Press books may be purchased in quantity for
educational, business, or promotional use. For information, please
e-mail sales.press@yale.edu (U.S. office) or sales@yaleup.co.uk
(U.K. office).

Set in Adobe Caslon type by Westchester Book Group.
Printed in the United States of America.

Library of Congress Cataloging-in-Publication Data
Schaeper, Thomas J.
Edward Bancroft : scientist, author, spy / Thomas J. Schaeper.
p.   cm.
Includes bibliographical references and index.
ISBN 978-0-300-11842-1 (clothbound : alk. paper)   1. Bancroft,
Edward, 1744–1821.   2. Spies–United States—Biography.
3. United States—History—Revolution, 1775–1783—Secret
service.   I. Title.
E280.B36S33 2011
973.3'86092—dc22
[B]
2010037928

A catalogue record for this book is available from the British
Library.

This paper meets the requirements of ANSI/NISO Z39.48-1992
(Permanence of Paper).

10   9   8   7   6   5   4   3   2   1

IN MEMORY OF MOM AND DAD
Who Sacrificed So Much for Us

History teaches us to expect spies among us and to anticipate that some of those spies will be of us. Espionage has not been invented by our recent adversaries, and it is not a sign of our political or moral decline. In fact, we have been beset by spies from within even before we had a Constitution to unite us. For instance, Edward Bancroft, a New England physician who served as secretary to the commission the American colonies sent to France during the Revolutionary War, was a confidant of Benjamin Franklin, an indispensable agent of John Adams, and a British spy. He sent London weekly communications in invisible ink and placed in a hole in a tree in the Tuileries Gardens. The rebellious colonies did not have to wait long for other disastrous betrayals, and, indeed, from our Country's early history on, the name Benedict Arnold has signified a traitor from within.

—WILLIAM H. WEBSTER, former director of the FBI, in a report on security submitted to the attorney general of the United States, 2002

Dr. Bancroft . . . you will find [to be] a very intelligent, sensible man, well acquainted with the state of affairs here, and who has heretofore been employed in the service of Congress. I have long known him, and esteem him highly.

—BENJAMIN FRANKLIN to Robert R. Livingston, 1783

Americans have committed a great injustice in making Benedict Arnold the archtraitor of the Revolution. That eminence rightfully belongs to Dr. Bancroft.

—BURTON J. HENDRICK, "Worse Than Arnold," 1935

Contents

Acknowledgments

The genesis of this book goes back nearly thirty years, to when I first met Claude-Anne Lopez. It was she who encouraged me to switch my research interests from the early to the late eighteenth century and to broaden my focus from French history to include Britain and America. Among other things, Claude spoke tantalizingly of the mysteries surrounding Edward Bancroft, and she wondered why no one had yet thoroughly investigated him. At long last I have finally taken up Claude's challenge and grabbed Bancroft before someone else did.

Many friends have aided me with advice and moral support as I worked on this project. Hearty thanks go to Jonathan R. Dull, James R. Taylor III, Cora Niver, and Kathleen Schaeper for their careful reading of drafts of the entire manuscript. Parts of it were also read by N. Gaye Redpath-Schaeper, Kate Ohno, Phillip G. Payne, and Rachel Engl. As I was nearing the end of this project, Elizabeth M. Nuxoll and Michael Sletcher went far above the call of friendship in tracking down answers to various questions, calling my attention to documents that I had failed to consult, and saving me from numerous factual blunders. As with all of my previous books, this one would not have been possible without the amazing work of interlibrary loan librarian Theresa Shaffer. If I were told that she was faster than a speeding bullet and could leap tall buildings in a single bound, I would believe it. Others who have helped me in sundry ways over the years include Ellen Cohn, Dennis Kent Anderson, Penelope Hunting, Tom Missel, Emily Schaeper, and Justin Schaeper.

A large part of this book is based on documents in about two dozen libraries and archives in Britain, France, and the United States. I owe a particular debt to the many staff members at the British Library and Britain's National Archives who answered my queries and cheerfully helped me in my sometimes clumsy efforts to find the materials I needed. In addition, I wish to give special mention to Jo Currie of Edinburgh University; Colin A. McLaren of the University of Aberdeen; Alison Rosie of the National Register of Archives for Scotland; Peter Carini and Barbara L. Krieger of Dartmouth College; Elizabeth Carroll-Horrocks of the American Academy of Arts and Sciences; Robin Wiltshire of the Sheffield Archives; Colonel R. D. Kinsella-Bevan of the Medical Society of London; Sophie Cawthorne of the Royal Society of Arts; Joanna Hopkins of the Royal Society; and Joan B. Ackerman of the Westfield Athenaeum.

Thanks to Google, I was able to locate several Bancroft descendants living in England. Not only did they welcome my interest in their ancestor, but they generously shared with me their private manuscript collections, family portraits, and genealogical research. Mere words fail to convey the debts I owe to John and Linda Green, Anthony and Daryll Bancroft Cooke, Ray and Alicia Salter, and William and Angela Moberly.

I have had the good fortune to work with some splendid professionals at Yale University Press. Lara Heimert was the executive editor who gave me an enthusiastic go-ahead at the start, while her successor, Christopher Rogers, offered calm encouragement and advice at the end. Associate editors Laura Davulis and Christina Tucker and manuscript editor Laura Jones Dooley provided cheerful and indispensable aid in the final stages of production.

Introduction

It was about nine o'clock on a Tuesday evening in Paris in January 1778. A rather ordinary-looking man could be seen strolling through the Tuileries Gardens. He appeared to be in his midthirties, a bit shorter and stouter than average. Any passerby who might have asked him for directions or the hour could have perceived that he spoke French with an accent that was British—or possibly American. The man seemed perfectly respectable, but a curious observer might have noticed him looking over his shoulder to see if he was being watched. When he was certain that he was unobserved, he darted over to a tree on the south terrace, took some papers from his coat pocket, placed them in a glass bottle, tied a string to the bottle, and deposited it into a hole in the tree.

Who was this man? If someone had asked him, he might have said that he was Dr. Edwards. This was the name signed on the papers deposited in the tree. If the curious onlooker had remained at the scene about an hour longer, he would have noticed that eventually another man stealthily made his way into the gardens, strode to the same tree, extracted the papers from the bottle, placed some other papers in the bottle, dropped the bottle back into the tree, and scurried away.

Who was this Dr. Edwards? What was in those papers? These questions form part of the amazing story of one of the most daring spies of all time. "Dr. Edwards" was one of the aliases used by Edward Bancroft. A native of Massachusetts, Bancroft had been living in London in the years leading up to the American Revolution. From 1776 to 1783 he spent most of his time in Paris, where he formed close associations with Benjamin Franklin, John Adams, John Paul Jones, the Marquis de Lafayette, and a host of other prominent Americans and Frenchmen. He became their friend, assistant, and confidant. Unbeknownst to any of them, he was working that entire time as a secret agent of the British government. The papers inserted into the tree in January 1778 provided intelligence about secret French aid for the Americans and details about a Franco-American alliance that was being negotiated. Thanks in large part to Bancroft, King George III's government would know of that secret treaty before it was formally signed a few weeks later. From 1776 to the end of the American Revolution, Bancroft worked relentlessly to keep the Crown informed of everything important regarding French participation in the colonial rebellion.

Remarkable as Bancroft's story is, until now it has never received the detailed examination it deserves. Indeed, only in 1889 did scholars discover the first conclusive bits of evidence regarding his espionage. In his lifetime, Bancroft was well known as a physician, natural historian, novelist, political commentator, businessman, and expert in inks and dyes. Not exactly an eighteenth-century James Bond. In 1889, however, an American researcher received permission to publish facsimile copies of thousands of previously closed British diplomatic archival documents. Only then did he and, soon thereafter, readers on both sides of the Atlantic discover the incredible story of "Dr. Edwards."

In the years since 1889, virtually all historians who have written about French involvement in the American Revolution have mentioned Bancroft briefly in their books. Two American students have written master's theses on him. A handful of authors have devoted book chapters or journal articles to him. Almost invariably, they have portrayed him as an arch-traitor to his country. They have described him as "villainous," "sinister," "devious," "dishonorable," and a "natural intriguer." Some have called him the greatest spy of all time. Others have said he was more despicable than Benedict Arnold. Many have also stated that the unprincipled Bancroft was a double agent, taking money from both the Americans and the British. A few have even accused him of murder, claiming that he poisoned one American who knew of his espionage.

Bancroft had access to nearly every important paper or conversation that such people as Benjamin Franklin, John Adams, Silas Deane, Arthur Lee, and John Paul Jones had in France. Through his bottles in a tree, special ciphers, invisible inks, and private messengers, the British government quickly learned of everything the Americans in France were planning. Bancroft provided intelligence on treaty negotiations at the start and at the end of the fighting, and in the intervening years he gave London advance notice of hundreds of ships leaving French ports. Because of his treachery, the Revolution lasted much longer and caused the loss of more lives and property than would have happened otherwise. So, at any rate, goes the standard view of this man.

But because no one until now has examined Bancroft's entire life and perused the thousands of relevant documents in American, British, and French archives, these assertions about him have gone untested. Was he a traitor to his country? Was he a double agent, working for both the Americans and the British? What motivated a noted scientist and author to give up his scholarly pursuits and for nearly seven years serve as a spy? Just how important was his secret intelligence to the British ministry? How did he operate and manage to keep his work hidden? Did Franklin or any other American know that he was a British agent? These are just a few of the questions that I endeavor to answer in this book.

In the 1990s I published two books involving the American Revolution—one on John Paul Jones and the other on Jacques-Donatien Leray de Chaumont. In working on those two books, I repeatedly came across Bancroft's name. After completing those books, I turned for a few years to other topics. But I could not get Bancroft off of my mind. Eventually I checked with a variety of experts in the field, and they assured me that Bancroft was still open for the taking. One even exclaimed that Bancroft was "the best topic out there."

Almost as puzzling as the man himself is that until now he has eluded a biographer. He has, however, attracted the attention of a novelist. In 1987 Arthur Mullin published *Spy: America's First Double Agent, Dr. Edward Bancroft*. As a novel, it is a melodrama—filled with lurid sex, violence, corruption, and one-dimensional characters. As historical fiction, it is a travesty.

Normally, when one reads a historical novel, one expects that the characters and events will stick fairly closely to the known facts. Those parts of a novel that depart from the known facts should at least be plausible. Mullin's novel, however, gets far more things wrong than right. For example, at the beginning of the story, one finds that the fictional Edward Bancroft is a tall, muscular man who is able single-handedly to fend off gangs of street thugs. He is in a loveless marriage to a wealthy woman named Olivia. In fact, however, Bancroft was not a man of heroic stature and action. His wife was named Penelope, and she did not come from a wealthy family. At the end of the novel the treacherous, devious main character suffers an unfortunate misadventure; he is assumed to be a homeless, deranged scavenger. The story ends in December 1777, with Edward Bancroft languishing away in the Bedlam asylum for the insane. The real Bancroft was never taken for a lunatic and was never incarcerated in Bedlam. Instead, he lived as a respected man of the world until his peaceful death in 1821.

Because of the many errors about Bancroft that exist in the pages of fiction and nonfiction, the time has come to give a full and accurate account of his life. The present book is much different from the one I first envisaged. My initial interest in Bancroft focused on his spy activities. When I began to delve into that story, however, it became clear that his years as a British agent in France were but a small part of a long and interesting career. Gradually I saw that his life was worth studying in and of itself. I realized, moreover, that many aspects of his espionage could be understood only when put in the context of his broader pursuits. Thus, my book on spying has evolved into a full biography.

1 *Early Life*

The Bancroft Family

The first thing to clear up about Edward Bartholomew Bancroft is the date of his birth. Depending on the book, article, or encyclopedia entry, one can read that he was born on the ninth or the twentieth of January, in either 1744 or 1745. All of these are correct. In the Julian calendar, still used in Britain and its colonies, he was born on 9 January 1744. The Julian calendar was at that time eleven days behind the Gregorian calendar, which had been adopted by all Catholic and most Protestant countries in the sixteenth and seventeenth centuries. Moreover, as late as the mid-eighteenth century in Britain and some other countries, the new year did not start until 25 March. In September 1752 Britain and its colonies switched to the Gregorian calendar and established 1 January as the start of the new year. Edward Bancroft's birth, when translated into the new calendar, occurred on 20 January 1745. The custom among historians when dealing with persons born in the first half of the eighteenth century is to change dates to the Gregorian. Benjamin Franklin, for example, was born on 6 January 1705 in the old style, but nowadays everyone who writes of him gives 17 January 1706 as his birth date. This book follows suit and uses the new style date for Bancroft.[1]

On his father's side, Edward was descended from John Bancroft and his wife, Jane, both of whom had left London in April 1632 in the ship *James* and arrived about eight weeks later in the Puritan Massachusetts Bay colony. They and their descendants appear to have been of solid yeoman stock—mainly farmers and tradespeople. One of these descendants, another John Bancroft, was born in Windsor, Connecticut, in 1679 but eventually moved to Westfield, Massachusetts, where he died in October 1749. He had eight children, seven from his first marriage and one from his second. The third eldest of his children was born in Westfield in August 1718 and was named Edward. In February 1744, Edward married Mary Ely, from Springfield, Massachusetts. In January 1745 they had their first child, the Edward who is the subject of this book. A second child, a boy named Daniel, was born in November 1746. By that time, however, the father had died, at age twenty-eight, of an epileptic seizure while working in a pigsty on his farm. Mary was left to fend for herself with the two infant boys.[2]

Prospects for the trio could not have looked good. The estate included about a hundred acres of land—scattered in twelve separate parcels in and around Westfield—plus a house, a barn, one cow, two heifers, one bull, and a few household items.[3] In January 1751 the young widow married David Bull, also of Westfield. Soon thereafter the family settled in Hartford, Connecticut. Through the 1750s they moved from Hartford to Springfield, back to Westfield, and then again to Hartford.[4] In Hartford, Bull became the proprietor of a tavern called the Bunch of Grapes. Little is known of the childhood and education of the two boys. Neither had much in the way of formal education. After the family moved back to Hartford, in April 1759, a tutor was hired for Edward. The instructor was Silas Deane, a recent graduate of Yale College. Edward was about fifteen years old, Deane twenty-two. The boy's studies with Deane probably lasted only a few months.

We know of Bancroft's early association with Deane only because many years later on two separate occasions Bancroft happened to mention it. The first came in the spring of 1778, when Bancroft met John Adams, who had recently arrived in France. In their conversations, Bancroft told Adams something about his background, and Adams recorded in his memoirs that Bancroft "had been a School Boy" under Deane.[5] The second occasion came in May 1790, in a letter Bancroft wrote to the famous clergyman scientist Joseph Priestley. Priestley had written to Bancroft to inquire about the circumstances of Silas Deane's death in September 1789. In his response, Bancroft mentioned that he had been "partly educated" by his deceased friend.[6] The relationship between Deane and Bancroft in the late 1750s therefore was brief and of little consequence. Many years later, however, the two men would become close friends and partners.

In October 1760 the Bancroft family moved to Killingworth, Connecticut. There, Edward was apprenticed to a local physician, Dr. Benjamin Gale. There is no indication of how much money the parents paid the doctor or of how many years Edward was obligated to work for him. At that time in colonial America, only a small minority of physicians and surgeons had degrees from medical schools in Britain.[7] The usual custom was for a boy to be apprenticed to a practicing doctor, usually for two to six years. When the young man felt competent to set out on his own, he established a separate practice. All this was done without any medical degrees or government licensing. There is also some evidence that either before or after the move to Killingworth Edward had some sort of relationship with a physician in Lebanon, Connecticut, one Thomas Williams.[8] Little is known of Edward's medical education over the next two and a half years, but evidently he was not happy with his situation. In June 1763 he broke his apprenticeship contract with Gale and sailed on the brig *Success,* bound for Barbados.[9] In December of that year he wrote two letters to Williams. In the first, he lamented that he had been "a friendless youth." In the second he recalled that "Insults received, a Haughty Disposition, and a Roving Fancy, conspired in effecting this Adventure."[10]

Travels in South America

Running away to sea did not make Bancroft different from countless thousands of other young American and European men. For Bancroft, however, it was the beginning of a career that would indeed mark him as exceptional.

After a few weeks in Barbados, where he was unable to find any suitable employment, he reboarded the *Success* and in September disembarked in South America somewhere along the River Demerara. Demerara (also spelled, Demerary) was also the name of the largest city in the region. Today that city is Georgetown. The eighteen-year-old Bancroft had landed in the western part of what was then Dutch Guiana. The eastern half consisted mostly of what was called Surinam. The western half contained three districts, named after the three major rivers: Demerara, Essequibo, and Berbice. In the 1790s the British would eventually gain control of these three provinces, which became British Guiana and later the independent country of Guyana. The hundreds of large plantations along the rivers produced vast quantities of sugar, coffee, cotton, and cacao. Bancroft would spend the next two and a half years here and would return to these plantations several times later in life.

On 4 December 1763 he wrote the following to Thomas Williams:

> I sailed for the River Demerara where I arrived about the middle of September. I had the good Fortune immediately upon my Arrival to ingratiate myself into the Esteem of Some gentleman of Note . . . by whose Recommendation added to that of a Celebrated Physician, from Edinburgh, I obtained in three days after my arrival the Employment of Surgeon to a gentleman of Fortune, Owner of two large Plantations and Near two hundred slaves in this River. This incident I esteem as one of the most Happy of my Life. My Employer is a gentleman of a frank, Obliging and condescending Disposition, by him I am treated as a Companion, I sit at his table, share his Diversions and in short lead a very agreeable Life. I have all my Medicins . . . am allowed a servant to attend me—a Nurse to administer my Prescriptions. My Practice being at the Door serves rather as an Amusement, than a Toil. By an intimate acquaintance with the afore named Physician I have a good Library at Command.[11]

In addition, Bancroft told Williams that he would be able to save "one hundred Pounds Sterling free of all Expense" in the first year and even more in the next. A few weeks later, he wrote to Williams that "I have been now for near three Months employed in the business of our Profession, & I have the satisfaction to find that my practice has been successful to my patients & agreeable to my employer."[12] While still in his late teens, Bancroft was demonstrating talents that would serve him the rest of his life: gaining the confidence of men of wealth and importance, having an eye for opportunity, reading voraciously, and being a quick learner.

The names of the rich plantation owner and the expatriate Edinburgh physician are not known. We do, however, know some of the particulars about where Bancroft worked. His first job, referred to in the above letters, was at the Plantation Providence. After a year there, in September 1764, he moved further up the River Demerara. He soon took medical charge of the

Plantation Retreeve. By July 1765 he was also tending to four additional plantations. At the age of twenty he was the sole physician caring for perhaps a thousand or more slaves and several dozen mostly Dutch colonists.[13]

On 20 February 1766 he suddenly gave up his medical practice on all the plantations.[14] He spent the next several months traveling through the Demerara, Essequibo, and Berbice valleys. With his savings from his medical practice, he could afford this hiatus from a regular job. He spent these months making observations of the animal and plant life of the region—studies he would incorporate into his first book.

In June 1766 he sailed to Barbados and from there to Boston and then Hartford. During this visit home he went to see Dr. Benjamin Gale and made amends for his abandonment of the apprenticeship.[15] In November he sold a small parcel of land near Westfield to his uncle John Bancroft for the sum of £22. In the deed recording the sale, Edward's profession is listed as "practioner of physick."[16] In February 1767 he boarded a ship bound for England. In succeeding decades he would revisit North America three times, but never again would it be his home.

The Natural History of Guiana

The story of his early years in London is the subject of the next chapter, but a discussion of his first book, published in London in 1769, is better placed here. That book was called *An Essay on the Natural History of Guiana in South America. Containing a Description of many Curious Productions in the Animal and Vegetable Systems of that Country. Together with an Account of the Religion, Manners, and Customs of several Tribes of its Indian Inhabitants. Interspersed with a Variety of Literary and Medical Observations, in Several Letters.* The title page states that the anonymous author is "A Gentleman of the Medical Faculty." The twenty-four-year-old Bancroft clearly was puffing up his credentials when he described himself thus. In the next two pages of the book Bancroft reveals his name and says that after most of the book was already in press his friends prevailed on him to reveal his identity. They told him that a book about strange things in a distant country would not have much authority coming from an anonymous author. Therefore he published his name, "not with a presumptuous expectation of acquiring Honour from the Work, but solely to add to its Credibility."[17]

This book is important not only for what it says of Guiana but also for what it tells us about the author. Along with Bancroft's later scientific publications, this volume made him a celebrated authority in scholarly circles, both in his lifetime and for several generations thereafter. The 404-page tome would have been remarkable no matter who wrote it, but the fact that its author was such a young, self-taught man from humble beginnings makes it extraordinary. It is written in the form of four long letters to his brother, Daniel. Bancroft thus was following the epistolary form used so often in both fiction and nonfiction in the eighteenth century. The four letters are dated 1766, though Bancroft probably wrote much of the text a year later, after his arrival in London.

Bancroft starts by acknowledging his deficiencies. He admits that he has no formal background in botany and says that his lack of skill in the "art of Drawing" means that he can include no illustrations of the plants and animals that he will describe. Though Bancroft knows the taxonomic terminology of pioneering Swedish naturalist Carl Linnaeus, he also gives the Indian names for many of the flora and fauna. Moreover, there is a distinctly informal, narrative flavor to many of the pages. His book could be read for pleasure and profit by both specialists and general readers.

He interjects himself and his personal experiences into nearly every page, making the book as much a travelogue as a dry classification of hundreds of animal and plant species. He laments the "unpardonable indolence" of greedy white settlers, who are content to stay on their lowland plantations rather than journey far up any of the rivers. Prizing firsthand observation, Bancroft reports that he has "spent many days . . . investigat[ing] the nature and qualities of these plants; and, by handling, smelling, tasting, etc." After eating some of the nuts of the *Ricinus Americanus* or Physick Nut Tree, which natives had told him was an emetic, he reports, "I believe it from my own experience."[18]

The first part of the book gives a wide-ranging history of European settlements since the early seventeenth century and a thorough account of geography and topography. Bancroft explains that the abundant rainfall makes for rich, verdant forests and an abundance of timber and all sorts of grains, fruits, and vegetables. This natural abundance plus the warm but not uncomfortable temperatures enable the native Indian peoples to feed and clothe themselves without much effort. About seventy-five pages are devoted to all the major trees, shrubs, and other types of vegetation that he has observed.

The second part is devoted to animals. The species native to the region include lynx, porcupines, hummingbirds, vultures, manatees, and so on. He also mentions some strange animals that he himself did not see but were reported to him by the natives. These include two-headed snakes that supposedly swim in the rivers and the notorious "Wild Man" (perhaps the South American equivalent of the North American Bigfoot). The natives have attested that this wild man stands about five feet tall and is covered with short black hair. The creature is said to attack Indian men and ravish their women. Bancroft drily notes that, unfortunately, none of these fantastic creatures has ever been captured.[19] Four varieties of animals garner his particular attention: insects, snakes, bats, and eels. He had devised a unique method for collecting snakes. By giving a glass of rum to every Indian who brought him one, within three months he accumulated three hundred of the creatures.

His thirteen-page discussion of eels soon became the most famous and important part of the book. He describes an eel native to the River Essequibo and names it the torporific eel. It measures about three feet in length and twelve inches in circumference. He learned of this eel from natives, who feared the shock they got when they touched it. Bancroft became the first person to investigate and explain this phenomenon in convincing fashion.

Since ancient times, Europeans had known about sundry varieties of "numb fish," as they often were called. The most famous of these was the torpedo fish, which could be found throughout the Mediterranean and along the Atlantic coasts of Spain and France. Many scientists and other observers over the centuries tried to explain the nature of its shock. By the mid-eighteenth century the most widely accepted theory was that of the renowned French scientist René-Antoine Ferchault de Réaumur (1683–1757). He claimed that this fish and other "numb fish" produced their effects through the swift movement of their muscles as they "slapped" a victim.

Bancroft writes that the testimony from all persons who have touched torpedo fish in Europe and torporific eels in South America indicates that the two creatures give off the same sort of shock. His methods for examining the eel's shock were so simple that, in retrospect, one wonders how previous observers could have overlooked them. He surmised that if the shock was purely mechanical, a person would have to be touching the eel to feel the sting. However, in a variety of ways Bancroft demonstrated that persons not in direct contact with the eel could also be affected. For example, a man who touched the eel with an iron rod got stung even though his hands were distant from the fish. Moreover, if that man held hands with a string of a dozen other persons, the shock was transmitted to all of them. Bancroft's conclusion was that the shock resulted from the transmission of electric particles. Réaumur thus had "amused the world with an imaginary hypothesis."[20]

When Bancroft's *Natural History* was published in 1769, the pages on the torporific eel had an effect in Europe and North America that one might very well call electric. Through the eighteenth century the study of electricity had been the focus of many scholars and amateur experimenters on both sides of the ocean. Hundreds of people were building and then getting shocks from touching Leyden jars. Of course, the most famous electrical experiments were performed in the late 1740s and early 1750s by a recently retired Philadelphia newspaper publisher named Benjamin Franklin. Writing recently on this topic, James Delbourgo notes that Bancroft's discovery spurred naturalists, physicians, and philosophers in Europe and North America to replicate his experiments.[21] In 1772 the Englishman John Walsh, a member of Parliament and also a scientist and member of the Royal Society, demonstrated that Bancroft's suppositions about the torpedo fish were indeed correct.[22] In 1773 William Bryant, like Bancroft an American physician working in Guiana, sent a paper inspired by Bancroft's discoveries to the American Philosophical Society in Philadelphia. The society eventually published the paper in its *Transactions*.[23]

Bancroft thus opened the field for investigations that within a few years would lead to the development of the battery, or Voltaic pile. Delbourgo affirms that "by providing a natural model that could be subject to experiment, the American eel played its own role in the invention of the modern electrical world."[24] Bancroft was also a pioneer in demonstrating the importance of electricity in animal physiology.

In the third section of the *Natural History* Bancroft turns to human beings. Although by the 1760s there were many white Europeans, black slaves, and persons of mixed race in Guiana, his focus is on the aboriginal natives, or Indians. There were four tribes living in the region claimed by the Dutch: the Caribbee, the Worrow, the Accawaw, and the Arrowauk. His opinions about these tribes are curiously mixed. On the one hand he says that all of them live "but little removed from" the ignorance and ferocity of a state of nature. They get drunk too often, they are sexually promiscuous, and because nature provides them with an overabundance of plant and animal food, they are indolent. They believe in gods who are always causing earthquakes or other natural convulsions, and thus the chief job of holy men is to appease the malevolent spirits.

Some of the Indians eat the bodies of enemies killed in battle. Bancroft says he abhors this practice but states that people who have never traveled outside their own country are in no position to criticize "the manners of distant unknown nations." He asks if natives who kill in self-defense and then eat their enemies are any worse than civilized nations that, with little remorse, "kill each other by unnecessary wars."[25] In arguing for cultural relativism, Bancroft situates himself in the mainstream of eighteenth-century Enlightenment thought. Voltaire made much the same point, in more humorous fashion, in the chapter in *Candide* where the main character discovers that in some countries it is natural for women to take monkeys as their lovers.

Although the red peppers and hot spices consumed by the natives would "excoriate the mouth" of persons unaccustomed to them, Bancroft observes that the natives eat a balanced, healthy diet. He discusses a broad range of health issues, including leprosy, yaws, worms, snake bite, "intermittent fever" (probably malaria), and "dry gripes" (most likely gastroenteritis). His analyses of the causes and cures for these ailments were remarkable for someone with so little medical training. He was perhaps the first to notice that yaws could be transmitted by flies, and he revealed that it could be cured with mercury treatments. Some of his remedies (such as using pepper to combat malaria) do not stand up to today's practices, but they were on a par with what the best European medical experts of that era recommended.

Bancroft devotes about thirty pages to an investigation of the poison arrows used by some Indians to kill animals or other Indians, but there is no record of these pages generating any interest among readers at the time. Only in the second half of the twentieth century have some historians focused on Bancroft's knowledge of poison. I shall return to this topic in a later chapter.

Despite the natives' occasional cannibalism or use of poison arrows, Bancroft fashions a picture of pastoral tranquility. The Indians spend endless hours dancing, telling fables, joking, or just resting in their hammocks. They are not acquisitive, and thus they do not have the jealousies and rivalries so prevalent in European society. Because their wants are few, the tribes rarely go to war with one another. He rhapsodizes that "if human happiness consists in contentment, these people must necessarily be, of all others, the most happy; where they have no wants but what are easily supplied, and where all are in a state of perfect equality, in which the tortures of discontent, envy, ambition, and avarice cannot possibly exist."[26] Bancroft notes, however, the pernicious effects of European colonization. He says that the Dutch are infecting the minds of Indians with European values and encouraging the tribes to fight with one another—so that the winners can capture the losers and sell them to the Dutch as slaves.[27]

Despite his lyrical ode to the joys of the simple life, Bancroft attacks those writers who have argued that "arts and sciences" have led to luxury, greed, and other kinds of corruption in civilized countries. Bancroft's readers would have known immediately who his chief target was. In the 1750s Jean-Jacques Rousseau had famously criticized "arts and sciences," saying that they had taken human beings away from a simpler, more natural kind of life. In short, Rousseau seemed to hate "progress" and all the modern trappings of civilization. Bancroft takes a middle-of-the-road approach. He maintains that the Indians' state of nature is admirable but that it cannot last. Progress is inevitable and not necessarily bad. Improvements in culture, technology, agriculture, medicine, and creature comforts are good, if used wisely. The evils of modern society, he maintains, result from the unequal distribution of wealth. This inequality leads to envy and violence among the poor and to avarice and a taste for useless luxuries among the rich. However, Bancroft is no nascent socialist. He says that without ambition and greed the rich would not be bringing improvements in the arts and sciences to the world and not providing jobs for those less well off. In short, Bancroft writes, "Good and evil are indiscriminately mingled in every cup."[28]

After offering these thoughts, Bancroft turns to his fourth and final section, which concerns the changes in Guiana brought by Europeans. He discusses the administrative divisions within the Dutch provinces. In some areas, to encourage settlement, land was given free to any settlers who developed working plantations. The Dutch West India Company, which controlled Guiana, welcomed English settlers. Nearly all of the hard labor was done by African slaves. Regarding slavery, Bancroft takes a two-sided approach. He notes that slaves outnumber whites five to one. Just weeks before he arrived in Guiana, there had been a huge slave rebellion along the River Berbice. The Dutch put it down brutally. Bancroft is aghast at the bloodshed, but he also says that it was necessary for the "self-preservation" of the whites. Here again, he more or less says that progress, in this case Western imperialism and capitalism, is inevitable; one must accept the bad with the good.[29]

He condemns the white men who force themselves on slave women and mentions that the women do all they can to prevent conceiving children. He reports that blacks are subject to many more illnesses than whites. As a physician on several plantations, he has witnessed the open sores caused by beatings, the sickness resulting from drinking bad water, and the snakebites that come from working barefoot in the fields.

In his ambivalent and often negative view of European settlement in Guiana, Bancroft ran against the current of popular opinion. Most of the adventurers and scientists who explored South America and other parts of the world from the sixteenth to the nineteenth centuries were filled with a sense of divine purpose. They were interested in the plants, animals, and people of exotic locales mostly because of how they could contribute to the wealth and power of the mother country. Europeans generally believed that native peoples failed to make full use of their natural resources. Bancroft, however, believed that the human beings and flora and fauna that he encountered were intrinsically interesting and valuable and were not simply underutilized tools to be used by "superior" Europeans.[30]

Another element in the *Natural History* that deserves mention is religion. Many of the historians who have written about Bancroft have assumed, because of his "treason," that he was an irreligious man of no moral principles. It should be clear from the above that he had severe misgivings about the cruelty, lust, and avarice of so-called civilized peoples. In numerous places throughout his pages he gives a clear indication of his own religious views. He had been born and raised in Puritan New England, but his *Natural History* reveals a far different kind of religion. In several places he reverently alludes to "the Author of our being."[31] In the book's conclusion he writes, "In taking a retrospect of Animated Nature, I cannot but admire the Wisdom and Goodness of that Power, who has so exquisitely adapted the Organs and Dispositions of all animal Beings to that life in which each is capable of enjoying the greatest portion of happiness, and who has caused each to be actuated with principles the least exposed to infringe the Order and Harmony of our material System."[32]

Bancroft's belief in a rational deity whose intentions could be grasped through an observation of nature is a religious attitude generally called Deism. With slight variations, this was the religious view of most of the philosophes of the Enlightenment. Voltaire, Diderot, Rousseau, Benjamin Franklin, George Washington, Thomas Jefferson, James Madison, and many of the other intellectual and political leaders of that era were Deists. Bancroft was therefore in good company.[33]

One final aspect of the book that should be noted is Bancroft's obvious acquaintance with classical and modern literature and with the writings of the major scientists of his era. The book is liberally sprinkled with English, French, and Latin quotations from such figures as Socrates, Plato, Virgil, Seneca, Pliny, and Celsus, as well as moderns like Philip Sidney and Alexander Pope. Though Bancroft did not write the book until he arrived in England, he obviously had access to the private libraries on the plantations where he worked. Colonial planters brought with them many of the books of the Old World, providing further evidence of the intellectual connectedness of the eighteenth-century Atlantic world.[34]

By his early twenties, then, Bancroft had mastered a huge amount of the accumulated wisdom of Western civilization and had written the first detailed scientific treatise on northeastern South America. Soon after his *Natural History* appeared, excerpts were reprinted in Britain's influential *Annual Register*—a sort of eighteenth-century scholarly *Reader's Digest*.[35] It was soon published in Dutch and German translations. In January 1783 a committee headed by James Madison recommended to the U.S. Congress a list of several dozen books that it should purchase, to establish a reference library for members. Bancroft's *Natural History* was included.[36] The book has been reprinted in the twentieth century and continues to be cited by numerous historians, natural scientists, and anthropologists.[37] The *Natural History* would bring Bancroft his first claim to fame and give an important boost to his budding career in London.

2 On the Rise in London

From May 1767 to the spring of 1777, Edward Bancroft lived mainly in the British capital. During this period he also made several extended journeys—to South and North America, Ireland, and France.[1]

Soon after he reached London, it became clear that this young man of humble origins was prepared to make it big in the great metropolis. In June 1767, just weeks after arriving unannounced and with no powerful friends or sponsors, he became a physician's pupil at St. Bartholomew's Hospital. That institution (commonly called "Bart's") was one of only two large hospitals in London at that time. (The other was St. Thomas's.) By the early eighteenth century, St. Bartholomew's had established a variety of informal instructional services for aspiring physicians. These included several lecture series and internships. Medical students from universities as well as physicians already in practice could make private arrangements to study with senior members of the hospital staff. On a lower level, interested young men could become apprentices to hospital physicians. It was this sort of informal apprenticeship that Bancroft acquired. The doctor he assisted on daily rounds was the prominent staff physician William Pitcairn. Few details of Bancroft's studies are known, but he seems to have developed a close relationship with his mentor.

Bancroft worked steadily at the hospital from the summer of 1767 to the fall of 1769, but he was also busy writing. During these years he wrote and published his *Natural History of Guiana*, dedicated to Pitcairn. He also published another, very different book.

The Looming Anglo-American Crisis

Edward Bancroft was nothing if not protean in his interests and abilities. There was little in his youth or background, however, to prepare one for the other book that he published in 1769. It was entitled *Remarks on the review of "The Controversy Between Great Britain and Her Colonies."* The 126-page volume was published anonymously, though persons in political circles soon knew the identity of the twenty-four-year-old author.

The book exhibits a thorough grounding in British political and constitutional history going back to the Middle Ages plus a firm grasp of current events. Its awkward title needs some explanation. Just a few months earlier a book entitled *The Controversy Between Great Britain and Her Colonies Reviewed* had appeared in London. That publication likewise appeared anonymously. Those "in the know" were aware that the authors of the *Controversy* were William Knox and George Grenville. Knox would go on to serve from 1770 to 1782 as undersecretary to Lord George Germain, the secretary of state for the colonies. Grenville had been prime minister from 1763 to 1765 and was best remembered for the Stamp Act. Bancroft's *Remarks* served as a rebuttal to their arguments.

In their book, Knox and Grenville stridently upheld the official British position regarding the American colonies. In its core, this position stated that a country could have but one source of sovereignty. All individuals and groups had to recognize their subservience to this highest power. In the case of the British Empire, since the settlement achieved after the Glorious Revolution of 1688, sovereignty lay in an inextricable connection between king and Parliament. When William and Mary surrendered all claims to divine right kingship, they acknowledged that Parliament was the senior partner in this sovereign entity. Knox and Grenville gave a historical defense of parliamentary supremacy and explained why it was the best and only way to rule Britain and its empire. They also defended Parliament's rights to govern and tax the colonists.

To understand Bancroft's refutation of Knox and Grenville, one must appreciate the general background. The 1760s were filled with numerous sources of conflict between the mother country and its North American colonists. Ironically, Britain's eventual loss of the thirteen colonies was directly linked to one of Britain's greatest diplomatic and military victories. Through the Peace of Paris of 1763, ending the Seven Years' War, Britain humiliated France. French prestige in continental Europe was gravely damaged, and France lost control of its North American possessions. Britain acquired formerly French lands along the Ohio and Mississippi rivers plus all of French Canada. Moreover, France ceded New Orleans and all of the Louisiana territory west of the Mississippi to Spain. This was done to compensate the Bourbons of Spain for coming to the aid of their cousin Louis XV in a losing cause. Britain thus controlled all territories from the Atlantic to the Mississippi River.

The euphoria from that victory, however, was short-lived. After 1763 the government in London was increasingly angered by colonial violations of the Navigation Acts. According to these mercantilist laws from the seventeenth century, colonists were supposed to trade exclusively with the mother country. British manufacturers and traders continually complained that the colonists violated these statutes and traded with whomever they wanted—in particular with the French in Martinique, Saint-Domingue, and other Caribbean islands. Another source of friction concerned native Americans. Numerous Indian tribes claimed the lands in the wide strip between the Mississippi River and the Appalachian Mountains. Now that this land was British, thousands of colonists were crossing the mountains and laying claim to new territory. To keep peace with the Indians and give his ministry time to figure out how to manage the situation, King George III signed the Royal Proclamation of 1763, which prohibited British subjects from traveling west of the Appalachians. Colonists ignored that proclamation and proceeded to move westward at a steadily increasing pace.

But the most grievous source of conflict concerned the royal finances. The British government had racked up a huge national debt during the war. Because much of the fighting had been done to protect the American colonists from the French and because the newly acquired lands in America would require money to protect and administer, it seemed obvious to the British that the colonists themselves should share in the tax burden. Prime Minister

George Grenville and his successors thus ushered in a series of parliamentary acts designed to raise revenue from the colonies. The first of these was the Sugar Act of 1764. This measure reduced customs duties on molasses entering the colonies, but it levied new duties on foreign textiles, wine, coffee, indigo, and sugar. The Stamp Act of 1765 went even further. It created revenue stamps, which had to be bought and attached to all kinds of printed matter and legal documents: newspapers, almanacs, licenses, deeds, death and marriage certificates, insurance policies, college diplomas, and even playing cards. Americans refused to buy the stamps and retaliated by organizing nonimportation agreements. When the colonists stopped buying British textiles, tea, and other products, thousands of British merchants and manufacturers felt the pain.

After British businessmen complained about the decline in their colonial trade, Parliament repealed the Stamp Act in 1766. But in order to save face, it passed a Declaratory Act, proclaiming Parliament's right to issue laws binding the colonies "in all cases whatsoever." Parliament also created a fictitious difference between "external" taxes that merely regulated trade and "internal" ones collected within the colonies. The Stamp Tax fell into the latter category, which Parliament was for the time being agreeing not to collect.

In 1767 the chancellor of the exchequer, Charles Townshend, mistakenly assumed that external taxes were acceptable to the colonists. He pushed through Parliament a series of bills that came to be called the Townshend Acts. One of these was a revenue act that placed duties on glass, lead, paint, paper, and tea imported into the colonies. Not only did this act impose new taxes on colonists, but it aimed to free colonial governors and other royal officials from control by colonial assemblies. Until then, governors and other officials received their pay from the assemblies. Townshend intended for these Crown servants henceforth to be paid from proceeds of the revenue act. The obvious result would be that governors and other royal officials would no longer be financially dependent on the assemblies.

The new Townshend duties met resistance from both moderate and rabble-rousing colonists. Among the moderates was John Dickinson, a Philadelphia attorney whose *Letters of a Philadelphia Farmer* (1767) opposed parliamentary taxation but urged conciliation. The rabble-rousers included Samuel Adams and James Otis, who succeeded in getting the Massachusetts assembly to distribute throughout the colonies a circular letter that called for

Americans to unite in rejecting the new taxes. The British government retaliated by dissolving the Massachusetts assembly, sending two regiments of redcoats to reside in Boston, and announcing its intention to bring all those accused of treason to London for trial. In 1769 the Virginia House of Burgesses declared that it alone could tax Virginians, and the Crown thereupon dissolved that assembly also. By that time Americans in all the colonies were adhering to new nonimportation agreements, hoping that, as in 1765, they could hurt British businessmen and thereby win their support.[2]

It was at this juncture that Edward Bancroft published his *Remarks*. Part of the book consists of the same sorts of arguments used by other leaders of colonial opposition to the new taxes. He presents a historical survey of the relative independence of the colonies from the time they were granted charters in the seventeenth and early eighteenth centuries. Those charters granted taxing rights to the local assemblies and guaranteed colonists "all the Liberties, Franchises, and Immunities" of free subjects of the Crown.[3] Over the years, the Crown "had granted the colonists the constitution and privileges of distinct states."[4] If colonists were going to pay taxes that were aimed at raising revenue, then the colonists deserved the rights of all British subjects. The mass of people in Britain might not be perfectly represented—as only a small minority of white males was eligible to vote—but at least each electoral district had one or more persons watching out for its interests in the House of Commons. The American colonies, with a territory far larger than the mother country's and a population of about two and a half million, had none. In short, "immense is the Difference between a Nation but imperfectly represented, and a People who have no Representation."[5]

The book trumpets the phrase "no taxation without representation," which probably owed its origin to James Otis. If Parliament wished to exercise direct control over the colonies, then every colonist who met the minimum requirements of land holding should be able to vote for a member of Parliament. The colonies should be divided into districts roughly the same size, in terms of population, as those in Britain.

If arguments from natural rights and British constitutional theory did not sway the British government, then Bancroft appealed to the self-interest of people in Britain. He repeatedly asserts that the "National Interest" of Britons would suffer if the government imposed "an Infringement of the Rights of my Countrymen." The colonies have flourished "under the benign

Influence of Freedom, and the Enthusiasm of Liberty grows in their Minds." If "they are made subject to the despotic Power of those whom they have neither delegated nor entrusted, and over whom they have no restraining Influence . . . their total loss of Freedom will be too palpable, and their slavery too real, too feeling, not to urge them to improve every occasion which may be favorable to a change of Government." He continues, "If our cause is just, Resistance is a virtue, . . . our fortitude is laudable." Moreover, he argues, the Americans occupy a continent far larger than Britain. Their numbers are growing far faster than those back home. Within just a few years, therefore, the Americans would be a wealthier, larger power than Britain.[6]

In these pages Bancroft does not, however, seek American independence. He aims "to establish a colonial dependence on a just and permanent basis." In this regard his views were identical to those of nearly all the leading colonial protesters of the late 1760s and early 1770s. No one was calling for independence. Americans simply wanted "the rights of Englishmen." Bancroft also asserts that the British Empire will be larger and stronger because it includes the American colonies. If the mother country does not acknowledge the rights of colonists, the colonists will be too strong to be subdued. Britain, he claims, is filled with "Effeminacy, Luxury, and Corruption." The smaller, weaker mother country needs the youth, health, and vigor of the colonies. Remaining united by "the Ties of reciprocal Affection" will benefit everyone.[7] This was to become an argument that Benjamin Franklin would often use in the years leading up to 1776.

The truly original and fascinating parts of the *Remarks* are those places where Bancroft offers his own distinctive solution to the impasse. Although he criticizes the injustice of Parliament in trying to tax the colonists, his ultimate solution differs from the one usually spouted by John Dickinson, Samuel Adams, and others. Bancroft realized that Parliament would accept no diminution of its sovereign powers to tax and govern. Moreover, even if Parliament agreed to let Americans send their own representatives to London, Bancroft was perspicacious enough to realize that this system would not work. Any American representatives in Parliament would be cut off from their constituents across the ocean. Unlike politicians today who can fly home on weekends and keep in daily touch with their districts via telephone, television, and the Internet, Bancroft states that American MPs would be more or less permanently stationed overseas. Bancroft realized therefore that

Americans would not long be satisfied even if they were to receive their wish of parliamentary representation. They would soon fear that their few representatives were out of touch with their needs or outvoted by the far larger number of men representing districts in Britain itself.[8]

Although Bancroft presents a solid case for colonial representation in Parliament, it is evident that he prefers a second, more radical defense of American rights. Through a careful reading of all the early colonial charters, he deduces that the colonies never were placed under the jurisdiction of Parliament in any regard. He concludes that the texts of the charters "abundantly prove, that the Colonies were not then considered as annexed to the Realm of *England,* or subject to its Laws." He shows that Elizabeth, James I, and Charles I granted charters personally and that whatever powers they retained over the colonies were vested solely in themselves as monarchs. The colonies were outside the realm of England but owed their allegiance to the Crown. To prove this, Bancroft cites numerous documents. These include royal decrees referring to Charles II as "king of England, Scotland, France, Ireland and Virginia." Virginia was thus a different state, under the king, but not under the "English" Parliament. And, unlike what happened to Scotland in 1707, the colonies were never annexed to England.[9]

Bancroft devotes several pages to instances in the seventeenth century that demonstrate the colonies' status as separate territories independent of Parliament. On numerous occasions from 1614 through the 1620s, Parliament passed bills regulating the importation and use of tobacco in England, without regulating its use in the colonies. In the 1620s and 1630s the House of Commons debated a bill that would grant English vessels the right to fish off the coasts of the colonies; both James I and Charles I rejected the bill, on the grounds that it would infringe on the rights granted to the colonists. In the early 1650s, in the era of Oliver Cromwell, Parliament signed a treaty with Virginia. The "country" of Virginia voluntarily agreed to be part of the Commonwealth. The treaty declared that "Virginia shall be free from all Taxes, Customs, and Impositions whatsoever; and none shall be imposed upon them without Consent of their General Assembly; and that neither Forts nor Castles be erected, nor Garrisons maintained without their Consent." In the 1660s Connecticut and New Haven petitioned the king to be united into one colony. At about the same time, Rhode Island and Providence Plantations asked for the same thing. Charles II, of his own authority, granted each request, retaining only for himself their allegiance, "without the smallest Share in the Legislative and Executive Powers of Government." Bancroft cites a vote taken in the House of Lords in 1734, concerning the newly revised constitutions of Connecticut and Rhode Island. The Lords agreed that "almost the whole Power of the Crown is delegated to the People, who make an Annual Election of their Assembly, their Councils, and their Governors." Furthermore, the Lords acknowledged that these assemblies had the power to make laws even without the assent of the royal governors, who were not mentioned in the original charters. The only stipulation in the charters was that colonial laws should not be contrary to the laws of England. In the revised Rhode Island charter, the monarch states that its inhabitants "did, by the Consent of our Royal Progenitors, transport themselves out of this Kingdom of England into America." Numerous clauses to this effect could be found in all the colonial charters. Bancroft says that the colonial assemblies were "their supreme Legislatures," with no appeals to king in council. Bancroft even notes that the practice of transporting felons to the colonies likewise proves they were outside the Realm of England; the goal of this punishment was to banish them from the Community (that is, Britain) that they had offended.[10]

Going back as far as the Middle Ages, Bancroft provides examples of territories or peoples besides just the American colonies that were not taxed by Parliament. For example, the principality of Wales and the county of Chester taxed themselves and sent portions of that revenue to the king. Eventually Parliament tried to tax those two regions, but the monarchs prevented this until Wales and Chester were represented in Parliament. Bancroft likewise mentions that in earlier centuries the English clergy taxed themselves rather than let Parliament do so.[11]

Bancroft does acknowledge one series of laws that violated the general practice of colonial financial and economic independence. These were the Navigation Acts first issued in the 1660s and 1670s and still in effect in 1769 (though often violated by American smugglers). These laws regulated imports and exports, placed limits on colonial industries (so that Americans were required to purchase finished goods from Britain), and stipulated that all trade between Britain and its colonies had to take place in British ships. Bancroft heatedly condemns these "unprecedented" and "inconceivable" laws that violated the "Spirit of the Constitution." He records that the colonists bitterly opposed them at the time, with Virginians even mounting a revolt in the 1670s. Once the violence subsided, Virginia sent delegates to London to meet with the king. In April 1676 Charles II issued a declaration affirming that "Taxes ought not to be laid upon the Proprietors and Inhabitants of the Colony, but by the common Consent of the General Assembly, except such Impositions as the Parliament should lay on the Commodities imported into England from the Colony." Thus, Bancroft concludes, the Crown admitted that such duties were aimed at regulating trade and not at collecting revenues in the colonies.[12]

Bancroft's solution to the controversy involves the establishment of a federal or commonwealth empire. All the parts of the empire (principally Britain, the North American colonies, Canada, and the Caribbean islands) would be united under the monarch. This "general Political League and Confederation" would serve the general good, especially in military and naval matters. But internal administration and taxation would be left to each constituent part of the empire. Britain's Navigation Acts would no longer regulate colonial trade and manufactures. Part of the tax revenue collected by colonial assemblies would be used for internal administration, and part would, by the consent of the colonies, be sent to London for royal expenses.

Would Bancroft's scheme have worked? In view of the temper of the times, almost certainly not. Given that Parliament and royal ministers rejected colonial protests against taxation, certainly they would have refused Bancroft's suggestion that the legal separation between Britain and its colonies be widened even further. With the perfect vision provided by more than two centuries of hindsight, today one can say that probably no proposed solution to the confrontation would have succeeded.

Bancroft's book attracted attention on both sides of the Atlantic. One of its readers was the young Alexander Hamilton. While an undergraduate student at King's College (later Columbia University), Hamilton wrote a letter to Alexander McDougal, a New York merchant and acquaintance of his. The undated letter was written sometime between 1774 and 1776. McDougal had lent some books to Hamilton. In his letter, Hamilton reports that someone had broken into his room and stolen several pamphlets. "What is worse the most valuable of them is missing," Hamilton lamented. The most valuable was "Bankroft's [sic] treatise." Hamilton hoped to purchase another copy and send it to McDougal to replace the lost one.[13] Many historians today continue to cite Bancroft's *Remarks* as a significant contribution to the rising chorus of American complaints against the mother country.[14]

How could the twenty-four-year-old Bancroft have produced such an erudite historical analysis so quickly—while also composing his *Natural History of Guiana* and studying at St. Bartholomew's Hospital? To explain Bancroft's incredible burst of energy and scholarship, some authors have conjectured that he must have had help, perhaps even a secret collaborator. Two candidates have been put forward. One is Paul Wentworth (1728–93). He was related to a powerful New Hampshire family, owned plantations in Surinam, and by 1769 was a resident of London. We know that Bancroft and Wentworth first met in 1769 in London. Other than that, however, there is no evidence to suggest that Wentworth played any role in composing Bancroft's book.[15]

The other possible "silent partner" is Benjamin Franklin. There is nothing in the surviving papers of either Bancroft or Franklin to suggest that Franklin participated directly in writing the work. The two men knew each other by the time Bancroft published it. Undoubtedly, Bancroft tried out his ideas on friends and asked for their advice—as he probably did in everything he published throughout his life. Thus it is likely that he discussed his ideas with Franklin before setting pen to paper. There is one place in the book where Bancroft staunchly defends Franklin, who spent fifteen years in London before the Revolution—1757–62 and 1764–75. Originally he had gone there as the agent (in today's terms, the lobbyist) for Pennsylvania, and eventually he also represented Georgia, Massachusetts, and New Jersey. By 1769 Franklin had become a vocal opponent of Parliamentary taxation and a resolute defender of American claims to the full rights of Englishmen. Franklin had made enemies in government circles, and therefore Knox and Grenville attacked him in their book. Hence Bancroft's retort in his *Remarks*, "It is a melancholy Reflection, that a Character the most respectable for Learning, Probity, and Honour, is no Security against those invidious Aspersions, which our Author [that is, Knox and Grenville] has directed against Dr. Franklin, who, will doubtless, think it unnecessary to descend to vindicate himself from such unmerited Censure."[16]

Franklin was far and away the most famous American in Britain at that time and so was singled out for blame by Knox and Grenville. It made perfect sense for Bancroft to defend his acquaintance. Some authors have claimed to see Franklin's ideas in the *Remarks*. But thousands of colonists as well as sympathetic Britons were making the same points about growing ministerial despotism and "no taxation without representation." Bancroft's argument about colonists being a separate realm and independent of Parliament is one that Franklin had considered on various occasions; indeed, Bancroft's proposed solution was in some ways similar to Franklin's Albany Plan of 1754.[17]

A handful of historians have claimed that the writing style in *Remarks* is "Franklinesque."[18] But it is hard to see that. Bancroft's style is clear and forceful, but stilted when compared to Franklin's. There is not one iota of humor in *Remarks*. Given Franklin's penchant for satire, puns, and other forms of humor, it is difficult to believe that he could have written 126 pages without winking at his readers on at least a few occasions. Moreover, if Franklin had wanted to publish a rebuttal to Knox and Grenville, he would have done so himself rather than hiding behind Bancroft. Franklin, after all, was never at a loss for words. His position as an official colonial agent might have made it awkward for him to voice many of his ideas publicly, but he could have done so without revealing his name. In fact, during his years in Britain he did that very thing on many occasions. He wrote numerous articles for London newspapers using pseudonyms like "Homespun."

Remarks is fundamentally Bancroft's work. It gives us further evidence of his insatiable curiosity and his ability to absorb vast quantities of information in a short time. The man's genius might not have been the equal of a Newton, a Voltaire, or a Franklin. But his accomplishments at such an early age were amazing, and he gave every sign of rising even higher in the intellectual firmament of his era.

Equally significant, this book tells us something about Bancroft's state of mind in 1769. In a few places he writes of Britons and Americans as "brothers" or "fellow subjects," but more often he refers to Americans as "us" and Britons as "them." In 1769 Americans might have forecast that he would become one of their leaders in the Continental Congress and the ensuing Revolution. True, Bancroft was living in London after 1767, but that would not have prevented him from returning home. After all, Franklin had resided in London even longer.

In later years Bancroft maintained that from the late 1760s to the early 1780s his fondest hope was that Britain would make concessions to colonial grievances and that America would remain a part of the glorious empire. His *Remarks* provides strong evidence to support this claim.

Further Travels and a Novel

Despite his foray into political discourse, Bancroft did not intend to forsake his medical career. Indeed, medicine apparently ran in the family. In 1769 Edward's brother, Daniel, came from America and enrolled in the medical school at the University of Edinburgh. He matriculated during the 1769–1770 academic year but left before obtaining an M.D. degree.[19] In 1771 he returned to America and, despite his lack of credentials, established a medical practice. In all probability Edward paid most or perhaps all of Daniel's expenses in Scotland.

Initially Edward planned to join his younger brother in Edinburgh. This is known because on 25 October 1769 Benjamin Franklin wrote a letter of recommendation for Bancroft to Dr. James Lind of the Edinburgh medical faculty. This letter is the first concrete piece of evidence that Franklin knew Bancroft by that time, and from the letter one can infer that they had known each other for at least a few months. Franklin stated that Bancroft was on his way to Edinburgh, "with a View of prosecuting his Medical Studies in your School of Physic now most celebrated of the kind in the known World." He lauded Bancroft as "an ingenious young American."[20]

But Bancroft never went to Edinburgh. Near the end of October he made another of his sudden and unexplained changes of career path. Instead of going to Scotland, he traveled to the Dutch Netherlands. From there, in January 1770, he sailed for South America.[21]

Why the abrupt departure from England? There are three explanations. One is that the medical school in Edinburgh was perhaps the most rigorous in Britain, requiring three years of residence before one could obtain the M.D. Bancroft was too restless for such a long-term commitment. Another is that Bancroft wanted to do fieldwork on the various plants in Guiana that could produce inks and dyes. A third is that Bancroft had been hired by his new friend Paul Wentworth to visit Wentworth's plantations in the region.

Paul Wentworth was later to become a major figure in Bancroft's espionage, and his life presents just as many mysteries. He was born in 1728 somewhere in the West Indies, probably Barbados. He spent a large portion of his youth in New Hampshire, where he claimed to be related to the colony's most powerful family. It has been said that the Wentworths were to New Hampshire in the eighteenth century what the Kennedys were to Massachusetts in the twentieth. Two Wentworths served as governors of the colony—Benning Wentworth (from 1741 to 1766) and John Wentworth (1767 to 1775). At some point in early adulthood, Paul Wentworth moved to Barbados. By the 1750s he was living in the eastern region of Dutch Guiana—the province called Surinam (Suriname today). Scattered records in the Dutch National Archives indicate that by 1756 he was a member of the Surinam Court of Civil Justice and the owner of three coffee plantations. The most prominent of these properties, called the Kleinhoop Estate, he acquired through marriage in 1756 to the widow of the previous owner. After his wife's death in 1766, he settled in London, accompanied by two of his household slaves. He left his plantations in the care of managers.[22]

In London he lived in grand style off the income from his South American properties. His rise in London society was aided by his family connection to the Marquess of Rockingham, whose family name was Charles Watson-Wentworth. Rockingham was a past and future prime minister (1765–66, 1782) and one of the leading opponents of Lord North's ministry during the Revolution. Rockingham's unpublished papers contain a handful of inconsequential, fawning letters from Wentworth.[23]

Wentworth was also said to be a close friend of Lord Suffolk, who served as a secretary of state in the 1770s. In 1774 Wentworth became New Hampshire's agent in England. He speculated heavily in stocks and other business ventures and often was seen in Amsterdam, Cadiz, Lisbon, Hamburg, and Berlin. He kept a mistress in an elegant townhouse that he owned in Paris. In 1777 the French playwright Beaumarchais commented that Wentworth spoke French better than he did and was one of the cleverest men in England.[24]

Wentworth first met Bancroft in London in 1769.[25] Evidently, he was greatly impressed by Bancroft's *Natural History of Guiana*. The principal reason for his sending Bancroft to Surinam was to find ways for improving the production of coffee and other crops on his plantations.

While in Surinam Bancroft pursued his personal field work, studied agricultural techniques, and did another of those things that astonish us. He wrote a three-volume novel and sent it back to London, where it was published in 1770. The novel is entitled *The History of Charles Wentworth, Esq., in a Series of Letters. Interspersed with a Variety of Important Reflections, Calculated to Improve Morality, and Promote the Œconomy of Human Life.*[26] The novel's three volumes come to 750 pages. Like his previous two books, this one was published anonymously. And like the *Natural History of Guiana*, the novel's format is epistolary. As with most first novels, Bancroft's is largely autobiographical. The story takes place in England and Guiana. Many of the words put into the mouths of its characters mirror Bancroft's ideas. And the surname of the main character is obviously taken from the author's friend, Paul Wentworth. One scholar has recently concluded that in writing this novel Bancroft performed "a significant act of self-translation."[27]

Admittedly, the work does not rank as a classic of the Western canon. However, it continues to be cited and discussed in works on the history of English literature, and it has been reprinted in the twentieth century.[28] The story creaks with improbabilities, but it contains many eloquent or amusing passages. For present purposes what is most important is what it reveals about the author.

The novel consists of letters exchanged between its principal characters, the chief one being Charles Wentworth. Both Charles's brother and his deceased father are, conveniently, named Edward. Charles is accused of seducing a young lady, and so he flees to Barbados. He ends up reaping great profits from his share in a privateering ship. (The story is set during the Seven Years' War.) He also purchases two lucrative plantations in Guiana. His mother writes to him from home, urging him to go into a sensible, respectable profession like the law. In one of the many satirical passages in the book, Charles answers her with the following observations on attorneys: "In spite of my inclination to conform to your opinion, I feel an insuperable aversion to the study of the law; as disagreeable, endless, intricate, and finally terminating in doubt and uncertainty; as a study which depends on an absurd mode of reasoning, from precarious, and often contradictory authorities, a mode which is happily exploded in every other science; and as a study which having for its object the decision of pecuniary controversies, inspires too great a sensibility to the value of wealth, and mechanically converts the mind to an habitual disposition to avarice."[29]

Soon after this, Charles acquires his plantations along the River Berbice, and just at that moment a widespread slave revolt occurs. Charles's slaves participate in that uprising, which the whites savagely suppress. In perhaps the most touching passage of the three volumes, a female slave is burned to death. As the flames engulf her, she cries out that her few months of freedom were worth far more than decades lived in bondage. Her courageous defiance and the brutality inflicted on the thousands of other recaptured slaves give Bancroft, through Charles, an opportunity to expand on the reflections on slavery made in the *Natural History of Guiana*. Charles admits that without slavery the plantations could not operate. Nevertheless, it is a vile business, and Charles determines to abandon his plantations and distance himself from slavery at the earliest opportunity.

Not long thereafter he travels upriver to remote regions where few whites ever ventured. He eventually encounters a white man named Mr. Gordon who lives among the natives and has taken an Indian woman for his wife. Gordon elaborates on themes addressed in the *Natural History*. He has settled far upriver in order to escape the greed, exploitation, and social injustices of "civilization." He condemns private property as the root of all evil and says that the natives live in relative peace and harmony because they are all equal.

Charles then leaves Gordon, journeys to the coast, and boards a ship headed for England. While at sea he falls overboard and is rescued by a vessel going to Philadelphia. Charles admires the hard work and energy of the Americans and predicts that America will rise to become a great world power. It will replace Britain, which is "enervated by luxury and vice."[30] Charles predicts, however, that eventually America will become corrupted and follow Britain into the same downward path.

In the end, Charles returns to England and is reunited with the woman he loves. He abhors the tawdriness and exploitation that he witnesses everywhere and retires to the countryside, where he will oversee the large estate that he has inherited from his uncle. He will use all the profits "to relieve the honest industrious poor."[31]

In addition to the autobiographical elements in the book, there are obvious ways in which the novel imitates Voltaire's *Candide*, which had been published eleven years earlier. Both stories have picaresque, labyrinthine plots, with the main characters being buffeted from one adventure to another. Like Voltaire, Bancroft was writing a philosophical tale rather than a realistic story. The events and characters were intended to be cardboard figures erected merely to allow the author to write satirically about serious topics. Mr. Gordon's isolated jungle hideaway and his critique of European society serve the same function as Voltaire's Eldorado, which also is located in the deep South American interior. Both Charles Wentworth and Candide sympathize with criticisms of European greed and imperialism, but they also yearn to return to familiar surroundings and values. Finally, at the end of both stories the main characters are cultivating their gardens.[32]

In numerous places throughout the book Charles ruminates on religion. Virtually every historian who has commented briefly on the book has said it proves that Edward Bancroft, in addition to being a devious traitor to his country, was also "irreligious," "anti-religious," or a "freethinker." But these charges are off the mark. While Charles is traveling upriver on the trek that will lead him to Mr. Gordon, he stops to admire nature: "Here we contemplated the wisdom and goodness of the Deity, every where visible in the various surrounding objects, discoverable in this immense, unexplored wilderness, whose every tree, shrub, and plant affords an object hitherto unexamined, though meriting the highest attention."[33]

Later, Mr. Gordon reflects: "I cannot . . . but think that every society that establishes a religion, and attempts to coutroul the opinions of its members to a conformity thereto, forgets and departs from the end of its institution; individuals did not divest themselves from their natural independence, to subject their consciences to the controul of others, in matters which depend on conviction, and are merely private or personal, and therefore ought to have no connection with government, as not being proper objects for the cognizance of political authority. Religion, in its native purity, is a voluntary tribute of gratitude and adoration to the deity."[34]

Gordon goes on to condemn forcing people in each nation to attend the ceremonies of one or other official religion, scaring them into compliance "by the fear of divine punishment, or bribed by the hopes of future reward." In all these civilized societies, he says, free inquiry into matters regarding God and nature are prohibited. Despite the "mild and charitable doctrines of christianity," no other religion on earth has shown such a "detestable spirit of intolerance and persecution." Christianity is fine for those who choose it. Gordon, however, declares that "it abounds with contradictions which are inconsistent with the truth, . . . And a very considerable part of it is so obscure and unintelligible" that all who study it understand and explain it differently. Nature and human reason, rather than the fallible writings of Scripture, are the best guides to the divine. Gordon then proceeds to ridicule numerous passages in the Bible. He wonders how a beneficent deity could punish all human beings to lives of misery and predestine most to hell simply because a woman ate an apple. Gordon views as preposterous the story of how the Jews were deemed a chosen people merely because a man named Abraham was willing to kill his son on orders received from a mysterious stranger. Citing Scottish philosopher David Hume, Gordon also denies that the Almighty would establish the laws of nature and then on a daily basis violate those laws. In other words, Gordon rejects miracles as the product of "the natural propensity of mankind to believe things which appear marvelous."[35]

It is easy to see why many in the eighteenth century were shocked by the novel's attack on established churches and some fundamental Christian tenets. Bancroft's deistic religious sentiments are even more pronounced here than in his *Natural History of Guiana*. He was a religious radical but certainly not an atheist. Through his characters, Bancroft fervently preaches love for the deity and his creation. He also advocates religious toleration and separation of church and state—ideas that were only slowly gaining acceptance among the educated classes of Europe.

In an excellent short essay on Bancroft written in the 1940s, Arthur S. MacNalty says this about the novel: "In *Charles Wentworth* Bancroft tried to do two things: to write an ethical and sociological treatise and a love-story. As a consequence, he failed in both aims and the novel, although interesting as a study of the author, cannot be regarded as a success. Probably Bancroft realized this, for he did not repeat the experiment."[36] Alternatively, however, one might conjecture that Bancroft did not write another novel because he had so many other irons in the fire. Over the years, he embarked on several projects or careers, only to break them off and start afresh on something else.

Two Americans who read the book soon after it was published were John and Abigail Adams, who purchased a copy for their library in Braintree, Massachusetts. Years later, in his memoirs, John castigated the work, charging that Bancroft wrote "a Novel which no doubt was recommended to many readers, and procured a considerably better Sale, by the plentifull Abuse and vilification of Christianity which he had taken care to insert in it."[37] The imperious Adams was not able, however, to dictate literary taste to his wife and daughter. Both Abigails recommended and lent the family's copy of *Charles Wentworth* to friends.[38]

A Man of Many Interests

In September 1770, after about seven months in Surinam, Bancroft sailed for Rhode Island. He spent the next several months traveling to various cities throughout New England. In February 1771 he left Boston for England, settling in London in April. The next several months contained more of the surprises that confront the biographer: Bancroft acquired a wife and became a business entrepreneur.

Sometime between April and September 1771 he married Penelope Fellows. She was from Shropshire, the daughter of William Fellows, Esq., and his wife, Penelope Wells. Born in 1749, Penelope was twenty-two at the time of the wedding. According to oral tradition among Bancroft's descendants, it was thought to have been "a runaway match," because the Fellows family was Catholic. The girl's parents would have had obvious reasons for rejecting her suitor: Bancroft was an American of undistinguished origins; he flitted from one location or career to another; he came of anti-Catholic Puritan stock; he was a freethinking Deist. There is no evidence to show that she ever reconciled with her parents.[39]

At about the same time as his wedding, Bancroft entered the business world. During his travels in North and South America one of the topics that had intrigued him the most was vegetable dyes—juices squeezed from various shrubs or trees that could then be used in inks or in the coloring of textiles. In Guiana he had experimented on linens with the juice of gardenia fruit. In North America he had become interested in extracts from the barks of three trees—the hickory, the red mangrove, and the black oak (also called the yellow or the dyer's oak). By 1771 he had become convinced that black oak showed the most promise. Bancroft found that when the inner bark of that tree was ground in a mill and the fibrous matter was then sifted out, what remained was a yellow powder. When mixed with the proper chemicals, this powder produced a dye that held fast to cloth. He named this new vegetable dye quercitron—after the Latin words for *oak* and *lemon* (*quercus* and *citron*). When mixed with other vegetable dyes, it could produce vivid greens, browns, and other colors. Moreover, quercitron was less expensive than other vegetable by-products that had been used previously. It was to become one of the most important dyeing materials in the world and would be used commercially until replaced by synthetic dyes in the mid-twentieth century.

Black oaks were plentiful in the forests of the middle and southern American colonies. In 1771, therefore, Bancroft dispatched his brother, Daniel, back to America to arrange for shipments of black oak bark to Britain. Little is known of this new entrepreneurial enterprise over the next few years. Daniel would have needed to purchase large stands of the trees and then have them cut down and the bark stripped from them. No information survives to tell us how he raised the money for these expenses. Daniel was unable to extract the dye from the bark himself. He was thus forced to ship the raw bark to Britain, where Edward could oversee the extraction process. In 1775 Daniel shipped twenty tons of the bark from Philadelphia. By 1775, however, much else had happened in Edward's life. We will return to the story of the dye in later pages.

In September 1771, not long after getting married and sending his brother to America, Bancroft traveled to Ireland. Leaving his wife, Penelope, in London, he remained in Ireland until February 1772. Lacking other information, one can only speculate that he visited the Emerald Isle to study its plant life, perhaps in search of new vegetable dyes.[40]

From February to April 1772, Bancroft was back in Britain. He seems to have spent most of these months at the University of Edinburgh. He did not officially matriculate there, but he attended lectures by the renowned Edinburgh chemist and physician William Cullen. Several hundred pages of Bancroft's scribbled lecture notes survive and are part of a collection owned today by some of his descendants.[41] Moreover, around this time Bancroft sent Benjamin Franklin a copy of one of Cullen's published books. Bancroft's letter states that the book contains a section on the gout, an ailment that hobbled Franklin frequently in his later years.[42]

In April 1772 Bancroft made a short trip to North America.[43] While he was away, his wife, Penelope, then living in London's Marlyebone parish, gave birth to their first child, Edward Nathaniel.[44] In all probability Bancroft returned to America to check up on the progress his brother, Daniel, was making with black oak bark. By late summer he was back in London, but within days of rejoining his wife and infant son he was gone again—returning to Ireland for several weeks. In October 1772 he was again in London, attending medical lectures on anatomy.[45]

Bancroft's dizzying series of travels now were over. With wife and son, he moved to new accommodations at Lisle Street near Leicester Square. He had become a minor celebrity. His findings about the electric eel were now being broadcast throughout Europe. One of his acquaintances was the famous botanist Joseph Banks, who had spent the years 1768–71 on the first great voyage of James Cook. Banks relayed some of Bancroft's ideas about medicine and nutrition to the Admiralty.[46] Bancroft was coming to be viewed as the premier expert on vegetable dyes of all sorts. Serving as a consultant to the East India Company, he helped to introduce lac dye into England.[47]

At some point in 1772 Bancroft invested in an American land company. This was to ensnare him in a confusing tangle of conflicting claims and illusory dreams over the next several years. But he was not alone. At the conclusion of the Seven Years' War, British North America suddenly came to include all the land between the Appalachians and the Mississippi. Who owned that land? There were many claimants. Several eastern colonies competed for large swatches of it, as their original charters did not specify clear western territorial boundaries. Virginia in particular claimed a huge territory west of the mountains. This led to quarrels with other colonies, which asserted ownership of some of the same lands. Both Virginia and Pennsylvania, for example, claimed the area around present-day Pittsburgh. The Crown was reluctant to let the colonies have any of this land, in part because this would lead to wars with the Indian tribes who lived there. Not willing to wait for the Crown, the Indians, and the colonial assemblies to sort things out, thousands of Americans began to cross into these territories. Many went as individual squatters, who would declare ownership of whatever parcels they settled on. Others went as agents of organized land companies. Some of these companies signed treaties with Indians, who agreed to sell significant chunks of their ancestral homelands in return for money, liquor, or promises of other lands. By the late 1760s the situation was a mess—colonies versus Crown, colonies versus each other, Indians versus whites, land companies versus colonies, land companies versus land companies, and land companies versus individual adventurers.

The land companies had names like Indiana, Illinois, Grand Ohio, Wabash, Mississippi, Susquehanna, and Transylvania. The names usually derived from rivers and do not reflect the boundaries of what eventually became some of the states in the Union. Pouring money into these companies became something like a mania: reckless, filled with illusory dreams of untold riches, and, in the end, financially disastrous. Nearly everyone who was anyone in colonial America from the 1760s to the 1790s risked modest or, in some cases, huge sums of money in these get-rich-quick schemes. This list included Benjamin Franklin, his son William (who after 1763 was royal governor of New Jersey), George Washington, Thomas Jefferson, the Lee brothers of Virginia, Aaron Burr, Alexander Hamilton, Patrick Henry, and Robert Morris, among many others.

In 1768 the six nations of the Iroquois Confederacy, feeling pressure from the onslaught of white settlers, signed a treaty with British authorities at Fort Stanwix (now Rome, New York). In this treaty, the confederacy ceded its rights to lands that today make up much of western New York, western Pennsylvania, West Virginia, and Kentucky. It was relatively easy for the Iroquois to do this, as their ownership of those lands was somewhat dubious. Other Indian tribes had traditionally resided in that vast territory. In signing away their titles to this broad stretch of land, the Iroquois preserved their ownership of most of central and northern New York. In a separate deal at Fort Stanwix, the Iroquois gave to some Pennsylvania representatives a piece of land east of the Ohio River (in today's West Virginia) to compensate that colony's residents for Indian attacks in 1763. This "suffering traders" tract came to be owned by a group calling itself the Indiana Company. The leading figures in this company included Indian agent and fur trader George Croghan, Philadelphia merchant Samuel Wharton, Pennsylvania Indian fighter and militia officer William Trent, and Benjamin and William Franklin.

In 1769 Wharton and Trent traveled to London to lobby for a royal charter recognizing their rights to the land. Together with Benjamin Franklin, they worked for several years in this effort. A royal charter was needed to validate what the Iroquois had given to the company and to fend off Virginia's supposed rights to the territory. To win government support, Franklin and his partners sold shares in the company to influential figures. These included Lord Camden (the lord chancellor), Lord Hertford (lord chamberlain), former prime minister George Grenville, Lord Rochford (member of the Privy Council), and Thomas Walpole. Son of Horatio, Lord Walpole, and cousin to the writer Horace Walpole, Thomas Walpole was a wealthy London banker, member of Parliament, and friend to America. The Indiana Company claimed about 2.4 million acres and offered the Crown £10,460 for title to the land. By 1770 the company had renamed itself the Grand Ohio

Company and was petitioning the Crown for 20 million acres. This land essentially makes up the state of West Virginia today. Walpole's key role in the company led it to become informally known as the Walpole Company. Walpole, Franklin, and their partners asked the government to establish this land as a new colony, volunteering to name it Pittsylvania, in honor of former prime minister William Pitt. The capital city would be named Charlotta, in honor of Queen Charlotte, wife of George III. In 1773 Colonial Secretary Lord Dartmouth voiced his support for the plan and suggested that the new colony instead be named Vandalia. This was a further ploy to win royal support: Queen Charlotte was reputed to be a descendant of the ancient Vandals. Vandalia is then what the company came to be called.

Sometime in 1772 Edward Bancroft purchased one or perhaps two shares in the company. The price for one share was approximately £200. He became not just a stockholder but an important lobbyist. As such, he expended both time and money defending the company's interests. The archival records for the company mention his name again and again.[48] Vandalia would loom large in Bancroft's life for the next decade. It would also tie him closer to Benjamin Franklin and Samuel Wharton.

Despite the support of various ministers, the company's petitions remained stuck in one committee after another. The government was still reluctant to encourage westward expansion, especially now that the colonies were creating so many problems with their objections to taxation. Moreover, Virginia's agents in London lobbied against Vandalia. Two rival groups of land speculators, from the Mississippi and Ohio Companies, likewise campaigned against Vandalia. George Washington and the Lee family were shareholders in these rival companies.[49]

While becoming an entrepreneur and a land speculator, Bancroft continued his medical and scientific pursuits. In May 1773 he presented a paper entitled "Observations on the Means of Producing and Communicating Colours" at the Royal Society, Britain's most prestigious scholarly organization. In this paper he challenged the accepted notion that the blackness of ink derived from the quality of astringency in vegetables. Within days of his delivering it, he was nominated for membership in that august body. Those who recommended him for admission included a member of Parliament, an artist, the royal astronomer, the king's physician, a Swedish botanist, several prominent physicians, and Benjamin Franklin. On 20 May, by a unanimous vote, he was accepted. A day later, Franklin wrote him a warm letter of congratulations.[50] In 1774 Bancroft delivered a follow-up paper to the society, entitled "Farther Conditions on the Black Dye." In it he demonstrated the advantages of using iron instead of vitriol in making ink. Over the next couple of years he presented at least two additional papers relating to dyes and inks.[51] For the rest of his life Bancroft proudly put the initials "F.R.S." (Fellow of the Royal Society) after his name in publications and official documents.

In the summer of 1773, Bancroft was invited to join the Medical Society of London, which had been established only a few months earlier. Its leading figure was John Coakley Lettsom, one of the most distinguished physicians in London. Lettsom was also renowned as an antislavery Quaker, a Fellow of the Royal Society, and a philanthropist. He had become disappointed with the medical societies already in existence. They tended to be narrow in focus. In the eighteenth century, physicians and surgeons still belonged to different professions. Physicians were the elite—they were academics who wrote books and prescribed remedies. Surgeons performed the manual labor in medical procedures. Apothecaries and midwives were also distinct groups. Each of these separate professions had its own societies. The most famous was the Royal College of Physicians, which admitted only graduates of Oxford and Cambridge.

Lettsom wanted to form a society that was broad in scope, one where experts from all medical fields could congregate and exchange ideas. From its inception, the members of the Medical Society included physicians, surgeons, apothecaries, and other men whose scientific or academic interests were related to medicine. Meetings were held twice a month. Usually a member or a guest presented a paper, which was followed by a general discussion.

Within a couple of months of the establishment of this society, Lettsom proposed Bancroft for membership. This was an extraordinary acknowledgment of Bancroft's reputation as a physician, especially since he had not yet obtained an M.D. It was also a testimony to Bancroft's character. Lettsom had freed the slaves on the West Indies plantation where he was born. In London he had established dispensaries that offered free medical care to the poor. He gave away vast portions of his personal fortune to worthy charities. Lettsom would not have taken Bancroft under his wing if Bancroft were known to be a shady character.[52]

By 1775 Bancroft had become the society's secretary, and that January he played a leading role in getting Lettsom elected president.[53] Although Lettsom had been the chief founder, he had not assumed the presidency in 1773. The first president, however, became a constant source of controversy. Therefore Bancroft helped to mount a coup that installed Lettsom at the top. A remarkable visual piece of evidence shows that Bancroft remained an active and respected member in the following decades. Down to the present day, the Medical Society holds its fortnightly meetings in its headquarters on Chandos Street. Prominently displayed on one of the walls there is a large oil painting composed around 1800 by Samuel Medley. The painting is entitled *The Founders' Picture*. That title is a misnomer. Not all the persons in the group were among the founders in 1773. What the picture shows are the more prominent members of the society from around 1800. Standing at the far left is Bancroft, who was about fifty-five at the time. His appearance is distinguished, though he is a bit shorter than average. He also shows signs of overindulging in good food and wine.

In 1774 Bancroft finally got around to obtaining his M.D. He received it from Marischal College at the University of Aberdeen. The two physicians who recommended him to the medical faculty there were John Coakley Lettsom and William Fordyce. Fordyce was one of the most distinguished physicians in London and a member of the staff at St. Thomas's Hospital. Why did Bancroft not obtain the degree in Edinburgh, where he had studied earlier? One possible reason is that Fordyce had taken his undergraduate degree at Aberdeen and may have recommended it to Bancroft. The other, and more probable, reason is that Bancroft was involved in so many affairs that he simply could not spend the required three years in attendance in Edinburgh. Aberdeen's medical school had perhaps the lowest standards of any in Britain at that time. Some of its professors were blatantly incompetent. Medical degrees were often conferred on persons who took no course of study and passed no final examination. In most cases the successful candidate needed only to provide letters of recommendation and pay a fee of about £20. Aberdeen was what today would be called a diploma mill. In fact, it is unlikely that Bancroft ever visited Aberdeen. He got in just under the wire. In the late 1780s, standards were tightened at the university, and at a minimum, an examination had to be passed before the degree was awarded.[54]

The Founders' Picture, ca. 1800. By Samuel Medley. Edward Bancroft is standing at far left. *Courtesy of the Medical Society of London*

Once Bancroft obtained his diploma, he could officially be licensed to practice medicine. He proceeded to do so. Except for another brief, unexplained trip to Ireland, in October 1774, Bancroft remained in London. In December 1774 he and his family rented a house in Downing Street.[55] Since 1730 the house at what is today No. 10 had been the official home of the first lord of the Treasury, who by tradition also was recognized as prime minister. (Still today the famous black door features a metal plate with the words "First Lord of the Treasury.") One of Bancroft's neighbors thus was Lord North. Several other prominent government officials lived on or near that street. Bancroft's motive for moving there, however, probably had more to do with his profession. Downing Street at that time also was a center for medical practitioners.

The year 1774 likewise saw Bancroft reenter the world of political affairs. Some years earlier he had already become a close friend of Benjamin Franklin. The two obviously had much in common. Both came from humble origins. Both had gone through years in an "unfree" status—that is, apprenticeships. Both had run away from their apprenticeships. Perhaps in reaction against those personal experiences, both were beginning to have severe doubts about slavery. Both were mostly self-educated. Both were Deists who rejected the superstitions and intolerance of established churches. Both were scientists. Both were jovial good company at the dinner table. Both were concerned about the growing conflict between the colonies and Britain. By early 1774 Franklin seems to have taken such a liking to the younger man that he took him under his wing, making him a sort of protégé.

Striking evidence of the strong bond between the two men came on 29 January 1774. On that date, Bancroft stood by Franklin as the older man was subjected to the most notorious public humiliation of his career. This was the culmination of what became known as the affair of the Hutchinson Letters. In December 1772 Franklin had sent a packet of letters to Thomas Cushing, speaker of the Massachusetts House of Representatives. The letters dated from the period 1767–69 and had been written by persons in America to an associate in Britain. The chief authors of the letters were Thomas Hutchinson and Andrew Oliver. Both came from distinguished Boston families and held appointments as royal officers in the late 1760s—Hutchinson as chief justice and then lieutenant governor, Oliver as colonial secretary. Their letters to Britain were filled with recriminations against colonial troublemakers. In one letter, Hutchinson even called for the suspension of the natural rights of Englishmen. The letters called for a strong show of force from the Crown.

It is not known how Franklin came to possess the letters. He said that an unnamed person had given them to him, on condition that Franklin not reveal the source. When forwarding them to Cushing, Franklin expected Cushing to show them to friends but asked that he not make them public. One can assume that Franklin knew very well that the letters would become public knowledge. Later Franklin said that by sending the letters to America he was hoping to promote reconciliation with Britain. He hoped to show American leaders that the British government was taking a hard line against the colonies because a small clique of Americans (that is, Hutchinson, Oliver, and others) were egging it on. Again, there is some reason to doubt that

Franklin sincerely believed that such inflammatory letters would actually douse the flames.

Soon after the letters reached America in early 1773, they were published in newspapers and had the expected consequence of rousing public protests. What made the situation even more explosive was that Hutchinson was now the governor and Oliver the lieutenant governor. Through the remainder of 1773 the Hutchinson Letters remained a source of controversy on both sides of the Atlantic. That fall, the Massachusetts House sent a petition to London stating that Hutchinson had lost the confidence of people in the colony and asking that the government replace him. In London, accusations were hurled from one person to another regarding the identity of the thief who had stolen the letters and sent them to America. In December two men, each accusing the other, even fought a duel. To put this controversy to rest, Franklin thereupon admitted that he himself had dispatched the letters to Massachusetts. He refused to name the person who had given them to him, and he stoutly repeated his dubious assertion that his motives for sending them to America were peaceful.

On 29 January 1774 the Privy Council assembled to deal with the matter. The ostensible issue at hand was the Massachusetts petition for the removal of Hutchinson and Oliver from their positions. The meeting took place in the Cockpit, which was a large building in Whitehall, the street on which most of the major government offices were located. The structure got the name because of cockfights held there in the reign of Henry VIII. On the assigned day, the Cockpit was filled with all the regular privy counsellors—current and past government ministers, the archbishop of Canterbury and other high clergy, and a variety of other royal officials—but also with lords and ladies from high society, who obviously had been invited to see the spectacle. The atmosphere was further charged by the news, received nine days earlier in London, of the Boston Tea Party.

Franklin, as Massachusetts's agent and the man who had leaked the purloined letters, was asked to attend. He brought a team of attorneys with him. He was prepared to explain in detail the many actions Hutchinson had taken that made it impossible for him to remain governor of the colony. Instead, Alexander Wedderburn, the solicitor general, arose and, rather than discussing the colonial petition, launched into a scurrilous one-hour attack on Franklin. Even by the raucous standards of political debate in that era, his philippic was withering—so much so that some eyewitnesses who later penned accounts of it felt obliged to omit some of the most blatant insults flung against the American. Wedderburn accused Franklin of being a disreputable thief, a liar, and a ringleader of colonial hotheads who were trying to rouse general hatred of Britain.

Franklin stood emotionless throughout this diatribe. Wedderburn's scathing attack had most people in the crowd jeering and laughing at the American. Franklin did have a few friends and supporters there, including the scientist Joseph Priestley and Edmund Burke, a staunch defender of America in the House of Commons. The friend who stood closest to Franklin throughout the ordeal was Edward Bancroft. Many years later, Bancroft provided Franklin's grandson, William Temple Franklin, with a written summary of the event. Temple (as he was usually called) included Bancroft's words in a six-volume edition of his grandfather's works that appeared in 1818. Bancroft recalled that

> [Franklin's] face was directed towards me, and I had a full uninterrupted view of it and his person, during the whole time in which Mr. Wedderburn spoke. The Doctor was dressed in a full dress suit of spotted Manchester velvet, and stood *conspicuously erect*, without the smallest movement of any part of his body. The muscles of his face had been previously composed, so as to afford a placid tranquil expression of countenance, and he did not suffer the slightest alteration of it to appear during the continuance of the speech in which he was so harshly and improperly treated. In short, to quote the words which he employed concerning himself on another occasion, he kept his "countenance as immovable as if his features had been made of *wood*."[56]

From the accounts of the affair by Bancroft and Priestley, it is also known that Franklin stored away the velvet suit that he wore in the Cockpit. He did not don it again until 6 February 1778, when he signed the treaty creating the Franco-American alliance.

Bancroft's attendance at the Cockpit that day took courage. For several days thereafter, Franklin was afraid that he might be arrested. If Bancroft had been an unprincipled social climber, he would have avoided a public appearance with Franklin, who had suddenly gone from popular celebrity to suspected traitor. Bancroft's written account of the affair dates from more than forty years later. Obviously, even after Bancroft had sided with the mother country in the Revolution and settled permanently in London, he still fondly remembered his old friend and mentor.

The Cockpit incident abruptly ended any chances for Franklin to continue working effectively as a colonial representative. The British government fired him from his post as deputy colonial postmaster. Most cabinet members and other royal officials refused to meet with him. Yet he remained in London. He received friends like Bancroft and Priestley privately in his rooms on Craven Street.

Bancroft joined with Franklin and other Americans in London in presenting a more united and forceful opposition to government policies.[57] In March and again in May 1774 Bancroft, Franklin, and a few dozen other Americans and their British friends signed petitions to the government asking for the repeal of the Boston Port Act and other measures that have come to be called the Coercive or Intolerable Acts. These acts were a retaliation against the Boston Tea Party. They closed Boston harbor to all trade, eliminated the local administration of justice, made all government officials responsible to the governor rather than to the provincial assembly, and called for the quartering and feeding of British troops by local citizenry.

Arthur Lee was the principal organizer of these two petitions. A scion of one of Virginia's most distinguished families, Lee had spent many years in England, studying at Eton and obtaining an M.D. at Edinburgh in 1765. Soon thereafter he took up legal studies and by 1770 had his own law practice. In these years he also began writing strident attacks on British colonial policies. Other Americans in London who signed Lee's petitions included Arthur's brother William, a London merchant and politician, and the wealthy South Carolinian Ralph Izard. On at least one occasion, in December 1774, Arthur Lee, Bancroft, and others met at Franklin's home to discuss the latest news from America and to plot new strategies for petitions to the Crown.[58] Later, in Paris, the Lee brothers and Izard would become enemies of both Franklin and Bancroft, but at least for now they all worked side by side.

Several writers have stated that Franklin used Bancroft as a secret agent in London during this period.[59] Supposedly, Franklin paid Bancroft to find out what British ministers were planning for America. There is no evidence for this. Indeed, it would have made no sense. During this period Bancroft had no contacts of any importance in the government. Franklin himself, despite his demoted status after the Cockpit, was still in a much better position to uncover what the government was doing. Franklin continued to meet with numerous important figures. These included former prime minister William

Pitt (now Lord Chatham), Edmund Burke, and Admiral Lord Richard Howe (who would soon become commander-in-chief of British forces in America).

In the summer or early fall of 1774, Franklin used his influence to return a favor for Bancroft's continued support. He recommended Bancroft to Ralph Griffiths, the owner and editor of the *Monthly Review*, a respected periodical that published reviews of important new books in all fields—politics, science, literature, religion, and the like. All of the reviews were anonymous; only Griffiths knew who the authors were. He did this so that contributors could express their views freely and readers could evaluate each piece on its merits rather than on whether they liked the author. Griffiths's contributors included dozens of the most respected men of letters in the kingdom, including Oliver Goldsmith, David Garrick, and Tobias Smollett. When a contributor sent in a piece, Griffiths scribbled the reviewer's name or initials on it. Many years later researchers gained access to the magazine's files and were thus able to discern who wrote what.

Bancroft's first review appeared in November 1774. Between then and the spring of 1777 (when he moved to France), he contributed approximately three dozen reviews.[60] He wrote about new books in medicine, science, and American history. In the April 1775 issue Bancroft published a long review of Oliver Goldsmith's eight-volume *History of the Earth and Animated Nature*. Goldsmith was a renowned poet, novelist, and playwright, but he also fancied himself a naturalist. Bancroft's review is scathing. He expostulates that this topic "requires a much more extensive knowledge than appears to have been possessed by this writer." He goes on to note that Goldsmith adopted "no methodical arrangement worthy of notice." Goldsmith was "wholly unacquainted with his subject" and "surprisingly ignorant." The review delivers this "censure . . . only from a sense of our duty to the Public."[61] Bancroft could dare to be brash. Not only was this review anonymous, but Goldsmith had died in 1774.

On a dozen or so occasions, Bancroft discussed books dealing with the growing American political crisis. In the fall of 1774 he wrote the first significant British account of Thomas Jefferson's *Summary View of the Rights of British America*.[62] In that review and later ones, Bancroft's views were similar to those he had expressed in his *Remarks*. About four years later, in France, Franklin confided to John Adams that Bancroft consulted with him before composing any reviews dealing with current American affairs.[63] One of Bancroft's final reviews was penned near the end of 1776. This was a review of Dean Tucker's *Certain Popular Objections against Separating from the Rebellious Colonies*. That book contained many intemperate attacks on Franklin. Bancroft staunchly defended the character and actions of his old friend.[64] What makes this review particularly curious is that at the same time that Bancroft was composing it he was also making arrangements to move to France, where he would serve the British government by spying on Franklin.

Franklin himself had returned to America in March 1775. By the time he arrived back in Philadelphia he seems to have made up his mind that the colonies could preserve their rights only by breaking entirely with Britain. Though he was nearing seventy, he quickly assumed a leading role in Pennsylvania politics as well as in the Second Continental Congress. In October 1776 Congress sent him back to Europe, as one of its three commissioners in France. In Paris he would join Silas Deane and Arthur Lee in petitioning the court of Versailles for assistance.

From the time of Franklin's departure from England until the summer of 1776, Bancroft remained in London and actively pursued his medical, scientific, and business enterprises. In April 1775 he and Penelope had their second child, a boy named Samuel Forrester.[65]

In 1774, Bancroft, Samuel Wharton, and Thomas Walpole became the Vandalia Company's most important spokesmen. After the disgrace of the Cockpit affair, Franklin withdrew from any public association with it, so as not to hurt its chances. By 1775 Bancroft and the others judged that the Vandalia claim to 20 million acres was, for the time being, dead in the water. Therefore they concentrated on the smaller chunk (2.4 million acres) that originally had been called the Indiana Company. That year Wharton and Bancroft published a pamphlet defending claims to that land (in what would be northern West Virginia today). Wharton and Bancroft argued that the land belonged to its original inhabitants, the Indians. By natural rights bestowed on them by the Creator, they had full title to it. If the Indians chose in 1768 to give 2.4 million acres to a group of whites, the Indians had a total right to do so. This bestowal of land did not need approval from Parliament, the Virginia assembly, or any other outside group. In the best of all possible worlds, this argument might have been valid. But one can readily see why the British government would never accept it.[66] The Crown was not going to make any decisions about the western lands at this point. Fighting had already broken out at Lexington and Concord in the spring of 1775. The land issue would have to await the end of the war before any resolution could be reached. Bancroft and all the other stockholders reaped not one farthing from their investments.

Bancroft also had yet to make any profits from his dyeing enterprise. In mid-1775 he petitioned Parliament for three patents. They would give him a full monopoly on the importation and sale of the dyes produced from three sorts of trees: the black oak, the American hickory, and the red mangrove. The first of these, which produced the yellow dye called quercitron, would be the most important for him. That October he was granted a fourteen-year monopoly for dyes from all three trees. At about that same time he received the shipment of twenty tons of black oak bark from Daniel. This must have been one of the final cargoes of anything to arrive from America. The king had declared the colonies to be in a state of rebellion, and virtually all trade with them was cut off. Bancroft extracted the quercitron dye from the twenty tons of bark and sold it to a calico printer named Arbuthnot.

Unfortunately, Arbuthnot soon thereafter went bankrupt. Only nine years later did Bancroft obtain any payment from him, and that was only 3 shillings to the pound of what he was owed. To make matters worse, no additional shipments of the bark could be sent from America for the duration of the Revolution. The tons of bark that Daniel had amassed in America sat where they were until redcoats confiscated them and used them for firewood.[67] Thus, for the time being, Bancroft's fourteen-year monopoly was worthless. He had invested heavily in getting the enterprise started. By mid-1776 Bancroft was in financial straits. His business losses exceeded whatever he earned from his medical practice and his publications.

It was at this juncture, in June 1776, that he received a letter from France. This letter would involve him directly in the American Revolution and, eventually, force him to decide which side he was on. Choosing sides led him into yet another career: espionage.

3 Initiation in Covert Activity

After Benjamin Franklin's departure for America in March 1775, Bancroft continued to show every sign of being a full-fledged supporter of the colonial cause. On 7 August 1775 from his home in Downing Street he wrote to Franklin condemning the British government's "Chains of Despotism." Bancroft decried the sending of additional British troops to America as a "hostile invasion" and asserted that the British would incite the Indians "to butcher the Inhabitants of the Colonies." Through this "Carnage" the colonists would "be reduced to submission." Bancroft condemned the 1774 Quebec Act, which permitted French Canadians to practice their Catholic religion and which extended Quebec territory through the Ohio and Mississippi valleys—thus placing another obstacle to the westward expansion of the thirteen colonies. In closing, Bancroft expressed the hope that the current ministry, which has "so unwisely and wickedly" conducted these actions, would be compelled "to Quit the Helm," so "that they may be succeeded by others who will contribute to a permanent and equitable reconciliation between Great Britain and the Colonies." A few months later, in December, Bancroft told Franklin that he wished for the parliamentary opposition to "act with Vigour" to topple the ministry. He assured Franklin "that under every Vicissitude and in every Place" he would always continue to be his most faithful, affectionate servant.[1]

All the evidence suggests that through mid-1776 Bancroft was planning to continue his various professional interests in London while remaining a friend and supporter of the American campaign for redress of grievances. It is important to stress this. In the light of what today is known about his later activities, most writers have postulated that his above-mentioned sentiments were a sham. Furthermore, with no evidence, they have surmised that he was already in contact with British ministers and waiting for his chance to gain access to American secrets. The truth is that Bancroft did not have to seek an entry into the Americans' camp. He was invited in.

The skein of events leading to his active involvement in the conflict started in the final months of 1775. In September, the Continental Congress established a Secret Committee to work clandestinely to acquire military and other supplies from abroad. The most prominent member of this committee was the merchant financier Robert Morris. Later this committee would be called the Commerce Committee. In November Congress created the Committee of Secret Correspondence, which in 1777 was renamed the Committee for Foreign Relations (precursor to today's State Department). This second committee aimed to make contacts with European governments and seek their help. (It should come as no surprise that numerous authors have confused these two secret committees.) Benjamin Franklin was appointed to the second committee and soon became its leader. Within weeks of its creation, this committee sent letters to two men in Europe asking that they work quietly to collect information relevant to the American cause. These were Arthur Lee, who still resided in London, and Charles-Guillaume-Frédéric Dumas. Dumas, a German-born scholar who had been living in the Dutch Republic for many years, was an old acquaintance of Franklin.

Both secret committees also decided to send someone to France, which was considered the likeliest prospect as a supplier and possible ally. The committees selected Silas Deane, who in effect became the first diplomatic envoy in the history of the United States. After his brief spell as a schoolteacher, Deane had been active as a businessman, lawyer, and politician. He served as one of Connecticut's representatives in the First and the Second Continental Congress. In October 1775 he failed to win reelection to Congress, a result of factional rivalries in Connecticut rather than any personal failings. Because of his experience in trade and government, he was selected in March 1776 for the French mission. For the Secret Committee he was to purchase items that could be traded to Indian tribes in order to keep them friendly. For the Committee of Secret Correspondence, his task was to obtain one hundred pieces of field artillery plus uniforms and arms for twenty-five thousand men. His larger assignment was to feel out the French crown regarding either secret or open help for the Americans.

From the outset, Deane faced numerous hurdles. He had never been abroad, and he spoke no French. Because the colonies had not yet declared independence, his mission had to be kept secret from the British minister in Paris. He had no money to purchase any of the supplies he was charged with obtaining. Instead he was expected to buy on credit, with Congress promising to send an equivalent value of tobacco, indigo, rice, and other products to France. Finally, he had no friends or acquaintances in France to advise him.

To help Deane overcome these obstacles, Franklin and the other members of the Committee of Secret Correspondence gave him a list of six men to contact as soon as he touched European shores. The first two were Arthur Lee and Dumas. The third was Jacques Barbeu-Dubourg, a physician and scholar who published a two-volume French edition of Franklin's works in 1773 and had been corresponding with Franklin for several years. The fourth was another old Franklin friend, Jean-Baptiste Le Roy, a scientist who had been exchanging letters with Franklin for almost a quarter of a century. The fifth was Charles-Jean Garnier, the French chargé d'affaires in London, yet another friend of Franklin. As instructed, Deane contacted them all and was offered their friendship and what little support they could muster.

The sixth person on the list was Edward Bancroft. The committee's instructions to Deane stated, "You will endeavor to procure a meeting with Mr. Bancroft by writing a letter to him, under cover to Mr. Griffiths at Turnham Green, near London, and desiring him to come over to you, in France or Holland, on the score of old acquaintance. From him you may obtain a good deal of information of what is now going forward in England, and settle a mode of continuing a correspondence. It may well be to remit him a small bill to defray his expenses in coming to you, and avoid all political matters in your letter to him."[2]

The reasons why Deane was referred to Bancroft are easily comprehended. Bancroft and Deane had an "old acquaintance," dating back more than fifteen years, to when they had been pupil and teacher. Not only had Bancroft demonstrated his keen support for the colonies, but he was a man of the world, fluent in French, and well placed to help an inexperienced Connecticut Yankee navigate the many shoals that lay in his path. The Griffiths referred to in the letter was Ralph Griffiths, editor of the *Monthly Review*, a friend of both Bancroft and Franklin.

Silas Deane arrived in Bordeaux on 6 June and immediately wrote to Bancroft, asking him to come to Paris and enclosing £30 to defray travel expenses. Bancroft responded on 25 June, stating that he had delayed responding earlier because he had been ill and because he had to take care of some business affairs with Thomas Walpole. Those affairs most likely related to land claims in America. On 3 July Bancroft departed for France, arriving in Paris on 6 July, one day ahead of Deane. Bancroft again fell ill and had to postpone meeting Deane until 8 July. Throughout his life, Bancroft frequently suffered from what he sometimes called "quotidian intermittent." It is not clear what this might have been—fever, malaria, migraine, or some other ailment.[3]

Deane's initial letter had not said anything about political affairs, lest the message be intercepted by the British post office. Yet Bancroft evidently guessed that Deane's mission in France must have something to do with the colonial crisis, for he brought with him a stack of pamphlets and newspapers to keep his former teacher up to date on events in London. The older man was pleased to discover that his former pupil had turned into a scholarly gentleman with an impressive knowledge of European affairs. Following instructions from Franklin, Deane informed Bancroft of everything that he was supposed to accomplish. Bancroft moved into the same Paris hotel and spent the next two weeks accompanying Deane everywhere.

Just three days after their reunion, they traveled the fourteen miles from Paris to the royal palace at Versailles. There Deane met with the foreign minister, the Comte de Vergennes. Bancroft discreetly stayed in an antechamber, leaving Deane alone with the minister. Vergennes's *premier commis* (chief secretary) Conrad-Alexandre Gérard translated for Deane. Vergennes welcomed Deane cordially and spent three hours with him. The minister listened to all of Deane's requests for arms, munitions, and uniforms. He told Deane that France was friendly to America's interests but that his government would have to act slowly and secretly. France could not afford to risk an immediate war with Britain. Moreover, France could not openly aid the colonists until they declared their independence from Britain and proved their determination to defend that independence. Vergennes also said that he would have to confer with the other ministers and with King Louis XVI before making any firm assurances. In closing, the minister warned that the British ambassador in Paris, Viscount Stormont, had informers all over. To conceal their dealings from Stormont, he instructed that henceforth Deane should meet secretly with Gérard rather than with Vergennes himself.[4]

After leaving the minister, Deane felt justifiably optimistic about what that first interview had accomplished. The details of this and other conversations are known because Deane invariably gave "a minute and faithful" report to Bancroft. In addition to follow-up meetings with Gérard and a second interview with Vergennes, Deane also conferred with two other men. They were Jacques-Donatien Leray de Chaumont and Pierre-Augustin Caron de Beaumarchais. Chaumont was one of the wealthiest businessmen in France, with several textile manufacturing operations and a small fleet of merchant vessels. He owned a magnificent Loire valley château as well as a spacious estate in the Paris suburb of Passy. He had held various government positions and was a friend of several past and present royal ministers. Beaumarchais likewise was a man of many talents. Of humble origins, he had risen from being a watchmaker to owning a large estate, becoming music tutor to the four spinster daughters of Louis XV, making a fortune in banking, and performing secret diplomatic missions in London for Louis XVI. He was a spirited adventurer with a somewhat shady reputation. Although he claimed to be a man of the people, rather incongruously he also remained steadfastly loyal to his monarch. Nowadays he is best remembered as a playwright—for *The Barber of Seville* (1775) and *The Marriage of Figaro* (1784). Despite their many differences, Chaumont and Beaumarchais shared an intense desire to serve their king.

Vergennes had recommended that Deane contact Chaumont and Beaumarchais for the supplies he needed. Through his own resources, Chaumont would be able to furnish all sorts of items, and he offered to sell these to Deane on credit. Beaumarchais was not a manufacturer or shipowner, but because of his energy, enthusiasm, imagination, and talent, Vergennes thought that he could also gather supplies for the Americans. Even before Silas Deane had arrived in France, Vergennes had sent Beaumarchais to London to collect information and hold preliminary discussions with Arthur Lee regarding America's needs. In the summer of 1776 the French and

Spanish crowns each gave Beaumarchais one million livres in start-up capital to purchase supplies and ships. In order to camouflage his own role and that of the two governments in this operation, Beaumarchais gave this new trading company the fanciful name of Roderigue Hortalez and Company.

From mid- to late July Bancroft joined Deane in negotiations with Chaumont and Beaumarchais. Bancroft served as translator and confidant.[5] By late that month, plans were afoot for Chaumont and Beaumarchais to send fifty tons of saltpeter, uniforms for thirty thousand men, two hundred tons of gunpowder, and all sorts of other materials to America. Vergennes authorized them to purchase cannons and other arms from French arsenals. Eventually the Continental Congress would be expected to repay Chaumont and Beaumarchais with money or tobacco and other goods.

To understand Deane's initial successes, one must realize why France and, to a lesser extent, Spain, were willing to help the Americans. To do this, one must first throw out some reasons given by earlier historians. France did not help the Americans because it shared the American ideals of republican liberty and equality. France was a divine-right absolute monarchy; neither Louis XVI nor any of his ministers had much, if any interest, in the fine sentiments of the Declaration of Independence or Thomas Paine's *Common Sense*. Only the Marquis de Lafayette and perhaps a handful of other Frenchmen who voluntarily served in the Continental Army showed any interest in democracy, equality before the law, and the rights of Englishmen. Nor did France get involved because it wanted to regain territories lost to Britain in the Seven Years' War. Neither in what Vergennes said to Deane and other Americans nor in what he communicated privately to the king and his fellow ministers is there the slightest hint that France wanted to reclaim its North American empire. France still held on to the parts of its American empire that were lucrative—that is, its share of the Newfoundland fishery plus sugar- and coffee-producing Caribbean islands like Saint-Domingue, Guadeloupe, and Martinique.

So why did France become involved? First, the crown wanted revenge for the mortifying defeat in the Seven Years' War. Worse than the loss of territories in 1763 was France's loss of face. France was no longer the diplomatic giant in European continental affairs of former years. Vergennes and other royal ministers felt humiliated when major events took place without their consultation or involvement. For example, France stood by helplessly in the

1770s when its traditional client state Poland lost huge chunks of land to Austria, Prussia, and Russia. Another reason why the French crown was interested in the Americans was trade. If the colonists broke from England, they might transfer most of their foreign commerce to France.

Spain's support for the Americans came more slowly and reluctantly. Since the signing of the Family Compact in 1761, Spain and France had been obligated to aid each other in the event of attack from a third party. It was a "family" compact because the Bourbon kings of the two countries were cousins. In 1775 Vergennes began working to interest Spain's king, Charles III, in the American cause. The Iberian monarch was extremely leery of the colonists' liberal ideals, fearing that they would seep into Spain's New World colonies. Furthermore, he suspected that the Americans wanted to expand into Spain's North American territories—East and West Florida and the lands west of the Mississippi. On the other hand, Spain held grudges against Britain as a result of the Seven Years' War and a brief conflict over the Falkland Islands in 1770. Moreover, Britain was friendly to Portugal, which was disputing Spanish claims to various territories in South America. Finally, Spain dreamed of reconquering Gibraltar, which Britain had acquired in the War of the Spanish Succession earlier in the century. Because of these considerations, in 1775 Charles III agreed to allow American ships to trade in Spanish ports. He also permitted Spanish merchants to funnel supplies to Americans through New Orleans and Cuba. In August 1776 he put up half of the two million livres that enabled Beaumarchais to purchase military supplies and ships. Nonetheless, in mid-1776 Spain was still far from committing itself to any overt participation in the American cause.

Vergennes knew that French entry in the conflict would have to be slow and gradual. One important reason for this involved the French navy. France could not hope to aid the Americans if the mighty British fleets dominated the seas. The capable French naval minister, Gabriel de Sartine, had begun extensive rebuilding programs even before Deane reached Paris, but he calculated that he would not have enough men, cannons, and ships of the line to risk confronting Britain until late 1777 or early 1778. The other factor was Louis XVI. The young monarch was both diffident and scrupulous. He disliked the idea of interfering in the internal colonial affairs of another country, even if that country happened to be Britain. The king would approve formal intervention only if it seemed the moral thing to do. Vergennes realized that this could be accomplished most easily if Britain appeared to be the aggressor. One fear that he planted in the king's head was the prospect that the Americans and British might reconcile and go on to conquer the French West Indies.[6]

Despite these factors, the volume of French support—whether through private individuals or government sponsorship—was already impressive by the summer of 1776 and would grow exponentially in the coming months. As early as 1775 Vergennes had sent a secret agent to America to meet with the Continental Congress and assure its members that France was friendly to their cause. The Americans especially hoped that the French government would tacitly allow its merchants to export war materials. Despite the absence of any formal French approval, dozens of French and American merchants rushed into this clandestine commerce. Ships brought arms, munitions, clothing, and other supplies to American ports directly from France or from the French West Indies. During one week in May 1776, for example, fourteen French vessels arrived in the Martinique port of Saint-Pierre, all carrying arms and munitions that would be transferred to smaller, faster vessels and then sent to the insurgents.[7] Britain knew about much of this traffic but could do little to stop it. France and Britain were not at war, and thus Britain could not prevent French ships from going to a French colony. Nor was the mighty British navy able to intercept much of the illegal trade that the Americans were conducting with merchants from the Netherlands and other European countries.

Chaumont and Beaumarchais therefore were not alone in this activity. They were merely the largest suppliers. They were "insurance." In the event that American and French merchants on their own initiative could not provide enough supplies, the French government wanted to make sure that Deane had the help of those two men.

Bancroft had a front-row seat and could see everything that was developing.

Return to London

On 26 July 1776 Bancroft left Paris and returned home to London. He did so for several reasons. Neither the Continental Congress nor Silas Deane had said anything to him about his remaining in Paris for an extended stay. Nor had any sort of official position been offered to him. Initially, he was merely one of six persons whom Deane was instructed to ask for help. To be sure, Bancroft did much more for Deane than any of the others. Three of the others (Lee, Garnier, and Dumas) were either in London or in the Netherlands and so not in a position to help Deane in Paris. For their part, Le Roy and Barbeu-Dubourg were scientists and scholars and little able to help in the areas of business and politics. So Bancroft had done as much or more than could have been expected of him. Moreover, his wife and children were in London. In the end, Bancroft told Deane that he needed to be in London to attend to his new dyeing business plus his other scientific and medical affairs.

Sometime early in August, Paul Wentworth discovered that his friend Bancroft had just returned from France. Wentworth approached him with a proposition. This was the start of Bancroft's career as a secret agent.

How did Wentworth become involved in this? It will be recalled that he owned plantations in Surinam, that he was related to the last royal governor of New Hampshire, and that in 1766 or 1767 he had moved to London. In the metropolis he used his family connections, his wealth, and his cosmopolitan flair to become a prominent and overtly ambitious man about town. In 1770 Governor John Wentworth received permission from London to add his relative Paul to the New Hampshire Council, even though Paul was living in Britain and would never again visit America. In 1770 Paul also was hired as a private agent by settlers west of the Connecticut River, in present-day Vermont, to defend their land claims against speculators from New York. In his authoritative account of colonial agents in London, historian Michael Kammen states that Wentworth did nothing in London to obtain official approval of their claims but instead used their needs as a pretext to get himself appointed the official New Hampshire agent. He garnered that appointment early in 1774, with help from his relative the governor. It is easy to see that the New Hampshire assembly and the residents of that colony had no idea what kind of man was representing them. When the issue of the land claims was finally brought before the London Board of Trade in 1775, Wentworth feebly defended his constituents' case, and before any decision was made the Revolution suspended the matter.[8] In 1774 and 1775 he repeatedly refused to side with his fellow colonial agents in presenting complaints to the Crown. He criticized one petition from the Continental Congress as having "a very high Tone

&... very offensive expressions." Edmund Burke, a member of Parliament who also happened to be the agent for New York, accused Wentworth of collusion with the government against the interests of New Hampshire. Wentworth also did some suspicious maneuvering in the aftermath of Benjamin Franklin's humiliation in the Cockpit in January 1774. Realizing that his influence in London was severely compromised, Franklin surrendered his appointments as colonial agent for New Jersey and Georgia and tried to retire from the Massachusetts agency. He recommended Arthur Lee for the Massachusetts position, but just at that moment Wentworth persuaded Lee to make a tour of Italy and gave him £300 to cover expenses. As a result, Franklin had to remain in the post for several additional months, until Lee returned. Wentworth seems to have wanted Lee out of the picture so that the discredited Franklin would have to continue in the job. In summing up Wentworth's service to New Hampshire, Kammen writes, "He was clearly a wretched choice for agent."[9]

By 1776 Wentworth had obviously thrown in his lot with the Crown. There is reason to suspect that his decision was rooted as much in self-interest as in genuine political and sentimental ties to the mother country. One author has labeled him "a man on the make, seeking money, position, and titles."[10]

In the early to mid-1770s Wentworth had been careful to befriend politicians both in and out of power so that his chances for success would be assured no matter how the political winds blew. In the government, his closest connections were with Lord Suffolk, the secretary of state for the northern department, and with William Eden, one of Suffolk's two undersecretaries. Once the colonial rebellion had commenced, Eden was charged with collecting information about Americans in England and France and with supervising the work of several secret informers. Eden realized that Paul Wentworth could be of use to him. Sometime in 1775 or 1776 Eden arranged for Wentworth to receive a modest annual retainer plus reimbursement for expenses. Eden and Suffolk also gave Wentworth some nebulous promises of a baronetcy, a seat in Parliament, and perhaps a sinecure in a government agency of some sort.[11]

Edward Bancroft's arrival back in London gave Wentworth his first major opportunity to demonstrate his worth to the government. He told Bancroft that he knew of his trip to France and his close association with Silas Deane. Wentworth probably knew of this because of regular reports sent to

London by the vigilant British minister in Paris, Viscount Stormont, and his chargé d'affaires, Horace St. Paul. Stormont knew about Deane from the moment the American arrived in the French capital.

Wentworth told Bancroft that the prime minister, Lord North, as well as Secretaries of State Lords Suffolk and Weymouth knew of Bancroft's sojourn in Paris. Wentworth was well aware of Bancroft's political sentiments—as a result of Bancroft's *Remarks,* his signing of petitions to the Crown, and other actions. But Wentworth also realized that Bancroft's support of American grievances stopped short of independence. Bancroft desired a reconciliation that would redress wrongs to the colonies but preserve the empire.

Somehow Wentworth prevailed on Bancroft to accompany him to a meeting with Weymouth and Suffolk. No record survives to reveal what transpired in that meeting. What does survive, however, is a document that Bancroft wrote a few days later. After completing it, he submitted it to the two secretaries of state.

The document is dated 14 August 1776. The original in Bancroft's hand has disappeared. A copy in the hand of William Fraser, an undersecretary to Suffolk, remains today in the British National Archives. It runs to nine manuscript pages. At the top of the first page is its informal title, "A Narrative etc." What it amounts to is a detailed summary of everything that Deane had accomplished in his first weeks in France. Bancroft lists the supplies that Deane was charged with obtaining; he summarizes the meetings with Vergennes, Gérard, Chaumont, Beaumarchais, and others; and he notes the strong French assurances of friendship and material support.[12] Though his report is remarkable for its detail, it also shows signs of having been written from memory some time after the events rather than being based on daily notes. Bancroft is off by a day or so in some of the dates he gives. This is an important point. Some authors have asserted that Bancroft was already a spy or preparing to be a spy during this first trip to Paris. If that were true, then one would expect him to have taken careful notes and been accurate in his dating. But the errors and general style of the document support Bancroft's later contention that he wrote it only weeks later, on the urging of Wentworth and government ministers. As a result of this report, the Crown knew just about everything that Deane was doing in France, and it knew this two months before the Continental Congress did.

One essential question that the "Narrative" does not answer is why Bancroft agreed to write it. The document itself is a matter-of-fact summary of Deane's actions in Paris; Bancroft's own opinions or motives are not discussed at all. Yet one must explore his feelings and intentions, for only then can one judge whether, like Paul Wentworth, he was an unprincipled opportunist, a traitor to his homeland, or someone driven by other sentiments.

A Traitor?

Virtually all American historians who have had occasion to mention Bancroft in the past hundred years have labeled him a traitor. And once they made their minds up on that point, it was easy for them to put a negative spin on all of his actions and personality traits. Even his seemingly most innocent or neutral deeds have been interpreted as revealing something devious, underhanded, unpatriotic, amoral, or immoral. Accordingly, they have considered his "Narrative" of 14 August 1776 to be just the beginning of his disgraceful betrayal of his country. The three historians of the first half of the twentieth century who did the most to establish this view of Bancroft were Samuel Flagg Bemis, Lewis Einstein, and Burton J. Hendrick. Unfortunately for Bancroft's reputation, all three were prolific, influential authors whose books and articles were widely read and discussed.

Bemis (1891–1973) was a diplomatic historian who spent most of his career at Yale University. He twice won the Pulitzer Prize for books on early American history and in 1961 served as president of the American Historical Association. Though he mentioned Bancroft briefly in several of his books, his most extensive analysis was contained in two journal articles. In "British Secret Service and the French-American Alliance," published in 1924, Bemis reprints two very important documents by Bancroft—a letter and a memorandum from September 1784. (These documents are discussed further below.) In his text preceding the two documents, Bemis discusses William Eden, Paul Wentworth, Edward Bancroft, and the general operation of the British espionage system. Bemis's view of Bancroft is unequivocal. He asserts that Bancroft possessed "a well-concealed but unrivalled genius for intrigue." Bancroft was a "double-dealing doctor" guilty of "perfidy." Bemis rejects any possibility that Bancroft might have had any motives other than money, power, and a taste for dirty dealing.[13] Bemis's 1961 article "Secret Intelligence, 1777: Two Documents" argues that the detailed secret intelligence Bancroft provided, via Wentworth, over several years was extremely important to the British military effort. In short, Bancroft betrayed his country and did it grave harm.[14]

Lewis Einstein (1877–1967) was a distinguished career diplomat in the State Department. In his spare moments, he managed to write more than two dozen books on diplomacy, Italian art, and American and European history. In 1933 he published *Divided Loyalties: Americans in England during the War of Independence.* The book is extremely well researched and offers fine analyses of the careers of several American artists, politicians, clergymen, and others who happened to be in England during the Revolution. Einstein's longest and most-often cited chapter is the first one, which deals with Wentworth, Bancroft, and their espionage in France. His approach to Bancroft is more nuanced than Bemis's sledgehammer treatment. Einstein is acutely aware of the difficulty that many Americans had in deciding, once the Revolution started, where their loyalties lay. He is genuinely sympathetic to the thousands of Americans who openly declared their loyalty to Britain. In the end, however, Einstein comes down on the same side as Bemis. Bancroft was a "traitor," indeed one of "the greatest villains," who was unable to erase the "stigma of . . . [his] crimes." His secret intelligence nearly cost the Americans their independence.[15]

Burton J. Hendrick (1870–1949) was a prominent journalist and editor who published more than three dozen books on American history. Three of his works won the Pulitzer Prize in the 1920s. His 1935 book *The Lees of Virginia* devotes more than twenty pages to Bancroft, but it was two articles published in mass-circulation magazines that did the most to darken Bancroft's reputation. In 1935 Hendrick's "Worse Than Arnold" appeared in *Atlantic Monthly;* in 1936 *Reader's Digest* printed his "Arch-Traitor of the Revolution." Hendrick declares that "Americans have committed a great injustice in making Benedict Arnold the archtraitor of the Revolution. That eminence rightfully belongs to Dr. Bancroft. Arnold was guilty of one act of treason, which failed, and so did no harm, while Bancroft for more than eight years was daily betraying his country, and doing so successfully. The prolongation of the contest was owing, more than to any other single cause, to the information which this man was constantly supplying—for money—to the Ministry in London."[16] According to Hendrick, Bancroft belonged to a "syndicate of betrayal"; all of its members were "intriguers" who bamboozled Benjamin Franklin and other American officials in France.

Scores of later historians have followed Bemis, Einstein, and Hendrick in condemning Bancroft for his avaricious, unprincipled betrayal of his country, a betrayal that almost helped Britain to quash the American rebellion. With a few exceptions, these later writers devote just a few sentences to him and add little or no new information.[17]

So was Bancroft guilty of treason? To answer this, one must ask: Why did he write the "Narrative" in August 1776? Fortunately, we have Bancroft's own explanation for why he did it. He provided it in the 1784 memorial that Bemis published in 1926. On 17 September 1784 Bancroft wrote a letter to the British foreign secretary, the Marquess of Carmarthen. The main purpose of the letter was to inform the minister that the government was in arrears in paying him his annual pension; he was still owed £1,000 for his services during and after the Revolution. In his letter and the accompanying memorial Bancroft cites approval from previous ministers for the payment of this pension, and he gives a brief overview of his work as a secret agent. The memorial deserves its reputation as an extraordinary document. Spies generally erase their tracks rather than leave a paper trail. This is one of the rare cases in which a spy put into writing what he did and why he did it. The memorial begins:

> In the month of June 1776, Mr. Silas Deane arrived in France, & pursuant to an instruction given him by the Secret Committee of Congress, wrote to me in London, requesting an interview in Paris, where I accordingly went, early in July, and was made acquainted with the purposes of his Mission, and with every thing which passed between him, & the French Ministry. After staying two or three weeks there, I returned to England, convinced that the Government of France would endeavour to Promote an Absolute Separation, of the then United Colonies, from Great Britain, unless a speedy termination of the Revolt, by reconciliation, or Conquest, should frustrate this project. I had then resided near ten years, & expected to reside the rest of my Life, in England; and all my views, interests & inclinations were adverse to the independency of the Colonies, though I had advocated some of their Claims, from a persuasion of their being founded on Justice. I therefore wished, that the Government of this Country, might be informed, of the Danger of French interference, though I could not resolve to become the informant. But Mr. Paul Wentworth, having gained some general

Knowledge of my Journey to France, & of my intercourse with Mr. Deane, & having induced me to believe, that the British Ministry were likewise informed on this Subject, I at length Consented to meet with the then Secretaries of State, Lords Weymouth and Suffolk, and give them all the information in my power; which I did, with the most disinterested views; for I not only, did not ask, but expressly rejected, every Idea of reward. The Declaration of Independency, was not then known in Europe, and I hoped, that Government, thus informed of the Danger, would prevent it, by some accommodation with the Colonies, or by other means. It had been my original intention to stop after this first Communication; but having given the first notice of a beginning intercourse, between France and the United Colonies, I was urged on, to watch and disclose the progress of it; for which purpose, I made several journeys to Paris, and maintained a regular Correspondence with Mr. Deane, through the Couriers of the French Government. And in this way, I became *entangled* and obliged to proceed in a kind of Business, as repugnant to my feelings, as it had been to my original intentions.[18]

Bancroft thus asserts that he did not seek to become a spy. He did so only because Wentworth and the two ministers prevailed upon him to give information. Bancroft likewise says he did not want the colonies to break away from the empire but hoped that their justified grievances would be remedied. Moreover, Bancroft says that if the colonies succeeded in gaining French support, this would greatly increase the chances of a general war. Bancroft hoped that, by informing the government of all that he knew, he would enable Britain to forestall French involvement and induce Britain to seek reconciliation with the colonies. His avowed motives for cooperating with the government are in line with all that is known about his earlier life and writings.

Bancroft also claims that when he arrived home in London from his first trip to see Silas Deane, he had no intention of returning to France. Only on the urging of the ministers did he consent to make additional trips to Paris. Here, too, the available evidence supports his contentions. Silas Deane's correspondence from the late summer and early fall of 1776 gives no indication that he expected Bancroft to return to see him anytime soon. Rather, Bancroft planned to resume his activities in London as a scientist, physician, businessman, husband, and father. Wentworth, Suffolk, and Weymouth changed his mind.

There is also reason to believe him when he says he did not like being a spy, which he calls a kind of business repugnant to his feelings. Although there had been spies, secret informers, and the like since ancient times, for the most part they were held in ill repute—even when doing valuable work for their own country. British archives from the Revolutionary era contain hundreds of letters from a small army of secret agents, and there are many instances where these other spies echo the same sentiments as Bancroft.[19] They felt ashamed of being involved in such sneaky, dishonorable affairs. Somebody had to do it, but it was still a dirty business. As late as the first half of the twentieth century most people continued to feel that way. Woodrow Wilson was one of them. He was a historian and president of Princeton University before he was elected president of the United States. In 1902 he published *A History of the American People* in five volumes. In it he devotes ample space to the dastardly deeds of Benedict Arnold, but, evidently out of embarrassment, he does not even mention the clandestine activities of a "good" spy like Nathan Hale.[20] When Henry L. Stimson became U.S. secretary of state in 1929, he closed his agency's cryptanalytic office, declaring, "Gentlemen don't read each other's mail." Only in the second half of the twentieth century did the profession of spy attain a sort of glamor—helped in large part by Ian Fleming's James Bond. So there is no reason to doubt Bancroft on this point.

Finally, Bancroft also was telling the truth when he maintained that he had sought no money or other rewards when he first met with Suffolk and Weymouth. He did eventually agree to a yearly pension, and this is discussed in the next chapter. The point here is that when he initially threw in his lot with Britain against the colonial revolt he had no mercenary motives.

If he believed in August 1776 that it was still possible to achieve reconciliation, he was not alone. Throughout 1775 and 1776, British ministers and members of Parliament remained convinced that most colonists sincerely wanted to remain connected to the glorious empire. The government believed that hotheads like John Adams and Benjamin Franklin were part of a small rabble-rousing cabal. If these intemperate rebel leaders could be silenced, then the great majority of Americans would come to their senses. Many American Loyalists held the same conviction. During the Revolution approximately seven thousand of them fled from the colonies to Britain, and most of them persisted in the notion that some sort of reconciliation could be brokered.[21] This might have been a chimerical illusion, but it was widely held.

Bemis and the many writers who followed in his path therefore have done Bancroft an injustice by automatically rejecting his claim to have the same illusion. The following chapters demonstrate that Bancroft had a variety of motives for what he did between 1776 and 1783. He was no saint. He did eventually acquire some mercenary motives, but money alone did not drive him. He did many things for which he was not paid and which gained him nothing in terms of financial or other types of reward. Despite his occasional inconsistencies, he retained affection for both America and Britain and endeavored to work for the good of both.

Let us return to the question: Did he betray his country in 1776 and thereafter? To answer that, one must ask, "What was his country?" Bancroft moved to England in 1767. Never again did he live in the colonies. Editors of scholarly biographical dictionaries in both Britain and the United States have claimed Bancroft as one of their own. Hence, for example, one can find entries for him in the *Dictionary of American Biography* as well as in Britain's *Dictionary of National Biography*.

So was he British or American? This question would not have made any sense to Bancroft. Nor would it have made sense to Benjamin Franklin, John Adams, George Washington, Thomas Jefferson, or any others in America until 1776. All would have answered that they were subjects of Britain and its empire. The word *American* had come into increasing use in the eighteenth century, but it did not denote a separate country. It was a useful shorthand way of referring to those subjects who lived on the western side of the Atlantic Ocean. Only in 1774 and 1775 did a small minority of colonists start to think of America as possibly being a separate entity, and only in mid-1776 did a majority of leaders and common people arrive at that decision.

In the eighteenth century, Americans were part of a strong transatlantic British community. This deep sense of Britishness had grown remarkably stronger in that century, and its distinguishing characteristics were its Protestantism, its reliance on a strong navy and merchant marine, and its adherence to the political structures and civil liberties that grew out of the settlement of 1688–89. Americans shared this sense of identity, which put them squarely on the side of the mother country against Catholic, divine-right, absolutist France.[22]

In the 1760s Boston jurist James Otis averred that "every British subject born on the continent of America . . . is entitled to all the natural, essential, inherent and inseparable rights of our fellow subjects in Great Britain. . . . We love, esteem, and reverence our mother country, and adore our King." In that same decade, Francis Hopkinson of New Jersey, later a signer of the Declaration of Independence, wrote, "Are we not one nation and one people? We in America are in all respects Englishmen, notwithstanding that the Atlantic rolls in waves between us and the throne to which we all owe our allegiance."[23] Until 1774 or perhaps even 1775 Benjamin Franklin continued to believe in something that he had written in the 1750s: "Britain and her Colonies should be considered as one Whole, and not as different States with separate Interests."[24] At the opening-night dinner of the Continental Congress in September 1774, the delegates in Philadelphia's Carpenter Hall drank a toast to "the union of Britain and the colonies on a constitutional foundation." On 5 July 1775 the Second Continental Congress passed what came to be called the Olive Branch Petition; in it the members appealed to King George III to rescue them from "irksome" and "delusive" royal ministers and proclaimed that "we mean not to dissolve that union which has so long and so happily subsisted between us, and which we sincerely wish to be restored." In October 1775 John Adams wrote to William Lee that "we cannot in this Country conceive that there are Men in England so infatuated, as seriously to suspect the Congress, or people here, of a Wish to erect ourselves into an independent State. If such an Idea really obtains amongst those at the Helm of Affairs, one Hour's residence in America would eradicate it. I never met one Individual so inclined, but it is universally disavowed."[25] After assuming command of the Continental Army, George Washington continued for months to offer toasts to George III when dining with his officers. As late as November 1775, Thomas Jefferson declared that "there is not in the British empire a man who more cordially loves a union with Gr. Britain than I do."[26]

One might almost argue that Bancroft and the thousands in America who came to be called Tories or Loyalists were the true patriots and that the Continental Congress was the seat of the real traitors. Admittedly, that would be a glib simplification. Perhaps it is more accurate to view the Revolution as a civil war just as divisive as that of the 1860s. No opinion polls existed in 1776, but it is likely that about 20 percent of Americans would have voted against independence, and perhaps another 20 percent would have abstained because of indifference, uncertainty, or fear. Some of the most ardent Revolutionary leaders also had the strongest ties to Britain and thus might well have become Loyalists. Horatio Gates had been born in England and had served in the British army; during the Revolution, however, he was appointed a major general in the Continental Army and, among other accomplishments, commanded the troops that forced the surrender of General Burgoyne at Saratoga in October 1777. As noted earlier, William and Arthur Lee were residing in London when the Revolution started. William was still serving as both a sheriff and an alderman in London; Arthur was practicing law and aspiring to become a member of Parliament. In earlier years Benjamin Franklin had contemplated settling permanently in England and attaining high government office, perhaps as an undersecretary in a ministry. Benjamin Rush, one of the most vehement American leaders in 1776, still harbored fond memories of his student days at the University of Edinburgh. It was Rush who suggested the title *Common Sense* to Thomas Paine, in memory of the common-sense Scottish Enlightenment ideas that he had admired so much.[27]

Just as the war of the 1860s often split families, so also did the Revolution. The most famous case of family division was that of Benjamin Franklin, whose son William was the last royal governor of New Jersey. William remained at his post and was arrested and imprisoned in 1776. Eventually he was released and made his way to England, where he lived until his death in 1813. Benjamin never forgave his son, and there developed a permanent breach between them.

While many Americans remained loyal to Britain, many Britons supported the American cause and criticized their government's harsh colonial policies. These included the radical London politician John Wilkes, MP Edmund Burke, and former prime minister William Pitt, known after 1766 as the Earl of Chatham.

In short, the argument that Edward Bancroft betrayed his country does not stand up to scrutiny. He was a subject of the British Empire, and he hoped that the empire would remain intact.

It is interesting to note that Edward's brother, Daniel, likewise had to make a choice. After his return to America in 1771, Daniel practiced medicine and worked to ship cargoes of black oak bark to England. Writing from Boston on 3 November 1775, he informed his brother Edward that he had finally reached a decision. He would remain loyal to the Crown. He was going to join the British army and serve under Brigadier General Timothy Ruggles. Because it would be hazardous for Edward to correspond with a Loyalist, Daniel recommended that they use aliases—A. Stuart for Daniel and S. Stuart for Edward. Given what is now known about Edward's eventual activities, the following passage in Daniel's letter is ironic: "Your total silence on political matters prevents me from a knowledge of your sentiments. But be assured, were you in my situation, you would think as I do."[28]

This was the last contact the two brothers had with each other for several years. Throughout the Revolution, Edward had no idea what had become of Daniel. The fact that his younger brother took a stand against independence might have had some bearing on Bancroft's thinking. When British ministers told him he could play an important role in keeping the empire intact, undoubtedly he must also have felt flattered. Thus he agreed to write his initial report in August 1776. He then found himself more or less trapped. The government expected him to continue the work he had started.

4 First Steps

Once Bancroft had submitted his initial report to the British ministry in August 1776, it was not clear what he was supposed to do next. Obviously, he could not collect information on American activities in France if he himself was in England. So what did he do from the late summer of 1776 to March 1777, when he moved to Paris?

Understanding his actions requires a basic grasp of the British ministry at that time. Starting with Robert Walpole in the 1720s, the person who was first lord of the Treasury usually came to be regarded as the chief minister. The title prime minister was not yet used, though in retrospect we now employ that term for Walpole and his successors. Lord North served as chief minister from 1770 to 1782. Britain did not have a foreign secretary—not until an administrative reorganization that took place immediately after North's fall from power. Diplomacy during the Revolutionary era was divided among three secretaries of state. These were the secretary of state for the colonies, whose chief concerns were Ireland, the Caribbean, and North America. Sometimes this secretary was simply called the American secretary. Lord George Germain held this post from 1776 to 1782. Relations with the Continent were split between the secretaries of state for the southern and northern departments, respectively. The southern secretary supervised dealings with

France, Spain, Portugal, the Italian states, and the Ottoman Empire. The northern secretary dealt with the Dutch Republic, Scandinavia, Poland, Russia, and the German states (including Austria and Prussia). In the early years of the Revolution, the southern department was controlled by Viscount Weymouth (1775–79), the northern by the Earl of Suffolk (1771–79). One other cabinet member with extensive involvement in the Revolution was the first lord of the Admiralty, the Earl of Sandwich (1771–82). There was a significant amount of overlap in the responsibilities of all these men, with great potential for conflicts and confusion. It was the prime minister's job to keep a lid on these internal rivalries and steer a more or less orderly course—while informing the king of everything.

The effect of Bancroft's "Narrative" of 14 August 1776 was immediate. On 16 August Weymouth dispatched a detailed missive to the British minister in Paris, Lord Stormont. Weymouth pretty much repeated Bancroft's information, sometimes word for word. He wanted Stormont to let the French crown know that Britain possessed details on everything that was going on.[1]

This does not mean Bancroft was the sole source of secret intelligence. Long before his first trip to meet Silas Deane, British agents were collecting information on activities in France that might be related to the American colonies. Who were these other secret agents? Most of them were not secret at all. Every British minister stationed in Continental capital cities was charged with sending home reports on any information that might be important. The same was true for consuls stationed in all the major ports of Europe. These officials made their own observations and also relied on information provided by paid informers. Most of these reports went to the southern or northern secretaries, but the Admiralty's Lord Sandwich also had a bevy of secret informers in dockyards throughout the Continent. As Britain and France were not at war, British government officials, sailors, merchants, and others were free to travel wherever they wished.

As early as the fall of 1774 Britain began to notice an increase in suspicious activities in French ports. In the spring of 1775 Suffolk ordered Stormont to inform French foreign minister Vergennes that Britain was concerned about news that French shipyards were constructing at least nineteen new ships of the line. In July 1775 Stormont informed his superiors in London that 32 million livres worth of goods recently had left French ports for Saint-Domingue, from which they would be dispatched to the British

North American colonies. In September Stormont reported that three hundred casks of gunpowder and five thousand muskets with bayonets plus other materials had been sent to America from Saint-Malo, Bayonne, and Bordeaux. In November 1775 the Admiralty sent orders to all naval commanders to be on the lookout for American ships bringing tobacco or other cargoes to Dutch, French, and Spanish ports and exiting those ports with saltpeter, gunpowder, and other war materials. Even without the looming American rebellion, such trade by British colonists with other countries was a violation of the Navigation Acts. When Beaumarchais commenced his secret trade in the summer of 1776, Stormont found out about it immediately. By August 1776 Stormont could report that France would soon have fifty-four ships of the line fit for service; the French navy, especially if coupled with that of Spain, then would be strong enough to confront Britain's.[2]

Again and again, both before and after Silas Deane's arrival in Paris, Stormont made the trek to Versailles to lay his complaints before the royal court. Stormont was one of the most adept and respected diplomats of his era. He was a regular guest at the prestigious Paris salons hosted by Madame du Deffand and Madame Geoffrin. The famed German art historian and archaeologist Johann Joachim Winckelmann once lauded Stormont as "the most learned man of his rank" of any that he had ever known[3]. At Versailles Stormont often conferred with the aging Comte de Maurepas, who was informally recognized as Louis XVI's chief minister. But more often he met with Vergennes. Stormont and Vergennes were equally adept in their knowledge of history and diplomacy and in their ability to decipher the veiled threats or assurances that they exchanged. Right up to the outbreak of hostilities in the spring of 1778, these two men played an elaborate cat-and-mouse game. France wanted to encourage the Americans, and Britain wanted to prevent it. But neither wished to go to war with the other. Britain hoped to crush the revolt before it generated a wider conflict with European powers. France for its part needed to continue its naval rebuilding program. So Stormont had to complain while not causing too much offense. Vergennes, on the other hand, had to assume a stony diplomatic countenance whenever the British minister visited him. Just as Claude Rains, the police chief in *Casablanca*, is "shocked" to learn that gambling is going on in Humphrey Bogart's bar, Vergennes professed utter astonishment when confronted by the details

Stormont laid before him. If some Americans were in France, Vergennes pointed out that they were breaking no French laws. He could not expel them. If French merchants were trading with the Americans, that was their private affair. He could not stop them. If France was rebuilding its navy, it had the right to maintain a strong military force. If France was sending additional warships to the Caribbean, they were going there for the defense of the French West Indies—not to protect illicit trade with British colonies. If American businessmen were violating British laws by trading with France, Britain was free to intercept that trade, confiscate the cargoes, and arrest the British subjects (that is, the Americans).

Vergennes knew full well that Britain could not stop this illegal traffic. Most of the ships involved in it flew the French flag when they left French ports. Either they actually were French vessels or they were American but using the French flag until safely in open waters. Britain could not risk stopping these ships, for that could precipitate war with France.

Thus, in terms of the volume of supplies leaving French and other European ports, and the names of the ships carrying them, Britain did not need Bancroft. Nor did it need Bancroft in order to keep informed of the French naval and army buildup. But it did need Bancroft to stay on top of what the French government was planning. Just how far would the French crown go in tacitly permitting private trade with America? How much secret aid would the crown itself provide? Would France be content to sit on the sidelines and offer supposedly secret aid, or would the Bourbon government eventually ally with the rebels and go to war with Britain? Neither Stormont nor any of the chambermaids, tavern owners, and minor officials whom he bribed could answer these questions. None of them had access to the inner circles of the American representatives in Paris.

Bancroft made two more short trips to Paris in the months following his initial reunion with Deane. The first came in October. The ostensible purpose of the trip was to help Deane as he set about obtaining supplies and official government support.[4] Bancroft received no salary or formal appointment, but Deane reimbursed him for some of his travel and other expenses. On 21 December Bancroft arrived in Paris yet again, this time remaining there until about 20 January 1777. At just about the same time, two other persons entered the French capital. They were Benjamin Franklin, arriving on 21 December from Philadelphia, and Arthur Lee, arriving a day later, from London. The Continental Congress had appointed them to join Deane as its commissioners in France.

Bancroft's reunion with Franklin must have been joyous. He served the three commissioners as a translator and facilitator and helped them get settled in their Paris hotels. He also accompanied them in their several trips to Versailles. They kept him fully abreast of what transpired in their conversations with Vergennes.[5]

When Bancroft returned to London after each trip, he conferred with Paul Wentworth, who then sent written reports to William Eden. That Eden received these communications is one indication of the bureaucratic confusion mentioned above. Eden was one of Lord Suffolk's two undersecretaries in the northern department. But it was the southern department, under Lord Weymouth, that supposedly handled all relations with France. It was Weymouth who corresponded and gave instructions to the British minister in Paris. So why did Suffolk's office take charge of supervising Wentworth, Bancroft, and several other secret agents watching the American commissioners in Paris? There are two possible explanations. One is simply that the bureaucratic divisions of responsibility were not clear-cut, and such overlappings in duties were not unusual. The other is that William Eden, a young and ambitious man on the rise, had taken lodgings in Downing Street to be near the source of power (that is, Lord North's residence). North and Eden had come to know each other well, and North perhaps suggested that Eden handle this business. Moreover, Bancroft also resided in Downing Street. He probably had no contacts with North, but he knew Eden. Given that, it might have seemed best to have Eden supervise Bancroft's work.

The results, however, could be cumbersome. Bancroft communicated to Wentworth, who reported to Eden, who reported to Suffolk, who then reported to the other ministers in cabinet meetings. From these meetings, Weymouth obtained Bancroft's information and then relayed it back to Paris for Stormont's use. Through his own army of informers Stormont continued to gather and send to London detailed intelligence on activities in French ports and in the capital.

The British ambassador knew about Franklin and Lee the day they arrived in Paris, and he kept track of their visits to Versailles—though he did not know what transpired in those interviews with Vergennes. In several letters to Weymouth, Stormont noted that a Dr. Bancroft was also in their company. And when Bancroft was back in London, Stormont was aware that Deane corresponded with him—largely about private business matters. Stormont likewise knew the aliases that Bancroft and Deane sometimes used.[6] What is somewhat amusing is that during all these months Stormont assumed that Bancroft was a rebel American; he did not realize that Bancroft was a British agent. Weymouth sent letters to Stormont, informing him of information obtained via Bancroft, but without revealing the name of the source. Weymouth himself knew Bancroft, as they met once early in August 1776. Sometime shortly after that meeting, Weymouth, Suffolk, and Wentworth began to use the alias "Mr. Edwards" or "Dr. Edwards" when referring to Bancroft. Not until months later, however, was Stormont told anything about either Bancroft or "Edwards."[7]

Bancroft did not initially settle in Paris for several reasons. His family and his sources of income were in London. He had not been given an official, salaried appointment by the British government. Nor had he been given any formal position by the American commissioners in Paris, and thus he had no plausible reason for remaining there permanently. These obstacles to his work as a secret agent would be resolved in February and March 1777.

A Double Agent?

Many of the authors who have written about Bancroft have maintained that he was a double agent, working for and betraying both the British and the Americans. According to this argument, when he was in Paris, he fed intelligence to the British. When he was in London, he sent information to the Americans in Paris. If indeed he was a double agent, working for both sides while mainly out for his personal gain, this must have occurred during the months from July 1776 to March 1777. From the latter date until June 1783 he lived in Paris, with the exception of one trip back to London in December 1777. In short, after March 1777 it would have been physically impossible for him to collect information in England.

But was he a double agent? Historians generally fall into two camps on this question. Some respond with a firm "yes." Editors of the Yale edition of *The Papers of Benjamin Franklin* have called Bancroft "one of the most successful double agents in the history of espionage."[8] Numerous other scholars have agreed, some even stating that the Continental Congress gave Bancroft an official appointment and a regular salary.[9] The obvious conclusion to be reached from this line of argument is that Bancroft had no allegiance to either side and was motivated by a desire for money and power.

The other camp of authors agrees that whenever Bancroft was in London in 1776 and 1777 he sent information about British political and military developments to Silas Deane in Paris. However, this did not make him a genuine double agent. Lewis Einstein, for example, states that the letters Bancroft sent to Deane contained nothing but "trivialities" and "idle gossip" about things that weren't secret at all but rather common knowledge to virtually everyone in London. Deane was "duped" into believing that these bits of intelligence were valuable and that Bancroft was risking his life in obtaining them.[10] Another author calls Bancroft's correspondence with Deane "bogus."[11] According to this line of thought, Bancroft's supposed role as a spy for the Americans was a mere ruse, calculated to win the confidence of Deane and Franklin. Hence the British ministers knew what Bancroft was doing and may even have fed him the misleading or useless data that he dispatched across the channel.

So was Bancroft an amoral double agent working for both sides, or was his espionage for the Americans a mere charade? The truth probably lies in a gray area between those two extremes. In the previous chapter it was noted that mercenary motives do not explain his decision to write his initial report for the British in August 1776. Only in February 1777 did the government arrange to compensate him for his work. (More on this below.) Similarly, Bancroft received no stipend from the United States. The Continental Congress never hired him as a spy and never paid him a salary. The American ministers in Paris reimbursed Bancroft for expenses he incurred when helping them— postage, travel, and the like—but never gave him a regular wage.[12]

What kinds of intelligence did Bancroft send to Deane in late 1776 and early 1777? He either brought to Paris or dispatched via the post copies of many of the most recent newspapers and pamphlets dealing with current affairs. These were designed to keep Deane abreast of what the government was doing and what the general public was thinking. Bancroft also sent Deane some long letters. He sent these in a secure fashion, so that they could not be opened by the London post office. Frequently Bancroft arranged to meet his friend Garnier, the French chargé d'affaires, at some secret location at midnight. Garnier took Bancroft's dispatches and stuffed them into the sealed diplomatic pouch that was taken several times per week to Versailles. From there Vergennes had the items delivered to Deane.[13]

The news Bancroft included in his missives ranged from details about parliamentary debates on the American rebellion to the latest gossip about battles between the Continental Army and redcoats or the captures of ships by one side or the other. On 13 September 1776, for example, Bancroft's voluminous letter to Deane contained a cornucopia of miscellaneous details. He reported that no news had yet reached London regarding the peace mission of Admiral Richard, Lord Howe, who had been sent to America to join his brother, Major General William Howe, the commander of British forces there, to seek reconciliation with the colonies; Bancroft said that a friend of his (probably Wentworth) had asked Lord Suffolk about this, and the secretary answered that he did not expect the American rebels to accept any agreement that fell short of recognizing full independence. (This conjecture was correct.) Bancroft then discussed General John Burgoyne, whose troops in Canada were planning an expedition to the South, but Bancroft doubted that Burgoyne would have enough time to mount his campaign that season. Bancroft also reported that London newspapers were full of stories about Deane's activities in Paris. The parliamentary opposition, especially Lord Grafton, was asking harsh questions about French aid for the rebels, in an effort to embarrass the government and perhaps to bring about a change of ministers. Bancroft then went on to warn Deane about some Americans who were actually British spies. One was Dr. Hugh Williamson, who had recently arrived in Paris and who, Bancroft said, was sending letters back to officials in London telling them about Deane's activities in France and warning Whitehall that Edward Bancroft was a close associate of Deane! Another spy was a Colonel George Mercer, a former lieutenant governor of North Carolina, who had fled to London and then declared himself a staunch supporter of the American cause. Bancroft alerted Deane that British ministers had sent Mercer to Paris to confer with Ambassador Stormont and collect information on Deane. More generally, Bancroft warned Deane that he would be surrounded by spies; Deane must use his "utmost circumspection" as he would be "assailed" by every shape and form of "artifice." Bancroft assured his friend that he was doing all possible to collect valuable intelligence. He regretted that he possessed no fund from which he could pay informers, but he was able to glean much information from his many personal connections in the government. Finally, Bancroft reported on various scraps of information about events in America. Moreover, Bancroft stated that if France intended to take part in the dispute, it must do so soon, for the Americans alone could not withstand the full force of Great Britain. Bancroft concluded the letter with a lament about his own safety: "how long I may be safe & quiet here I really do not know; there are so many rascals to recommend themselves to Government by Tale bearing, that if they can get no intelligence, they may perhaps forge Lies, & throw me out of that State of Security in which I had imagined myself to be."[14]

Did this letter and others provide merely trivial or easily obtainable information, as claimed by Lewis Einstein and others? According to this interpretation, Bancroft fed Deane such banalities in order to make it seem that he was busy working for the American cause. But a closer examination of the letters reveals a more complex picture. Neither in this letter nor in any other did Bancroft provide false information. If he were strictly a British agent working against the Americans, one might have expected him to feed the American commissioners some details that might lead them astray. It is true that much of what he wrote was the kind of information that any reasonably well-read, well-connected person could have learned. However, the fact that what Bancroft wrote was not "news" to some people in London does not mean that it was not news to Deane in Paris. Deane and the other American representatives in Paris were always starved for information from America and London. Thus Bancroft's accurate prediction that the Howe peace commission would fail was useful for Deane. And Bancroft's surmise that Burgoyne would not attempt his march from Canada down the Hudson River valley until 1777 let Deane know that an attempt at a knockout blow by the British would not come until the next year, thus giving him time to acquire more French aid.

Some authors have gleefully noted the irony of Bancroft warning Deane about other spies. He knew that Deane could become suspicious about how the British knew so much about American activities in France. Just in case Deane wondered if the leaks came from Bancroft, Bancroft himself, according to this line of thought, quickly diverted attention to two other Americans and accused them of being the spies. But were Williamson and Mercer merely Bancroft's innocent victims? In late July, six weeks before Bancroft sent a warning about those two men, Arthur Lee also wrote to Silas Deane from

London. He alerted Deane to the omnipresence of British agents, stating, "In these times it is necessary to abstain from trusting those of whom there is the least suspicion." Taking a scattergun approach, Lee listed seven Americans who were living in London and possibly visiting France. These included merchants and former colonial agents plus Sir James Jay (a physician and older brother of John), Paul Wentworth, and the same Colonel Mercer whom Bancroft had mentioned. Lee noted that Mercer "is always with ministerial people and should not be trusted."[15] The other person Bancroft was suspicious of, Hugh Williamson, went to Paris in August 1776, sought out British minister Stormont, and offered to serve the British cause in some capacity. Stormont considered using him, though nothing seems to have come of it.[16] In short, there were valid reasons for Deane to distrust both Mercer and Williamson, and historians have been wrong to reject Bancroft's warning as a slanderous shifting of blame to two innocent bystanders.

At first glance, one might wish to dismiss out of hand Bancroft's concluding passage in the above letter, where he says he is afraid that Loyalists in Britain will suspect him of helping Deane and report him to the government. Of course, the government knew about Bancroft's dealings with Deane. Even if some bitter Loyalists did turn against Bancroft, he had nothing to fear from Suffolk and other ministers, who knew what he was up to. Nonetheless, the Loyalists were on a witch hunt and could have made trouble for Bancroft if they targeted him with their suspicions.

But a puzzle remains. North, Weymouth, Suffolk, Eden, and others knew that Bancroft was sending reports to Deane. They knew that he met with Garnier. However, they did not see the contents of Bancroft's letters. If they had, they would not have been pleased. Bancroft was sending Deane accurate information about political events in London and also the freshest news from America. Deane treasured the intelligence he received from his former student. He completed his first report to Congress on 18 August 1776. In it he discussed Bancroft's services to America and noted that at present Bancroft was back in London. Deane then wrote, "This gentleman is certainly capable of giving as good, if not the best, intelligence of any man in Great Britain, as he is closely connected with the most respectable of the minority in both Houses, not particularly obnoxious to the majority, and for his abilities, they are too well known to Dr. Franklin to need any attempt to do them justice in a letter."[17]

Deane was laying it on a bit thick, but his general point about Bancroft being well informed and having important connections was accurate. Bancroft did not move in the highest political circles, but he had some well-placed acquaintances in the parliamentary opposition—for example, Lord Camden in the upper house and Edmund Burke and Thomas Walpole in the lower. In letters to Congress in the fall and early winter of 1776, Deane stressed that Bancroft "merits much of the Colonies" and "has been of very great service to me." But Deane added that all this "costs something."[18] By this Deane did not mean that Bancroft was demanding a salary and official appointment as a secret agent. Rather, Deane simply felt bad about having few funds with which to compensate Bancroft for his expenses.

After Benjamin Franklin arrived in France near the end of 1776, he placed the same confidence in the information Bancroft sent from London. On 8 February 1777, for example, Franklin and Deane wrote to Congress and enclosed a copy of intelligence that Bancroft had just sent them.[19] Deane thought the material so important that he also sent a copy to Vergennes.[20] In his dispatch, Bancroft reported on an increased level of warlike preparations. Ships were being readied to carry additional British and German troops to America. He noted that the British planned to crush the northern colonies before help could arrive from those in the South or from France. This was an accurate assessment of British war plans for later in that year. Understandably, Franklin and Deane wanted to make sure that the Continental Congress had as many details as possible to help them best determine how to stop the imminent invasion led by General Burgoyne. Similarly, Franklin and Deane hoped that Bancroft's intelligence might prod Vergennes into speeding up French assistance.

While in London Bancroft did something else that exhibited a genuine affection for America in general and Franklin in particular. Along with a letter of early March 1777 to Franklin, Bancroft enclosed a copy of one of his final contributions to the *Monthly Review*. It was a review of a pamphlet published late in 1776 by Josiah Tucker, the dean of Gloucester. In earlier years Tucker and Franklin had become bitter foes; their differences over British-American relations eventually led them to ridicule each other personally. Bancroft used the publication of Tucker's newest pamphlet as an excuse to launch a four-page personal assault on its author, accompanied by a resounding defense of Franklin. If Bancroft's sympathies lay solely with the British and if he had totally "betrayed" America, he would never have written that piece.[21]

In short, he was never a paid secret agent of the American commissioners, but he did send them valuable information and exhibit a genuine interest in their welfare.

John the Painter

For Bancroft to fulfill his commitment of August 1776 to inform British ministers about what the Americans were doing in Paris, he would need to do more than make occasional visits to France. Lacking any official appointment or salary from the Americans, he had no plausible excuse for settling in Paris for the long haul. The bizarre story of John the Painter would provide such an excuse.

James Aitken, whom the popular press later dubbed "John the Painter," was born in Edinburgh in 1752 to a poor but respectable working-class family. At age fourteen he was apprenticed to a house painter. After completing his seven-year apprenticeship, early in 1774 he set out for London. There he soon turned to a life of crime and vagabondage. In the space of just a few months he shoplifted, burglarized homes, robbed stagecoaches, shot a dog, and raped a shepherdess. Later in 1774 he made his way to America as an indentured servant. However, he ran off shortly after reaching shore and wandered through the colonies before making his way back to Britain in 1775. He read widely, though unsystematically, and developed some sort of sympathy for the American cause. Nevertheless, in 1775 on three separate occasions he joined the British army, pocketed an enlistment bonus, and thereupon deserted.

He craved fame of any sort and in 1776 came up with a wild scheme that would eventually set Britain ablaze, both literally and figuratively. He determined to burn down the six royal dockyards, where naval vessels were built and repaired. He would start with the two most important of them, at Portsmouth and Plymouth. The result would be the crippling of the navy and consequently a swift victory for the American rebels. In October he traveled to Paris, where he hoped to gain support for his plan from Silas Deane. The first two times he showed up unannounced at Deane's hotel the valet would not let him in. The third time Aitken forced his way into Deane's quarters, and the American commissioner had little choice but to speak with him. Deane considered Aitken a reckless young man but nevertheless agreed to meet him again the following day. He thought that Aitken's scheme for burning the two major naval dockyards was, at best, an improbable gamble. But the young man was determined to carry it out. And so in mid-November Deane gave him his informal approval plus just enough money to get back to England. Finally, Deane told Aitken that if he needed any protection or a little more financial help, he could look up his friend in London, Edward Bancroft.[22] Deane thought he would never hear of Aitken again and assumed the plan would amount to nothing. Thus he did not even bother to write to Bancroft and tell him that Aitken might possibly contact him.

Using a primitive delayed-action incendiary device, Aitken was able to set fire to the Portsmouth ropeyard on 7 December. The complete sets of rigging for two ships were destroyed, along with many other materials. In the immediate aftermath, everyone assumed that the fire had been an accident. Even though no one yet suspected arson, Aitken panicked and remembered the friend Deane had mentioned to him. The volatile Scotsman swiftly made his way to London and found Bancroft at his home in Downing Street. When Bancroft learned what Aitken had done plus the fact that Deane had given Aitken his name and address, the doctor was seized with fear. If he offered to help Aitken, he himself might be implicated in the incendiarism. On the other hand, to reject Aitken completely would be to risk losing the confidence of Deane and other Americans. Not knowing how to respond to Aitken's plea for money and aid in avoiding capture, Bancroft agreed to speak with Aitken again the next day. Curiously, Bancroft chose as a rendezvous spot the Salopian Coffee House, a popular establishment on Charing Cross Road almost adjacent to the Admiralty offices. Bancroft seems to have thought that it was safer to meet Aitken there than in some dark, secluded hideaway. If anyone later recalled seeing him with the arsonist, Bancroft would always be able to come up with some plausible explanation—for, surely, if he had been involved in Aitken's plot, he would never have met the man in so conspicuous a location. Bancroft responded to Aitken with vague, noncommittal chatter. He refused to give Aitken any money or other kinds of help. The Scotsman then left, disappointed and even angry with Bancroft.[23]

From London, Aitken headed for his second main target, Plymouth. After reaching that city he decided to forego setting fire to its dockyard. Instead he went to Bristol in mid-January 1777, where he set fire to some merchant ships, warehouses, and private homes. At about the same time, on 15 January, a dockworker in Portsmouth found one of Aitken's primitive incendiary devices—one that had fizzled out before it could burn down the hemphouse situated next to the ruined ropehouse. This discovery proved that the fire resulted from arson. That bit of news plus the Bristol fires led newspapers and government officials to conclude that the blazes were the result of a vast terrorist network of Americans and their sympathizers. Pandemonium spread throughout Britain; the hunt for these terrorists was the primary topic of discussion for weeks. The government suspended the writ of habeas corpus.[24]

In this atmosphere Bancroft surely regretted his brief contacts with the pyromaniac. His heart must have pounded with fear when Aitken was arrested late in January. Under harsh questioning and possibly torture, would Aitken mention Deane and Bancroft? Even worse, to placate his jailers, might Aitken fabricate some story about Bancroft assisting him?

Sometime in early February Bancroft took the extraordinary step of visiting Aitken in the London prison where he was incarcerated. It is not known what excuse Bancroft gave for wanting to see the prisoner. What is known, however, is the purpose of the visit. He wanted to find out what Aitken would say at his trial. In all probability, he urged Aitken to avoid mentioning Deane or himself. The trial of "John the Painter" was held at the assize court sitting in Winchester. During the proceedings, Aitken defiantly proclaimed his innocence. Only after he had been found guilty and sentenced to be hanged did he reveal his true name and confess all that he had done. He admitted that Silas Deane had given him a limited amount of support. He also acknowledged that after setting his first fire, he had sought out Bancroft in London. But he insisted that Bancroft had given him "no countenance."[25] On 10 March Aitken was taken to Portsmouth, where he was hanged.

When Bancroft learned of this, he felt relief. But he had real reason still to be afraid. Popular hysteria was at such a pitch that American Loyalists who had fled to Britain were feverishly looking for clues about anyone who might have had ties to the arsonist. Apparently believing that some persons had mentioned him as a possible accomplice, Bancroft planted articles defending himself in several newspapers in mid- to late March. They were published anonymously, and nowhere in them did Bancroft mention his own name. The articles simply said that various people were maliciously spreading rumors about an innocent man who had had nothing to do with the terrorist.[26]

Although Bancroft genuinely feared that public opinion might turn against him, there is no evidence that British ministers suspected him of having had anything to do with the fires. Bancroft thus feared the mob rather than the government.

The documentary testimony supporting this narrative of Bancroft's limited involvement in the saga of John the Painter is ample. Numerous authors, however, have reported a different scenario. Some have stated that Bancroft was indeed suspected by government officials and that for a time some police agents were appointed to follow his movements. However, there is no evidence to support this claim. Several writers also have maintained that at some point in early to mid-March Bancroft was arrested and thrown in jail. The only evidence for this comes from a letter that Silas Deane wrote on 16 March to Robert Morris, head of the Secret Committee in Congress. Deane exclaimed that poor Bancroft, to whom America owed so much, had been incarcerated in "the Bastille of England."[27] Presumably Bancroft himself or someone else had written Deane a now-lost letter informing him of the imprisonment. There is no indication of how or why or where Bancroft was arrested and placed in custody.

Bancroft's supposed incarceration is open to various interpretations. Because Deane's letter is the only surviving evidence, it is possible that Deane based his statement on a false rumor. It is also possible that Bancroft himself was guilty of a falsehood. Why lie to Deane about it? If Deane thought the British government believed that Bancroft was a zealous American, this would greatly increase the confidence that Deane, Franklin, and others would have in him. It is also possible that the government did have Bancroft arrested, but as a ruse, to make it seem they suspected him—thereby achieving the same result. There are surviving letters from Paul Wentworth to former New Hampshire governor John Wentworth as well as to Secretary of State Suffolk indicating that the royal ministers had absolutely no suspicion that Bancroft had anything to do with John the Painter.[28]

Bancroft's movements in late 1776 and early 1777 also demonstrate that he had nothing to fear from the government. James Aitken had visited him sometime shortly after 7 December—after the Portsmouth fire. Bancroft was in Paris from 21 December to about 20 January, when he returned to London. If he genuinely feared being tied to the incendiarism, he would not have traveled back to England. He moved to France in March, but he did not hurriedly flee there for safety. He spent weeks settling his affairs in England and arranging for his family to join him in France.

Thus, even though Bancroft was in no grave danger in London, he led Deane and Franklin to believe that he was. The Americans became even more firmly convinced of his loyalty to their cause. On 26 March Bancroft left London for Paris. Early in May his wife, Penelope, and their two children crossed the channel to join him.[29] Not until June 1783 would he and his family reside in England again.

One final issue regarding John the Painter needs brief mention. Some authors have asserted that Silas Deane and Edward Bancroft played a much larger role in the plan to set England ablaze than what has been described above. When Aitken showed up at Bancroft's door in Downing Street in December 1776, say these authors, Bancroft knew all about him and was expecting him to come. This line of thought has no foundation in any of the surviving evidence.[30] The relevant letters by Deane and Bancroft clearly demonstrate their reluctance to have anything to do with this stranger who had barged into their lives. In fact, Aitken's plans seemed so far-fetched that Bancroft suspected that the man might be a British spy charged with collecting evidence against both him and Deane.[31]

Payment for Services Rendered

The John the Painter episode gave Bancroft a plausible reason for needing to leave England. But he would also require an income. His varied scientific interests, memberships in learned societies, freelance contributions to the *Monthly Review,* and part-time medical practice brought him recognition and friendships, but little income. The time and money he had expended in his vegetable dye venture thus far had brought debts rather than profits.

Bancroft had not initially asked Wentworth, Eden, or Suffolk for payment for his services. He did the work because he believed that if he let the British government know how determined the Americans were to pursue their revolt and attain French assistance, the Crown would offer suitable terms for reconciliation. Until March 1777 his only significant expenses had been his trips to Paris in October and December–January. However, if he were to leave England for an extended period, he would lose his modest sources of income there.

A solution to this monetary obstacle was reached in February. Early that month, Bancroft wrote to Wentworth and explained his situation. He stressed that his "first and principal motive" for agreeing to work for the government had not been "pecuniary considerations." However, he would need a steady income if he was to move to France. He requested a lifetime annual allowance of £200 and a one-time initial grant of £600. Suffolk considered the request reasonable and approved for him a life pension of £200, retroactive to 25 December 1776—making it a sort of belated Christmas present. Bancroft would receive it in quarterly installments. To aid Bancroft in settling his debts and setting up a household in France, Suffolk also approved an immediate gift of £500—slightly less than what had been requested. Furthermore, Suffolk said that Bancroft's permanent annual pension would increase to at least £500 either when the revolt ended or when France openly entered the war.[32] (Suffolk kept his word. After France openly entered the war in the spring of 1778, Bancroft's pension was increased.) Suffolk also gave Bancroft some vague assurances of other possible rewards—money, government sinecures, and such—depending on how successful his work might be. Translating eighteenth-century currency into twenty-first-century equivalents is a hazardous business. Very roughly, £200 in 1777 would be in the neighborhood of $40,000–50,000 today. The fragile state of Bancroft's finances was revealed when it came time for his wife and children to join him in Paris in May 1777. To pay for her travel expenses, Penelope had to borrow £41 from Paul Wentworth.[33]

The fact that Suffolk decided to establish a regular salary for Bancroft at this moment is significant for another reason. Suffolk approved it in February, when public outcries about John the Painter were at their height. This further demonstrates that the government itself knew Bancroft to be innocent of any involvement with the arsonist.

Intent on stressing Bancroft's greedy motives for his treason, Samuel Flagg Bemis and other authors have erroneously stated that he demanded money from the start or soon thereafter. It is thus important to stress again that he asked for and received no money when he wrote his initial report in

August 1776. The available evidence indicates that it was Suffolk who first suggested that he should receive regular compensation. Finally, even after the pension was raised to £500 in 1778, Bancroft was receiving barely enough for a growing family to support itself modestly in one of the most expensive cities in the world.

By March 1777 Bancroft therefore had a credible excuse for "fleeing" to France, and he had a steady income. The natural scientist, physician, and author was now about to become a full-time spy.

5 *Our Man in Paris*

Edward Bancroft's most active and important period of espionage took place during his first year of residence in Paris—from April 1777 to the open break between France and Britain in April 1778. How did he operate? What was his relationship with the various American representatives in France? What kinds of information did he collect?

The Cast of Characters

To follow the story, one must know the major personalities involved. First there is the Bancroft family. Bancroft's wife, Penelope, arrived in Paris a few weeks after her husband, in May 1777, in tow with five-year-old Edward Nathaniel and two-year-old Samuel Forrester. Bancroft had a marvelous ability to compartmentalize. He kept his family apart from his public life. In fact, Bancroft was so secretive about his family life that some of his acquaintances thought that Penelope was his mistress. Paris being Paris, it was easy to assume that a man about town would bring a mistress rather than a wife to such a city. When John Adams arrived in Paris in the spring of 1778, for example, he decried the fact that Bancroft lived with "a woman" who bore him several children. Adams admitted that he never met this "woman," but nonetheless he disapproved of what he considered Bancroft's open defiance of decency and religion.[1] Some later historians, eager to think the worst of a traitor, likewise assumed that Bancroft kept a mistress whom he declined to make into "an honest woman."[2]

During their first weeks in France the family probably lived in rented rooms in a Paris hotel. Sometime in the summer or early fall the family rented furnished rooms in a house in the suburb of Chaillot. There, Penelope and the children enjoyed privacy and fresh air; also, the rent was cheaper there than in Paris. In October 1777 Penelope gave birth to the couple's third child, Maria Frances, who was baptized in the Chaillot parish church[3]. Though Bancroft himself was a non-churchgoing deist, his wife (as noted earlier) appears to have been a Catholic.

With the family in Chaillot, Bancroft seems to have spent most of his days and nights elsewhere. What did Penelope think that her husband was doing? Certainly she suspected nothing of his espionage. She knew that he spent much of his time with Franklin and his associates and probably figured that he was on their payroll. Very probably she also knew bits and pieces about his ongoing business speculations and assumed that these were profitable.

The three American commissioners who represented Congress in France were Benjamin Franklin, Silas Deane, and Arthur Lee. The seventy-year-old Franklin had brought with him his two grandsons. The elder was William Temple Franklin (called "Temple"), the sixteen-year-old illegitimate son of Franklin's own illegitimate son, William. Not only had Benjamin broken all ties with his Loyalist son, but the old man had taken complete control of his grandson. Temple was a spoiled teenager but devoted to his grandfather. From 1776 to 1785 he served as Benjamin's personal secretary and aide. The other grandson was seven-year-old Benjamin Franklin Bache, the son of Franklin's daughter Sarah. "Benny" had been brought along to obtain a Continental education. Franklin installed him in a boarding school just outside Paris. After a few months, Franklin was aghast to notice that Benny was becoming a Frenchified dandy, and so the grandfather shipped him off to a more straitlaced school in Protestant Geneva. There Benny would learn to be "a Presbyterian and a Republican."[4] In 1783 Franklin brought the boy back to live with him. Determined to ensure that the youth would acquire a useful trade, Franklin oversaw his training as a printer at the printing press and foundry that had been installed in their residence. A few years later the young man went on to become one of the most powerful and controversial newspaper editors in late eighteenth-century America.

Initially the three commissioners lived in Paris hotels. Late in February 1777 Franklin and Temple moved to the suburb of Passy, where they would reside until their return to America in July 1785. In Passy they lived in a spacious garden pavilion that was on the grounds of the elegant Hôtel de Valentinois. (In 1779, after his appointment as American minister, Franklin moved into a wing of the main building.) This estate belonged to Jacques-Donatien Leray de Chaumont. He was a jack of all trades—a wealthy ship-owner, proprietor of mines and manufacturing enterprises, former holder of several midlevel government positions, friend of many current and former royal ministers, and proud bearer of a noble title acquired through purchase of a government office. Passy was also on the road leading from Paris to Versailles, making it a convenient place for going to meetings in either location. Adjacent to the back gardens of the Hôtel de Valentinois was the estate of Ferdinand Grand, who was the chief banker for the Americans. Nearly all of the 47 million or so livres that the French government gave or loaned to the Americans were channeled through Grand's hands.

Another major advantage of the residence was Chaumont and his family. Madame Chaumont, her daughters, and son would provide a surrogate family for Franklin and his grandsons. Chaumont himself shared many of the same interests as Franklin, and the two men became close friends as well as associates. He was an ardent Anglophobe—a result of British damage inflicted on his and his father's ships in the Seven Years' War. Even before Franklin arrived in France, Vergennes had told Deane to contact Chaumont for many of the cannons, uniforms, and other supplies that he sought. Chaumont was to become the single most important supplier of the Continental Army. What he could not produce himself, he helped to obtain from others.[5]

Silas Deane moved into the garden pavilion sometime in July 1777. Even after his move to Passy, he retained his Paris lodgings and sometimes stayed there for the night. He had many official dealings in the capital with American ship captains, French businessmen, and French military officers. Where Deane went, so also went Bancroft. While establishing his family in a Chaillot apartment, Bancroft also kept a room in the same hotel with Deane. When Deane took rooms in the Passy estate, Bancroft did so as well. From the summer of 1777 Bancroft seems to have lived mostly in the garden pavilion, with occasional visits to his family in nearby Chaillot and to his pied-à-terre in Paris. Until his departure from France in 1783 he rented a succession of different rooms in the city.[6]

The third commissioner, Arthur Lee, played a smaller role in official business than Franklin or Deane. There were two principal reasons for this. The first is that he was absent for extended periods. From early February to mid-July 1777 he was gone most of the time, on two self-appointed missions to Spain and Prussia. His goal was military aid and possibly even an alliance with one or both powers. For reasons mentioned earlier, the Spanish government was extremely hesitant regarding the American cause. Lee was not allowed even to enter the city of Madrid, but he was given some general assurances of money and supplies. The trip to Berlin, on the other hand, was a total failure.

The second reason for Lee's lesser importance was his personality. It would have been hard for Congress to appoint a more undiplomatic person for a sensitive posting. Lee was a chronically cantankerous, suspicious troublemaker. Many of his contemporaries admired his intelligence, his integrity, and his fervent attachment to the American cause. But exceedingly few would have called themselves his friends. Even a sympathetic biographer has admitted that Lee's view of the world was Manichean: a few people were on the side of light and virtue, but he thought most represented darkness and corruption.[7]

Lee was a scion of one of Virginia's most prominent families, but he always seemed to lie in the shadow of his talented and ambitious older brothers—Richard Henry, Francis Lightfoot, and William. Living in England in the 1760s and 1770s, Arthur discovered that there, too, he was overshadowed—this time by his fellow colonial agent, Benjamin Franklin. Before he arrived in Paris, Lee had also started to harbor negative thoughts about Silas Deane. Lee suspected—wrongly—that Deane and the playwright-adventurer-businessman Beaumarchais were raking huge and unwarranted profits from the cargoes of supplies that they were arranging for shipment to America.

Franklin and Deane liked each other and worked together well. By mid-1777, however, Lee was openly feuding with them. Instead of living in Passy, he took rooms in Chaillot and later in Paris. Franklin and Deane largely ignored him. They often neglected to invite him to meetings and made important decisions without consulting him. Of course, this merely confirmed Lee's belief that those two were part of a wide conspiracy of "plundering knaves" who were more concerned with lining their own pockets than with advancing the American cause.[8] By extension, Lee also distrusted anyone else who was friendly to Franklin and Deane. This came to include Bancroft.

In addition to Arthur Lee, two other American officials in Paris helped to guarantee the dysfunctional operation of the American delegation. These were Arthur's older brother William and Ralph Izard. Since 1768 William Lee had lived in London, where he became involved in the radical politics of John Wilkes and where, as a British subject, he won election to serve as a sheriff in London in 1773 and as an alderman in 1775. Thereafter he was often referred to as "Alderman Lee." In June 1777 he arrived in France to work as a congressional commercial agent in Nantes. He gave up that post in February 1778 when he received notice of his appointment as American commissioner to Berlin and Vienna. In March 1778 he set off on a tour of German cities, but nowhere was he formally received by a royal court or other official body. Izard was a South Carolina merchant who had been working in London but who moved to Paris in the fall of 1776. In the early summer of 1777 he received word of his appointment as American commissioner to Florence. Knowing that he would not be received by the Tuscan government, he stayed put in France. As a result, both William Lee and Izard spent most of 1777 through 1779 in Paris, where they devoted much of their time to complaining of their situation and arguing with Franklin and anyone associated with Franklin. Like William's brother Arthur, they were hot-tempered and quick to see conspiracies everywhere. After Congress revoked their useless diplomatic appointments in 1779, William Lee eventually moved to Brussels to continue his mercantile business, and Izard returned to America. But before they left, they had plenty of time to create problems for Bancroft—a topic for the next chapter.

Jonathan Williams Jr. is another person requiring mention. Born in 1750 to a wealthy Boston merchant family, he was a grandnephew of Benjamin Franklin. In 1770 Williams moved to London, where he served part-time as his great-uncle's clerk and bookkeeper. By 1775 the young man had become a rising businessman in London. He traveled to France in December 1776 to see what aid he might be able to give the newly arrived Franklin. Early in 1777 Franklin and Deane thought to make use of his commercial expertise and sent him to Nantes. There he inspected the merchandise being readied for America in Beaumarchais's ships. The earnest, hard-working young man was also instructed to keep an eye on the official American commercial agent in that city. This was Thomas Morris, the alcoholic, unreliable half-brother of Robert Morris. Among other things, the commercial agent dealt with the sale of British prize vessels brought to port by American privateers and supervised the shipment of supplies purchased by Congress (via money distributed by Ferdinand Grand).

The situation in Nantes was even more dysfunctional than in Paris. By the late summer of 1777 there was a three-way struggle to control American commercial affairs in that important port—the contestants being the official agent Morris, the unofficial agent Williams, and the newly appointed co-agent whom Congress had sent to work with and control Morris. This new co-agent was William Lee. Morris helped to end some of the confusion in January 1778, when his abused body gave out and he died. William Lee relinquished his claims to the post in February 1778 to concentrate on his nonexistent duties as commissioner to Berlin and Vienna. Having had enough headaches as a result of the imbroglio, Williams spurned any suggestion that he accept the official position. A French merchant then was appointed to watch over congressional business in Nantes. Thereafter Williams remained in Nantes as a purely private merchant and shipowner. On a commission basis he handled some shipments of congressional supplies. Starting in 1778 Bancroft became Williams's partner in several commercial ventures. The Lee brothers and their allies lumped Williams into the evil cabal that they imagined.[9]

A final American requiring introduction is William Carmichael. Up to the spring of 1776 Carmichael had been living a rather debauched life as a young student in London. In May 1776 Arthur Lee entrusted him with some letters to be taken to America. But instead of traveling west, Carmichael headed east, to Paris. There he met and befriended Silas Deane. From then to early 1778 Carmichael performed numerous duties for Franklin and especially for Deane. He lived in Deane's Paris hotel and served as the commissioner's unofficial secretary and aide. Deane sent him on trips to the Netherlands and Prussia to drum up commercial support for America, but these missions proved failures. Franklin and Deane often had him carry dispatches to American agents or ship captains in French ports. Bancroft rented a room in the same hotel and often worked in tandem with Carmichael performing various tasks for Deane. Carmichael and Bancroft became boon companions until Carmichael returned to America in February 1778.[10] Carmichael would also be a target of the poison pens of the Lees and their allies.

Methods of Operation

How did Bancroft ingratiate himself with Franklin and the other Americans? What exactly did he do from day to day? How did he collect secret information and then transmit it to his superiors?

Bancroft had formed a close personal bond with Deane and Franklin, both of whom appreciated his many abilities and his apparently fervent attachment to the American cause. His desire to help them plus his supposed need to escape Britain after the John the Painter episode more than adequately explained why he and his family had moved to France.

Bancroft also could be a fun person to have around. Several tantalizing scraps of firsthand testimony to his qualities as a lively dinner companion have survived. With his friend William Carmichael, Bancroft sometimes could be downright rakish. Carmichael was notorious for his love of drink and women and often could be found in taverns frequented by American ship captains. In June 1777 Carmichael wrote to Captain Joseph Hynson, one of his merchant marine pals, about the life he shared with Bancroft. Carmichael reported that he and Bancroft kept "a decent house." They saw "none but ladies of the 1st Quality." They had not seen a mere strumpet in the past three weeks.[11] Certainly, Bancroft's recreational activities with Carmichael gave him added reason to tuck Mrs. Bancroft and the children away in the suburbs.

By the late spring of 1777, Bancroft had rapidly made himself indispensable to both Deane and Franklin. In the age before computers and photocopiers, making clean original copies plus duplicates of long letters and other documents was a laborious process. After he moved to the Hôtel de Valentinois, Franklin hired a French clerk who did much of that work. The two Frenchmen who, successively, held that post up to 1785 were reasonably conscientious, but they had a poor command of English and made many errors in their work. Moreover, keeping up with the flow of paperwork was more than one clerk could handle. The three-person American commission (and, after February 1779, Franklin alone, as the newly appointed minister plenipotentiary) handled an incredible array of duties. Besides high-level dealings with the French and other governments, these chores included distributing modest sums of money to American sailors and others who were stranded in Europe, working for the release or the improvement of conditions of American prisoners of war in England, handling requests from European soldiers, sailors, and engineers who wanted to volunteer in the American war effort, issuing safe conduct passports to Americans about to sail from French ports (such passports guaranteed that French or other friendly parties would not bother them, but they offered no help if one was captured by the British), aiding American privateers in their sale of British prize vessels, arbitrating disputes between American and French merchants, and paying for and supervising the shipment of cargoes purchased by Congress.

Temple Franklin helped out with much of the copying and record keeping. So did Bancroft, who copied all sorts of sensitive materials—letters to Congress and to Vergennes, proposals for treaties with France and other powers, and so on.[12] It is evident in some cases that he was more than a copyist. He translated items from French to English or vice versa. Sometimes he participated in the actual composing of the documents. In April 1777 he helped Franklin write a proposal intended for the Holy Roman Emperor.[13] The following September Bancroft informed Paul Wentworth that "we" were working on a memorial to be submitted to Vergennes and Count de Aranda, the Spanish ambassador in Paris. By "we" Bancroft meant himself, Franklin, and (probably) Deane.[14] So not only was Bancroft in the best position imaginable to find out what was transpiring between the Americans and the French ministers, but he even had a hand in formulating those discussions! No fox ever had better access to a henhouse.

Bancroft also performed a host of little chores or favors. In February 1777, while still in London, he sent Deane a sketch of Franklin. The drawing was a gift from Thomas Walpole, the businessman and member of Parliament who was the partner of Franklin and many others in various land companies. Walpole's son had drawn it. Franklin liked the sketch so much that he let it be used as the model for the famous terra-cotta medallion created by the Italian artist Jean-Baptiste Nini. Franklin's image in that medallion, showing him in his fur hat, remains today one of the most familiar likenesses of him.[15] In February 1778 Samuel Wharton, then in London, dispatched a

Stilton cheese to Franklin and Deane. He sent it to them in care of Bancroft.[16] More substantially, the commissioners also sent Bancroft on missions to French ports, where he helped to purchase supplies, arrange for repairs of ships, and assemble crews. He was later reimbursed for his expenses.[17]

Most historians who have written of Bancroft have said that he was Deane's secretary, Franklin's secretary, or, more generally, the secretary of the entire delegation. This is only partially true. It would be more accurate to say that he worked occasionally and informally as a secretary. But he was more than a mere clerk. His status as a respected man of letters and personal friend of Deane and Franklin ensured that he was viewed as a social equal. Some historians have claimed that from the start he received a regular salary for his services and held an official congressional position.[18] Neither of these suppositions is true. Congress never appointed an official secretary for Franklin, not even after he became the minister plenipotentiary. This became a major source of irritation for the old man. In short, Bancroft never received a salary or a title.

Proof of Bancroft's unofficial status can be seen in an episode that occurred in October 1777. On the third of that month he wrote a letter to the three commissioners. In it he recounted his many services to them, starting from the summer of 1776, when Silas Deane first contacted him. Since then he had "endeavoured to serve the interests of our Country as far as my very limited Abilities and opportunities would permit." It was not he, but rather the Continental Congress, who had first called upon his services, and his work had caused him some financial "embarrassments." "I flatter myself," he wrote, that Congress or its representatives in France "would have thought me not unworthy of some regular appointment or employment." It is "neither reputable or decent in me to attach myself any longer to the business of a Commission which I have no proper right to meddle with; and as my want of Fortune moreover will not permit me to do it; I therefore intend to withdraw myself from all Political pursuits; of which I beg leave to inform you, and to request that you will Convey my grateful thanks to the Congress for the Notice which their Committe[e] formerly were so pleased to bestow on me. I shall ever consider myself as highly honored, though I may not have been benefitted by it."[19]

In short, because he had no appointment or salary, he was quitting. It is possible that he was bluffing. If he actually had carried through on it, he would have lost his access to Franklin and Deane and all their confidential papers. In consequence, he would have become useless to the British ministry, which undoubtedly would have stopped paying him. Moreover, he would no longer have had advance notice of commercial and political affairs that he used in his stock speculations. So why did he write it? Perhaps he really did need the extra money and assumed that the commissioners could easily give him a job title and a modest stipend. Or perhaps his vanity was wounded by his lack of any official position. Finally, he might have done it to throw off suspicions about his loyalty. Through the summer and fall of that year the commissioners had strong evidence that someone close to them was leaking information. If Bancroft were indeed a British agent, he would not have threatened to give up his close relationship with them—or so Bancroft might have hoped they would think. There is nothing in the papers of Franklin, Deane, or Lee to tell us what they thought of his letter. All we know is that shortly after writing it Bancroft did indeed depart. He went to the Netherlands, where he consulted with Paul Wentworth. Wentworth might have ordered or persuaded him to withdraw his resignation. By early November Bancroft was back in Passy and working with the commissioners as though nothing had happened. One can only guess at the excuse he gave them for his change of heart.[20]

For Bancroft's biographer, his services to the American commissioners prove a maddening puzzle. Without a doubt, his primary allegiance lay with the British Empire, and his major goal was to stop the rebellious colonies from breaking away from that empire. But that does not mean he was anti-American. He genuinely believed that it was in America's best interest to stay united with Britain. To help Britain retain the colonies, he needed to win the confidence of Franklin, Deane, and others. Therefore, in his work for them, he had to do a decent job.

What is so puzzling is that he did more than just a decent job. He gave advice that Franklin and Deane valued highly. There is no indication that he ever tried to sabotage their work. He genuinely liked them and, in his own fashion, wanted to help them. He might even have played a role in badgering France to commit itself to more open aid for the rebels. This occurred with two articles published in July 1777 in the *Affaires de l'Angleterre et de l'Amérique*, a periodical printed by the French foreign affairs ministry. One was simply entitled "Memoir" and the other "Supplemental Observations." The two pieces called on France to declare war on Britain immediately. The authorship of these documents is not certain. They might have been written by Franklin, Deane, Bancroft, or all three of them. Vergennes professed anger at the appearance of these pieces in one of his own publications, for he had already told the Americans that France was not yet prepared for an open commitment. That might be why Franklin denied any connection to them and quietly intimated that Bancroft had written them. When John Adams arrived in Paris in 1778 he learned of the two writings and had no doubts about their provenance. Later he wrote in his autobiography, "Bancroft had a clear head and a good Pen. He wrote some things relative to the Connection between France and America, with the Assistance of Franklin and Deane as I presume, which were translated into French by Mr. Turgot or the Duke de la Rochefoucault . . . and which were very well done."[21]

When not working as a clerk, adviser, or general facilitator and friend, Bancroft made trips to various cities to inspect the quality, quantity, and readiness of shipments of uniforms, cannons, and other materials ordered at public expense. For example, in mid-May 1777, just weeks after he moved to France, Bancroft was sent to Rouen to inspect merchandise being loaded on ships for America.[22]

While in Rouen Bancroft also took the time to compose a long letter and send it, with several enclosures, to the man who had been assigned to oversee his work, Paul Wentworth. Nowadays, in the language of secret intelligence, Wentworth would be called his handler. Through the spring of 1778, virtually all of Bancroft's secret information was communicated directly to Wentworth. Upon receiving dispatches from "Dr. Edwards," Wentworth often made his own summaries of them, added personal comments, and forwarded everything to Secretary of State Suffolk. Suffolk then communicated the intelligence to the other ministers; Lord North usually passed the materials along to George III.

Bancroft wrote from Paris, Rouen, or other French cities, whereas Wentworth was in London. How did Bancroft transmit the letters safely to Wentworth? Certainly not through the regular postal system, where both French and British inspectors were likely to read them. In some letters Bancroft refers vaguely to the agreed-upon method of communication. Bancroft was intentionally vague, because if the letters were intercepted by French police or spies, he did not want to reveal the names of places or persons involved.

Bancroft and Wentworth generally used private messengers—sometimes their servants. France and Britain were still officially at peace, and so people could travel freely between the two countries. During this twelve-month period, Wentworth often complained that Bancroft was not sending him enough information. This was not for lack of energy on Bancroft's part. He was busy working for the commissioners. He had access to all their papers, but in those days a spy did not have miniature cameras with which to copy hundreds of pages per hour. Bancroft had to find times when Franklin, Deane, and others were not in the rooms where all the records were kept. Whenever he heard footsteps, he had to stop his work. Then there was the problem of sending his lengthy reports to London. If Bancroft sent a messenger to London, it might be two weeks before that person arrived back in Paris ready to take a new batch of materials. On average, a one-way trip between the two capitals took four or five days.

Impatient to obtain news as quickly as possible, Wentworth visited Paris himself. Between May 1777 and February 1778 he traveled to France at least eight times.[23] In addition, on three occasions he met with Bancroft in other cities, once in London and twice in the Netherlands. In his visits to Paris, Wentworth posed as an apolitical, wealthy man of the world. He stayed with his mistress and engaged in his sundry stock speculations and other business investments. To all appearances, he seemed unconcerned with the diplomatic and military issues stirring between the United States, France, and Britain. Some of his meetings with Bancroft were clandestine, late-night affairs. Others were out in the open. The two men, after all, were old friends, dating back to Bancroft's work on Wentworth's plantations in Surinam. After a few days in Paris, Wentworth either returned to London or went on to Amsterdam, where he also had business interests. Only a handful of Bancroft's reports to Wentworth have survived.[24] In Paris, of course, Bancroft's reports were given orally. Wentworth apparently destroyed most of the letters he received from Bancroft once he had summarized them in his own hand for Suffolk.

Secret Intelligence

What information did Bancroft give Wentworth during this twelve-month period? It would be tedious here to recount all the bits of information he dispatched. Most of what he sent is now part of the well-known story of Franco-American relations during the Revolution. It will suffice to discuss just some of the particulars of his reports.

Bancroft had arrived in Paris on 1 April 1777, and on 6 and 10 April he dispatched his first letters to Wentworth. Most of the men's subsequent correspondence would be conveyed by private messengers, but Bancroft sent these initial letters through the regular post. He hoped that the letters would look innocent and thus not be opened by either the French or British postal inspectors. Their innocent appearance was due to the fact that the envelopes indicated that the sender was a man named J. Jones and the recipient a Mr. George Carlting at the Café Marlboro in London. These were two of the numerous aliases used by Bancroft and Wentworth. In these two messages, Bancroft reports that he is winning the confidence of the American commissioners and coming to learn all their secrets. Supplies for America are being loaded in ships anchored off the French coast. The court at Versailles is very friendly to the rebel cause. France is not yet ready for war against Britain, but it has promised substantial financial aid. The Continental Congress will send commissioners to seek alliances with other continental powers. The senior French minister, the Comte de Maurepas, is no longer averse to war. The impetuous Marquis de Lafayette has, against the wishes of his family and the government, equipped a vessel at his own expense and sailed for America with a group of other military officers. Bancroft says that the crown only pretends to disapprove of what Lafayette did, and all the ladies at court, especially Marie-Antoinette, excitedly applaud the valor of the dashing young marquis. Arthur Lee has returned from Spain with promises of some secret aid. Prussia has expressed some interest in trading with America. Tuscany has agreed to refund some of the duties it charged to American ships entering its ports. Lambert Wickes and captains of other American ships have entered French ports with captured British merchant vessels and are preparing to set out on new expeditions. Franklin and Deane have let him (that is, Bancroft) view French police reports on the clandestine activities of other British agents working in Paris! A Captain Nicholson has arrived in Paris with letters for the commissioners; on his voyage from America, he captured two British vessels.[25]

One of Bancroft's most voluminous communications came a few weeks later, near the end of May. He was in Rouen, inspecting ships and cargoes for the commissioners. While there, he sent Wentworth a letter plus a four-page memorandum and copies of several important documents via private messenger. The letter is unsigned but in Bancroft's hand. In it Bancroft says he will do his best to follow Wentworth's instructions. He will make his communications as "sparing" as possible, so that he will avoid being detected. He will send his intelligence to Wentworth through the "usual channel." Then Bancroft commences to jump from one topic to another. He says he will attempt to learn what transpired in a conversation between a French military officer and Franklin. Sometime soon he will furnish Wentworth with a new supply of invisible ink. (That seems to indicate that Bancroft, a chemist, made the ink himself, along with the chemical wash that rendered it visible.) Ferdinand Grand has told the commissioners that France remains favorable to their cause and that the crown is building eight to ten new warships to protect American trade from the British ships that cruise along the coast. Bancroft assures Wentworth that the Continental Congress has no secret agents in Britain; Deane corresponds with no one there, and Franklin's British correspondents are merely old acquaintances. Bancroft provides the names of the congressional agents in Nantes, Le Havre, Bordeaux, Marseille, and Martinique who are aiding American privateers and arranging for shipments of supplies. Congress has written to the commissioners that they should discourage any French military officers from seeking employment in the American army unless they have a good command of English; otherwise, they will be useless. The commissioners in Paris have almost been "persecuted to death" by thousands of Frenchmen trying to volunteer.

Bancroft ends his letter by noting that he was prevented from copying even more papers because of "the presence of certain persons, in a certain place all the afternoon." Nonetheless, he is proud of the amount of intelligence he is able to forward. He declares that he is providing more than "all the other secrets" from "other sources." In other words, he is confident that he is more valuable than all the other British agents working in France put together, and he hopes that Wentworth will make Lord Suffolk aware of this. In a postscript, Bancroft adds that he will be returning to Paris and that Wentworth can contact him by writing to Mr. George Chalmers (another Bancroft alias) at the Café du Conti.[26]

The copied documents that were enclosed with the letter were items to which Bancroft had easy access at the Hôtel de Valentinois. One of these was a list of the French army officers who sailed with Lafayette. The most famous of these was a major general, the Baron de Kalb. A second document was a recently signed contract between the American commissioners and the French Farmers General, a cartel of tax collectors who had a monopoly on the importation and sale of tobacco in France. As a way of concealing part of its aid for the rebels, the French crown had instructed the Farmers General to advance 1 million livres to the commissioners in return for future shipments of tobacco from America. (As it turned out, very little tobacco was shipped during the Revolution, due to the heavy presence of British cruisers off the American coast.) A third document was a letter from the three American commissioners to the Baron de Rullecourt; they authorized him, in the name of the United States, to seize the Zaffarin Islands off the coast of Morocco and use them as a base for attacking British shipping. Bancroft's final copied document is a letter from Baron Schulenberg, a minister in the Prussian government, to the American commissioners; Schulenberg politely discourages proposals for Prussian-American trade. The four-page memorandum that also accompanied Bancroft's letter contained a summary of all that he had learned since his move to France.

In their correspondence, Wentworth and Bancroft could conceal their true meanings by using either an invisible ink or an agreed-upon code. Bancroft used code in the attached memorandum. Most of the persons and places mentioned in it are designated with numbers or symbols. After he received the document, Wentworth consulted his code book and made interlinear notations on the paper, filling in what the missing words should be. Thus, for example, 136 meant Spain, 93 was Arthur Lee, 57 was England, 122 was Paris, □88nn4x was "woollen," and 7n802adx6 was "cloathing."After deciphering the document, Wentworth forwarded it to William Eden.[27]

Bancroft begins his memorandum with information regarding aid that Spain is giving to the rebels. Bancroft reports that Spain is willing to give the Americans a stockpile of supplies sitting in New Orleans—two thousand barrels of gunpowder, a quantity of lead, and a large amount of clothing. Moreover, Spain is sending five vessels laden with military supplies to America. They are to be paid for by bills of exchange to be honored by Arthur Lee or Benjamin Franklin (who would ask Ferdinand Grand to furnish the funds). Spain wishes the colonies well but cannot assist them openly, in particular because Spain could not risk endangering a large, richly laden fleet

I now set down my dear Friend to recapitulate shortly, the substance of my different late Conversations, that you may be inabled with more certainty to communicate them to 137. — To begin then with 136 — The Duke who met 93 told him that there were lodged at new-orleans ... 2000 Barrels of gunpowder ... in a quantity of ... a large quantity of Cloathing &c for all which 35 might immediatly send, as an order from 37 of 136, would be instantly dispatched for their delivery: He said other Supplies of necessary commodities would be sent to America from 136; and accordingly, we have been lately advised of the actual sailing of 4 Vessels from Bilboa directly, for 36, with Colonys sailCloth Cordage ... Coarse Linnens, Woollens ... &c &c; & also that a fifth is going for the same purpose — All these as I understand were dispatched under the direction of Mess.rs Guardiloqui ... & Son of that Place, and the same Gentlemen have lately sent us Bills to the amount of about £100,000. Livres tournois, They say that much more is to follow as fast as good paper can be purchased, but that this is difficult to be found: These Bills were indorsed payable to the order of 93 — but it has been desired that all future remittances from that quarter may come to the order 58. (& of which the Bills in question are apart) The Duke told 93 that this sum wc. we might expect, would be considerable but no sum was specified, nor is do we know any thing about quantity that can authorize the forming of any Conclusion — He assured 93 that 36 had the utmost good wishes of 136; but that the latter could not as yet openly succour & assist the former or quarrel with England, because a very large & rich Flota was soon expected, & might be endangered by a less cautious mode

First page of a report from Edward Bancroft to Paul Wentworth, May 1777. *British Library, Auckland Papers* due to return soon from South America. Bancroft also notes that Spain is "prejudiced" against Arthur Lee, whose prickly personality fared no better there than in France. Bancroft's source says that Spain might be more receptive to American overtures if Franklin were to go there, and Bancroft states that Franklin is considering the trip. Bancroft goes on to say that France and Spain are planning an important "diversion" in favor of the colonies. This will take place in the near future. Bancroft does not know what it will be, and the American commissioners also are not let in on the specifics. (Even today we are not sure what this was.) Franklin and Deane have recently sent new proposals to Vergennes and Aranda without consulting Lee. Thus far neither the French minister nor the Spanish ambassador has responded. Bancroft has not seen the letter given to Aranda, but he is sure that soon Deane will tell him the details—in particular, what, if anything, the United States will offer to Spain in return for open assistance.

Bancroft also notes that the Americans' earlier request for eight ships of the line has been rejected by the French ministry, because it would lead to war with Britain. France, however, has promised pecuniary assistance along with the hope that it might be able to offer something more "decisively effectual" at a later date. In the meantime, France has already provided a free gift of 2 million livres. In addition, Versailles has promised an additional 2 million livres for this year and again for next year to enable the commissioners to pay for all the supplies they were ordering from private merchants.

Following this, Bancroft offers some personal reflections. He exclaims, "It seems to me impossible to conjecture the real intentions of 60 [France] & 136 [Spain]. The former is so much addicted to deception that it would appear to me very doubtful whether its assurances to America ought to be more candid than those to 57 [England]." That is a highly amusing statement, coming as it does from someone who himself was no mean practitioner of deception. He says that France for the moment is backing up its words to the commissioners with money, and if a war does come, France will probably justify it on the basis of some supposed British hostile action in Europe. Bancroft surmises that Spain is more inclined to go to war against Portugal, a result of ongoing boundary disputes in South America.

Next Bancroft reports that a large merchant ship is preparing to sail from Dunkirk but that he does not know its destination. Another large ship, this one belonging to Beaumarchais, is about to depart from Marseille. A smaller vessel has left Nantes. Bancroft surmises that the latter two mer-chantmen will pass near Ireland before heading to America. Bancroft also notes that a man named Boux is supervising construction of two uncom-monly large, well-armed ships; they are to be constructed in the Netherlands, but Bancroft is not sure precisely where. Boux is doing this under the direc-tion of Georges Grand, a prominent banker in Amsterdam and the brother of Ferdinand Grand. These two ships will be for the use of the Americans.

Bancroft then relates that a Mr. Galvan has been sent from South Caro-lina to France to buy a large quantity of heavy cannons that will be used to fortify the city of Charleston. He is also purchasing a significant amount of military stores from Beaumarchais and others. All of these materials are due to sail for South Carolina from Marseille within a few days.

The list of things Bancroft reports continues. A Frenchman named Holker is producing twenty thousand uniforms, which will bring to eighty thousand the number being sent to America. Franklin's landlord, Chaumont, has re-cently agreed to furnish packet boats that will carry monthly messages plus cargoes of supplies to Congress. There is a French agent in America who cor-responds with the Comte d'Artois (one of Louis XVI's brothers), and Silas Deane sometime soon will meet with d'Artois. The American commissioners have sent circular letters to the courts of Austria, Spain, Prussia, and Tus-cany, asking for recognition of American independence. Those courts have not yet made any response. The commissioners hope to gain use of a Prussian port, where American privateers can bring their prize vessels and from which supplies can be shipped to the colonies. In the last letter received from Con-gress, the delegates appear to be in high spirits and determined to resist Britain to the end. In order to get Americans to buy loan office certificates (government bonds), Congress has had to raise the interest it pays on them to 6 percent. In Boston a Mr. Cushing is building a seventy-four-gun ship of the line and a thirty-six-gun frigate, but Cushing does not know if he will be able to procure enough sails, cordage, and other materials.

The several paragraphs above summarize just one communication from Bancroft—sent to Wentworth from Rouen near the end of May 1777. Most of the information was accurate and up to date. Some of the things Bancroft reported turned out to be false leads, but that was not his fault. Franklin, for example, did ponder a trip to Spain, but he never made it. Cushing's ship-building plans did not come to fruition. The commissioners did give their blessing to the Baron de Rullecourt's planned invasion of the Zaffarin Islands, but that quixotic scheme never got off the ground.

Every two weeks or so from the spring of 1777 to the spring of 1778 Bancroft had a similar cornucopia of both big and small news for his handler. His secret intelligence covered everything: the personal relations among Franklin, Deane, and Lee; the meetings between the commissioners and Vergennes in Versailles; the incoming and outgoing correspondence; the various American and French visitors at the Hôtel de Valentinois—all this and more.[28]

Supplies for America and Attacks on British Shipping

The three most crucial topics on which Bancroft provided details were: the American and French ships leaving French ports with supplies for America, along with the degree to which the French government supported this clandestine trade; American privateering vessels that brought British ships to French ports for sale; and the question of whether France would eventually give open support and recognition to the United States.

Bancroft supplied news about dozens of merchant vessels ready to depart from French ports. These included the *Heureux,* the *Amphitrite,* and other bottoms being dispatched from Marseille by Beaumarchais. Some of the ships leaving France sailed to the French West Indies and then transferred their goods to other vessels, which then tried to elude British cruisers and enter North American ports. Others leaving France went straight to the rebel colonies. Bancroft sometimes provided the names of the ships, sometimes the names of the captains, sometimes just the ports where ships were scheduled to disembark. He could not give specific departure dates. No one could have done that. A ship's departure depended on how fast its cargo and crew could be assembled and how quickly any repairs could be accomplished. Even when all those were ready, a ship might be unexpectedly stuck in port because of storms or contrary winds. Nonetheless, the hope was that, armed with this information, British ships cruising near the major French ports would be able to capture many of these merchantmen. If the vessels were American, the British had a clear right to take them. If the ships were French, they were still fair game if they were transporting military supplies to a rebellious part of the British Empire.

Through the summer and fall of 1777, American privateers proved to be the most contentious issue between France and Britain, and Bancroft played a pivotal role in this drama. Privateers held a status halfway between outright pirate ships and naval vessels. One might call them licensed brigands. These privately owned ships were supposed to carry letters of marque from their governments; these letters authorized them to prey on enemy merchant shipping. Many privateers bypassed this legal nicety and simply seized as many enemy ships as possible. They took these captured vessels into ports of their own country or into friendly ports elsewhere, sold the ships and cargoes, and divided the money between the captains and crews.

Scores of American privateers cruising in European waters captured more than five hundred British vessels in 1776 and 1777.[29] Occasionally, the Americans sent their prizes into Spanish, Dutch, Prussian, or Scandinavian ports. The vast majority of the prizes, however, were taken to French ports. There were obvious reasons for this: French ports were usually the nearest at hand, and France was giving every sign of favoring the American cause. Vergennes was willing to close his eyes to these activities as long as the privateers kept a low profile and avoided implicating the French government in what they did.

The capture of British merchant vessels caused severe diplomatic frictions between Britain and those countries permitting American privateers to use their ports. Because France was the number one safe haven for these semi-piratical vessels, the crisis became most acute there. Letting the American privateers use ports for repairs, purchase of supplies, and the sale of prize ships and cargoes was a violation of neutrality. Britain generally was successful in compelling the Netherlands and Baltic countries to return British prizes to their "rightful" owners and to stop harboring American privateers. The larger question was: How far would Britain go in pressuring powerful, pro-American France? In addition to the privateers, there were also American naval warships seizing British merchant bottoms.

Through the early fall of 1777 Britain put more and more pressure on France to stop aiding the American commerce raiders. This proved to be a delicate issue, because neither Britain nor France wanted all-out war against the other—at least, not yet. Britain still hoped to quell the rebellion before any Continental countries got involved. France's navy would not be fully prepared to face Albion's until the following spring. France also did not want its

Newfoundland fishing fleet to be seized before it could return home. Britain, however, could not countenance an affront to its honor and serious damage to its maritime commerce. On the other hand, France was still smarting from the humiliation of 1763 and could not seem to cave in to British huffing and puffing. If France wanted to weaken the British Empire and win American trade for itself, it could not simply abandon the Americans.

Throughout these months Bancroft collected voluminous data on the privateering crisis, but he was not the only British agent involved. As noted previously, British ambassador Lord Stormont had numerous paid informers in most of the ports. British consuls stationed in other countries also gathered particulars on the comings and goings in French ports. The information Bancroft supplied confirmed all of this activity, often adding specifics as to what ships were captured and sold, where this was done, and which American ships were responsible for the seizures.

Bancroft proved even more important, however, in another way. Only he was in a position to pinpoint the degree to which the American commissioners and the French ministry colluded to encourage the preying on British maritime commerce. This was crucial for Britain. Otherwise, Franklin, Vergennes, and their colleagues could have successfully claimed that they had little knowledge or control over what private Americans and Frenchmen were doing in ports strung out over hundreds of miles along the Atlantic and Mediterranean.

One of Bancroft's first major finds came late in May 1777. On 25 May, Franklin and Deane dispatched a long letter to the Committee for Foreign Affairs. It was customary in those days to send two or more copies of any letter across the Atlantic, in different ships, in the hope that at least one would reach its destination. Both copies that Franklin and Deane sent managed to reach Philadelphia. Those two copies can be found today in the Papers of the Continental Congress in the National Archives in Washington, DC. Interestingly, however, two other copies can be found in William Eden's papers in the British Library. One of these is entirely in Bancroft's hand, and the other is partly in his and partly in Paul Wentworth's hand. Shortly after Franklin and Deane wrote the letter, Bancroft evidently "borrowed" a copy of it and took it to Wentworth, who was making one of his regular visits to Paris. The letter was so important that they wanted to make sure it reached Eden and the British ministry. Therefore they hurriedly made two copies. Wentworth took one copy with him on his return to London, and the other traveled via another route (probably with one of Stormont's diplomatic couriers).[30]

In the letter Franklin and Deane reported on sundry matters. In particular, they discussed activities in French ports. They remarked that ordinarily when American naval ships or privateers entered harbors for repairs or the sale of prizes these activities "may be cover'd and conceal'd by various Pretences" so that they could be "wink'd at" by the French court. However, American use of French ports as a base of activity for attacking British shipping had gone too far. In order to avoid "immediate War," Versailles had returned some of the prize vessels to their British owners. However, Franklin and Deane assured Congress that France had offered "the most substantial Proofs of . . . Friendship." Once the current flap died down, the commissioners were sure that American privateers again would be able to operate out of French ports.

In the same letter, Franklin and Deane summarized what was happening regarding the purchase and shipment of supplies. They were ordering saddles and other accouterments for horses. They hoped to have uniforms for eighty thousand men manufactured and shipped by the end of the year. They were negotiating with French, Swedish, and Dutch merchants for pistols and cannons. If Congress needed money, it could sign bills that would be payable in France—with money that the crown had given to Ferdinand Grand. Versailles was still declining to sign a treaty of commerce, for that would be an acknowledgment of American independence, which would bring immediate war with Britain. However, Versailles assured them that even without such a treaty they could depend on "every Indulgence" in treating America as, in effect, a most favored trading nation.

Thanks to Bancroft, British ministers knew all of the above weeks before the same letter reached Philadelphia. It gave them concrete proof that the French government was aiding and abetting the seizure of British bottoms and the dispatching of supplies to America. It also told them that, for the moment, neither France nor Spain wanted open war. Thus Lord North's government knew that if it kept the pressure up, the French crown would, for the time being, back down. The privateering would continue, but at a lower level.

In addition to contending with France, Lord North had to confront public opinion at home. British newspapers ran sensational stories about the dangers to shipping in Britain's home waters. These accounts occasionally sent panic throughout the country. If Americans, aided by the French, could freely roam these waters, they might also make land raids. And, with French and perhaps Spanish help, there might even be a major invasion. These considerations would be an important factor throughout the Revolution. Neither in 1777 nor later could Britain send all of its men and ships to quell the American rebellion, because it needed to defend its coast against Americans and their possible allies. Britain also had to protect its West Indies possessions. Bancroft's information helped to keep these fears alive and thus was important in Britain's strategic planning. To the extent that Bancroft contributed to the retention of men and ships in Britain and in the Caribbean, one might say that his information had the unintended effect of actually helping the American cause.

Through the summer and fall of 1777 Bancroft continued to supply details regarding American privateers. In mid-July Wentworth visited Paris and immediately forwarded to Suffolk what Bancroft had learned of the latest goings-on in Versailles. According to Bancroft, the diplomatic dustup caused by American attacks on British shipping had led to a heated disagreement in the king's council. Naval minister Sartine was, along with Vergennes, a vehement Anglophobe who argued strongly for continuing to support the Americans. Senior minister Maurepas and finance minister Jacques Necker argued for caution. They maintained that any eruption of hostilities at that moment would endanger the fishing fleet still across the Atlantic plus a large fleet bringing essential naval stores to France from the Baltic. Sartine lost the battle of wills, and orders went out for all American warships and privateers to depart from French ports. Thanks to Bancroft, however, Wentworth was able to inform his superiors that, although French fear of an immediate war was genuine, Versailles did not cave in entirely. The orders to expel American ships were not strictly enforced. Franklin and Deane, with Sartine's private approval, were still supporting the purchase and outfitting of privateers and encouraging them to continue their work, even if that meant temporarily shifting some of their activities to Spanish ports. Additional reports from Bancroft through the fall demonstrated the same kinds of French subterfuge. Official orders would go out for the expulsion or seizure of American ships and their prizes, but private, usually oral, instructions would also go out, letting port officials know that they could safely close their eyes to what the Americans were doing.[31]

This game of brinkmanship, with Britain and France pushing each other just to the edge of war, might have continued indefinitely. But in early December news reached both London and Paris that in mid-October General Burgoyne's army had surrendered to American troops at Saratoga. That event would have a significant impact not only on the course of the war in America but also on Anglo-French-American diplomacy in Europe. Moreover, it would add to Edward Bancroft's workload.

6 The Franco-American Alliance

The Battle of Saratoga is often considered a major turning point in the Revolution. The British goal was to take control of the Hudson River valley and thus separate New England from the middle and southern colonies. After suffering defeat in two battles in mid-September and early October, General John Burgoyne surrendered to the American commander, General Horatio Gates, in the town of Saratoga, New York, on 17 October 1777.

The standard view of the battle holds that it accomplished two things: It helped to turn the tide in favor of Washington's Continental Army, and it persuaded France to give open support to the fledgling United States. But this view is overstated on several counts. Militarily, it is true that the battle was important. The British loss virtually guaranteed that the rebellious colonies would be free from any future attacks coming from Canada, and it ended British hopes for separating New England from the other colonies. The surrender of an entire British army gave the Americans a major morale boost. But few at that time would have called it a turning point. While Gates and his subordinate commanders (including a heroic Benedict Arnold) were surrounding Burgoyne's troops, George Washington's army was suffering defeats in Pennsylvania at Brandywine Creek and Germantown. The horrible winter at Valley Forge still lay ahead, as did the bloody British campaigns in the southern colonies.

Nor was the battle a turning point in terms of French involvement. Enough has been said in earlier chapters to show that France was already committed to the Americans and was anticipating open involvement in the war by the spring of 1778. Of course, the American victory was good news. When word of Saratoga reached Paris in early December, Vergennes was as happy as Franklin and the other Americans.[1] So if France was planning to enter the war anyway, what did the battle accomplish in terms of American diplomacy? It sped up processes already at work. It led the British government to make some last-minute attempts at reconciliation, and it gave Vergennes a final opportunity to persuade Louis XVI to approve open involvement.

Oddly, Bancroft's importance to the British at this juncture was initially felt through his absence rather than his active involvement. On or about 4 December, just as the news of Saratoga reached Paris, Bancroft departed for London. This is known because a few days after his abrupt disappearance from Paris, Paul Wentworth arrived there. William Eden had dispatched Wentworth as a secret emissary to feel out the American commissioners about some sort of Anglo-American reconciliation. Wentworth was counting on help from Bancroft, only to find him missing. Bancroft had suddenly gone to London on public as well as private affairs. (More on these below.) He did not return to Paris until 23 December.[2]

Wentworth arrived in Paris on 10 December and took rooms in a hotel near the place Vendôme. Within his first twenty-four hours there he dispatched three letters to Eden. He reported that he went to "Edwards's" (that is, Bancroft's) Paris lodgings but was told by the landlady that he had moved and she did not know where. Wentworth then happened to meet Bancroft's maid walking along a street. She informed him that Bancroft had gone to Rouen to pick up some chests that had arrived for him there. Not believing that, Wentworth asked around town and was told that Bancroft had taken wing to London on some business ventures in which he and Silas Deane were involved. Wentworth was reluctant to proceed without Bancroft and spent the next few days preparing his plan of action and picking up gossip on political events from an unnamed friend. Wentworth told Eden that this friend had been giving him reliable information from inner ministerial doings at Versailles for some eight years. Now the friend was telling him that the news from Saratoga had no impact on French-American relations. Those at Versailles who opposed direct involvement in the rebellion, chiefly the

Comte de Maurepas, were holding their own against the war party led by Vergennes and naval minister Sartine.[3]

That dispatch to Eden reveals just how harmful Bancroft's absence from the scene was. Wentworth's anonymous informant was badly mistaken. If Bancroft had been present, undoubtedly he would have told Wentworth that on 6 December Vergennes's secretary Gérard had visited the Hôtel de Valentinois and asked the American commissioners to resubmit their proposal for an alliance. Two days later Franklin's grandson Temple carried a new copy of the proposal to Versailles, where Vergennes welcomed him warmly and promised a reply within forty-eight hours.[4] The reply came as an invitation for the commissioners to meet with him in person. On 12 December Franklin, Deane, and Lee traveled to Vergennes's country home near Versailles. There he gave them a strong assurance of official support but said that first he must await word from Madrid. France was hoping that Louis XVI's Bourbon cousin Charles III would agree to join an alliance with the United States. A response from Spain was expected in about three weeks.

France was inching closer to the edge of war, and yet, without Bancroft, neither Wentworth nor Stormont, despite their numerous paid informers, was aware of it. Not having Bancroft to act as intermediary, Wentworth plunged ahead on his own. On 12 December he wrote an anonymous letter to Silas Deane, who was thought to be the most conciliatory of the three commissioners and with whom Wentworth apparently had some previous acquaintance. He asked to meet Deane either on the road to Passy or at an art exhibition in the Luxembourg Gallery or in a bathhouse on the Seine. Deane responded to the writer, who identified himself only as "ABC," and said that he could receive him at his Paris hotel on the rue Royale the next morning.[5]

Wentworth kept that appointment on the thirteenth, and the two men spent hours discussing the history of British administration in the colonies. They agreed to meet again the next morning, at a nearby café. When Wentworth arrived there, he found Franklin and Lee sitting at a table with Deane. At Wentworth's approach, Franklin and Lee walked away—probably a snub intended to display American defiance. Wentworth acknowledged that he was there as a purely private individual, but he gave assurances that the British ministry had indeed sent him. He revealed that Britain would undo all the offensive taxes and other measures that had been instituted since 1763 and grant the colonies more autonomy in regulating their internal affairs. Deane recommended that Wentworth reread Bancroft's 1769 book *Remarks* for a persuasive exposition of the colonial position. To sweeten his offer, Wentworth mentioned that Britain would be willing to grant Deane and his colleagues various honors in America, including high political office and honorific titles. Deane was noncommittal on every point, and the two men agreed to meet again two days later.

Wentworth's report to Eden on these conversations extended to twenty pages. Indeed, many of the letters Wentworth sent Eden through 1777 and early 1778 ranged over so many pages that British ministers and even George III started to complain of his inability to stick to the main points. In those letters Wentworth often complained of being overworked and of having to stay up through the night to write his reports. It is easy to see that Wentworth had himself to blame if he lost sleep, with his meandering, repetitive, trivia-filled missives. It was bad enough that Wentworth spent precious time with Silas Deane discussing the battle tactics of Roman emperors Claudius and Vespasian, but he also summarized that discussion in one of his reports to Eden. Other letters contained irrelevant digressions about Parisian pawnshops, the Comte de Maurepas's gout, and the Comtesse d'Artois's pregnancy. Usually he also called attention to the promises made to him in London for a pension, a seat in Parliament, a baronetcy, and other favors. He admitted that he could be "prolix" and "perhaps too diffuse" and that Eden might want to wait until he had "a vacant hour" at his "pleasure" to spend reading his "trifling reflections."[6]

After consulting with Franklin, Deane did not show up for his follow-up rendezvous with Wentworth. Franklin himself declined to meet with anyone less than an accredited emissary, and he refused to consider anything less than complete American independence. Franklin sent news of Wentworth's entreaties to Vergennes. This is a fine example of Franklin's cunning diplomatic acumen. If Versailles was fully informed of British peace overtures, this could speed up open commitment to America. The stratagem worked. Vergennes immediately dispatched his secretary Gérard to assure the commissioners that France would take a major step very soon.[7]

Wentworth thus got nowhere with Deane or Franklin, and he did not even try to approach the bilious Lee. What was worse, Wentworth was upset at being taken for a lowly spy—which in that era placed him at about the same level as a brothel keeper or an actor. To soothe Wentworth's hurt feelings, Stormont wrangled an invitation for Wentworth to be presented at court in Versailles. Vergennes also flattered Wentworth by inviting him to a private dinner. Wentworth's feelings were assuaged, but without Bancroft to intercede or ply him with insider information, he failed to achieve any substantial negotiations. Without Bancroft, Wentworth vainly endeavored to ferret out the reasons why various Americans in Paris—including William Carmichael and Silas Deane's brother Simeon—were being sent to America and what dispatches they might be carrying.

On 25 December Bancroft, recently arrived back from London, finally went to see Wentworth. Franklin, Deane, and Vergennes all knew in advance of this visit. It seemed natural for the two old friends and business partners to meet. It was also expected that Bancroft would try to find out from Wentworth any pieces of information that Wentworth had not yet revealed in his conversations with Deane. Bancroft's main motive, however, was to assure Wentworth that he was back on the job for his British masters. Bancroft said that no treaty of alliance had yet been arranged. The most important piece of news that Bancroft gave Wentworth was that the three American commissioners were adamant in their demand that Britain recognize complete and immediate independence. They would not negotiate with Wentworth or any other British agent without London's initial accession to that point. This information disappointed Wentworth, who had hoped that his persuasive skills might still have had some chance to succeed.[8]

Every few days thereafter Bancroft and Wentworth continued to meet secretly, in an unnamed location where they hoped to avoid detection by French spies. Bancroft kept his handler informed on the progress of treaty negotiations. He reported that the American commissioners sometimes made clandestine late-night trips to Versailles or that Vergennes's secretary Gérard stealthily came to Passy under cover of darkness. Wentworth was incredulous when Bancroft revealed, accurately, that France was willing to ally with America without the promise of much in return. France did not aim to reclaim any of its lost territories in America; all that it hoped for was increased trade with an independent United States plus American help in protecting French possessions in the Caribbean. When British ministers learned of this from Wentworth, they, too, were incredulous. Bancroft also provided more details on ships laden with supplies destined for America. Wentworth told Eden that he kept much of this information secret from Lord Stormont, because the hot-blooded British ambassador was likely to go straight to Vergennes to complain of French treachery. This would alert the French that there was a "leak" in Passy, thus endangering the ever-nervous Bancroft. While treasuring the intelligence he received, Wentworth nonetheless had doubts about Bancroft. He suspected that Bancroft might be allied with parliamentary opposition leaders who were much more conciliatory toward America, and he complained that Bancroft sometimes showed more interest in his private commercial ventures than in the Crown's service. Yet Wentworth declared to Eden that "in so great and critical a moment," we "entirely depend" on him.[9]

At the end of December and again early in January 1778 Bancroft obtained for Wentworth what he could not achieve on his own: meetings with Benjamin Franklin. On condition that Wentworth not repeat the insulting offer of bribes or noble titles that had been mentioned to Deane, the senior commissioner reluctantly agreed to meet the British agent under the guise of their being "private friends and well wishers." In their initial interview, Franklin asked Wentworth if he had any formal powers to agree to terms and whether Britain was prepared to recognize American independence. Wentworth admitted that he was merely an unofficial envoy, and he nervously avoided directly answering any of the old man's other questions. Bancroft attended the meeting, as Franklin's aid and adviser, and participated in the discussions. Today's diplomats, schooled in the art of obfuscation, would appreciate Bancroft's efforts to achieve some sort of compromise. He suggested several phrases that the British could use for the status of the United States; these words would seem to recognize independence without actually doing so. Bancroft's attempt to broker an agreement is a further indication of his desire to defend American rights while preserving the British Empire. Franklin, however, was a plain speaker and demanded a clear, unequivocal acknowledgment of independence.[10]

Despite growing testy with Wentworth, Franklin assented to a second meeting. On 31 December news reached Paris that Spain declined to join the alliance with America. Vergennes delayed in sending word that France was prepared to go it alone. Franklin knew that French spies would report to Versailles about any meetings with Wentworth. So in conferring with the British agent a second time, on 6 January, the sly senior commissioner had no hopes for any meaningful discussion; his real aim was to frighten Versailles into thinking that an Anglo-American reconciliation might be on the verge of taking place. This might also be why Franklin met with two other British envoys sent by Lord North's government during the first days of January. Franklin met with them as well as with a phalanx of other Britons who, on their own authority, trekked to Passy in vain attempts to head off a French alliance. To everyone Franklin gave the same response: he would negotiate terms to end the fighting only after London gave immediate recognition of American independence. The old sage correctly surmised that Vergennes would know about all this activity and use it to nudge the timid, punctilious Louis XVI into finally agreeing to ally with America, even without Spanish aid. The minister indeed did use this information, warning his monarch that the Americans and British might join together and make war on France.[11]

Bancroft's nineteen-day absence from Paris in December did not, in the long run, destroy any chances of an Anglo-American rapprochement. Even if he had been there and brought Wentworth together with Franklin several weeks earlier, the chances for reconciliation were nil. The American commissioners were dead set on total independence, and France had long been heading toward war. France's delays were more a matter of waiting for the right time than of deciding whether to intervene.

It was on 8 January 1778 that Gérard arrived at the Hôtel de Valentinois to announce that France was now prepared to enter into negotiations for an alliance. A flurry of comings and goings between Passy and Versailles occurred over the next four weeks. Bancroft kept Wentworth informed of everything. Wentworth dutifully reported all to Lord Suffolk. He sometimes used his own servant as courier and sometimes the couriers of Ambassador Stormont. The ambassador and other British agents likewise sent reports to London, chiefly to southern secretary Lord Weymouth. Without the benefit of Bancroft's insider information, Stormont and the other agents could not be nearly as precise as Wentworth in their analyses of the details. Nor could they know for sure whether an alliance had already been signed, whether it was to be signed within days, or whether obstacles of some sort had further delayed it. Although Wentworth and Stormont professed mutual friendship and cooperation, they were jealous of each other. Stormont was proud of his intelligence-gathering network and resented the fact that his superiors had felt the need to send Wentworth and others to Paris. Thus the two men sometimes did not share their information with each other.[12]

On 6 February 1778 Gérard met with Franklin, Deane, and Lee in foreign ministry offices on the quai des Théatins, just across the Seine from the Louvre. There the four men signed two treaties. The first was a treaty of amity and commerce, in which the two nations guaranteed most favored nation status to each other. The second was a treaty of alliance, in which France agreed to fight until American independence was recognized. France likewise renounced any desire to reclaim Canada or other territories in America. The United States, for its part, vowed to help in protecting the French West Indies from British conquest.

The treaties would go into effect once war broke out between Britain and France. Until then, they were to be kept secret. Vergennes insisted on this for several reasons. He wanted to make sure that the Continental Congress ratified the treaties before France openly committed itself. He also hoped that Britain might stumble into taking the first hostile act, thereby enabling France to declare that it was fighting a defensive war. Moreover, he held out hope that Spain still might join the alliance before fighting commenced. Last, he wanted to give France's army and navy as much time as possible to complete their preparations.

It was Edward Bancroft who first sent news of these treaties to London. The final wording of the two treaties was worked out on 27 January 1778. Within hours of that, Bancroft (using his commercial alias "Benson") wrote a private letter to his business partner in London, Samuel Wharton, briefly informing him that the two treaties had been worked out. News that a Franco-American alliance was formalized surely would make stocks fall, and so Wharton would sell stocks before their values declined or purchase insurance wagers betting that war would come. The British post office intercepted Bancroft's letter, and it was sent immediately up the chain of command to Lord North and George III.[13]

Some authors have taken this letter from "Benson" as evidence that spying always took a back seat for Bancroft, with stockjobbing and other private interests topmost in his mind. It should be pointed out, however, that William and Arthur Lee and Ralph Izard were also busy at this same time making London stock wagers based on their insider knowledge. In addition, what Bancroft's critics seemed to have missed is the fact that when he sent his private letter to Wharton he also sent Wentworth an "official" letter. Wentworth had returned to London in mid-January. In a letter started on 22 January and completed six days later, Bancroft gave Wentworth a full rundown of all the details in both treaties and reported that, as of 28 January, they were being translated into English, so that they could be signed in both languages. He also gave Wentworth the latest news about French military preparations. Army battalions were being sent to fortify the French Atlantic coast; a squadron commanded by La Motte Picquet was preparing to convoy merchant ships to America; and naval minister Sartine was issuing new guidelines for French privateers. On receiving this letter, Wentworth sent it to Eden, who shared it with government ministers.[14]

In late January and early February Bancroft worked feverishly as Benjamin Franklin's friend, adviser, and unofficial secretary. He helped to arrange for copies of the treaties to be made and dispatched immediately to America.[15] Within an hour or two of the official signing of the treaties on 6 February, he hired a special courier to speed the news to his London superiors. Years later, in his 1784 memorandum to Lord Carmarthen, Bancroft boasted that the government in London knew of the treaties within forty-two hours of their signing.[16] Numerous historians have assumed this was correct and taken it as another sign of Bancroft's importance to the British cause.[17] Several others have dismissed Bancroft's claim, noting that a trip from Paris to London took four or, more often, five days.[18] Thus Bancroft again was inflating his importance and writing things that could not be believed. While it is true that the trip between the two capitals usually took about five days, it could be done in much less time. If one could find a coach ready to depart immediately, if the roads were not too muddy, if there was a boat sailing just when one arrived at the coast, and if the winds in the channel were favorable, the trip could be made in under forty-eight hours. Paul Wentworth gave proof of that in November 1777. Needing to make one of his frequent visits to pick up intelligence from Bancroft, he left London for Paris on 11 November, reached Paris on the thirteenth, and was back in London on the sixteenth.[19] There is also more direct confirmation of Bancroft's veracity on this point. On 9 February 1778, Lord North communicated the contents of Bancroft's letter of the sixth to George III; Wentworth had probably received the letter from Paris on the eighth.[20]

With information from his paid informants, on 6 February Ambassador Stormont also wrote with news of the alliance. His two letters of that date, both to Weymouth, were not, however, as precise as Bancroft's. He did not know the specifics of the treaty, and indeed he was not aware that there were two separate treaties. In fact, although Stormont felt sure in his heart that there was a treaty, he could not state that this was absolutely certain. His letters did not reach London until 12 February.[21]

Private Trade and Stock Speculations

While working as an assistant to the American commissioners and a spy for the British, Bancroft was also occupied with private business matters. It was these that led him abruptly to head for London on 4 December 1777, just as the news of Saratoga reached Paris. Some writers have surmised that Bancroft hoped to take advantage of his advance knowledge of this American victory to make new speculations in the London stock market. This was also a charge that Arthur Lee later made.[22] That explanation, however, makes no sense. The news of Burgoyne's surrender had spread throughout Britain at the end of November, and Bancroft did not arrive in London until around 8 December—much too late to profit from his knowledge of that event. It seems, rather, that Bancroft went there primarily to collect winnings from earlier speculations and to try to cover losses from less successful ones. It was possible in that era to make wagers in the stock market as to whether a particular military campaign would prove successful. A win or a loss on the battlefield could drive stocks or maritime insurance rates up or down. Bancroft evidently had "picked the right horse" and, even before Saratoga, had bet against Burgoyne; he was eager to pocket his winnings. He also seems to have made new speculations, based on his guesses about future events. Some weeks after Bancroft's trip to London, Silas Deane met with Paul Wentworth and mentioned that Bancroft had gone there "on great business" with 300,000 livres in credit, to be used on behalf of Deane's and Bancroft's joint dealings. That figure is astoundingly large. Neither of the two men had that kind of money. One can only conclude that several other, unnamed investors also were involved, that Deane was exaggerating the size of his business transactions, or that Deane was engaging in wishful thinking about the extent of his potential profits.[23]

Obviously, Bancroft used his access to privileged information in his stock speculations—or "stockjobbing" as many at that time called it. This brings up one of the complicating factors regarding his actions and motives.

Was he predominantly a British agent? Or was he a double agent who cared little for political causes and was mainly interested in being paid by both sides? Or, again, was he a double agent who somehow was sympathetic to the people and political interests of both sides? Or, last, was he primarily a stock-jobber who took up espionage as a sideline to obtain insider information and profit in the London stock market? There is evidence for all of the above, and one cannot say for sure how much any of these possible interpretations conflicted with or complemented each other in his mind. It is even possible that Bancroft himself could not say which impulses drove him most strongly.

Before Bancroft moved to Paris in the spring of 1777, he had already displayed a penchant for business dealings. Even though the outbreak of Anglo-American hostilities had stymied plans to import large quantities of quercitron bark to Britain, through 1777 he still struggled for ways to make a killing using his knowledge of vegetable dyes. He was so optimistic that his friend William Carmichael said, perhaps partly in jest, that Bancroft would become the richest man in Europe.[24]

Not willing to put all his hopes into one venture, by 1777 Bancroft expanded his business interests into other areas. His chief partners were the entrepreneur and politician Thomas Walpole, the brothers Samuel and Joseph Wharton, and Jonathan Williams Jr. The Wharton brothers were Philadelphia merchants and speculators who spent much of the 1770s in London. Joseph's movements are difficult to track, but it is known that Samuel went there in 1769 as an agent of the variously named Ohio/Indiana/Vandalia/Walpole land companies—in which Franklin, Bancroft, and many other prominent Americans were investors. Though his and Walpole's lobbying for the territories met with no success, Samuel Wharton stayed on in London and became involved in numerous commercial ventures and stock speculations.[25]

Both he and, to a lesser extent, Joseph Wharton were partners with Bancroft in several schemes. Correspondence with the Whartons was usually conducted through private couriers. But these messengers could be careless or susceptible to bribes from government agents. At least once, in November 1777, Samuel Wharton entrusted a man named James Van Zandt with a letter for Bancroft. Van Zandt was an American businessman on his way to Paris. He also was a British spy, and before departing London he made sure that William Eden had a copy of the letter. Thus one spy was being employed to keep an eye on the private business operations of another spy. At least initially Van Zandt did not realize that Bancroft was also a British agent.[26]

Aware of these dangers, the Whartons and Bancroft generally used aliases in their correspondence. Bancroft was usually addressed as "Mr. Benson" or "Mr. St. Pierre." Joseph Wharton was "William Bell" and Samuel was "Mr. White." Alas, the British postal inspectors who regularly opened mail going back and forth across the channel were not deceived. They knew who the senders and recipients were. Anthony Todd, secretary of the General Post Office, regularly sent reports to ministers and remarked that he and his inspectors sometimes were compelled to work through the night opening and reading letters going to or from France.[27]

Of course, the British government was not alone in opening the mail of suspected enemy agents as well as that of many ordinary citizens. Other governments also did a remarkable job of opening letters, deciphering secret codes, and reattaching wax seals without the recipients being able to detect the tampering. Only when Bancroft or someone else used invisible ink did the government have a problem. Postal officials could easily tell that some pages had hidden writing. However, if the "snoops" applied fire or a chemical wash to reveal the writing, the eventual recipient of the letter would know that someone had already read it. Fortunately for postal inspectors, Bancroft and his correspondents used invisible ink only rarely, preferring to rely on codes and aliases.[28]

Bancroft and the others were well aware that some of their letters would be intercepted by postal officials. In one letter of October 1777 Bancroft wrote, "I dare not write a syllable of politics."[29] Shortly after that, Joseph Wharton closed a letter to Bancroft by noting that he had much to say but could not put it on paper.[30]

It should also be mentioned that the use of aliases, invisible ink, and ciphers or codes was not unusual in that era. Most diplomats, politicians, and businessmen used one or the other of these methods for camouflaging their activities at one time or another. Businessmen feared that their competitors would find out about their activities. So the mere use of aliases and the like did not automatically imply that the letter writers were doing anything shady, unlawful, or unpatriotic.[31]

It was probably Samuel Wharton who initially got Bancroft involved in stock speculations. Though Wharton was chiefly interested in his own personal gain, he was a steadfast supporter of the American rebellion and a friend of several members of the British opposition—a loose confederation of Lords and Commoners who opposed the North ministry's clumsy handling of the conflict. Wharton's continuance in London and Bancroft's removal to Paris seemed perfect for their mutual political and financial interests. Not knowing that Bancroft was a British agent, Wharton assumed that the news he sent Bancroft would be relayed to the commissioners and thus help them in their diplomatic work. The information that Bancroft (as "Benson" or "St. Pierre") sent to Wharton concerned the same sorts of information that Bancroft (as "Edwards") gave to Paul Wentworth: ships about to leave France with supplies for America, British prizes brought to French ports for sale, the ups and downs in Versailles's willingness to commit more openly to the American cause. Wharton used all these details in his decisions on how to invest his and Bancroft's money in the London stock market. Bad news for the British war effort meant that bears would start selling their stocks as fast as possible; good news meant that bears became bulls and suddenly were buying again. One could also invest in maritime insurance. The greater the risks to British shipping, the higher the insurance rates would be in a given week. One could even place what were, in effect, wagers on whether open war with France would commence by a certain date.[32]

By late 1777 Bancroft had even coaxed his friend Silas Deane into investing in some of these London speculations. Deane did not know Bancroft was a spy—contrary to what some historians have said. (This is a topic for later discussion.) There was nothing unusual about a government official using his advance knowledge of events for personal profit. Laws prohibiting such actions did not exist in those days. As long as one's private investments did not conflict with one's public duties, there generally was no problem. Indeed, the Continental Congress would have had a hard time getting enough citizens to work for it if today's standards existed back then. Congress had no established professional bureaucracy to use, and it could not pay large salaries. It desperately needed men with experience in military, political, and commercial affairs, and so it had to allow many of them to continue with their private business activities.[33]

It would be wrong to assume that Bancroft got involved in espionage simply to gain secret information for his business speculations. He had a keen interest in Anglo-American affairs long before his stockjobbing. As far as can be determined, he never fed false information to the British government in order to change government policies, and hence the stock market, in directions that would fill his pockets. Thus historian Julian P. Boyd errs in stating, for example, that Bancroft kept Stormont in the dark about progress on a Franco-American treaty of alliance, in order to use secret information for his own financial gain. Boyd likewise maintains that in December 1777 Bancroft informed his London superiors of the cargo that Beaumarchais's *Amphitrite* would be carrying to America but that he withheld from them the date of its departure and the route it would take. Boyd asserts that Bancroft concealed this information because he and Deane owned some of the cargo and did not want the British to capture the vessel. There is no evidence for such assertions. If Bancroft did not want the *Amphitrite* captured, he would have avoided giving the British any information about it. Moreover, there is no proof that Bancroft and Deane owned any of the cargo. Finally, persons in Paris could never be sure of the exact departure date or routes of ships departing from distant ports.[34]

Nonetheless, it can be said that on occasion Bancroft's private pecuniary interests took center stage in his mind. On occasion he devoted so much time to his private affairs that he neglected his official duties. The most glaring incidence of this has already been mentioned—when Paul Wentworth arrived in Paris in December 1777 only to discover that Bancroft had hurriedly skipped away to London. How much profit did Bancroft reap from this episode? One set of surviving records indicates that he and Silas Deane each gained more than £5,000. However, there is also evidence that Bancroft had to use much of these winnings to cover losses from other investments. One source indicates that he was trying to buy insurance to cover a possible loss of £10,000 in a deal where his partner was Silas Deane.[35] Like many speculators, he tended to hedge his bets. He laid down large sums, guessing that news from America, interest rates, or insurance rates would go in one direction. When additional news reached him, he then sometimes wagered in the other direction, to ensure that any losses would not be too large. In December 1777, Lord North reported to George III that, on balance, Bancroft had suffered a net loss from his investments.[36] On the other hand, near the end of that month, when Bancroft arrived back in Paris and met up with Wentworth, Wentworth reported to William Eden that "Edwards" was "not as he should be. He offered to repay all He has received. The cursed journey to London has spoiled all."[37] In other words, Wentworth surmised that Bancroft was awash in money and no longer needed his government pension. It is possible, however, that Bancroft had threatened to quit simply out of pique, because Wentworth had scolded him for being so long in England. At any rate, one cannot say, in the end, whether Bancroft won or lost money in his trading ventures and stock speculations. Like most gamblers, he never let his losses stop him from hoping for a killing.

To be fair to Bancroft, one should note that Wentworth was wrong in assuming that private investments were the only reason for the trip to London. Bancroft had official business as well—both in his service for the Americans as well as his service to Britain. On behalf of the American commissioners he tried, unsuccessfully it seems, to plant in British newspapers copies of various documents that might prove embarrassing to the North government. The commissioners also wanted him to find out just how strong the parliamentary opposition to the North ministry was. When Bancroft arrived back in Paris on 23 December, he brought with him the news that North was preparing to send to Philadelphia a three-man peace commission led by Lord Carlisle, charged with offering the colonies virtually everything they wanted except full independence.[38] This was a crucial piece of information, as Vergennes was able to use it to help persuade Louis XVI of the urgency of allying with the Americans sooner rather than later. While aiding the Americans, Bancroft did double duty in London by also serving his British masters. He met with Undersecretary William Eden and filled him in on all that had been transpiring at Passy.[39]

Here is another example of the kinds of business correspondence that passed back and forth across the channel. This letter of 8 December 1777 was sent from Paris to a London merchant named Thomas Rogers:

> As things seem to be from strong appearances in all quarters in a very unsettled state there is a probability, if not a certainty, that . . . a great stroke may be made and very considerable advantages gained by your stocks, and as it may fall in my way to see how things will turn as soon as most people, with your aid in London, ye business might be successfully accomplished, and having a high opinion of your judgement, honor, integrity, secrecy and caution, would willingly engage with you in a scheme of that kind, you to be one third interested, and ye other two thirds here, for which two thirds I must stand answerable or to be the receiver. This I must enjoin you never to mention to any person breathing. . . . If you decline the proposal, I request this may be immediately committed to the flames.[40]

This letter was written not by Bancroft but by William Lee. The irony here is overwhelming. The two Lee brothers and Ralph Izard adopted a holier-than-thou attitude and bitterly condemned Bancroft, Deane, and others for using their public positions for private gain. Yet the Lees and Izard also invested in land companies and stock speculations. Little wonder, then, that William Lee stressed secrecy in the above letter—lest his hypocrisy come to light.[41]

Bancroft was not the only British secret agent to mix private and public affairs. When he departed from Paris on 4 December, he was joined by James Van Zandt, known as "George Lupton" in his secret correspondence with Eden and Suffolk. Van Zandt/Lupton was on his way to London to collect on some of his own speculations.[42]

Late in February 1778, Samuel Wharton wrote to "Benson" that their business affairs in England generally were going well but that they were hampered because of the lack of communications from "Benson."[43] One reason for the slowness of communications is that the private messenger they had been using, a man named Boquet, had just died. In his letter Wharton lamented the death of this trusted courier and hoped he could find a reliable replacement. Neither Wharton nor Bancroft guessed that Boquet had not been so trustworthy after all. William Eden bribed Boquet and his successor to turn over copies of all the dispatches they were carrying.

In mid-March 1778, Wharton wrote to "Benson" that British stocks were falling on unfavorable news from America and the prospects of war with France. Wharton was quickly selling some stocks while it was still possible to profit from them. But, on the whole, their speculations were not going well. Wharton exclaimed that "only war can save us"—a clear indication that the two men had been making wagers in maritime insurance and other funds that would pay off only in the event of hostilities with France. As per usual, a copy of this letter also ended up in Eden's hands.[44] Despite access to privileged information, Joseph Wharton's speculations likewise were faltering. Sometime early in 1778 he lost nearly £10,000, when the trading house of Richard Ford and Company went bankrupt. He hoped to recoup his losses by betting on the outcome of future political events.[45]

During these months Wentworth likewise continued to use his insider's access to information to make sundry speculations, sometimes on his own, sometimes with Bancroft.[46] In a letter to Eden late in March, he noted that the government was late in paying his pension and had not yet found him a seat in Parliament. War with France was imminent, and so his role as a secret agent traveling frequently across the channel would come to an end. He remarked that in his most recent round of stock parlays, he himself had lost £1,300, whereas Bancroft stood to gain £700. Wentworth ruefully exclaimed that he would never speculate again.[47] We do not know if he kept his word on that point. What is perhaps most interesting about this letter is that Wentworth openly discussed with the undersecretary the private investments he was making while employed by the government. The conclusion seems inescapable. In that era, it was common practice.

Bancroft's London stock speculations appear to have ended sometime around March 1778. As war between France and Britain loomed, private correspondence of any sort across the channel became dangerous and difficult. In the months following March, Samuel Wharton sent a handful of letters to Bancroft and Benjamin Franklin. Outside of a couple of brief mentions of his business matters, he mostly relayed news that he had picked up regarding the war in America or political squabbles in London.[48] Repeatedly he said that he had to be careful what he wrote, because he knew he was being watched. Evidently, the British government allowed this correspondence to continue because Wharton did not have access to any top-secret intelligence and could do no real harm; besides, the government thought it might learn something useful from the letters. Eventually both Samuel and Joseph Wharton concluded that they were no longer safe in London and moved to Paris.[49] Joseph returned to America in April 1779, and Samuel followed in December 1780.

The Tree in the Tuileries Gardens

Paul Wentworth departed from Paris on 15 January 1778 and did not anticipate returning. He left, in part, because he was afraid of being arrested as a British spy. He knew that French agents and informers, including his servants, had been tracking his every movement since his arrival more than a month earlier. His attempts to reach an agreement with Deane and Franklin had gone nowhere, and thus he could serve no useful purpose in France. The question then became: how to continue communicating with Bancroft? With good reason, Wentworth distrusted not only the regular postal system but also private messengers.

This brings us to the story of the tree in the Tuileries Gardens. This is perhaps the most famous episode in the career of Edward Bancroft. Many historians have written briefly about it. Unfortunately, they have gotten much of it wrong.

The only source for this story is a document written by Wentworth. The original manuscript copy is located in William Eden's papers in the British Library. In 1889 Benjamin Franklin Stevens published a photographic reproduction of it in his magnificent twenty-five-volume collection of *Facsimiles of Manuscripts in European Archives Relating to America, 1773–1783.*[50] The document has no title, no signature, and no date. The four-page memorandum lists the topics Bancroft is supposed to report on and the method by which he will transmit this information to Wentworth in London. Bancroft's name is not mentioned. Rather, he is referred to as "Dr. Edwards."

The document states that Edwards is supposed to communicate to Wentworth all that he finds out about the following: progress toward a Franco-American alliance; French aid for the colonists; trade with America carried on in French, Spanish, or any other European ports; trade between non-French Caribbean islands and the thirteen colonies; the activities of American congressional agents in obtaining credit in France and Spain; Franklin and Deane's correspondence with Congress and with other congressional agents abroad; and all transactions between American agents and the courts of Versailles and Madrid.

The document then lists some of the matters that Edwards should find out about and report directly to Lord Stormont. These include any details about ships and cargoes departing from French or other European ports and destined for America plus any specific information about British vessels captured by American privateers and brought to French ports. Stormont would use all this information in the complaints that he regularly lodged with royal ministers in Versailles.

The final and most famous part of the document describes how Edwards is to convey his information to his superiors. Letters are to be addressed to Mr. Richardson (a fictional name). The letters are to be written "on gallantry"—in other words, they should be innocuous love notes. However, in the empty spaces on the papers, Edwards is to use invisible ink to write down his copious secret intelligence. Lord Stormont would be given the chemical wash that could be applied to the paper to make the secret writing appear.

The document instructs Bancroft to take all his papers to the Tuileries Gardens each Tuesday evening before 9:30. He is to place them in a bottle and then drop the bottle into a hole near the base of "the tree pointed out on the South Terrace of the Tuileries." Sometime after 9:30, a Mr. Jeans will come to that spot and retrieve the letters. (Thomas Jeans was Stormont's chaplain as well as a courier who transported official diplomatic pouches between Paris and London.)[51] Jeans will then insert into the bottle any communications from Stormont to Edwards. Finally, Jeans will place the bottle back in the hole of "the Box-Tree agreed on." After viewing the secret intelligence, Stormont will send the letters immediately to Wentworth in London, via diplomatic messenger.

In this document Wentworth also asks Bancroft to perform a private errand. Bancroft is supposed to obtain letters for Wentworth from a Mr. Mary, a Paris banker with whom Wentworth was engaged in sundry investments. The letters from Mary should also be deposited in the tree. Stormont will include these unopened letters in the packet that his messenger will carry to London.

Virtually all writers who have discussed this document have used the Stevens reproduction, without noting the qualifications Stevens mentioned. Stevens conjectured that the document was written in December 1776, but he put that date in brackets and included the abbreviation "qy"—short for "query," indicating that he was not sure of the date. Most later historians have taken that date as an established fact. Some have even been more precise, stating that the agreement was written on 13 December 1776.[52]

It is easy to see why many writers settled on December 1776. The original document is located in the archival volume of Eden correspondence that covers the months January 1776 to May 1777. The document is placed among letters and other materials from the month of December. The slip of paper immediately following the last page of the Wentworth-Bancroft agreement has written on it the date 13 December 1776. However, that sheet belongs to another document entirely and has nothing to do with the item in question here. At the bottom of the dated sheet is a note indicating that it accompanied a copy of orders sent to Sir William Howe on that date. Furthermore, a glance at this and other volumes of Eden papers shows that the clerks who organized them (perhaps years later) frequently put undated items in the wrong places—sometimes filing them in boxes that were off by years from where they belonged.

There are strong reasons to believe that the document was composed much later than earlier supposed. In December 1776 Bancroft was making visits to Paris but was not living there and had not yet even made plans to live there. But this document clearly assumes that he will be—or already is—residing in France. The document also instructs Bancroft to find out as much as he can about the activities of Franklin and Deane. Franklin, however, had just landed in France early in December and did not join Deane in Paris until later that month. If Wentworth was composing the memorandum in mid-December, he most likely would not have known that Franklin was in France, much less that Franklin was a congressional agent sent to work with Deane and Arthur Lee. Indeed, when British ministers first learned of Franklin's arrival in France, they assumed that the aging rebel had gone there principally as a private citizen, to retire and escape the fighting in America. Franklin brought two of his grandsons with him, which seemed to indicate that he was also trying to save at least some members of his family.[53]

The fact that the document speaks of Stormont and Thomas Jeans also raises a problem. The obvious inference from the document is that Stormont was aware of the arrangements and would instruct Jeans to carry out the weekly assignment in the Tuileries Gardens. Yet in none of Stormont's letters through all of 1777 does he give any indication that he knows anything about this. His dispatches to Lord Weymouth contain many references to his unnamed informants, but the few particulars that he provides about them indicate that they were not Bancroft. These other informants seem to have been merchants in port cities or servants, clerks, or friends of various ministers in Versailles. Stormont never indicates that he obtained any of his intelligence from someone living with the American commissioners in Passy. In a handful of his letters from 1777 he does mention Bancroft, but he portrays Bancroft as a friend and agent working for Franklin and Deane.[54]

As noted earlier, Wentworth and Stormont had a frosty relationship. They were reluctant allies, competing for the claim of providing the best intelligence to London. Stormont knew that Wentworth made trips to Paris to see someone named Edwards. Wentworth took Edwards's information back to London, gave it to Eden, who gave it to Suffolk, who communicated it to Weymouth and North; Weymouth then often summarized Edwards's reports and conveyed the information back to Stormont. Stormont then scurried to Versailles to confront Vergennes, Maurepas, and Sartine with evidence of France's complicity with the rebels.

Not until late in 1777 did Stormont get to meet Edwards. Through September and October Bancroft had been growing increasingly fearful that he would be discovered and arrested. What especially alarmed him was that Weymouth's letters to Stormont often quoted at length from reports Bancroft had written. Bancroft's dispatches contained numerous exact copies of letters and other documents that he found in the Hôtel de Valentinois. Stormont took these verbatim reports to Versailles. Thus it was easy for French ministers to suspect that Stormont was getting his information directly from someone in the Franklin or Deane household. As a confidante and unofficial secretary who spent many unsupervised hours in the rooms where heaps of official papers were left sitting on tables, Bancroft might be the first person suspected.

To calm Bancroft's jittery nerves, Wentworth made another of his numerous trips to Paris. On 13 November 1777 at his lodgings in the rue de Richelieu, Wentworth arranged a meeting between "Edwards" and Stormont. In a whisper (presumably to avoid the ears of curious servants) Wentworth introduced the two men to each other. He did not tell Stormont that Edwards and Bancroft were the same person, and Stormont himself did not guess this. Stormont had heard and written about Bancroft previously, but he had never seen him before. Stormont still did not realize the truth a few weeks later, when on 4 December, Bancroft abruptly left Paris to take care of business affairs in London. The ambassador quickly wrote to Weymouth, reporting that Bancroft was on a secret mission to London on behalf of the American commissioners.[55] Stormont's failure to realize that Bancroft was on "his" side or to deduce that Bancroft was Edwards were undoubtedly the biggest failures of his otherwise impressive intelligence network.

In the meeting on 13 November, Wentworth wanted to introduce the two men so that the ambassador recognized Edwards's face. That would be important, because if Edwards ever felt that he was in immediate danger, Wentworth wanted him to flee to Stormont's home. The ambassador would then take him under his protection and arrange for his safe passage to England. Stormont agreed to this, and then Edwards explained why he was afraid. Edwards proceeded to summarize the information he had been giving Wentworth over the previous six months. Edwards said he had copied all this data from papers belonging to Franklin and Deane. When (via Suffolk and then Weymouth) this intelligence was sent to Stormont, Edwards expostulated that Stormont must have used the very same words that had been in the original documents, because Vergennes recognized them. When the minister informed Franklin of this, Franklin agreed that there must be a spy in his midst.[56]

For the time being, Edwards said that he had managed to escape detection. Vergennes conjectured that the culprit might be someone else. There were two possible suspects. One was William Carmichael, the young Marylander who had spent more than a year helping Deane and Franklin with various chores. Through 1777 Carmichael had some contacts with Wentworth and Stormont. Carmichael and Wentworth lodged in the same hotel, and so they probably saw each other every time Wentworth came to Paris. Apparently the garrulous, womanizing, bibulous, self-important Carmichael offered Wentworth and Stormont some inside information on what was transpiring between Passy and Versailles. Wentworth and Stormont never fully trusted him, however, and never considered him a British agent. Carmichael's motives and actions remain murky. He hated France and seems to have hoped somehow to precipitate an Anglo-French war. That, in turn, would lead Britain and America to patch up their differences and join together against their common Catholic foe—or so he apparently thought.[57]

The other suspect was Beaumarchais's secretary, Théveneau de Francy. It was Bancroft himself, afraid of being detected, who threw Vergennes and the Americans off the track by hinting that Francy was the traitor. Beaumarchais was heavily involved in sending shipments of supplies to America. Francy thus was in a position to know the kinds of things about which Stormont complained in Versailles. False though the charges against Francy were, they created enough of a temporary diversion to let Edwards/Bancroft off the hook.[58]

But the suspicions about Carmichael and Francy could not camouflage his activities for long. Francy had already left for America, in October, on a mission to collect from Congress money owed to Beaumarchais for the several cargoes he had sent there. Vergennes wanted Carmichael out of France, and after several delays Carmichael finally returned to America in February 1778. With both of those men gone from the scene, Edwards told Stormont, he would have difficulty deflecting attention from himself.

There is no record of how Stormont responded to all that Edwards said, but he must have taken it to heart. In his future visits to Versailles, he altered his wording enough to make it impossible to determine his sources. Edwards was sufficiently satisfied by this long interview to return to his espionage activity.

Given the above, it is highly unlikely that the Wentworth-Bancroft agreement was written before Stormont had been brought into contact with Edwards. Another factor that works against putting the document in December 1776 is that it speaks of a particular box tree in the Tuileries Gardens. This tree, conveniently, had a hole in it, wherein one could deposit a bottle containing papers. Both Wentworth and Bancroft knew Paris well. However, it is unlikely that in their earlier visits to Paris they would each, independent of the other, have inspected all the trees in the gardens and spotted the same tree as a good place for hiding messages. (Nowadays such a spot would, in the vocabulary of espionage, be called a "dead drop.") The document contains no specific details that would enable someone to make sure he had found the correct tree. It does not say, for example, that the tree is located a particular distance from a certain fountain or staircase. The document simply refers to "the tree pointed out" and "the Box-Tree agreed on."

Given these vague descriptions of the tree, it is extremely probable that Wentworth and Bancroft were walking together in the gardens and jointly decided which tree to use. When would they have walked through the gardens? Wentworth made at least eight trips to see Bancroft in Paris between April 1777 and January 1778. It could have happened during any one of them. However, there are strong reasons to believe that their promenade to find a dead drop location occurred near the end of Wentworth's last trip, in January 1778. Because Wentworth was visiting Paris virtually every month before that, there would not have been any need to work out some other system for communication. Not trusting private messengers and eager to impress William Eden and Lord Suffolk with his zeal, Wentworth wished to deal with Bancroft in person.

Only in January 1778 did Wentworth realize that a change was needed. He himself was afraid of being arrested as a spy. In a letter of 1 January to Eden, Wentworth indicated that he and "Edwards" had arranged for secret meetings. Wentworth did not name the place, but he reported that the meetings were scheduled for Tuesday evenings.[59] It must have been during an evening stroll through the Tuileries Gardens that the two men spotted the tree and Wentworth drew up their agreement. On 7 January Wentworth wrote to Eden that "I have settled a plan for Ed[wards's] future correspondence, I think safely."[60] The inescapable conclusion is that Wentworth was referring to the Tuesday evening bottled messages in the boxwood tree. With the new communication system in place, Wentworth departed for London on 15 January.

A few other things about the Wentworth-Bancroft agreement should be noted. As mentioned already, the document is untitled and unsigned. For lack of better words, Stevens called it the "Engagement of Dr. Edwards to correspond with Paul Wentworth." Actually it was not an engagement, an agreement, a contract, or anything similar. The four pages have some words crossed out and others inserted between the lines, and the final page ends in midsentence. In other words, it is a rough draft. Wentworth probably scribbled it during one of his late-night letter writing marathons and then showed it to Bancroft. Not wishing to leave a paper trail that could lead to them, neither man signed it. It is unlikely that Bancroft would have kept a copy for himself. Wentworth gave the document to William Eden sometime shortly after he reached London. There is no record of what Eden thought of it. In the absence of any comment from the undersecretary, one can assume that he approved of the plan.

This revised dating of the document sharply alters what most historians have said about Bancroft for the period 1776–77. Virtually all have mistakenly assumed that the dead drops in the Tuileries Gardens commenced shortly after December 1776 and that George III's government knew everything that was happening in Versailles and Passy within less than a week after it occurred. Writing in the 1950s, one historian belittled this message system as "a sort of schoolboys' secret ritual." Nonetheless, he admitted that through this method "the line of communications for great secrets of state from Bancroft to the British cabinet was drastically shortened both in time and distance."[61]

Did the system work once it was put in place in January 1778? It did, at least at first. A letter that "Edwards" wrote to Wentworth late that month arrived in London via Stormont's diplomatic pouch.[62] Bancroft/Edwards would never have visited Stormont's home, for French spies would have spotted him immediately. So one can assume that Bancroft had deposited the letter in the tree, where Thomas Jeans later picked it up.

Just as earlier historians have mistakenly dated the Wentworth-Bancroft agreement, so also have they gravely exaggerated its importance and the length of its operation. They have surmised that Bancroft wrote dozens or hundreds of letters "on gallantry," with the secret intelligence hidden by invisible ink. They have assumed that this correspondence started late in 1776 and extended to the end of the war and the signing of the final peace treaties in 1783.[63] The plain fact is that no such amatory epistle from a Dr. Edwards can be found anywhere. None exists in the papers of William Eden or Lord Stormont.[64] Surely, if they had existed, some copies would have survived. Nor can one find even a reference to such love letters in the correspondence of Wentworth, Eden, Stormont, Suffolk, or anyone else.

Thus after Wentworth left Paris in mid-January 1778, Bancroft does appear to have left messages in the boxwood tree. But he did not disguise them as love letters; nor did he put them in code or invisible ink. Knowing that they would travel in Stormont's secure diplomatic pouch, he must have concluded that such ruses were unnecessary.

How long did he continue to make his weekly trips to the Tuileries Gardens? Previous scholars should easily have been able to see that the system could not have lasted for long. After 6 February 1778, all of Paris and London were abuzz with speculation about a Franco-American alliance. Vergennes finally realized that his aim of keeping everything a secret would no longer be possible. Early in March he agreed to make the treaties public. In doing so, France was recognizing the rebels as an independent country. This meant an immediate rupture of diplomatic relations between France and Britain.[65] On 13 March, the French ambassador in London officially notified the British government, which then immediately sent orders for Stormont to leave Paris and return home. Stormont and his staff departed from the French capital on 22 March.[66] On 20 March, Franklin, Deane, Arthur and William Lee, Ralph Izard, and more than a dozen other Americans were granted a private audience with Louis XVI. Later that day they were treated by Vergennes to a sumptuous banquet. One of the Americans who accompanied the commissioners to these festivities was Edward Bancroft.[67]

What earlier writers have failed to grasp is that the Tuesday evening visits to the boxwood tree in the Tuileries Gardens inevitably ended after Stormont and his staff left France. Hence the saga of the Tuesday evening love letters, filled with the kind of cloak-and-dagger aura that makes a good mystery, was one that lasted no longer than a couple of months.

Late in February Bancroft sent what was perhaps the last letter deposited in the tree. In it he reported on the delays encountered by the ship that was supposed to carry copies of the two treaties to Congress. Incidentally, it was Bancroft himself, the ever helpful friend of Franklin and Deane, who had laboriously made those copies. When the delegates to Congress finally read the texts of the two treaties that were so important in the birth of the United States, they were reading the handwriting of the chief British spy![68]

After Stormont's departure for London, Bancroft had no safe and regular method to communicate with Wentworth. Somehow late in March he managed to get word to London about a futile final effort by Britain to reach some accommodation with the American commissioners. William Pulteney, a Scottish MP, met with rejection when he visited Franklin at the Hôtel de Valentinois.[69] In April at least three dispatches from Bancroft reached London. In them Bancroft informed Wentworth that Silas Deane had been recalled to America. Deane had been well liked in Versailles, and the French court was giving him many gifts and other signs of appreciation. Sailing with Deane would be Conrad-Alexandre Gérard; Vergennes had appointed his secretary to be the first French minister to the United States. Bancroft also told Wentworth that Deane's successor arrived in Paris just a day or so after Deane had left. The new commissioner was John Adams. Bancroft reported that Adams's presence in Paris did not bode well for the American cause. The cantankerous American had already begun quarreling with Franklin and Vergennes.

It was in one of his April letters that Bancroft also gave London what, years later, was one of his biggest pieces of news. He reported that Deane and Gérard would be sailing from Toulon, on the flagship of a fleet commanded by the Comte d'Estaing. D'Estaing would deliver his two distinguished passengers in America, but his larger purpose was to attack the fleet of Admiral Howe in New York and, it was hoped, cut off the British in New York from any reinforcements. This would mark the first major blow that France struck on behalf of its new ally.

How did Bancroft transmit these messages to London? One cannot be sure. Late in April Wentworth sent a long memorandum to Eden, summarizing what Bancroft had written. Wentworth noted that "the enclosed were a long time getting to me through various channels." Edwards had written that soon all correspondence with Wentworth would be "impracticable." After the rupture of diplomatic relations between France and Britain, it would be difficult for a courier to travel directly across the channel. The messengers

Bancroft used therefore traveled to Ostend and other Dutch ports and sailed to London from there.[70] Near the end of April, Wentworth planned to journey back to Paris in order to set up a new method of communication with Bancroft. There is no evidence to show whether he made this trip or whether he succeeded in arranging a secure method of conveyance for Bancroft's future letters.[71]

After Stormont and his staff returned to London, Bancroft was, as far as can be determined, the only full-time British agent left in Paris. He continued to work there until the summer of 1783. To paraphrase novelist John Le Carré, he was the spy left out in the cold.

7 Gauging Bancroft's Role

The vast majority of all the materials concerning Bancroft's espionage come from the period up to the spring of 1778. The questions historians have asked about him likewise have been based primarily on this early period. How important was Bancroft to George III's government? What did British ministers do with the information he provided? How did he avoid being detected?

Putting Bancroft in Context

Scholars have varied widely in their estimates of his importance. Most have asserted that he did great damage to the American cause. Depending on which author one reads, Bancroft was the most important British spy of the American Revolution, the spy of the century, or even the most remarkable spy of all time. According to this view, everything that transpired in Passy, Paris, and Versailles was known in London within days, thanks to his messages in the Tuileries Gardens. His pilfering of documents ensured that London knew more about activities in French ports than Versailles did. An untold number of ships leaving French ports were captured as a result of Bancroft's advance news of their sailings. His secret intelligence helped the British so much that the American Revolution lasted far longer and killed far more men than it would have otherwise.[1]

Other authors have taken a middle-of-the-road approach. They agree that Bancroft's information was accurate and extensive. However, it was not as crucial as it could have been. The reason is that George III himself and others in his government distrusted Bancroft because of his speculations in the stock market. Lewis Einstein has remarked, for example, that "no Government has ever been so well informed of the most secret doings of its enemies as was the British Cabinet," but the "royal horror of gambling" led the British cabinet to ignore much of what Bancroft reported. Hence his work was important, but not nearly as significant as it could have been.[2]

A handful of scholars have taken a third position and greatly belittled Bancroft's role altogether. One has written that Bancroft primarily was a stock jobber and only a "half-hearted" spy.[3] Another has asserted that most of the intelligence he provided was already common knowledge and hence virtually useless.[4] Yet another has posited that Bancroft distorted or concealed from his British superiors any information that might hurt his business interests; for example, he did not give notice of the sailing of ships that were carrying his own trade goods.[5] One author has even stated that Britain had so many agents collecting information throughout France that Bancroft and Wentworth "were supernumeraries, whose value may be discounted almost one hundred percent."[6]

A close examination reveals that Bancroft's role does not fit neatly into any of these interpretations. Yes, he was a stock speculator. However, enough has been said in previous chapters to demonstrate that he became interested in the Anglo-American controversy long before he became a spy and long before he started his stockjobbing. It is true that he sent advance news of events to his business partners in England, particularly Samuel Wharton. Wharton and the others then made all the decisions as to what to buy or sell. There is not a single example of Bancroft's giving secret intelligence to Wharton that he was not also providing to the British ministry. Similarly, no evidence exists to support the charge that he withheld information about ships sailing when particular vessels were carrying his own merchandise. Last, there is the fact that Bancroft remained in France as a British agent for another five years after war between Britain and France broke out. His business investments in London declined sharply after the spring of 1778, and yet he continued his work as a spy. Thus it is wrong to view him merely as a stock-jobber and businessman who cared little about one side or the other in the Revolution.

Regarding the question of his importance, it is true that Bancroft was far from being the only British agent or informer in France. Ambassador Stormont and the first lord of the Admiralty both had networks of informers throughout France. There were also a handful of men who, like Bancroft, were more or less full-time British spies. One who has already been mentioned is James Van Zandt. The son of a wealthy New York businessman, he happened to be in London when the Revolution started. Van Zandt claimed to have been a courier sent by the Continental Congress with dispatches for Benjamin Franklin. As far as can be determined, that claim was spurious, but he attracted the attention of William Eden. The undersecretary recruited Van Zandt and dispatched him to Paris early in 1777. In his correspondence with his London superiors, Van Zandt adopted the alias George Lupton. For nearly a year, until January 1778, he lived mostly in Paris, with two or three short visits back to London. In Paris he lodged in the same hotel as Silas Deane and William Carmichael. He became close to both men, and in rather careless fashion they told him more than they should have about negotiations with the French and about ships leaving various ports. "Lupton" also wormed his way into the confidence of numerous American ship captains who came to Paris to seek aid of one sort or another from Deane and Franklin. His letters cover much of the same topics as the intelligence that Bancroft gave to Wentworth. However, Lupton's reports do not have anything close to the precise details of Bancroft's. Lupton lacked access to Benjamin Franklin and the official papers stored in the Hôtel de Valentinois.

Virtually all of Lupton's letters to Eden are filled with pleas for money. Lupton apparently was not paid a regular stipend, but Eden had promised to supply him with funds so that he could keep up the ruse of being a businessman engaged in buying and selling cargoes going to America. In dribs and drabs through 1777 Eden forwarded a few hundred pounds to the agent. By December 1777, however, Lupton's cover had been blown. This was probably the result of his debauched lifestyle, his loose lips, and his failure to fool anyone into believing that he was actively engaged in commerce. He begged for Eden to send him to America, where he could spy on his own father, a prominent merchant, and send valuable information back to England. In

January 1778 he reported that French spies dogged his every move. Then his letters suddenly stopped, and Lupton disappeared from the pages of history. He probably returned to London or America.[7]

Another agent was Joseph Hynson, an American ship captain who somehow had become stranded in France early in 1777. There he befriended fellow Marylander William Carmichael. Knowing that Deane and Franklin were seeking a reliable method for transporting their dispatches to Congress, Carmichael hit upon the idea of hiring Hynson for the task. Deane and Franklin agreed to supply Hynson with funds to purchase a lugger in England and then bring the vessel to a French port, where it could be outfitted as a fast packet boat. Hynson would then carry the dispatches to America.

Hynson traveled first to London, where he spent time in a boarding-house of low repute. He bragged to the ladies in residence that he was on a secret mission for the Americans. The proprietress of the establishment took this bit of gossip to the Reverend John Vardill, an American living in London when the Revolution commenced. Vardill had come to London for his ordination into the Anglican priesthood, and he stayed on and spent much of his time writing pamphlets against the American rebels. He came to the attention of the government, and William Eden hired him to spy on other Americans and to recruit, for British service, those who might be flexible in their allegiances. One of the Americans whom Vardill "turned" into a British agent was James Van Zandt. In return for his services, Vardill received a modest stipend plus the promise of the Regius Professorship of Divinity at King's College (later Columbia University). Given the outcome of the Revolution, of course, he never received his professorship.

Vardill had little trouble in "turning" the vain and greedy Hynson. He gave the ship captain an undisclosed amount of money, with assurances that more would come. Hynson purchased a lugger in Dover and sailed it to a French port. He then went on to Paris to await instructions. The plan devised by Eden and Vardill called for Hynson to let his ship be captured by British ships when the time came for the trip to America. A variety of delays kept Hynson on hold for several months. The lugger he had bought was deemed unsuitable for packet service, and Hynson rejected as unseaworthy several other vessels that the commissioners proposed to buy for him. He spent his time hanging out in taverns, running errands for the commissioners, and surreptitiously meeting with Ambassador Stormont to report on all he learned.

Finally, in October 1777, Franklin and Deane decided that the time had come to dispatch a huge pouch of letters and other papers to Congress. They sent the sack to Hynson in Le Havre. Hynson's proposed ship was not yet ready to sail, so he was instructed to give the pouch to a Captain Folger, whose vessel was about to depart for America. To ensure that Congress was kept aware of all that the commissioners had been doing, the pouch contained copies of about seven months' worth of letters and reports. Folger dutifully delivered the sealed pouch to Philadelphia about two months later. When members of the Committee of Correspondence opened it, they were astonished to discover a large stack of blank paper. In Le Havre, Hynson had managed to open the sack, replace the official documents with empty sheets, and tie the pouch shut again without Folger noticing anything amiss.

As soon as Folger sailed, Hynson immediately set out for London, where cabinet ministers and George III could read for themselves the abundant, explicit evidence of dozens of cargoes departing French ports and destined, directly or via the Caribbean, for North America. The papers also provided details on American privateers outfitting in French ports. Last, they offered clear proof of Versailles's complicity in all of this activity. This was the largest batch of secret intelligence that the British were to gain in 1777.

William Eden found Hynson to be "an honest rascal and no fool though apparently stupid."[8] Judging that Hynson could be of no further use, the undersecretary sent him back to Paris early in November, giving him vague instructions to continue spying on the American commissioners. Eden did not keep his promise of an annual stipend of £200 for the seaman. Hynson found himself in France with little to do and no funds. What was worse, his abrupt trip to London had raised suspicions in Deane and Franklin. They stopped having anything to do with him. Clearly inept and befuddled, Hynson offered to become a spy for the Americans! They refused even to dignify this proposal with an answer. Hearing that the uncouth, garrulous sea captain was becoming a nuisance and an embarrassment to the British, Eden had him brought back to England. Hynson was given a minor position in the navy, and, like Van Zandt, he soon disappeared into obscurity.[9]

There were also other British agents in Paris. One was John Thornton, who worked as Arthur Lee's private secretary through most of 1777 and the first half of 1778. Thornton was so trusted by Lee, Franklin, and Deane that in late 1777 and early 1778 he made at least two trips to London to try to arrange for prisoner exchanges or for the improved treatment of Americans held in British jails. In these trips he used his insider information to speculate in stocks. While in London he also reported in person to Lord North and other ministers regarding all that he had learned in France. Despite many warnings, only in the summer of 1778 did Arthur Lee finally admit that his secretary—by then safely back in London—was a British informer.[10] Lee thereupon replaced Thornton with a fellow Virginian, Hezekiah Ford, an Anglican priest who also turned out to be a Loyalist and probably a British agent. In April 1779 Lee sent Ford to America with a bundle of dispatches for Congress. Lee warmly recommended Ford, as someone who had "faithfully" served him for eight months. In America, however, evidence of Ford's Loyalist activities came to light. The Virginia legislature brought charges of treason against him, but Ford judiciously disappeared from the scene before the case could be resolved.[11]

Another agent active in Paris was Nathaniel Parker Forth, whom one historian has described as a "profligate Irish stock speculator."[12] He was an unusual choice for a spy. Even William Carmichael, whose personal life bordered on the dissolute, regarded Forth as a "low-lifed criminal."[13] Forth was a stockbroker and speculator, a wine merchant, an owner and rider of a string of prize racehorses, and a skilled player of the violin and viola. By the time of the Revolution, he was residing chiefly in Paris, though his business affairs frequently called him back to London. He was a friend of Lord Mansfield, the lord chief justice, who happened to be the uncle of Ambassador Stormont. By early 1777 Forth had also become a British secret agent. Using his commercial contacts throughout France, he supplied information that Stormont claimed was "the greatest use" to him.[14] Somehow in January of that year Forth was introduced to the Comte de Maurepas, Louis XVI's senior minister. The two men liked each other immediately, partly because they shared a wry sense of humor. Maurepas had come to detest his meetings with the obdurate, demanding Stormont and much preferred dealing with Forth. The French minister therefore took the extraordinary step of asking the British government to appoint Forth as a secret special envoy who would deal exclusively with him. Lord North's government approved this arrangement and gave Forth an initial grant of £1,000 and a yearly pension of £600. This money was supposed to cover Forth's own expenses plus the bribes he distributed to informers he engaged in French ports.[15]

Forth's appointment as special envoy was bizarre for two reasons: first, because Britain already had an official representative in Paris, Lord Stormont; and second, because Maurepas did not inform Vergennes or anyone else about it. One can only speculate as to Maurepas's reasons for secrecy. Most likely, he wanted to find a way to stay in the center of diplomatic activities. He favored a more conciliatory relationship with Britain, whereas Vergennes and naval minister Sartine were more determined to ally with the Americans. Forth regularly met with Maurepas throughout 1777 and early 1778 and relayed his findings to Stormont.

So does the presence of this phalanx of part- and full-time British agents demonstrate that Bancroft and Wentworth were mere "supernumeraries, whose value may be discounted almost one hundred percent"? Would Britain have obtained all the information it did without the Bancroft-Wentworth tandem? The clear answer is "No." To begin with, since ancient times, governments seeking secret intelligence about the enemy have always sought to have as many sources of information as possible. By placing numerous agents in the field, a government can use the data collected from one source to double check the data collected from another. That does not necessarily imply distrust of one agent or another; it is just standard operating procedure. There is ample evidence to show that Lord North collated all the information coming from Bancroft, Lupton, Thornton, Forth, Stormont, and others and felt more confident of his conclusions when all or most indicated the same thing.[16] North, Weymouth, Eden, and Stormont also sometimes had Lupton and others spying on Bancroft, without telling them that Bancroft was "one of ours."[17] Again, this was standard procedure.

Bancroft's Uniqueness

The evidence now available amply demonstrates that Bancroft's reports to London were more numerous, more detailed, and more accurate than those of any other agent. In the previous chapter it was noted, for example, that his reports on the signing of the Franco-American treaties were superior to those of Stormont. Bancroft's intelligence reports had the authenticity of an "insider," while Stormont and others had to make do with what they could glean from the outside. Lupton's letters on the comings and goings of ships in French ports provided little or nothing of value that Bancroft did not reveal.

John Thornton sent to London things he learned from working with Arthur Lee, but one must remember that Lee himself was an outsider who sometimes knew little of what was going on. Moreover, some of Thornton's information proved to be drastically wrong. Several of his reports from December 1777 through March 1778 indicated that there was still a good chance for reconciliation with the Americans on terms suitable to Britain. These reassuring but inaccurate missives helped to lull the ministry into believing that its peace overtures had a chance for success.[18] Though Hezekiah Ford was a Loyalist, there is no solid evidence that he succeeded in providing any information to London.

Nathaniel Parker Forth perhaps did more harm than good for the British. Even before he started to work as a secret agent at the start of 1777, Bancroft let Franklin and Deane know about him. In February, before Bancroft had moved to Paris, he wrote from London to warn the American commissioners about Forth.[19] This remains one of those peculiar things that the sometimes inscrutable Bancroft did during his years in espionage. He might have done it to divert suspicion from himself. Or it might be a further indication that, though he was primarily a British agent, he nonetheless performed some valuable services for the Americans. Beaumarchais and his secretary Francy, who had commercial dealings with Forth, also knew from the start that Forth was a British agent. Though Maurepas did not inform Vergennes of Forth's status as a special envoy, the foreign minister discovered the truth almost immediately.[20]

From the start, therefore, Forth was hardly a "secret" agent. Most of the intelligence he gathered was information that the Americans and the French wanted him to collect. Francy declined to accept the bribes Forth offered him, but he freely supplied Forth with details about shipping in various ports; many of those details were trivial, misleading, incomplete, or totally false.[21] In selecting Maurepas as his special "inside" source, Forth, an equine enthusiast, had simply picked the wrong horse. Maurepas was a wily old character, and one cannot be sure why he did some of what he did. On occasion he either intentionally misled Forth or, because he was not kept in the loop by Vergennes, unintentionally gave Forth wrong information. In July 1777 Forth proudly assured his superiors that he had managed to get Maurepas to promise that France was sending only one ship to fortify defenses at Martinique; the truth, however, was that over the next few months France dispatched to the West Indies three frigates carrying five infantry battalions plus auxiliary companies of cavalry and artillery.[22] In August 1777 Maurepas assured Forth that France would accede to British demands that prizes captured by America privateers be returned to their British owners and that the privateers not be allowed into French ports. Forth again trumpeted this news to London. Unlike Bancroft, Forth did not realize that this was a ruse. Despite the official order sent to French port officials, Versailles quietly let everyone know that this was temporary and that port officials could, unofficially, close their eyes to the Americans' activities.[23] In December and January Maurepas assured Forth that no alliance with the Americans was being negotiated, and Forth seems to have been unaware of the signing of a Franco-American treaty on 6 February until weeks afterwards. By the time Forth departed from Paris early in April 1778, he realized that he had been duped. He complained frostily of this in his final meetings with Maurepas and Vergennes.[24]

In brief, Bancroft was the only agent to win the full confidence of Franklin and Deane. He was the only one who could spend hours alone at the Hôtel de Valentinois in the room filled with confidential papers. He was also the only one to escape detection by the Americans and the French.[25]

On numerous occasions throughout 1777 and early 1778, William Eden, Lord Suffolk, and Lord Weymouth stated that Bancroft's intelligence, channeled through Wentworth, was of the utmost importance. For example, on 21 July 1777 Suffolk wrote to Eden telling him to give Wentworth's most recent reports immediately to North and Weymouth, so that they could take appropriate action.[26] Throughout July and August, armed with information from Wentworth, Eden alerted the Admiralty's Earl of Sandwich regarding the imminent departure of numerous vessels from French ports. A large ship at Nantes, under a Captain Nicholson, was about to leave Nantes, with papers showing it was headed to Martinique, but it would change course for North America once it was safely out of French waters. Captain Lambert Wickes was preparing to sail from Saint-Malo. A Captain Johnson would soon leave Morlaix in a heavily armed ship. Fourteen merchantmen were scheduled to disembark from Nantes in late September or early October. Eden hoped that Sandwich would instruct naval ships to intercept all of these American vessels.[27] It has been noted already that Stormont often borrowed Bancroft's exact wording when he met with Vergennes to complain of French secret aid to the rebels. The fact that Stormont used information provided by Bancroft was a tacit admission that Bancroft's intelligence in many ways was better than Stormont's.

More important, Lord North himself placed high value on all the Wentworth-Bancroft dispatches. Although initially he had reservations about the two men because of their stockjobbing, eventually he dropped such misgivings. On 29 September 1777 he wrote to Eden that any doubts about the reliability of their intelligence were removed when their reports were compared to another cache of information. A couple of months earlier, while Arthur Lee was in Berlin on his fruitless mission to gain Prussian support, the British minister there, Hugh Elliot, sneaked into his room, broke open a locked box, and made copies of all the documents Lee kept therein.[28] Lee's papers confirmed just about everything that Wentworth had reported. North hoped that Suffolk would reward Wentworth and Bancroft for their services.[29] Two weeks later North informed George III that further corroboration of Wentworth's information had arrived from two separate sources. The British minister in Madrid, Lord Grantham, had submitted data his agents collected regarding movements in French and Spanish ports, and a British ship newly arrived from America confirmed the arrival in ports there of ships whose departure from French ports had earlier been reported by Wentworth.[30]

On 28 October 1777 North dispatched a detailed set of instructions to Admiral Lord Howe, commander of British naval forces in North America. He listed ships leaving French ports, along with their cargoes, sailing routes, and probable destinations. He instructed Howe to use all these details in capturing as many of the vessels as possible. A close comparison of North's dispatch with letters and memos of Wentworth and Bancroft demonstrates that the bulk of the intelligence came from them, with corroborative details supplied by Lupton, Hynson, the stolen papers of Arthur Lee, and other sources.[31]

Early in 1778, as Wentworth submitted Bancroft's intelligence regarding the imminent Franco-American alliance, Lord North immediately took all of this information to the king. The prime minister asserted that Wentworth was "our truest informer" and that all of his (and Bancroft's) reports had been confirmed by other sources.[32] North glumly concluded that war with France was imminent and Britain must take immediate action to prepare for it.

The British Government's Use of Secret Intelligence

Many other examples could be cited to demonstrate the faith that the British ministry had in the intelligence provided by Bancroft. The next questions to be asked are these: What did the government do with this information? How important was it in capturing supplies destined for America? Did Bancroft's reports materially aid the British in any way at all? The answer to all these questions is "Not much." But the fact that Bancroft's information made little difference in the duration and the outcome of the war had nothing to do with any deficiencies or failures on his part. There were a host of other reasons why, in the end, his coded messages, secret rendezvous, and notes in a tree had only a modest impact.

The most often cited reason why a few historians have belittled Bancroft's role is that George III distrusted both him and Wentworth. The British monarch was similar to his French counterpart, Louis XVI. Both thought that the government as well as private individuals should behave in an upright, moral fashion. They were also doting husbands and fathers. In short, they were not cut from the same cloth as many of their predecessors. George III detested money-grubbing stockjobbers who gambled on getting rich in the "Alley" (the shorthand term for Exchange Alley, site of the stock exchange). The king was certain that Wentworth and Bancroft tailored their intelligence to send stocks up or down, depending on how they had invested their money. Throughout the fall of 1777, he believed that the two rascals were "bearing" the market, providing false, gloomy news from France so that stocks in London would plummet; this would enable the two stockjobbers to make a killing by buying up stocks at low prices. In September, George III told Lord North that "the two letters from Mr Wentworth are certainly curious, but as *Edwards* [Bancroft] is a stock jobber as well as a double Spy no other faith can be placed in his intelligence but that it suits his private views to make us expect the French Court mean war, whilst undoubtedly there is good ground to think that Event is more distant than we might suppose Six months ago. Mr Wentworth I suspect also is a dabbler in the Alley and as such may have, views, I am certain he has one, the wish of getting some Employment."[33]

On 31 December the king sent back to North another of Wentworth's letters, remarking that Wentworth "is an avowed stock jobber and therefore though I approve of employing him I never let that go out of my mind. I cannot say his dispatch which I return contains anything to build upon, but it convinces me that Bancroft is entirely an American and that every word he used on the late occasion was to deceive."[34]

In short, George III distrusted every word coming from Wentworth and Bancroft and repeatedly said so. The result, as Lewis Einstein summarizes it, is that "the royal horror of gambling helped to free America."[35] But Einstein is guilty of a grave oversimplification. No one in the British government had any proof for believing that Bancroft was an American agent, and as far as can be determined, the king himself was the only one to believe it.

George III's distrust of Wentworth and Bancroft must be qualified in several respects. He distrusted all spies. As mentioned previously, most spies before the twentieth century came from the lower depths of society and performed their work for purely mercenary reasons. The monarch occasionally expressed the same doubts about Hynson, Forth, Lupton, and other agents. He disdained them because they were, like Bancroft, stockjobbers or because he suspected they were working for the Americans and feeding false information to their British handlers. On 6 April 1777 George III told his ministers, "I have ever doubted whether any trust could be reposed in Hynson. I am now quite settled in my opinion that He as well as every other Spy from N. America is encouraged by Deane and Franklin and only gives intelligence to deceive."[36]

Furthermore, George III was averse to accepting any information that he deemed unpleasant. He tended to accept as reliable any intelligence that indicated success for British military or diplomatic efforts. Conversely, he tended automatically to distrust any sources that brought unfavorable news. When Wentworth and Bancroft provided good news—for example, about frictions between the American commissioners and Vergennes—he liked their reports. In November 1777 he even approved the granting of an extra £500 to Bancroft.[37] But most of the intelligence Wentworth and Bancroft sent was unpleasant—hence his added distrust of them.

By focusing on George III's distrust of Bancroft, however, historians have been asking the wrong question entirely. The fact is that George III's likes or dislikes often meant little in terms of what his government actually did. Lord North kept the king well informed about all that was happening, and the king gave his opinions. However, the king rarely, if ever, instructed

North or his other ministers about what they should or should not do regarding the American rebels. Almost invariably, he acceded to what his ministers desired. The conduct of British military and diplomatic efforts thus was almost completely in the hands of the prime minister, the secretaries of state, and the first lord of the Admiralty. Cabinet ministers never changed what they thought of Bancroft as a result of the king's misgivings. British historian Ian R. Christie describes the general status of George III in all areas of government this way: "It is evident that there was constant dialogue over policy between the king and the cabinet (as well as between the king and individual ministers); but this was more a process of participation than of direction. On some occasions the king got his way, but there were other equally significant occasions when he failed to do so or swallowed an unpalatable recommendation. The 'mixed monarchy' of the eighteenth century presupposed an active king; but it seems an exaggeration to regard the nature and extent of George III's activity in the 1760s or 1770s as justifying the description 'personal rule.'"[38]

In his authoritative account of the British war effort, Piers Mackesy asserts that George III's "contribution to the war was a moral one. He could try to see that the Ministers held together and did their duty. He would put heart into the hesitant, stir up the idle, and check the treacherous. . . . His own firm spirit helped to hold the Ministry together and encouraged resolute measures; in the darkest crises he never lacked confidence or courage. . . . His aim was not to direct policy, but to infuse his own energy into those who ought. He knew the importance of pushing slothful administrators, and gained his servants' respect."[39] In short, by the 1770s the British monarch was more a cheerleader or morale booster than a commander.

Focusing on George III's distrust of stockjobbers like Wentworth and Bancroft likewise is totally wrong for other reasons. The plain truth is that the British government took little action in response to the intelligence being gathered by any of its agents in France and elsewhere on the Continent. This includes the voluminous reports submitted by the British ambassador in Paris, Lord Stormont. Like Bancroft, Lupton, Hynson, and others, Stormont reported on innumerable ship arrivals and departures in French ports. Lords North, Suffolk, Weymouth, and Sandwich collated all the information submitted by their various agents and thereby had an extremely clear idea of which ships were sailing from which ports on approximately which dates. Yet outside of using this information to complain to Vergennes and Maurepas, the British government did little with Bancroft's or anyone else's secret intelligence.

With its superior navy, Britain was in a position to seize many or even most of the ships carrying supplies to the insurgents—or so it might have seemed. Yet nowhere in the British archives is there a single piece of evidence to show that a tip from Bancroft, Stormont, or any other informer led to the capture of a particular vessel. British squadrons regularly patrolled the entire French coast, both in the Atlantic and the Mediterranean, but even the mighty British navy could not be everywhere at once. Moreover, that navy was spread thin. Some ships were deployed in European waters, others in America, and yet others in the Caribbean. The largest part of the navy, however, was kept along the British coast to protect the homeland.

But there was an even bigger reason why the intelligence sent by Bancroft and others was not acted on. The British government was afraid to use it. Both France and Britain wanted to postpone open hostilities: the French, because their naval buildup would not be complete until the spring or summer of 1778; the British, because they hoped to quash the rebellion before France entered the fray. The result was that British squadrons were ordered not to risk any confrontation that could cause an open rupture with France. Thanks to Bancroft and his cohorts, Britain knew all about the scores of ships leaving French ports. But the British also knew that seizing these ships was risky. Some of the vessels were owned by Americans, whereas some were French-owned. Stopping the French ones would be a violation of French neutral rights, especially since the official French papers on board indicated that the ships were heading toward the French West Indies—and not to America. Stopping the American ships was also risky. Most of these ships carried papers indicating that they were French-owned; those papers were a sham, but they still gave a semblance of legality. Moreover, there were likely to be some Frenchmen among the crews of American vessels, and thus capturing them could force a showdown of some sort. British ships did stop and search many merchantmen leaving French ports. But before the vessels were stopped, the merchant captains, whether they were American or French, threw overboard any incriminating documents. Thus the "official" papers shown to British sea captains indicated that the ships were French and destined for French islands. Once the merchantmen were safely out in the

Atlantic, some of them changed course and headed straight to North America. The others continued on to Martinique or Saint-Domingue, from where the cargoes were transshipped to America. Many Dutch and Spanish ships also brought supplies to America during this period, using the same subterfuges.

The result was that the British squadrons patrolling in the North Sea and along the French coast seized relatively few vessels. The vessels sent out by Beaumarchais are a case in point. Because of his notoriety as a playwright and because it was well known that Versailles was "secretly" subsidizing his purchase of ships and cargoes, the British knew all about his activities—thanks to Bancroft and others. Between the spring of 1777 and the spring of 1778, Beaumarchais dispatched eight merchantmen to America. Only one was seized by the British. The tactics used by Beaumarchais's vessels were typical. One of his ships, for example, was *L'Heureux*. It set sail from Marseille on 26 September 1777. According to its papers, it was armed with eighteen cannons and carried a cargo of wine, sulfur, vegetables, and other merchandise. Ostensibly it was bound for Martinique. Once it was safely out to sea, it took on a new name, *Le Flamand*. It actually carried thirty-four cannons, and its hold was filled with muskets, brass cannons, medicine, uniforms, tents, tools, and gunpowder. It changed course for Portsmouth, New Hampshire, where it arrived safely on 1 December.[40]

If capturing vessels on their departure from French ports was too risky, there was no such danger in seizing merchantmen as they approached the American coast. All vessels owned by rebels were ripe for capture. Moreover, French or other foreign vessels entering American harbors also were fair game. Such vessels lost all the protection of neutrality once they attempted to bring military supplies to Britain's rebellious colonies. Here too, however, the intelligence provided by Bancroft, Stormont, and others was of little use. When a merchantman left a French port there was no way of predicting when or where it might put in once it reached American shores. And the American seaboard contained hundreds of large and small harbors where a trading vessel could put in. As noted above, in late October 1777 Lord North sent Admiral Lord Howe a lengthy dispatch containing information collected from Bancroft and others. He instructed Howe to capture as many of those vessels as possible. After receiving the orders in January 1778, the admiral wrote back to the Admiralty with a list of complaints: his ships needed repairs, the

American coast was too long for him to patrol with the number of vessels in his command, many of his men were sick, and his fleet was sorely in need of supplies. In leaden bureaucratic prose, he bleakly concluded that "I am unable to assure you . . . that such sufficient precautions have been taken as promise those advantageous consequences which, from the circumstantial nature of the intelligence, might be reasonably expected."[41] The result was that the information provided by Bancroft and others had little effect on either side of the Atlantic.

Lord North and His Cabinet

Beyond the fear of precipitating war with France and the insufficiencies of its navy, there were yet additional reasons why the British government did not make more use of the information so painstakingly collected by Bancroft, Stormont, and others. One of these has to do with the character of the cabinet ministers themselves.

Let us start with chief minister Lord North—who, incidentally, always shunned the title "prime minister." Before his assumption of the leading ministerial position in 1770, he was widely regarded as the ideal man for the job. Respected for his personal integrity, he was a devout Anglican and a loving husband and father. He was urbane, witty, and good-natured. In the House of Commons, he was a sharp debater and parliamentary infighter. He had been appointed chancellor of the exchequer in 1767 and first lord of the Treasury in 1770; he retained these two posts and continued to lead his party in the Commons until his resignation from office in March 1782. He was a gifted financial administrator and had the firm support of the monarch.

It is ironic and unfortunate, then, that he has gone down in history with the label "the prime minister who lost America." For over a century after his ministry, one of the standard insults that could be hurled at any of his successors was that he was "the worst prime minister since Lord North." Why did this gifted man fail so miserably in the single largest crisis of his dozen years at the helm? Part of the failure was his personal fault, but an even larger part had little or nothing to do with him. He suffered innumerable crises of confidence throughout his ministry. Although some historians have called him inept, it is probably more correct to say that he was temperamentally unsuited to handling a national crisis and leading a war effort.[42] On perhaps dozens of occasions he beseeched George III for permission to resign, and at least a few times he suffered what appeared to be nervous breakdowns.

These requests to retire started before the American revolt but became more frequent in the years after 1775. For example, North piteously begged to retire in December 1777 (upon the news of Saratoga) and again several times in the early months of 1778 (as war with France became imminent). On 29 January 1778, writing of himself in the third person, he wrote to the king that "the anxiety in his mind for the last two months has deprived Lord North of his memory and understanding. . . . The whole of this matter has been an additional proof to Lord North of his incapacity for the high and important office in which he is placed."[43] Parliamentary opposition to the government's handling of the war rose to such a pitch in May 1778 that North warned "if your Majesty does not allow me to retire, you and the country are ruined."[44]

Each time that the king refused his request, North became paralyzed with indecisiveness. One illustration of this will suffice. With intelligence from Bancroft indicating in January 1778 that a Franco-American alliance was definitely in the offing, North realized that the moment had come for one final effort to reconcile with the Americans. He decided to send envoys to Philadelphia with authority to repeal all the measures imposed since 1763 and the power to grant home rule within the empire. Yet he waited until 17 February 1778 to propose it in the House of Commons. One reason for his delay was that he simply could not bring himself to believe that the French had finally taken the ultimate step of allying with the rebels.[45] Only in mid-April did three commissioners at last depart. They were headed by the Earl of Carlisle, and together they came to be called the Carlisle Commission. Their journey was doomed before it began, for the Americans were determined to settle for nothing less than complete independence. The point here, however, is that North delayed for months in what he perceived to be an urgent task.

Another problem with Lord North was that he did not see himself as the driving force in his ministry. He considered himself a convener of cabinet meetings, an adviser to his colleagues, and their liaison to the king, but he did not see himself as their boss. In general he went along with whatever decisions they made for their departments. As a result, there was no unified direction for British diplomacy or the war in America. Diplomatic relations with Continental countries were divided between the northern and southern secretaries of state. The northern secretary was Lord Suffolk until his death in March 1779; in the fall of that year North named as his successor the erst-while minister in Paris, Lord Stormont. The southern secretary was Lord Weymouth, until November 1779, when he was replaced by the Earl of Hill-sborough. All aspects of the war in America were under the control of the American secretary, Lord Germain, who held that office until it was abol-ished in a cabinet reshuffle following North's resignation in March 1782. The navy was controlled by the first lord of the Admiralty, the Earl of Sandwich, who left office when North stepped down.

If the intelligence provided by Bancroft and others in France often was not used, that was due in part to the caliber of these officials, their working relationships, and the size and quality of the staffs at their disposal. The number of undersecretaries and clerks working for the cabinet ministers was exceedingly small by Continental standards. Each secretary of state, for ex-ample, had on average just a couple of undersecretaries and seven to ten clerks. Moreover, several of these undersecretaries and clerks were lazy and incompetent, having obtained their jobs through family connections and pa-tronage. Often they were swamped with work, and as a consequence letters went unanswered and communications between departments were poor. Harmful delays often occurred, and frequently the government's left and right hands were clueless as to the actions of the other. Sometimes there was no clear line of demarcation between the responsibilities of the different departments; the secretaries of state, for example, occasionally issued direc-tions to naval commanders who, theoretically, were under the control of the Admiralty.[46]

Lord North's government was not just small and disorganized but also dysfunctional. Suffolk generally gets high marks from historians for being intelligent and conscientious, but often he was absent and incapacitated due to painful eruptions of gout. Weymouth, on the other hand, is generally re-garded as an inept, lazy, often-inebriated political hack.[47] In his magisterial book on the British navy in that era, N. A. M. Rodger states that "through-out the American war, British strategy was influenced and constrained by political tension within the ministry, and in particular between North, Sand-wich, and . . . Germain. . . . Cold, arrogant and isolated, distrusted and dis-trustful, Germain habitually intrigued to undermine other ministers. . . . tension within the cabinet was inevitable. What made it really damaging was North's inadequacy as a war leader."[48]

A prime example of the paralysis that often infected the government concerns the French fleet sent to America under the Comte d'Estaing in the spring of 1778. British informers in French, Spanish, and Italian ports had been sending reports of a naval buildup in Toulon since early in the year. No one, however, knew whether it was destined for North America, whether it would attack British islands in the Caribbean, or whether it would it join with a Spanish fleet to mount an invasion of Britain itself.

In mid-April Bancroft sent a dispatch to London revealing that d'Estaing's flagship would have two important passengers: Silas Deane, who had been recalled to America by Congress, and Vergennes's former secretary Conrad-Alexandre Gérard, who had just been named minister to the United States. Thus d'Estaing was headed for North America, where he would deliver his distinguished passengers and then attack the naval force of Admiral Lord Howe. Bancroft's 1784 memorial to Lord Carmarthen recounting his services to the crown mentions this dispatch as one of his most important.[49] Stormont and virtually all other British secret agents had left France by this time, making Bancroft the only person able to provide this kind of intelligence. In fact, Bancroft knew more about all of this than did Arthur Lee, who was angry to learn the details only after the fact.[50]

D'Estaing's squadron of 12 ships of the line and 5 frigates sailed from Toulon on 13 April 1778 but did not clear the Straits of Gibraltar until 16 May. With the war in America chiefly his responsibility, Germain latched on to Bancroft's information and argued strenuously in the cabinet that part of the home fleet should be sent to destroy d'Estaing's ships before they reached the open ocean. Sandwich and Admiral Augustus Keppel, commander of the home fleet, cared less about America and more about their own chief area of responsibility—namely, the protection of the British Isles. The result was a deadlock. Sandwich and Keppel refused to detach any vessels from the home fleet, and thus d'Estaing's squadron sailed freely out of the Mediterranean. Once it became clear in late May that Bancroft had been correct regarding d'Estaing's destination, Germain argued that part of the home fleet should be dispatched to catch the French squadron before it could attack Howe, whose ships were fewer in number and in poorer condition. Germain lost this argument also. Not until June was a squadron under Admiral John Byron sent in pursuit of d'Estaing. During two months of cabinet bickering, Lord North declined to take a firm stand and order his colleagues to take action of one sort or another. By mid-April he had come to agree with Germain, and yet in corresponding with Sandwich the most he could bring himself to say was that "I am rather inclined to run the risk [of detaching part of the home fleet] and wish you would consider it."[51]

In this particular episode, the British were lucky, and the indecision at the top did no great harm. D'Estaing's squadron reached the mouth of the Delaware River nine days too late to catch the British fleet and army, both of which had retreated from Philadelphia to the relative safety of New York. If d'Estaing had arrived earlier, a victory over the British fleet or the bottling up of the army might well have ended the fighting more than three years before Yorktown. Failing to trap either Howe or Clinton, d'Estaing spent the next several months attempting, in conjunction with the American army, to take Rhode Island; when that failed, he rather ingloriously sailed for the French West Indies.

The British Secret Service

Even those historians who agree about the deficiencies of Lord North and his cabinet tend to insist that at least the Secret Service was well run and effective. Its head, William Eden, was, by all accounts, intelligent and ambitious. Born in 1744, he was still a young man and in the early stages of his career during the Revolution. An Oxford-educated lawyer, in the early 1770s he came to the attention of Solicitor General Alexander Wedderburn, who obtained for him the position of undersecretary to Lord Suffolk in 1772. Historians differ regarding Eden's relationship with his new boss. One author has claimed that Eden was lazy and that Suffolk frequently had to coax him to carry his part of "the labouring oar."[52] However, the bulk of the available evidence suggests that the two men had a good working relationship. Suffolk obtained a royal pension for his protégé, plus a seat in Parliament and a sinecure as auditor of Greenwich Hospital.

Eden was a schemer and opportunist who aspired to ever higher office. Soon after he became undersecretary, he took a house at 17 Downing Street, where he could be close to Lord North. When North's personal secretary was ill, Eden filled in on that job while still working for Suffolk. In gratitude, North appointed him to the Board of Trade. One author states that Eden further aided North by pandering in the chief minister's secret love affairs.[53]

Clearly, Eden was a young man on the make. His rising star was helped by his expertise in the law and his excellent knowledge of American affairs. His brother, Robert Eden, had served as royal governor of Maryland and had married into that colony's prominent Calvert family. It was natural then, once the Revolution began, that he be given charge of watching over many of the American Loyalists living in England plus the secret agents working in France.

The vast majority of historians writing about Eden's Secret Service have agreed that it was large, efficient, and potent. They have called Eden or the Secret Service in general "argus-eyed," in reference to the Greek mythological giant who had a hundred eyes. They have admired Eden as a genius. His espionage agency was ruthlessly powerful, with bureaus throughout Europe. Thanks to this army of spies, Eden and his superiors knew more about what Franklin and other Americans were doing in Paris than did the Continental Congress. Eden's right-hand man was Paul Wentworth, who controlled the entire operation in Paris (or, depending on which historian one reads, in all of France). Bancroft headed the cell working in the Hôtel de Valentinois. The annual Secret Service budget grew to astronomical proportions during the Revolution, to at least £80,000 and perhaps even to £200,000. (The average total of government expenditures in peacetime was around £8 million, rising to about £20 million during the Revolution.) In short, most historians portray Edward Bancroft as a key figure in a large, well-oiled, tightly controlled espionage machine.[54]

There is just one problem with the above scenario: there was no Secret Service! There was no spy agency or department under Eden or anyone else in the government. The term "secret service" (with no capitals) was often used in the correspondence of that era, but this referred to the work of various individuals, not to an established government office of any kind. In this regard Britain lagged behind France and several other countries. Paris had an official police force in the eighteenth century, and most French spies worked for it. Even the Continental Army under George Washington had a better-organized espionage system than did Britain. Washington supervised an impressive network of spies in New York, Long Island, and elsewhere throughout the Revolution.[55] Britain had no police force until the nineteenth century and no MI6 until the twentieth. The British government's use of secret agents went back centuries, as it did everywhere, but this had always been ad hoc. Government ministers hired or bribed individuals for particular tasks, but these spies and informers generally were not formal employees on the payroll. Richard Van Alstyne is one of the few historians to have realized the decentralized and often haphazard nature of the British intelligence system. Regarding William Eden, he concludes: "He was certainly not the mastermind at the head of a nonexistent secret service."[56]

The "Secret Service's" annual budget of £80,000 to £200,000 was not what most historians have perceived. There are sundry documents referring to these sums for particular years during the Revolution, but they do not refer to the budget of a particular office. They are summaries of what were variously termed "extraordinaries," "secret services," or "special services." It is impossible to know for sure what the individual expenditures were used for. Undoubtedly, some of this money reflected pensions given to Bancroft, Wentworth, Lupton, Forth, and others, plus bribes given to numerous informers. Some of these secret funds, however, were used for things totally unrelated to espionage. For example, through the 1770s George III often gave Lord North money to pay off the chief minister's personal debts, and these "secret" payments form part of what some historians count as the "Secret Service" budget. Other expenses often cloaked under the general rubric "secret service" included gifts (that is, bribes) to foreign statesmen as well as to members of Parliament. There were also payments to Grub Street hacks who wrote pamphlets or articles favorable to the government. What in the eighteenth century was called "special" or "secret" services is more likely today to be called "discretionary" or "slush" funds. Moreover, espionage activities could also be covertly paid for through the king's privy purse, through post office funds, or through the discretionary funds of the individual cabinet ministers. In short, no one then or now could say with any confidence how much the government spent for secret intelligence activities.[57]

There was no Secret Service, but there were spies. Both full-time agents and part-time informers were hired by each government agency. Every army general had his own spy chief, usually an adjutant-general. The first lord of the Admiralty and the secretaries of state hired their own agents and had their own "secret services" budgets to pay for them. Every ambassador or consular official stationed abroad was also charged with the bribing of local informers. No one in the government at that time and no historian today could estimate how many secret agents were employed or how much they were paid.

There is no doubt that Britain invested a lot of money and time in spying on real and potential enemies. The problem was that all this work was disorganized. Neither William Eden nor anyone else was in charge of all of it. Eden himself had no experience in espionage. In 1776 North and Suffolk informally charged him with keeping an eye on Americans living in London. He was to find out what he could about them and make use of some of them if that was feasible. The person whom he asked to do much of this for him was the aforementioned clergyman John Vardill. Vardill had more to do with supervising agents in Britain and in France than did Paul Wentworth. Wentworth therefore did not run the "Secret Service" in France. He was the handler of just one agent, Bancroft. And Bancroft certainly did not run the cell in Passy. There was no cell, just him.

The nonexistence of a British Secret Service is further demonstrated by the fact that William Eden was appointed to the Carlisle Commission that left for America in April 1778. If he had been so important as the crafty, all-knowing head of the entire British intelligence system, then certainly he could not have been spared for an extended voyage to America. It is not clear whether he lobbied for the new job or whether North beseeched him to take it.[58] Being a peace commissioner was a step up from being an undersecretary, and before his departure he demanded and was granted a salary equal to that of an ambassador.[59] Technically, he remained in charge of Wentworth, Vardill, Bancroft and other secret agents, even though he would be in America. In his papers there are two curious letters that were sent to him after his departure and that caught up with him in America. One, dated 23 April 1778, was from North. The chief minister was enclosing a letter that Eden could give to General Henry Clinton, who had replaced William Howe as the army's commander in chief. That letter instructed Clinton to give Eden money from army contingency funds "for secret service use." North added, however, that he did not see what use such money would be to Eden in America.[60] On 24 April Wentworth dispatched to Eden a short letter enclosing extracts of recent reports from Bancroft. Wentworth noted that it was now difficult to get information out of France and that he himself would soon go to Paris to try to work out a new method of communication.[61]

These two letters demonstrate just how unorganized and amateurish the British intelligence service could be. In an era when a message could take up to two months to cross the Atlantic, how would Eden be able to supervise espionage activities in Britain and France? The obvious answer is that he could not and did not. Eden's papers for the remainder of 1778 and subsequent years reveal that he turned his attention to the work of the Carlisle Commission and other matters; never again did he deal with espionage.[62] In the mid-nineteenth century Eden's son published a two-volume edition of his papers. Perhaps in part because spying still was not respectable and in part because that profession had occupied such a small part of Eden's life, the son did not include even a single reference to his father's brief involvement in espionage.[63]

After the failure of the Carlisle Commission in Philadelphia, Eden arrived back in London at the end of 1778. He found himself out of a job, for his post as undersecretary to Suffolk had been filled by someone else. Eden beseeched Lord North for employment, but the minister offered him nothing. For the next two years Eden made trouble for the North ministry, often siding with the parliamentary opposition. Finally, at the end of 1780 he was appointed secretary to Lord Carlisle, the new lord lieutenant of Ireland. There is no need to track Eden's career further. Suffice it to say that his work as an overseer of spies ended in April 1778, and no one was appointed to succeed him as head of the nonexistent "Secret Service."

If the secret intelligence that Bancroft gathered up to the spring of 1778 did not significantly aid the British cause, the reasons for this therefore had little to do with Bancroft himself. He worked hard at his task, taking significant risks. He was the most important British agent in France and the only one with insider access to the American commissioners. The British government's fear of sparking an early war with France, Lord North's indecisiveness, the dysfunctional nature of the cabinet, and the lack of a centralized Secret Service ensured that the government would take little action on the information at its disposal.

Last, even if Lord North's cabinet had made immediate use of the secret intelligence provided by Bancroft and others, Britain probably would have lost the American colonies anyway. Once France, and later Spain and the Netherlands, joined the war, Britain found itself isolated diplomatically, without a significant European ally. North and his cabinet devoted more time, money, and naval resources to fighting the war in European waters and to protecting valuable West Indies islands than to holding on to the troublesome Americans. Britain simply lacked the resources to wage war successfully on all these fronts. The logistics of fighting a large-scale war more than three thousand miles from home would have been staggering even if Britain could have given North America its undivided attention. Moreover, the British soon learned that the number of Loyalists in America was not as large as had been hoped. British historian H. T. Dickinson has provocatively concluded, "In retrospect, the American War appears almost unwinnable."[64]

Thus even if George III's government had made full use of the intelligence provided by Bancroft and other agents, there is little likelihood that the outcome would have been different. Nonetheless, Lord North's cabinet continued to collect as much information in France as was possible throughout the Revolution. After the spring of 1778, however, that task became more daunting. Ambassador Stormont and most British secret agents had scurried back to London once France openly declared its alliance with the fledgling American republic. Only a handful of part-time informers remained in some French ports. Bancroft was the sole active British agent stationed in Paris after April 1778.

8 *In for the Long Haul, 1778–1783*

Serving Britain

After Ambassador Stormont and his staff left Paris in March 1778, Bancroft's work became more dangerous and difficult. Most of the details of how he communicated with London remain unknown. Putting messages in a tree in the Tuileries Gardens ended in March, for there was no longer anyone left in Paris to retrieve them. In early April 1778 Bancroft wrote to Paul Wentworth that "all communications with you will soon be impracticable."[1] He managed to get that letter to London by sending a private messenger through Ostend. Until the United Provinces entered the war against Britain in December 1780, travel between Dutch cities and Britain and France was legal and less guarded by British and French agents. Undoubtedly, some of Bancroft's couriers also slipped onto small boats along the French coast and made their way to England under cover of darkness.

Benjamin Franklin Stevens's widely used twenty-five-volume collection of documents from European archives gives a very misleading impression of Bancroft's espionage career. Stevens reprinted many items by or about Bancroft up to April 1778, with only one letter from a later date. The basic reason for this is that Stevens made extensive use of the papers of Undersecretary of State William Eden. As noted in the previous chapter, Eden left for America as part of the Carlisle Commission in that month and never again had any-thing to do with spying. Thus Eden's papers for later years contain nothing about Bancroft or Wentworth. Because nearly all historians writing on the diplomacy of the American Revolution have relied heavily on Stevens, most of what has been written about Bancroft is limited to the period up to April 1778. But he remained in France five more years. Despite the difficulty of communicating with London, there is ample evidence to show that a shallower but nonetheless steady stream of his reports did reach the British cabinet.

To whom did Bancroft send his dispatches? Most of them went to Wentworth. After the spring of 1778, Wentworth devoted most of his time to his private business speculations, but he continued, in his toadying way, to hope for a baronetcy and a seat in Parliament. Thus he frequently passed on to the secretaries of state whatever information he received from Bancroft. Virtually all of the Bancroft's letters from these years have disappeared. What remain are Wentworth's summaries of them or brief references to them. Lords Suffolk and Stormont forwarded the information to North, who on dozens of occasions forwarded the documents to the king. When ministers mentioned Bancroft specifically, they continued to use his alias, "Edwards."[2] Wentworth finally received at least a partial reward for his efforts. On the resignation of the member of Parliament for Saltash, Cornwall, in July 1780, Wentworth won the special election to succeed him. His prized position lasted less than two months. On 1 September Parliament was dissolved. In the general election held on 11 September, Wentworth came in a poor fourth in the balloting. He challenged the results, charging the two men who won seats from that district with opening "Houses of Entertainment" for all who would vote for them and preventing some of Wentworth's supporters from being able to vote.[3] Given the lax electoral standards of that era, it is not surprising to learn that the House of Commons rejected Wentworth's petition.

During this five-year period Bancroft kept George III's government well informed on a wide range of people and on the ups and downs of the Franco-American alliance. The activities of Americans in France during these years have been chronicled extensively by many other writers, and there is no need to give an exhaustive analysis here.[4] Regarding Benjamin Franklin, the chief development was his promotion to minister plenipotentiary. Once France recognized the independent United States and sent Conrad-Alexandre Gérard to Philadelphia as its minister, the United States had to respond in kind.

Thus in September 1778 Congress voted to elevate Franklin's status, and Franklin received official word in February 1779.

Franklin's new prominence meant that the other two commissioners were no longer needed. Silas Deane had already been recalled to America. Congress was upset by the volume of French volunteers whom he had sent to serve in the Continental Army. Just as Deane was departing in April 1778, his replacement, John Adams, was arriving. After word came of Franklin's new appointment, Adams was left jobless. He returned to America in June 1779.

The other commissioner, Arthur Lee, likewise lost his position but nonetheless remained in Paris. He was still the commissioner to Spain, though the court in Madrid would have nothing to do with him. In Paris he spent much of his time with his brother William, the commissioner to the Holy Roman Empire and Prussia, and Ralph Izard, the commissioner to Tuscany. None of the three had much to do in any official capacity. Arthur Lee and Izard eventually left for America in 1780, while William Lee moved to Brussels and finally, in 1783, back home to Virginia.

Bancroft reported extensively on naval, military, and diplomatic affairs. During the tortuous peace negotiations of 1782 and 1783, he kept London well informed about the goals, feelings, and bargaining points of the American commissioners.

As in the previous chapter, the important question is: Did the British government value and use this intelligence? Again, the answer is mixed. There is no specific incident where one can say with certainty that Bancroft's information was a key factor in a British victory on land or sea. By the time his dispatches wended their way to London by various circuitous routes, any news that he had about particular ships departing from French ports would likely have been outdated. Moreover, although Bancroft was the most important agent in France during these five years, Lord North, his secretaries of state, and the first lord of the Admiralty continued to collect information from other sources as well—from ship captains, from government officials stationed in Holland or the Italian states, and from British sympathizers or part-time informers in French ports. George III persisted in distrusting Bancroft and disliking the bad news that his messages often brought. In August 1779, for example the king wrote to North that Edwards's news for a long time has been "calculated to intimidate . . . without foundation . . . [and] exaggerated."[5]

But the monarch's misgivings did not deter North and his cabinet from relying heavily on Bancroft for details about French and American actions. In April 1781, for example, North sent George III two letters from Bancroft and Wentworth and stressed that the information was very important, even though it was now too late to take any direct action. When North received news from Bancroft about French naval movements, he always forwarded the information to the Earl of Sandwich so that the British navy could take appropriate steps. Bancroft kept his superiors abreast of Spain's slow but steady steps toward joining the war and, after Spain officially entered, of Franco-Spanish plans for an invasion of England. (That project was aborted in the summer of 1779.) Bancroft's importance is also indicated in a negative way. If weeks went by with no news from him, North's cabinet bemoaned the lack of intelligence about enemy plans.[6]

He also reported the doings of John Paul Jones, who arrived in France in December 1777, expecting to be given command of a newly built Dutch frigate. The Dutch were still neutral and thus not supposed to provide warships to the Americans. Thanks to intelligence from Bancroft, the British were able to pressure the Dutch into canceling the sale. Jones therefore had to make do with the sloop *Ranger,* which had brought him to France. His plan was to terrorize the enemy through daring raids on coastal towns. In April 1778 Jones achieved this goal with his famous expedition around Britain and Ireland. Bancroft's dispatches to London warning of Jones's departure from Brest arrived just a few days too late to aid in capturing the *Ranger* before it reached the British coast. Bancroft likewise kept his superiors informed about Jones's subsequent actions—his triumphal return to France, his disappointments in waiting months for the French government to supply him with a larger ship, and his eventual acquisition of the *Duc de Duras* (which he renamed *Bonhomme Richard*). In September 1779, off the coast of Flamborough Head, Jones commanded a small squadron that encountered two British warships. In the ensuing battle Jones issued his daring cry, "I have not yet begun to fight!" and he managed to capture both the *Serapis* and the *Countess of Scarborough.*[7]

Despite intelligence sent by Bancroft and other informers, the British navy performed miserably against Jones. British ships could not be everywhere, and thus even with some advance warning they could not blockade every French port and protect every stretch of British shoreline. However, in a broader way, Bancroft did have a concrete impact. The details he sent regarding planned raids or invasions gave the Earl of Sandwich ample reason to keep large numbers of naval ships in home ports or on coastal patrols. This reassured the British people of their security. However, Bancroft's dispatches had the unintended result of helping the United States. Naval squadrons that could have been used to quash the American rebellion instead were kept at home.

Bancroft's work was considered so important that in June 1780 his annual pension was doubled in size. In addition to his permanent pension of £500 he was to receive an additional £500 for every year that he remained in France. There was also some vague promise that part of this additional £500 would be added to his permanent pension, providing that the government continued to be satisfied with his services. All this money was paid through Lord North's discretionary special or secret service accounts.[8]

Peace Negotiations

The final stage of Edward Bancroft's work as "Edward Edwards" lasted from the start of peace negotiations in the spring of 1782 to the signing of the preliminary peace accord on 30 November of that year. To understand his role, one must first know the general context.

In mid-November 1781 word reached London that Lord Cornwallis's army had surrendered on 17 October at Yorktown, Virginia. Britain's desire to continue the fight soon evaporated, and Lord North's discredited and dispirited government collapsed in March 1782. The new chief minister was the Marquess of Rockingham, who had been a leader of the opposition. In an effort to coordinate foreign affairs more efficiently, the northern and southern secretaryships were combined into one secretary of state for foreign affairs. That position went to the young Charles James Fox, renowned as an orator and Francophobe. The plan to have a unified foreign policy was wrecked, however, by retention of the American secretary. That office was renamed "secretary of state for home and colonial affairs" (today simply called the home secretary). The new holder of this post was the Earl of Shelburne, another former opposition leader.

Fox and Shelburne soon became bitter rivals in the peace negotiations. Fox favored granting independence quickly to the Americans so that Britain could turn all its might against France, Spain, and the Netherlands. Shelburne, for his part, hoped to persuade the Americans to agree to some continued link with the mother country. He also favored a conciliatory policy toward France, because he wanted a peace settlement that would leave no resentments and thus enable British trade with Europe and America to flourish. Fox and Shelburne vied with each other for the upper hand in parleys that would take place in France.

Congress selected five men to serve as its peace commissioners. These were Franklin, John Adams, John Jay, Henry Laurens, and Thomas Jefferson. Through the spring and early summer of 1782, Franklin was the only member of the group in France; acting alone, he commenced talks with British envoys. John Jay had been serving as American minister in Spain since early 1780 and, with his family in tow, arrived in Paris in June. Immediately on his arrival he came down with influenza and was bedridden for several weeks. John Adams arrived in Paris in October 1782, having spent the previous two years in the Netherlands acquiring loans and a commercial treaty for his country. Henry Laurens was a South Carolina planter-businessman and member of Congress who arrived in Paris only on 28 November 1782, just two days before the signing of the preliminary articles of peace. The last of the commissioners, Thomas Jefferson, never arrived. For personal reasons, he declined the appointment and remained in America.[9]

The British envoys sent to deal with Franklin and the others reflected the rivalries and changes within the British cabinet. The first to come was Richard Oswald, an elderly Scot whose liberal open-mindedness and practicality were bound to appeal to Franklin. Eager to upstage Fox, Shelburne had sent Oswald as an unofficial representative whose task was to make initial contact with the Americans and establish some ground rules. Shortly afterward, Fox sent his own representative, Thomas Grenville, who was to deal with Vergennes plus the Spanish and the Dutch. Though Grenville was authorized to deal only with European powers, he also had several meetings in May and June with Franklin.

With both Oswald and Grenville, Franklin was adamant on one topic: the independence of the United States was not a bargaining point. Britain would have to accept it, at least tacitly, before any meaningful discussions could commence. Another sticky issue was whether Britain would negotiate separately with the Americans or whether there would be an all-party conference. The instructions drafted by Congress told the peace commissioners not to act alone but to do everything with the advice and consent of the French court. Franklin was grateful to France for its indispensable aid, but he also realized that an all-party conference would involve the United States in squabbles over affairs that did not concern it—for example, Spain's desire to regain Gibraltar. Thus in June Franklin quietly agreed to deal separately with Britain.

But would he deal with Oswald or with Grenville? Late in June, Franklin decided on Oswald, which was a major blow to Fox's pretensions. At the same time that news of Franklin's choice reached London, an even bigger development occurred. On 1 July Rockingham died of influenza and was succeeded as prime minister by Shelburne, which prompted Fox's resignation. This also led to a new phase of the negotiations. As chief minister, Shelburne took direct control of the peace talks. He wanted a quick end to hostilities and decided to recognize American independence and offer generous terms to France as well as to Britain's other enemies. He recalled Grenville to England. Oswald remained in Paris, where he would serve as Shelburne's representative to the Americans. To assist him, Shelburne sent Benjamin Vaughan, a close friend of Franklin as well as his English editor. Shelburne's secretary of state for foreign affairs was Baron Grantham, and Grenville's replacement as chief negotiator with the French was the experienced diplomat Alleyne Fitzherbert.

Just as cross-channel discussions seemed to be progressing, another crisis occurred. John Jay recovered from influenza in early August at about the same time that Franklin was sidelined for several weeks by another of his many attacks of kidney stones and gout. This left Jay as the only active American representative. Jay distrusted both Vergennes and Shelburne. He demanded that Oswald's official credentials contain an explicit recognition of American independence. This led to an impasse that lasted to mid-September. Jay finally agreed to a revised, fuzzily worded alteration of Oswald's instructions.

Official negotiations resumed early in October, by which time Jay had been joined by a recovered Franklin. Late that month Adams arrived from the Netherlands, and in November British undersecretary of state Henry Strachey came to work with Oswald. The main topics of discussion were the western and northern boundaries of the United States, compensation to

Loyalists who had lost their property and been forced into exile, removal of British troops, and American fishing rights off the Newfoundland coast. Bancroft was present at some of the meetings that occurred, though it is difficult to say whether he participated in the give-and-take.[10]

After weeks of contentious counterproposals, the American and British representatives reached accord. On 30 November they met at Oswald's Paris hotel and signed the preliminary articles of peace. These would not become binding until terms between Britain and France were reached. On 20 January 1783 British hostilities with France, Spain, and the Netherlands ended, with the signing of preliminary articles in Versailles. It took another nine months for all the governments officially to ratify the terms of the peace settlement. Britain's new peace commissioner, David Hartley, signed formal treaties with the American commissioners and representatives of the other belligerents in Paris on 3 September 1783.

The United States did remarkably well in the settlement. Britain acknowledged America's complete independence and recognized the American western boundary as extending all the way to the Mississippi. Even more, Britain granted Americans the right to navigate on the Mississippi.[11] The Americans did not, however, gain all that they wanted. Shelburne rejected their claims to acquire Canada and granted them only limited fishing rights off Newfoundland. Furthermore, the Americans conceded that prewar debts to English merchants still must be paid. The issue of payments to Loyalists ended in a draw. Franklin's resentments against Loyalists (who included his own son William) were so strong that he resisted English demands for full compensation. The result was a weakly worded clause that "earnestly recommended" that the individual states make whatever payment was deemed suitable. Last, Britain promised to withdraw its troops from American soil. In the years to follow, the flaws in the treaty became clear. The failure of states to compensate Loyalists gave Britain an excuse to keep troops in the Northwest Territory until the mid-1790s. Nonetheless, from the American perspective, the peace settlement was a triumph. When news of the preliminary treaty reached London late in 1782, there was a huge outcry against it. Shelburne was accused of being much too generous to the Americans. In February 1783 he was forced to resign and was replaced by a coalition government headed by his enemies Lord North and Charles James Fox.

At first glance, one might assume that, if the Americans won so much, Bancroft must have been of little or no use to the British. Yet, even though the British seemed to lose more than they gained, Bancroft did perform significant work. This is revealed by an issue that occurred regarding his pension. As the initial peace feelers commenced in the spring of 1782, Bancroft discovered that his annual pension of £1,000 pounds had been eliminated. This happened in April, when Rockingham's new paymaster-general, Edmund Burke, introduced in Parliament a bill for "economical reform" that included numerous measures designed to cut government expenses and eliminate waste, especially in the various "special" or "secret" service accounts. One of the budgets that suffered as a result was the one from which Bancroft's pension came. When he stopped receiving his quarterly payments, he immediately complained. Sometime early in 1783 chief minister Shelburne ordered foreign secretary Grantham to restore the pension. That was a clear indication of Bancroft's value.[12]

We do not know much about the specifics of what Bancroft transmitted to Shelburne, Oswald, Vaughan, Strachey, and Fitzherbert. He conferred secretly with them in Paris through the latter half of 1782 and early 1783 and gave them oral reports. From the few letters that survive, however, one can see that he let the British know the issues about which Americans were truly adamant and those on which they might be willing to compromise. For example, early in August 1782 he informed Benjamin Vaughan that the Americans genuinely were open to negotiating apart from France. Bancroft said that Franklin and his colleagues were not "yet" ready to make a separate peace, owing to "some sense of fidelity" to France. However, if France insisted on continuing the war or posed any other obstacles, the Americans would "desert" that country and proceed alone. Furthermore, Bancroft told Vaughan that the Americans had "no sort of bonds" to Holland and Spain.[13] In September Bancroft wrote directly to Shelburne that Franklin and the others would reject any settlement that did not grant western lands to the United States. The Americans wanted their new country to stretch all the way to the Mississippi, without those lands becoming part of Canada or being ceded to Spain. Knowing how strongly the Americans felt on this issue, the British realized that it would be pointless to haggle over it.[14] Bancroft also assured the British that the Americans were sincere in their general bargaining positions. They had no clandestine plans or surprises and were not secretly conniving with France.

One of Bancroft's most important contributions was letting Shelburne's negotiators know of the rift between the Americans and the French court. Adams and Jay distrusted Vergennes and considered Franklin too beholden to French wishes—even though before those two appeared on the scene the elder statesman had already tacitly agreed to violate Congress's orders to work in concert with France.[15]

Knowledge of such things was significant for Shelburne and his successors in the Fox-North ministry. Via Bancroft, the British realized that the new United States was not a puppet of France. This fit right into Shelburne's far-sighted hopes. He knew that the new country would be weak politically and economically. Without a strong bond to France, it would remain dependent on trade with England. This is precisely what occurred in the years after the Revolution. Thanks to Bancroft's secret intelligence, Shelburne's representatives could confidently forge ahead to make a generous peace with the Americans.

In the months following the signing of the preliminary treaty, Bancroft continued to furnish important information. For unknown reasons, he seems to have dealt mostly with Alleyne Fitzherbert rather than with Richard Oswald or any of the other British representatives.[16] From December 1782 through early 1783 he met secretly with Fitzherbert and gave him written summaries of all developments. Fitzherbert considered Bancroft "a man of sense and education and in point of address and appearance far above the ordinary run of persons of his class."[17] On 14 December Fitzherbert wrote to Shelburne that Bancroft was "a valuable treasure to government both as a source of intelligence of all sorts and as an instrument to be employed in guiding indirectly . . . the views and conduct of the American Commissioners."[18]

A few days later he wrote to Henry Strachey, who by that time was back in London. The preliminary accords with the Americans had been signed nearly three weeks earlier. But things were still being sorted out, and there were opportunities for changes before the signing of the definitive treaty. In this letter Fitzherbert recounted what had happened in the days immediately before and after the signing of the provisional treaty. He alluded to several obstacles raised by Henry Laurens, who had arrived in Paris just in time to participate in the final meetings. Laurens was taking an extremely hostile position against Britain. Fitzherbert also noted, with disgust, that in the days following the signing of the provisional treaty Benjamin Franklin had brought up additional clauses to be included in the final settlement. In particular, Franklin wanted statements about reciprocal trade privileges for American and British ships. We know from other sources that Franklin, Adams, and Laurens were also asking for yet other new clauses to be inserted in the formal treaty. Franklin in particular was still clamoring for compensation as a result of British "depredations" to the property of private American citizens.[19] (In the end, the official treaty signed on 3 September 1783 did not include any of these revisions.) Thanks to Bancroft, Fitzherbert was given advance warning about these things plus other information about what was going on in the minds of the Americans. Thus Fitzherbert was able "to remind them [the Americans] that nothing can be farther from our thoughts than to submit tamely to so scandalous & unwarrantable a proceeding as the foisting in any fresh articles (much less such very obnoxious ones) into our treaty." Fitzherbert went on to say that Bancroft had told him that Vergennes greatly resented that the Americans had proceeded on their own to negotiate with Britain rather than working in concert with France. Thanks to Bancroft, Fitzherbert could assure his superiors in London that relations between the United States and France would not be entirely cordial; hence, Britain could hope for friendship and trade from America once the treaty was signed. The letter concludes as follows, "I have only one word more to say about Mr. Bancroft which is that I have strongly recommended to Lord Shelburne to advance him immediately the arrears of his stipend, as he has richly deserved, and is I believe in great want of it.—the truth is that he is at this moment an invaluable treasure to us, and though the double game he has been playing with P. Wentworth is certainly against him, yet it should seem from his eagerness to get out of that Gentleman's hands, that it must now be at an end, unless his game in testifying that eagerness be a very refined one indeed."[20]

One can only speculate as to what sort of trouble had developed between Wentworth and Bancroft. A few days earlier Bancroft had told Fitzherbert that Wentworth was a "bad man." Their stock speculations had brought more losses than gains, and this might have led to friction between them. It is also possible that Bancroft chafed at being controlled by Wentworth. Wentworth always wanted to receive Bancroft's information, so that he (Wentworth) could then communicate it to government ministers, thereby currying favor with them. Bancroft might also have objected that his quarterly pension payments came through Wentworth, rather than coming directly to him. During the peace negotiations, Bancroft dealt directly with Shelburne and with the British negotiators in Paris. This growing independence from Wentworth might have further strained their relationship. Fitzherbert recommended that henceforth Bancroft should send his reports directly to Shelburne or some other minister, without having to deal with Wentworth.[21]

As things turned out, Bancroft's relationship with Wentworth had become irrelevant by the end of January 1783. The war was over, and except for a few minor changes, the terms of the general peace settlement had been determined. Within a few months Bancroft and his family would be living again in London.

Serving America

While Bancroft was aiding the British government through all these years, how was he regarded by the Americans and the French? What did they think he was doing in France? As pointed out earlier, Bancroft never received a salary or an appointment either as a secretary or as a secret agent from the Americans. Given that he was a British spy, one might suppose that he helped the Americans only to learn their secrets and to sabotage their efforts. But there are mounds of evidence to demonstrate that he had strong affection for Franklin and most of the other Americans and that the services he provided them were valuable.

He spent most of his time working with Franklin's grandson Temple as the elder statesman's general assistant. Clearly Franklin needed help. He not only had to deal with the French court nearly every day, regarding loans, ships, supplies, and other matters, but he also had to offer whatever succor he could to the scores of American merchants, ship captains, stranded sailors, and others who ran into one problem or another while in France. Most of the time Franklin employed a Frenchman as clerk; this person made copies of his letters and tried to keep some order in all the files. Given Congress's failure to send him an official secretary, in March 1781 Franklin decided to reward Temple for his work and give him a regular salary, retroactive to December 1776. Finally, in November 1782 Franklin and the other peace commissioners made Temple their formal secretary.[22]

Next to Temple, Bancroft was the person who saw Franklin most often. Early on, Bancroft seems to have had a room near Franklin's in the Hôtel de Valentinois. When not spending nights there, he could be found with his family in nearby Chaillot or in his Paris apartment. On the few days when he did not see Franklin in person, the two men exchanged messages via servants.[23] In August 1779 Bancroft and Franklin's landlord, Leray de Chaumont, jointly purchased an estate adjacent to the Valentinois. Chaumont put up the money for the property, though the deed was in Bancroft's name. Thereafter, on days when Bancroft could not make it back to his family or his Paris lodgings, he could simply retire to his home next door.[24]

In March 1778 Bancroft sent a strongly worded letter to Congress, demanding that he be paid a salary. He said that he had been working full-time for more than a year for its cause. America, he declared, was "my native country." He needed to support his family and would have to return to his private pursuits unless Congress compensated him for his time. When the letter reached Philadelphia, it was sent to a committee, where it died.[25] Bancroft never raised the matter again; nor did he stop working for the Americans. As with his threat to quit the previous October, this might have been a bluff, intended merely to show the Americans how much he was sacrificing for their cause. It might also have reflected his genuine need for money. His business speculations brought as many losses as gains. Bancroft always seems to have lived beyond his means.

In the summer of 1779 Franklin recommended to Congress that Bancroft be appointed his official secretary in Paris. In September Congress voted instead to appoint John Laurens to that post; Laurens declined the assignment, and no replacement was ever named. At that same time Congress considered Bancroft for appointment as secretary to John Adams, who was preparing to return to France as a peace commissioner. But Francis Dana eventually got the nod for that job.[26] The fact that Bancroft was passed over for these two positions did not necessarily reflect any adverse judgment by the delegates in Congress. It is true that Arthur Lee had already sent negative letters to Congress about him, but William Carmichael, Silas Deane, Benjamin Franklin, and others had reported very favorably on him. His failure to receive an appointment probably had more to do with the fact that he had lived outside America for so many years and did not have as many supporters in Congress as did Laurens and Dana. If Bancroft had been named Franklin's official secretary, this would have created an unprecedented situation. As secretary, he would have assumed the position of chargé d'affaires in the event that Franklin was absent or incapacitated. In other words, a British spy would have been in charge of American diplomacy in France!

But Bancroft had to satisfy himself with being an unofficial assistant, friend, and adviser to Franklin and others. Again and again, when Franklin's American, French, British, and other friends or acquaintances wrote to him, they closed their letters asking him to give their compliments to Temple and "Dr. Bancroft."[27] In the summer of 1779 Franklin's friend Charles-Guillaume-Frédéric Dumas planned to make an extended visit to see the American minister. Living in Amsterdam, Dumas was a teacher and scholar who had met Franklin several years earlier and had become an important supporter of the American cause. He wrote to Franklin that he had heard much about Dr. Bancroft and hoped to rent a room in his home or somewhere near it. He knew that Bancroft was Franklin's "good bosom friend." If he was accompanied by Bancroft, he would be able to pop in to see Franklin "without ceremony" whenever he wished.[28] As things turned out, Dumas did not make this trip, but his letters reveal how widely Bancroft's intimacy with Franklin was known.

Persons who needed Franklin's help for one thing or another knew that a sure way to get his attention was to use Bancroft as an intermediary. Thus they approached Bancroft when they required Franklin's approval for passports to travel to or export wine to England, when they wanted to see Franklin on some important matter, when they sought employment from Franklin, when they wanted Franklin's help in obtaining clothing for state militias, and so on.[29]

Franklin depended on Bancroft for a myriad of tasks. The old man's command of French was far from perfect, and so on occasion he used Bancroft as a translator.[30] Many of the private individuals and public officials with whom Franklin corresponded used their own special codes or ciphers. Some of these were so elaborate that Franklin found it impossible to read them. (He was not alone in his exasperation at the complexity of some of the systems invented by Americans and Europeans in that era.) He therefore gave Bancroft control of the books containing the keys for decoding the messages.[31] This, of course, greatly aided Bancroft in his work as a British agent.

One of Franklin's special concerns through his years in France was the well-being and release of American sailors who had been captured and imprisoned in England. In February and March 1779 he engaged in a lengthy correspondence with various officials in London to arrange for an exchange of prisoners. British sailors incarcerated in France would be sent to Britain in return for the release of Americans. To complete the final details, Franklin planned to send Bancroft to England. On 22 February Franklin wrote to David Hartley, asking him to obtain a passport so that Bancroft could make the trip. He extolled Bancroft as "a Gentleman of Character and Honour."[32] As things turned out, details for the exchange were worked out more quickly than expected, and Bancroft did not need to make the trip.

In the summer of 1779 Franklin called on Bancroft to aid in judging a business matter. John Ross was an American merchant working in Nantes. Ross had arranged for the shipment of numerous cargoes of supplies purchased by Congress. He complained to Franklin that Congress was refusing to pay him all that was owed. Franklin appointed Samuel Wharton and Edward Bancroft to examine Ross's accounts. They decided in Ross's favor. Calling Wharton and Bancroft "Men of Integrity," Franklin duly informed Congress that it owed Ross £18,000.[33]

Sometimes Franklin sent Bancroft on missions to French ports. In March 1780, for example, Bancroft traveled to Nantes, La Rochelle, and Lorient. He worked to gather supplies needed for the Continental Army. In Lorient he helped John Paul Jones outfit the *Alliance*, which was scheduled to take many of those supplies to America. While there, Bancroft distributed money to Jones's crew. They were owed much in back wages and prize money, and so Franklin, using part of the loans received from France, was advancing them enough to keep them fed and clothed. Bancroft also hired and paid American sailors to join Jones's crew. To cover his personal expenses incurred on that trip, Bancroft was reimbursed 1,000 livres by Ferdinand Grand.[34] On another occasion Bancroft received 6,000 livres for military supplies he had purchased and sent to America. At another time Franklin paid him 320 livres for English newspapers that he furnished. He was also given 99 livres for a wax seal he obtained for John Adams.

There are many other pieces of evidence to demonstrate what John Adams's called the "indissoluble" and "confidential" friendship between Franklin and Bancroft.[35] Scattered through Franklin's voluminous papers are numerous short notes exchanged between the two men. Many of these are undated, informal invitations to dinner. Bancroft was a regular participant in the Sunday dinners that Franklin hosted for prominent Americans staying in Paris. Beyond that, Franklin, Temple, and Bancroft often dined casually together. On one occasion when Benjamin and Temple were coming to dine with him, Bancroft sent a hastily scribbled note to Temple, asking him to bring along two bottles of claret and one of sherry; Bancroft promised to repay the loan after his wine cellar was restocked. Sometimes Bancroft invited Franklin to his Chaillot home for a meal with his family or with friends who were visiting him. On one occasion, for example, Charles-Jean Garnier, the former chargé d'affaires in London, was visiting Bancroft, and Franklin was asked to sup with them; on another, Franklin was invited to Chaillot to dine with Thomas Walpole.[36]

Late in the evening of 19 November 1781, news of the American victory at Yorktown reached the Hôtel de Valentinois. A young American merchant named Elkanah Watson happened to be visiting there, and in his diary he recorded that the only other American present that night to join Franklin in a joyous celebration was "the celebrated Dr. Bankroft."[37]

It is easy to see why Bancroft and Franklin got along so well. They shared wide-ranging interests and had been friends since the late 1760s. Bancroft's writings and actions in London had demonstrated his firm support of American grievances. Beyond that, Bancroft was a jovial conversationalist and dinner companion. One amusing example of Bancroft's wit occurred in April 1782, when Leray de Chaumont escorted Franklin, Temple, and Bancroft on a tour of his limestone quarry in Passy. The workers there had just discovered the bodies of several toads that apparently had been buried in a cavity of the rock for thousands of years. To the amazement of all, one of the toads was still alive. Franklin took the live toad plus a dead one back with him to the Hôtel de Valentinois. On the way home, the live toad expired. Franklin thereupon placed it in a bottle and poured some spirits of wine on it. The toad suddenly came back to life and flopped around for a couple of minutes before expiring for good. Bancroft cheerfully remarked that the toad "was in high spirits."[38]

When Franklin rose to prominence in French Freemasonry, he did not forget his boon companion. In 1778 the elder statesman was admitted to the Neuf Soeurs, the most prominent lodge in Paris. (The nine sisters were the

Greek muses.) Whereas in America Masonic lodges tended to be mostly so-cial clubs for the political and business elites, in France and elsewhere in Europe the lodges led campaigns for Enlightenment reforms. These included humane law codes, governmental efficiency and accountability, freedom of thought, and attacks on the greed and intolerance of both the Catholic and Protestant churches. The Neuf Soeurs lodge generally attracted prominent writers and thinkers. In 1779 Franklin agreed to serve as the lodge's *Vénérable*. Over the next year he used his leadership position to get four of his closest friends elected to membership. These were his grandson Temple, Ferdinand Grand, John Paul Jones, and Edward Bancroft. After his induction in 1780, Bancroft appears to have taken an active part in lodge meetings for the next three years.[39]

There was little that Americans were doing in Passy, Versailles, or Paris to which Bancroft was not privy. As he was returning to America in June 1779, John Adams, ever jealous of the popular Franklin, complained that the senior statesman was so old and lazy that very soon "the entire Guidance of our Affairs" would be in the hands of Leray de Chaumont and Bancroft.[40] Of course, that was an extreme exaggeration written in one of Adams's choleric moods, but it reflects Bancroft's central position in American affairs.

Because Bancroft helped the Americans while also spying on them, most authors who have dwelt on this topic have dismissed him as a double agent who served both sides while being loyal to neither. As one historian has written, Bancroft was neither wholly British nor wholly American but wholly Bancroft.[41] According to this view, he despicably sold his services to both sides, while gaining insider information he used for his private speculations. In his defense, it must be said that there is no evidence that he ever lied or withheld information from one side or the other in order to serve his own interests. He worked hard to provide good services to both sides. But does this mean he was disloyal to both or that, in some twisted way, he was trying to be loyal to both? It is true that he used his insider information to speculate on the London stock market. But so did several others, including his critics the Lee brothers. And his stock speculations ended after the spring of 1778. Thus for the next five years his privileged access to secret intelligence gained him nothing personally.

Readers of this book might perhaps be disappointed to learn that after unraveling so many parts of Bancroft's activities, one still cannot answer definitively what is perhaps the most important question: What motivated him? Was it money, power, adventure, or an egotistical desire to be highly esteemed by men in authority on both sides of the conflict? Or, once he had agreed in 1776 to start providing information to the British, did he find that he was caught up in something from which he could not escape? Perhaps all of these factors played a part. In his 1784 letter to Lord Carmarthen, he said that initially he had agreed to become a British agent because he hoped that by doing so he could provide information that would enable George III's government to find a way to reconcile with the colonies. As mentioned earlier, all the available evidence supports that contention. The degree to which that continued to be important for him after 1777 is open to conjecture. After 1784 he never again spoke or wrote about his espionage career, and thus he took his secrets to the grave with him.

John Paul Jones

Next to Silas Deane and Benjamin and Temple Franklin, the American who became Bancroft's closest friend was John Paul Jones. The intrepid, hot-blooded American naval captain first arrived in France in December 1777, aboard the twenty-gun sloop *Ranger*. Congress had promised him a new, powerful frigate in France. Upon his arrival in Brest he discovered that this was not to be. The British had learned of the new Dutch ship, the *Indien*, and pressured the still-neutral Dutch not to sell it to the Americans. Therefore the Dutch sold it to the French navy. Disappointed in this setback, Jones traveled to Paris at the end of the year and remained there for about two weeks. When not making the rounds of parties in the capital, he visited the Hôtel de Valentinois. He beseeched Franklin, Deane, and Lee for help in obtaining a more powerful ship. It was during this time that he and Bancroft became friends. The commissioners could not give Jones a new ship, but they did provide funds for repairs and supplies on the *Ranger*. In mid-January Jones returned to Brest and spent the next couple of months supervising work on the sloop and planning some daring adventure. When he sent reports to Deane, Benjamin, and Temple Franklin he usually asked them to give their compliments to Dr. Bancroft.[42]

In April 1778 Jones took the *Ranger* on the first of his soon-to be-famous cruises in European waters. He sailed through the Irish Sea and led raiding parties ashore at Whitehaven in Cumbria and at the Earl of Selkirk's estate on St. Mary's Isle. In a brief but fierce action he captured the British naval sloop *Drake*. He regained Brest in May, with many prisoners and seven prizes. Most important, he had managed to spread terror through every British coastal town.

There is evidence that the British Admiralty had been forewarned about Jones's cruise. It is not clear whether these notices came just from Bancroft or also some other informer used by the Admiralty. But, as noted previously, advance warnings about ships departing French ports were often of dubious value. Ships might sail earlier than predicted or, more likely, later—due to delays from adverse weather, lack of supplies, unfinished repairs, and so on. Moreover, Jones had not told anyone in Passy—not even Bancroft—precisely where he had planned to sail.[43]

Jones's triumphant cruise made him the talk of France. The next several months, however, would also prove to be among the most exasperating of his life. Despite his newfound celebrity, Jones felt betrayed. Upon arrival in Brest, he sent the commissioners a draft for 24,000 livres to be used for feeding and clothing his crew. The commissioners refused to honor it. Arthur Lee and John Adams were upset at Jones's effrontery in expecting them to pay his bills. There were already too many demands on the funds that Versailles provided them. Jones would never forgive Lee or Adams for their lack of support, and he came to call the former "the Wasp" and the latter "Mr. Roundface." It was at this juncture that the friendship between Jones and Bancroft bloomed. Adams noted that Bancroft was one of the people most loudly trumpeting Jones's triumphs.[44] On his own, Jones was getting nowhere with the commissioners, Vergennes, or naval minister Sartine. His choleric temperament, his constant complaining, and his overripe sense of personal honor (deemed vanity or egotism by his enemies) did not help his cause. Furthermore, his crew was in a state of near revolt, writing to the commissioners to complain of his harsh treatment. Jones needed a friend to whom he could confide his rage and impatience. This friend would be Bancroft. In May 1778 Jones started to use Bancroft as his intermediary with Franklin. He knew that Bancroft would know when and how to present the captain's case most diplomatically. His first request for help came late that month, when he bitterly complained about the commissioners' rejection of his bill. This was a "damn'd disgrace." He could not afford to feed his crew or his British prisoners. He closed by asking Bancroft if there was any hope at all of obtaining the Dutch frigate that originally had been promised to him. Soon thereafter Franklin managed to send money for the crew. He also informed Jones that France was now willing to let the American captain take command of the *Indien*.[45]

In June, Jones was summoned to Versailles to confer with Sartine. The minister warmly congratulated him on his successes and promised him a fast frigate. Jones spent several weeks in Passy, lodging in a room near Franklin's in the Hôtel de Valentinois. On 4 July he helped to celebrate the second anniversary of the Declaration of Independence. When he was not with Franklin and Bancroft, he was socializing with the top nobility (male and, in particular, female) in Paris and Versailles. Again and again he pressed his case. If he could frighten the British people, make raids on shore, and capture ships with the small *Ranger*, imagine what he could do with a powerful frigate.

In early August 1778 he returned to Brest, to await news of a suitable ship. Soon thereafter he was jolted to learn that for a second time the timid Dutch still could not be persuaded to sell the *Indien* to the Americans. The next several months were filled with high hopes and deep disappointments. Sartine repeated his promises, sometimes saying Jones would have not just one ship but an entire squadron. Jones made detailed plans for daring raids on the British coast. Repeatedly, however, the news from Paris was negative. The French navy desperately needed to keep all available ships for itself. Sartine actually did offer Jones several different ships, but when the captain examined them he found them too small, too old, too slow, or too decrepit. He began to think that Sartine was lying to him. He even suspected that Franklin, despite his sympathetic words, was not working hard for his cause.

During these long months of frustration, Jones considered Bancroft his one true friend. Knowing that he had to control his temper when he wrote directly to Sartine and Franklin, Jones unloaded his true feelings in his letters to Bancroft. Again and again Jones wrote to Bancroft, defending himself against charges of cruelty made by his crew, complaining about the slowness of French port officials in giving him the money due from prizes he had brought to French ports, and bemoaning his lack of a fast, powerful fighting ship. He charged that Sartine had "violated . . . [his] sacred honor," and he suspected that Franklin was merely "trifling" with him. He asked Bancroft to use his good judgment in determining how best to present his case to them. Bancroft was his "good friend," his "worthy friend." Bancroft replied that Sartine had dealt Jones "scandalous treatment." By the fall of that year Bancroft was actively working with Leray de Chaumont to find a ship and arrange for the French government to purchase it. Several times Bancroft went to Versailles to see Sartine. On one occasion he had to borrow a sword from Temple Franklin. Just about anyone could enter the grounds of the Palace of Versailles, but men had to wear swords—a sign of gentlemanly status. Bancroft's sword was being repaired.[46]

In the fall of 1778 Jones, Leray de Chaumont, and Bancroft finally settled on a ship that Jones deemed suitable. It was an old East Indies merchant vessel named the *Duc de Duras*. Eventually Jones would rename it the *Bonhomme Richard*, partly to honor Franklin. The elder statesman's *Poor Richard's Almanack* had been published in France as *Les Maximes du Bonhomme Richard*. The French government formally purchased the vessel in February 1779. Over the next several months much work would need to be done to transform it into a warship—purchasing cannons and other supplies, cleaning the hull, and hiring a crew. Franklin, Leray de Chaumont, and Bancroft worked closely with Jones to arrange these details.[47]

In March 1779 Jones revealed to two persons a dark secret he had been harboring for several years. In 1773 in Tobago he had killed a member of his crew on the merchant ship he was commanding. The crew was on the verge of mutiny, and Jones probably would have been cleared of any wrongdoing. But rather than wait for a court's decision, he had fled to the American colonies and changed his name from "John Paul" to "John Paul Jones." The two people to whom he unburdened himself were Franklin and Bancroft. To Bancroft he wrote, "The Misfortune of my life will not I am assured Sink me in your Opinion, nor loose me in the esteem of a Man whose friendship I so much Value."[48]

In the spring of 1779 the French government decided to mount a powerful raid on the English coast. Jones would be given command of a squadron of ships. The army troops who would go ashore were to be commanded by the Marquis de Lafayette, who had returned to France several months earlier to lobby for more aid for the American cause. During his stay in France, Lafayette came to know Bancroft well and to like him just as much as Jones did. Together Jones and Lafayette asked Bancroft to accompany them on their expedition. As a portly scientist and man of letters, Bancroft would have cut an odd figure in such an adventure. Jones and Lafayette wanted to reward him for all his work on their behalf.[49] One can imagine what Bancroft's superiors in London would have thought of his participating in a raid on their shores. As things turned out, the raiding expedition was canceled when France and Spain decided instead to mount a joint full-scale invasion of England. Bancroft therefore never got his chance for military glory. Due to a variety of problems relating to logistics, the weather, and other factors, the large invasion likewise never took place.[50]

In August 1779 Jones was authorized to take his squadron of five ships on a raiding expedition around the British Isles. His aim was to attack British naval ships and capture as many merchant vessels as possible. This was to become his most famous voyage. On 13 August, just as his squadron was about to sail, Jones sent off a letter to each of the three men with whom he felt closest—Lafayette, Franklin, and Bancroft. To Bancroft he wrote, "I can assure you that it has given me Real concern to be deprived of the pleasure which I had in expectation from your Company on Board here on our Famous expedition." Over the next several weeks the squadron captured about two dozen prizes. Late in September, in a bloody encounter off Flamborough Head, Jones captured two British warships, the *Serapis* and the *Countess of Scarborough*. On 3 October Jones anchored off the island of Texel, in Holland. Immediately he sent off triumphal reports to Bancroft, Lafayette, Franklin, and a handful of others.[51]

In November Bancroft performed another valuable service for Jones. During the action against the *Serapis*, Jones's *Bonhomme Richard* was joined by another of the ships in his squadron, the frigate *Alliance*, captained by Pierre Landais. Jones and Landais were comparable in their pride and bilious tempers, and numerous times earlier in the cruise they had quarreled. In the aftermath of the Flamborough Head battle, Jones charged that the rebellious Landais had purposely fired broadsides at the *Bonhomme Richard* rather than at the *Serapis*. Immediately upon reaching Texel, Jones reported all this to Franklin and Bancroft and demanded a court martial for Landais. Though French, Landais was an officer in the Continental Navy. Franklin was, in effect, the commander of the U.S. Navy in Europe. Landais denied Jones's charges, claiming that if any of his shot hit the *Bonhomme Richard* this was purely an accident—after all, the *Bonhomme Richard* and the *Serapis* were latched together during much of the battle. Landais stoutly rejected accusations that he was a coward or a traitor.

In mid-November Franklin conducted a hearing on the matter in Passy. Jones himself could not attend. British ships had blockaded his squadron at Texel, and not until late December would he be able to escape. Jones, however, had sent lengthy reports to Franklin. Landais traveled to France by land and presented his case in person. To ensure fairness, Franklin asked two persons to join him as judges in the hearing. One was a close friend of Landais— Leray de Chaumont. The other a close friend of Jones—Edward Bancroft. After reviewing all the testimony, Franklin decided that he did not have sufficient evidence or authority to make a decision. He therefore forwarded the matter to Congress.[52]

Jones's reliance on Bancroft continued once the commodore made it back to France in February 1780. His ship was the frigate *Alliance*, formerly commanded by his archenemy Landais. Jones immediately set to work in Lorient ordering repairs and new supplies for the vessel. His exploits made him the toast of France, but once again he was dissatisfied. Several things upset him. First, he bitterly condemned an agreement that Leray de Chaumont had made him sign on the eve of his departure from Groix, near Lorient, on 14 August the previous summer. Among other things, this agreement stipulated the manner in which prize money would be divided between officers and crews of the squadron. Working on behalf of the French navy, Leray de Chaumont had been the chief organizer of the expedition, outfitting the ships, obtaining supplies, hiring crews, and so on. Chaumont was also charged with handling all subsequent revenues and disbursements—including prize money. Jones detested the "concordat," as the agreement was called. He objected to the proposed method for dividing up the prize money—partly because he, as the overall commander, would not receive as high a percentage as he wanted. Once the cruise was over, Jones had yet other reasons for detesting Chaumont. The chief grievance concerned prize money. The prizes included three merchantmen sent to Bergen in Norway, a handful of others that had been sent to French ports, plus the *Serapis* and the *Countess of Scarborough*. Early in 1780 the latter two ships had managed to escape British patrols and make their way from Texel to French ports. All of these vessels were supposed to be sold, with the profits going to the officers and crews who had served in the squadron. But months went by, with no news of prize money or wages.

Whereas earlier Jones had considered Chaumont one of his best friends and supporters, now he came to view him as evil, incompetent, or both. It was to Bancroft that Jones addressed many of his letters on these matters. Jones could not write in French, and Chaumont could not read English. Thus Bancroft was needed both as an interpreter and as an intermediary. Jones often relied on Bancroft's good judgment when it came to knowing how and when to approach Chaumont. Bancroft did his best to allay Jones's suspicions. He told Jones that Chaumont was not intentionally keeping money from the crews. In some cases the prize money was tied up in bureaucratic disputes within the naval ministry. In other cases there were even bigger problems. For example, rather than being a safe haven, Bergen turned out to be the worst place where Jones could have dispatched some of his prizes. British officials immediately threatened neutral Denmark (whose king also ruled Norway) with war unless the prizes were returned to their British owners. Norwegian officials quickly complied with that demand, to the consternation of Franklin, Jones, Vergennes, and Sartine. Bancroft explained all these matters to Jones and did his best to reconcile the two former friends. In the end, this proved impossible.[53]

As noted earlier, Bancroft traveled to Lorient in March 1780, to assist Jones with repairs on the *Alliance* and the rounding up of some additional men for the crew. Without blaming Leray de Chaumont for the delays, Bancroft nonetheless supported Jones in pleading that at least some of the overdue prize money be given to the crew. At around the same time, Bancroft joined Franklin and several other Americans in signing a petition asking that the *Serapis* be given or lent to the American navy so that it could convey much needed supplies to the Continental Army. That petition failed, as the French navy purchased the ship for itself at the prize auction.

Upset over his supposed mistreatment by Chaumont and the French court, Jones headed to the capital in mid-April 1780. He installed himself in the home Bancroft owned adjacent to the Hôtel de Valentinois.[54] There the two men lived for the next six weeks. When Bancroft was not accompanying Jones in visits to see Franklin or naval officials in Versailles, the two men went to dinner parties held in Jones's honor. It was also in this period that the two were inducted into the Neuf Soeurs lodge. Tucked away in a collection of Bancroft's papers owned today by some of his descendants is a scribbled copy of the words to one of the songs composed in the commodore's honor. The song is in French. Translated, its title is "Couplets Sung for the Commodore Paul Jones at a Dinner." From its first stanza one can imagine the boisterous setting in which it was sung:

> Let us empty all our bottles
> To the health of the hero
> Whose exploits and marvels
> Cause the despair of our rivals.
> In fable and in history
> Nothing equals his great feats.
> If you don't believe me
> Just ask the English.[55]

Early in June 1780, Jones returned to Lorient. Soon after he arrived there his old nemesis Landais seized control of the *Alliance*. Landais claimed that the ship was rightly his, having been given its command by Congress. Landais was egged on by Arthur Lee, who would at last be returning to America in the *Alliance*. Lee detested Franklin, and because Franklin supported Jones, Lee in turn opposed Jones. In a letter to Bancroft, Jones exploded in rage at this turn of events and blamed Franklin and French officials for letting it happen. Bancroft made the mistake of showing that letter to Franklin, who then scolded Jones for his tendency to blame everyone whenever things seemed to go wrong.[56] Early in July Landais sailed the *Alliance* from Lorient to America, leaving Jones stranded.

Through the summer and fall of 1780 Jones continued to rely on Bancroft for help in the matter of prize money. Bancroft met often with various naval officials, with little success. Jones also needed a ship. In July Franklin and Bancroft managed to obtain from the French a small frigate for him, the *Ariel*. The captain spent the next three months transforming the warship into a cargo vessel, so that he could transport gunpowder and other supplies to America. Bancroft aided him, meeting with French officials and cutting through bureaucratic red tape. As Jones prepared to return to America, he gave Bancroft control of all his financial dealings. Bancroft was charged with paying thousands of livres that Jones owed to various creditors. Jones also gave Bancroft and Franklin full power of attorney to receive the prize money he was due. Jones's letters to Bancroft repeatedly expressed his "real affection" for his friend. The captain assured Bancroft that "No man loves you more." He praised Bancroft's "great and good heart." After months of delays, including those caused by a tempest that nearly sank the *Ariel*, Jones finally sailed for America in December 1780.[57]

The bluff, thin-skinned sea captain accumulated many conquests among members of the opposite sex. Among men, however, Jones had few close friends. His letters to Bancroft reveal a male bonding that was perhaps unequaled in Jones's life. One recent Jones biographer has stated that Bancroft only "pretended" to be Jones's friend; Bancroft "was a turncoat whose devious maneuverings could have sunk the rebel cause, not to mention Jones."[58] Bancroft certainly was devious, but there are reasons to believe that he genuinely liked Jones and wished him well—while also hoping that the Americans would lose and thereby remain in the empire. One reason involves his family. When Bancroft and his wife, Penelope, ensconced themselves in their Chaillot residence in mid-1777, they were accompanied by their two children, five-year-old Edward Nathaniel and two-year-old Samuel Forrester. In October 1777 and January 1779, respectively, Penelope gave birth to daughters, Maria Frances and Julia Louisa. In April 1780 they had another son and named him John Paul Bancroft. A sixth child, Catherine Penelope, was born in September 1781. The newborn children were baptized in the nearby Catholic church, Saint Pierre de Chaillot. It stretches the limits of credulity to believe that Bancroft would have named one of his children after Jones if he had not harbored some real affection for the naval hero.[59] Moreover, the two men continued to have friendly relations, via correspondence, long after Bancroft had ceased to be a spy.

John Adams

Bancroft's relations with John Adams ran hot and cold. When Adams first arrived in Paris in April 1778, as Silas Deane's replacement, Bancroft was one of the first Americans to visit him. Before his departure, Deane had left a welcoming letter for Adams. Among other things, Deane stated that "Doct. Bancroft can be very useful to You, and as soon as You know him You will find that he merits Your Friendship and Confidence." Deane lamented seeing "merit like . . . [Bancroft's] neglected" by Congress. On about the same day Adams received that laudatory missive, he was visited by Lee ally Ralph Izard, who proceeded to blacken Bancroft's name. Izard admitted that in earlier years in London Bancroft had been a firm supporter of the American cause. Since his arrival in France, however, Bancroft had been "duped" by the corrupt, greedy cabal headed by Franklin and Deane.[60]

The general situation in the French capital was not one destined to suit the choleric Adams, who even in the best of circumstances was never one to enjoy unalloyed contentment. There is some evidence showing that his emotional outbursts, nervous breakdowns, and general cantankerousness might have been caused by a thyroid ailment called Graves' disease.[61]

In Paris in the spring of 1778, Adams was immediately disappointed to learn that an alliance with France had been cemented before his arrival. He almost decided to turn around and go home. What was worse, he discovered that Franklin was lionized in France. When Franklin took his new colleague to salons and dinner parties to meet government officials and high nobles, all that Adams could do was complain of "these incessant Dinners, and dissipations."[62]

But Adams was no Arthur Lee. The latter was venomously paranoid, whereas Adams could at least try to be open-minded and admit, grudgingly, that even Franklin sometimes performed valuable services. One can almost feel sorry for Adams upon his confronting the two armed camps of Americans that hurled insults at each other. On his arrival in Paris he said he found animosities between Deane and Arthur Lee, between Arthur Lee and Franklin, between Ralph Izard and Franklin, between Bancroft and Arthur Lee, and between William Carmichael and everyone else. He endeavored to remain "untainted with these Prejudices." He was told that Bancroft had made a fortune "dabbling" in stocks and trade.[63]

The ever punctilious Adams was shocked by the disarray of official papers sitting around openly in the Hôtel de Valentinois. He considered Franklin lazy, not realizing that the older man's way of doing business suited the French temperament. To succeed in France, one needed to bide one's time for the right diplomatic moment, and one had to attend the many dinner parties to which one was invited. Adams's no-nonsense way of doing business would never have worked there. Even a sympathetic recent biographer has admitted that "Adams was too plainspoken for diplomacy and too honest for politics."[64] Like the Lees, Adams never overcame his suspicions of French motives, and he repeatedly charged that Franklin was much too subservient to Vergennes. Arthur Lee and Adams were so combative in their dealings with the foreign minister that eventually Vergennes refused to have anything to do with them. As one of the few Founding Fathers not to invest in land companies or commerce, Adams was genuinely dismayed to learn that Deane and Franklin had engaged in private trade while holding public office. (Adams was incorrect about Franklin, who, outside of holding on to his old shares in the Vandalia Company, did not engage in any business while in France.) Because Bancroft likewise was a businessman, Adams easily concluded that he was part of the Franklin-Deane-Chaumont-Beaumarchais gang of thieves.

In his memoirs Adams castigated Bancroft's "Abuse and vilification" of Christianity in his *History of Charles Wentworth*. On the other hand, Adams admitted that Bancroft had "a clear head and a good Pen" and had written some pro-American pieces for the French-language newspaper *Affaires de l'Angleterre et Amérique*—though the ever suspicious Adams assumed that Bancroft had had help from Deane and Franklin in writing them. When Adams made his daily trips to the Hôtel de Valentinois to work with Franklin, he nearly always found Bancroft there. Adams confirmed that Bancroft was a convivial dinner companion—indeed, much too lively for Adams. He had this to say of Bancroft:

> He often dined with Us especially when We had company. Here I was not so well pleased with his Conversation, for at Table he would season his food with such enormous quantities of Chayan Pepper, which assisted by a little generous Burgundy, though he drank not a great deal, would set his tongue running at a most licentious rate both at Table and after dinner, as he gave me great paine. The Bible and the Christian Religion were his most frequent Subjects of Invective and ridicule, but he sometimes fell upon Poli[ti]cks and political Characters, and not seldom expressed Sentiments of the Royal Family and the Court of France, particularly the Queen, which I thought very improper for him to utter or for Us to hear. Much as Mr. Lee was censured for freedoms of Speech, I never heard a tenth part so much from him as from Bancroft. The Queens intrigues with Madame the Duchess of Poli[g]nac, her constant dissipation, her habits of expence and profusion, her giddy thoughtless conduct were for a long time almost constant Topicks of his Tittle Tattle.[65]

Thanks to Adams, one can see a tiny sliver of Bancroft's family life: "He also had with him in France, a Woman, with whom he lived, and who by the french was called la Femme de Monsieur Bancroft. She never made her Appearance. She had several Children, very handsome and promising whom I saw in France and two of whom I have since seen in America, with complexions as blooming as they had in their Childhood. One of them behaved very well—the other has been much censured, I know not how truly."[66] Like some others, Adams assumed that Bancroft's woman was not his wife.

There are just a few scraps of evidence to show that any of the prominent men with whom Bancroft dealt might have met Penelope. In May 1783 Lafayette invited Dr. and Mrs. Bancroft to dinner. It is not known if Penelope accepted the offer.[67] She and the children were never mentioned in any of the letters Bancroft exchanged with Franklin, John Paul Jones, and others. About all that is known of the children is that those born in France were baptized in Catholic churches in Passy or Chaillot.

Paradoxically, although Adams disliked Bancroft's business speculations and supposed irreligion, he appreciated Bancroft's talents and loyalty to the American cause. In February and March 1779 Adams supported Franklin's choice of Bancroft to travel to England to arrange for an exchange of prisoners. Although Adams rejected some of the worst accusations against Bancroft made by Arthur Lee and his allies, by the time Adams left France the first time, in June 1779, he had come to believe that Chaumont, Bancroft, and several others were greedily controlling American policies in order to favor their business investments. He declared he had "an entire distrust" of Bancroft, who had "too irregular and eccentric a character." Back in his home in Braintree, Massachusetts, in the fall of 1779, Adams learned that Congress was considering appointing Bancroft official secretary either to Franklin or himself—Adams was preparing to return to France as a peace commissioner. Adams exclaimed that if this happened, America ought to "retire and weep." He wrote to his friends in Congress about Bancroft's low character as a stock-jobber and his failings in religion and morals. Adams must have breathed a sigh of relief when he learned that Congress had finally settled on other men for the two positions.[68]

Surprisingly, when Adams hurried to Paris in the fall of 1782 to take part in the peace negotiations, he seems to have forgotten all his old misgivings. Adams, Bancroft, Franklin, and John Jay sometimes dined together to discuss negotiating strategies. Occasionally Bancroft sat in on the meetings between the Americans and the British representatives. Adams even sought out Bancroft for advice. He wanted Bancroft's insights on the character of George

III, his ministers, and the British peace commissioners. He found that Bancroft was extremely knowledgeable on issues like Gibraltar and other European affairs. Moreover, Bancroft's friendships with persons in Versailles provided Adams with details about Vergennes's personality and motives. As far as can be determined, Bancroft never gave Adams any false or misleading information.[69]

The Mission to Ireland

Like most of the Americans in Paris, the French also trusted Bancroft completely. Throughout these years Bancroft had easy access to ministerial offices in Versailles. This was demonstrated in a remarkable way in 1779, when Vergennes selected Bancroft for a secret mission to Ireland. As mentioned earlier, in the spring of that year John Paul Jones, Lafayette, Vergennes, and Sartine were busily preparing for a full-scale Franco-Spanish invasion of England. They knew that many in Ireland were chafing at British rule. Irish merchants abhorred the embargo on all trade with America. Presbyterians in the North were clamoring for an independent Irish parliament. Catholics in the South had disliked Protestant dominion since the sixteenth century. Lafayette and the ministers therefore thought that if an Irish rebellion could be mounted, this would create a distraction for British forces, benefitting the Franco-Spanish invasion. But the French government would need to send someone to Ireland to investigate the situation there. The person Lafayette recommended was Bancroft. The marquis's letter of 23 May to Vergennes is worth quoting in detail:

> None of the Americans in Paris (Mr. Bancroft excepted) has earned our confidence enough to be charged with such a commission. I have convinced the latter to run the risks of the undertaking, and his intelligence combined with his honesty has made me look upon it as a great good fortune that he should be willing to do this. He will pay you his respects tomorrow or the day after and will leave Paris Wednesday to go to Calais. The passport you will give him, as if he were an English merchant . . . will enable him to get to Dover. He will cross England under the same disguise and embark at Liverpool for Dublin, Londonderry, and other important places. . . .
>
> I advised Dr. Bancroft to go very slowly with the Irish, to dismiss at first any idea of independence, to speak only of redressing wrongs and

bringing the English government back to reason. I told him to emphasize America's interests and French disinterestedness, to trust only a few of those people who lead others, and finally, to incur no obligations and proceed with moderation and circumspection. . . . I was obliged to mention the plan [to Dr. Franklin] in order to obtain Dr. Bancroft's services. . . . I shall add that since this negotiation must be kept very secret, the secret should remain among you, M. le Comte de Maurepas, and me, and I told the Doctor [Franklin] only what was absolutely necessary.

I believe Mr. Bancroft's speedy departure is all the more important as it seems that Irish affairs must soon take a decisive turn.[70]

Franklin gave his full assent. He urged Bancroft to tell the Irish they were welcome to immigrate to America and that America would welcome their trade. He suggested that Bancroft write some discreet pieces for Irish newspapers—nothing too inflammatory, but enough to stir up some "good Effects."[71] Bancroft left Paris around the first of June and returned a little more than three weeks later. His actual time in Ireland was less than two weeks. But that was enough for him to travel to several cities, meet with a variety of political and religious leaders, and canvas public opinion. Upon his return to Paris, he sent a detailed report to Vergennes. He stated that the Irish were not yet ready for a major rebellion. The Presbyterians and Catholics detested each other and thus would not cooperate in a fight against the British. Furthermore, many Irish volunteer troops would probably side with Britain against any French invasion. Bancroft said that with French aid a few thousand troops could take the city of Cork. But his general conclusion was that France should abandon any plans involving Ireland.[72]

As in so many other instances with Bancroft, one can interpret his Irish mission in various ways. On the one hand, one could say that he was merely giving an honest statement of the facts. Historians of eighteenth-century Ireland agree that his assessment of the situation in 1779 was accurate. But one could also postulate that his report aided his British superiors. By dissuading the French from meddling in Irish affairs, he was keeping the British from sending more troops and ships there—forces that could be used in America. Finally, one can argue that his report also helped the French and the Americans. Persuading America's ally not to waste men and money in a hopeless rebellion in Ireland freed up additional French resources for the war in America.

Personal Affairs

By the spring of 1783 Bancroft realized that his work in France was done and that the time had come to take his family home—that is, to London. He also had financial reasons for the move. His quarterly payments from the British government had been stopped a year earlier. Early in 1783 Shelburne ordered them reinstituted. However, Shelburne was forced to resign almost immediately thereafter. The new North-Fox government did not honor his pledge. Apparently this had nothing to do with Bancroft personally. The new ministry felt no obligation to continue payments promised by predecessors. Numerous secret agents, peace commissioners, and other mid-or lower-rank officials met the same problem once the war was over and the government tried to put its finances back in order.[73]

During his years in France Bancroft had little time for his medical and scientific interests. His earlier achievements in these areas won him election in 1779 as a corresponding member of the Société Royale de Médecine, though there is no indication that he ever participated actively in that body's meetings. On occasion he offered medical advice to some of the Americans in France who fell ill at one time or another.[74]

He devoted much more attention to business investments, but they profited him little or nothing. Like so many gamblers, whenever he did make a killing, he plowed the winnings back into another speculation, which, as often as not, proved a disaster. In the spring of 1778, both John Adams and John Paul Jones remarked that Bancroft was making a fortune through his stock speculations and trading.[75] That was, as it turns out, only half true. Whenever Bancroft was flush with cash, he seems to have let it show, buying drinks for everyone and persuading some friends to join him in his ventures. Like many businessmen, however, he tried to keep up a good front, concealing the times when he suffered deep losses.

In May 1778 Paul Wentworth sent Bancroft's Paris banker 30,000 livres as Bancroft's share in a recent investment. Thereafter, however, the joint ventures of those two men led to losses of far greater amounts. Throughout the Revolution Bancroft purchased sundry goods for shipment to America, to be sold to merchants or to Washington's army. One can find dozens of letters exchanged between Bancroft and his various partners. In December 1778, for example, Joseph Wharton congratulated Bancroft upon the recapture of a brig that was carrying some of his merchandise; the brig had been taken by the British and then recaptured by an American ship. The merchant with whom Bancroft dealt most regularly was Franklin's nephew, Jonathan Williams Jr., stationed in Nantes. Working on commission, Williams arranged for the shipment of Bancroft's items on whatever ships happened to be sailing for America. These items included medical supplies, cambrics, silks, shalloons, hardware, plus other types of goods. In November 1779 Williams mentioned that Bancroft currently owed him 804 livres. In payment for his services, Williams was charging his friend a low commission rate of just 1 percent; this means that recently he had dispatched at least 80,000 livres worth of Bancroft's merchandise. In other letters Williams referred to some trunks carrying Bancroft's goods; the trunks were valued in livres at 5,000, 16,500, 22,000, and 23,000.[76]

From these bits of information it is obvious that Bancroft was heavily involved in trade. It should be pointed out, however, that his privileged position in the Passy household won his personal business no guarantees of safety. Once out of Nantes or other ports, the ships that carried his merchandise faced the same risks as any others. Most of Bancroft's goods apparently did reach America, though sometimes they suffered water damage and had to be sold at discount.

There were few American products available for sale in Europe, especially after 1778, when the British took control of most of the southern colonies and their tobacco. Moreover, there was always the risk that ships leaving America might be captured. Therefore, Bancroft, Williams, and scores of other American and French merchants who succeeded in getting their cargoes to America chose to invest their money in Continental loan office certificates. This initially looked like a safe decision. By December 1779, however, Williams was informing Bancroft that the depreciation of American currency was so drastic that all their profits were evaporating; Williams bemoaned the "mournful picture" of their situation. The biggest blow came after March 1780, when American currency was officially decreased to one-fortieth of its previous value. Over the next several years many American and French businessmen complained to Congress of how they faced financial ruin because of the rampant inflation that destroyed the value of the money they were paid for their goods. Bancroft even published a short pamphlet exposing this injustice. It seems, therefore, that his trade with America ended up hurting him deeply. In August 1781 he wrote to Franklin asking for a loan of 1,500 livres. He said that the total volume of his trade had been about 1 million livres but that he was still owed 200,000 livres. Franklin lent him the money, and somehow Bancroft was able to repay it two months later. In all probability, he never recovered most of the 200,000 livres.[77]

Williams and Bancroft also engaged in another type of business—privateering. They owned shares in several ships that preyed on small English merchant vessels in the channel. In May 1780 Williams reported that their privateering ventures were doing well and asked Bancroft to reinvest their profits in additional expeditions. In August Williams praised Bancroft as "an excellent partner" and again told him to keep reinvesting their winnings. One can only guess how large their profits were. Most of the captured ships were small and brought in what Williams called "trifling" amounts when sold at auction. Since neither Williams nor Bancroft was wealthy at the end of the war, it is probably safe to conclude that their privateering profits were just enough to liquidate their losses from other investments.[78]

Bancroft kept a hand in sundry other types of business also. Hoping to revive his quercitron import enterprise once the war was over, sometime in 1780 he enticed John Paul Jones to invest in it.[79] Bancroft retained and in some cases increased his shares in the Vandalia, Indiana, and Illinois and Wabash land companies.[80] These speculations in land companies would never prove profitable for him or for any of the hundreds of other persons who invested in them over the years. Once the Revolution was over, the United States government refused to acknowledge the charters granted earlier by the British government or by the various colonies. Eventually, all of the original thirteen states relinquished their claims to western lands, and most of that vast area became the Northwest Territory in 1787.

Sometime in the fall of 1780 Bancroft, Samuel Wharton, Francis Coffyn, and Jan Ingenhousz invested heavily in the shipment of linens to America. Coffyn was a Flemish merchant based in Dunkirk. Ingenhousz was a Dutch physician and scientist as well as an old friend of Franklin. Wharton himself was returning to America, where he would handle the sale of these goods as well as future shipments. Ingenhousz invested £1,000 in the venture, with the others investing even more. Eleven of the initial fifteen parcels of linens reached America, but there was water damage to some of those that did arrive. Coffyn, Bancroft, and Ingenhousz eventually received just a small part of what they were owed. Over the next couple of years Ingenhousz pestered Franklin with numerous letters, beseeching him to make Wharton or Bancroft give him a full report on what had happened to the linens. There is some indication that Wharton was an unscrupulous scoundrel in this and other affairs, offering flimsy excuses for not sending his partners their fair shares of the profits.[81]

In March 1783 Bancroft began to make preparations to move back to London. After getting his wife and six children settled there, he planned to travel to America. There he hoped to take care of a host of private business matters. Because he had been absent from America so long and because he might need the help of some prominent people there, he needed letters of introduction from persons who knew him in France. He had no trouble obtaining such testimonials. The lodge of the Neuf Soeurs gave him a certificate praising his abilities and zeal and asking that all lodges in America welcome him.[82] From Benjamin Franklin he obtained a letter to Robert R. Livingston, the secretary of foreign affairs. Franklin lauded Bancroft as "a very intelligent, sensible man, well acquainted with the state of affairs here, and who has heretofore been employed in the service of Congress. I have long known him, and esteem him highly."[83]

John Jay gave Bancroft letters for Livingston, as well as for Robert Morris (superintendent of finances), Elias Boudinot (president of Congress), and George Clinton (governor of New York). To Boudinot, Jay wrote, "You will I hope recieve [sic] this Letter from the Hands of Doctor Bancroft, whom I take the Liberty of recommending as well as introducing to your Excellency. I have had the Pleasure of being intimately acquainted with this Gentleman, for this Year past, and assure you that in the Course of it, he has to my Knowledge been a useful and zealous Friend to America. His long residence in this Country, and his acquaintance with our Affairs in Europe from the Beginning of the War, enable him to afford you much interesting information."[84]

Matthew Ridley, a merchant and Maryland's agent in France, likewise provided Bancroft with a letter to Robert Morris. Ridley wrote that Bancroft "is a gentleman with whom I have been long acquainted and flatter myself from the Knowledge I have of him you will receive mutual pleasure in being known to each other."[85]

Finally, Bancroft carried with him a letter from Lafayette to George Washington. In it the marquis stated, "I have long known him, first of all in

England and afterwards in France where he ever appeared to me a Sensible and a warm friend to our Cause. Agreeable to that party Spirit, which to my great concern has ever divided our ministers or envoys in Europe, Doctor Bancroft has been praised by some and criticized by others. But I owe him the Justice to Say that his public opinions, and his Conduct have always appeared to me Such as becomes a Citizen of the United States."[86]

Bancroft asked Temple Franklin to forward to him in London any letters that might arrive for him in France. On 14 June 1783 he and his family finally left their home in Chaillot, taking a coach to Dunkirk and from there sailing to England.[87] Bancroft's days as a spy were over at last.

9 *Arthur Lee: Spy Catcher? Benjamin Franklin: Traitor? Edward Bancroft: Murderer?*

Arthur Lee and the "Outing" of Bancroft

Over the years many historians have wondered how Edward Bancroft managed to fool everyone, both the Americans and the French. There was nothing new in his methods. Ciphers, aliases, invisible inks, and the depositing of messages in hiding places had been standard fare for centuries. Certainly Bancroft's intelligence and perhaps his carefulness helped him. But his daily intimacy with so many important figures nonetheless has led many to speculate that his undercover work must have been spotted by someone.

As a consequence, numerous authors have argued that indeed Bancroft did not escape detection entirely. It has long been known that Arthur and William Lee charged Bancroft with treason. With their ally Ralph Izard, the Lees lumped Bancroft, Franklin, Deane, Beaumarchais, Leray de Chaumont, Jonathan Williams Jr., and numerous others into what they considered an evil cabal of profiteers who put their private business interests above patriotic duty. Because the Lees and Izard did not have much to do in Paris, they had ample time to imagine conspiracies and dispatch innumerable scathing reports to Congress. Most of their charges were well off the mark. Congressional investigations into the financial records of Franklin and Deane never turned up any malfeasance. Most of the Americans working in France—and most of the delegates in Congress—spent time on private enterprises while also working for the public cause. Franklin was an exception to that, which made the charges against him doubly wrong. The accusations by the Lees and Izard were also hypocritical, given their own participation in land companies and trade.

At any rate, this meddlesome trio in mid-1777 claimed to have proof that Bancroft was a British spy. Several scholars have picked up on this and concluded that Franklin and others were negligent in not accepting the charges. Arthur Lee was the first to make this allegation, but no one besides his brother and Izard believed him. Part of the reason lay in Lee's personality. He tended to assume the worst about everyone, except for his relatives and closest friends. As one author has written, for Lee "suspicion was addiction."[1] He saw spies everywhere. Even John Adams, who abhorred Bancroft's religious views and stockjobbing, refused to believe he was a traitor. Instead, Adams complained that the Lee brothers and Izard's "Prejudices and violent Tempers would raise Quarrells in the Elisian Fields if not in Heaven."[2]

Until now, historians have been satisfied in concluding that, if Franklin and others rejected the "proof" against Bancroft, the reason was Arthur Lee's personality. However, what no previous author has realized is that Arthur Lee's evidence was faulty. In other words, he and his allies happened by accident to reach a correct conclusion.

The skein of events in this story began in the summer of 1777, when the Lee brothers received information indicating that about a year earlier Bancroft had met with George III's Privy Council. Supposedly this had happened on two separate occasions soon after Bancroft's return to London following his initial meetings with Deane. To the Lees, there was but one conclusion: Bancroft was passing secrets to the enemy. When Bancroft heard what the Lees were reporting about him, he was livid. He and Arthur Lee nearly came to blows. Bancroft asked his friend and London business partner Joseph Wharton to track down the source of this calumny. In September 1777 Wharton had a long conversation with a Dr. Ruston, who had given the original story to Arthur Lee. On questioning, Ruston admitted that he himself had not seen Bancroft enter the Privy Council chambers. Instead, Ruston said he was told this by a sea captain. Ruston refused to name this mysterious sea captain, other than to say that he was an American who had come to know Bancroft years earlier in Surinam. Ruston conjectured that the captain had learned of the Privy Council visits from Bancroft's servants. Ruston told Wharton that he was sorry for any trouble that he had caused, and he promised that he would try to clear the matter up. But he said this would be difficult, for the sea captain was no longer in England.

It was clear to Wharton that Ruston's story was hardly credible. After their initial meeting, Ruston avoided seeing Wharton again. Moreover, Wharton concluded that if Bancroft was indeed a secret agent he would never let his servants know about it.[3]

When Bancroft received Wharton's report in November 1777, he immediately showed it to Franklin and to the Lees. It had the desired effect of refuting the charges against him. The Lees and Izard apparently realized the weakness of their case, and they never raised this issue again. What is known today, but not by the Lees and others in 1777, is that whenever Bancroft was in London he met with Paul Wentworth and occasionally with William Eden. As much as was possible, his identity was kept a secret from others. He certainly never met with the Privy Council. That body was much too exalted ever to have met with a lowly spy.

That did not mean, however, that the bothersome trio gave up in their campaign against Bancroft and the other supposed war profiteers. In April 1778 the Lees and Izard, for example, accused Bancroft of having leaked information in London about the Franco-American alliance a couple of weeks before its actual signing on 6 February. In early April an out-of-work American ship captain named Musco Livingston had just arrived in Paris from London. He told Izard that while he was in London he had seen a letter in Bancroft's hand intended for one of the Wharton brothers. Bancroft tipped them off about the treaty of alliance, which was due to be signed early in February, and he told them to invest their money accordingly. Both the Whartons and Bancroft denied this, though it is now clear that they were lying. The three had indeed been using their insider information to guide their investments.[4]

Arthur Lee righteously sent a copy of Livingston's report to Congress. What Lee did not reveal to Congress was that his own brother William had also been using insider information for speculations on the London market. Nor did Arthur mention that early in February 1778 William probably also had leaked details about the treaty to his London partners. Finally, Arthur did not tell Congress that at the very time that the alliance was being signed, on 6 February, he himself had written to the Earl of Shelburne, then a leader of the parliamentary opposition, giving him full details of the treaty. Lee was an ardent anti-Catholic Francophobe, and he urged Shelburne to push the English government to try one more time for reconciliation with the Americans. French postal agents intercepted that letter and gave a copy to Vergennes. This fueled Vergennes's distrust of the dislikable Virginian. Apparently Vergennes did not show the letter to Franklin and Deane. If he had done so, Franklin and Deane would most likely have concluded that, if anyone was a traitor, it was Arthur Lee.[5]

This matter continued to boil for another year. Bancroft extricated himself from any suspicion by blaming Arthur Lee's secretary, John Thornton, for divulging early news of the alliance in London. Like so many others, Thornton also was using his insider information to speculate in the London market. As a result of these suspicions, Thornton eventually fled to London. Lee reluctantly had to admit that his secretary had been a British agent.

Previous historians have failed to note John Paul Jones's role in exonerating his friend Bancroft. In the early months of 1779 Jones had several meetings with Musco Livingston and Joseph Wharton. (Wharton had by then moved to France, before his return to America.) Jones was able to get Livingston to retract his statements about Bancroft and admit that he was unsure whose handwriting he had seen on letters in January 1778.[6]

Benjamin Franklin as a Fellow Traveler

Several writers have asserted that not just Arthur Lee but also Benjamin Franklin and Silas Deane knew that Bancroft was an enemy agent. They not only knew about Bancroft but were his partners in crime. The case for each of these men will be dealt with separately.

Shortly after Franklin arrived in France, he was warned about British spies who would follow his every step. The person who alerted him to this danger was Juliana Ritchie, an American living in France. Although she had never met Franklin, she wrote to him on 12 January 1777. She stated, "I proceed to the purpose of this letter, which is to inform you Sir, that you are surrounded *with Spies,* who watch your every movement who you Visit, and by whom you are visited. Of the latter there are who pretend to be friends to the cause of your country but *that* is a mere pretense. Your own good sence will easilly infer the *motive* of *their conduct.*"[7]

A week later Franklin responded to her: "I am much oblig'd to you for your kind Attention to my Welfare, in the Information you give me. I have no doubt of its being well founded. But as it is impossible to discover in every case the Falsity of pretended Friends who would know our Affairs; the more so to prevent being watch'd by Spies, when interested People may think proper to place them for that purpose; I have long observ'd one Rule which prevents any Inconvenience from such Practices. It is simply this, to be concern'd in no Affairs that I should blush to have made public; and to do nothing but what Spies may see and welcome. When a Man's Actions are just and honourable, the more they are known, the more his Reputation is increas'd and establish'd. If I was sure therefore that my Valet de Place was a Spy, as probably he is, I think I should not discharge him for that, if in other Respects I lik'd him."[8]

Numerous authors, both admirers and detractors of Franklin, have parsed every phrase in his letter, as if they were clues to the Holy Grail. In doing so, they have given the letter much more importance than it deserves. Ritchie was a rather impecunious American expatriate living in a Benedictine convent in Cambrai, about a hundred miles from Paris. She had no connections with the British, American, or French governments, knew nothing about espionage, and did not even know the purpose of Franklin's trip to France. Franklin did not need her advice in order to know he would be surrounded by both British and French spies. Finally, he knew the likelihood that Ritchie's letter and his own, both being sent through the regular post, might be opened and read by postal inspectors.

Historians have ranged widely in their interpretations of Franklin's response. Some have said his letter reveals his old age; he was getting lazy and careless. Some have said it reflects his customary humor and bravado. A handful have said that Franklin welcomed having British spies like Bancroft in his midst, so that he could feed them false information.

There is some ground for believing that the insouciant tone of his letter really did reflect his beliefs. Throughout 1777 Franklin might have wanted the British to know about French secret aid. This would have either of two consequences. It might prompt the British to grant American independence before a general European war erupted. Or Britain, armed with intelligence "stolen" from Franklin, might put pressure on the French, forcing Versailles to enter the war more quickly than it intended. Either option would have suited Franklin. Similarly, he had reasons for desiring French spies to know much of what he was doing. He wanted Vergennes to be aware that British emissaries were coming to Passy, seeking reconciliation. If Versailles thought that there might be an Anglo-American rapprochement, that could bring France into the war earlier rather than later.

But all of the above is mere speculation. One of Franklin's most famous maxims from *Poor Richard's Almanack* was "Let all men know thee, but no man know thee thoroughly." Throughout his life Franklin could be taciturn, often keeping his innermost feelings a secret even from his closest friends and colleagues. Why then would he reveal his true thoughts on an important matter to a lady who was a total stranger? The most that one can deduce from his letter is that he was trying to put at ease a worried fellow American.

Still, the question of how this astute, perceptive statesman could have been fooled by Bancroft ceases to go away. Most of his biographers simply note that this was a monumental error of judgment. Or they say that, like so many others, Franklin was duped by the clever Bancroft. Franklin had a weakness for admirers and for talented young men who shared his wide-ranging interests. Thus, in Franklin's eyes, Bancroft was just one among dozens of acolytes who sought the elder man's support and companionship.

Over the past several decades, however, a handful of authors have maintained that Franklin was not duped. According to them, Bancroft accomplished what he did because Franklin himself was a British agent. Readers will not find this topic even mentioned in any of the mainstream biographies of Franklin. All of the most highly respected scholarly and popular books on Franklin stress his American patriotism and, after 1776, his hatred of the British government. Authors like Edmund S. Morgan, Walter Isaacson, Gordon S. Wood, H. W. Brands, Stacy Schiff, and J. A. Leo Lemay, among many others, do not give as much as a sentence to the theory that Franklin was a British agent. Is there a conspiracy of silence? Are they hiding Ben Franklin's nasty little secret? No. The basic reason why mainstream historians do not mention this topic is that it has no merit. The so-called evidence that Franklin himself was a spy is so flimsy as to be virtually nonexistent.

The thesis that Franklin was a spy began to surface in the 1960s. In a general history of the British Secret Service, Richard Deacon confidently asserted that Franklin was "an active secret agent for the British."[9] Furthermore, he noted, Franklin allowed Bancroft to organize a Secret Service cell in Passy. Deacon provided not one iota of evidence to support his claims. As noted in an earlier chapter, there was no British "Secret Service" in the eighteenth century and no "cell" in Passy. Deacon apparently based his judgment on the theory that, because Franklin knew Bancroft for so long and so well, he "must" have known what Bancroft was up to.

It is easy to see the flaw in such an assumption. If Franklin "must" have known about Bancroft, then John Paul Jones, John Adams, Lafayette, and numerous others should have been able to do so likewise. But no one has ever accused those persons of being British agents. Even more, Vergennes and the chief of police in Paris, Jean-Charles-Pierre Lenoir, should have discovered Bancroft's clandestine work. Paris almost literally crawled with secret agents and informers who worked for the Paris police. A common saying in eighteenth-century Paris was that when two people spoke to each other, a third was listening.[10] Yet, as noted earlier, Vergennes trusted Bancroft so much that he sent him on a secret mission to Ireland in 1779.

The most famous and most detailed "exposé" of Franklin's treachery appeared in 1972, with Cecil B. Currey's *Code Number 72/Ben Franklin: Patriot or Spy?* Currey is guilty of so many factual errors, illogical inferences, and groundless suppositions that it is hard to know where to begin. His basic thesis is that Benjamin Franklin was a greedy opportunist who cared little about American independence. He traveled to France in 1776 for selfish reasons. Afraid for his own skin, he wanted to escape the violence in America and avoid British retribution against him—in the event that Britain won. In France he saw endless opportunities for personal gain. He was a full-fledged partner of Bancroft, Deane, Chaumont, Beaumarchais, and other war profiteers who sold rusty muskets and other inferior goods to the needy Americans for inflated prices. With his business associates, he continued to lobby endlessly for the land companies in which he had invested. He heedlessly rejected warnings about spies from Juliana Ritchie and Arthur Lee. By appointing his nephew Jonathan William Jr. to a position as commercial agent in Nantes, he thereby came to control all the comings and goings of ships and cargoes from there and other ports. Franklin's nepotism was boundless; in addition to favoring his nephew, he lobbied for an official diplomatic appointment for his grandson Temple.

Before leaving America in 1776, he showered favors on his son-in-law Richard Bache, winning for him a contract to print the new paper currency and appointing him his successor as postmaster general. Because Arthur Lee was on the scent of Bancroft and perhaps even of Franklin himself, Franklin did all that he could to keep Arthur Lee out of Paris and uninformed about what was going on there. Finally, Franklin never cared about American independence. In meetings with Paul Wentworth in December 1777 and January 1778, Franklin was willing to scuttle the pending alliance with France if Britain could offer him sufficient money and land in bribes. In 1782 and 1783 Franklin again held out the hope for reconciliation with Britain. He would sacrifice American independence if he saw it might be in his personal interest. Finally, according to Currey, Franklin professed allegiance to both England and America, so that he would come out ahead regardless of who won the war.

There simply is not space here to deal completely with the startling range of Currey's allegations. I must limit myself to a few specific examples of his arguments and their specious foundations. The title of his book refers to the code number that Paul Wentworth used in his letters to William Eden. When Wentworth wrote from Paris, he generally used the number "72" when referring to Franklin, but the conclusion Currey draws from this fact is ludicrous. A glance at letters from Wentworth as well as from other British agents reveals that they used code names or numbers for most of the persons and places they discussed. Thus, for example, in his letters to William Eden, Wentworth did indeed use the number 72 when referring to Franklin. In addition, Wentworth used 51 for Silas Deane, 116 for Arthur Lee, 201 for Vergennes, 103 for Stormont, 138 for Lord North, 71 for France, 64 for England, and 202 for Versailles.[11] Even a schoolchild should be able to see that this does not mean that Franklin was a spy any more than any of the other persons were. If Currey had been on to something important, what he should have been able to demonstrate is that Franklin used this code number for himself when writing to other British agents or William Eden. However, no such letters exist. Indeed, Currey does not appear to have visited any British archives while doing his research.

Some of Currey's facts are accurate—up to a point. It is true that Franklin dismissed the warnings of Arthur Lee and Juliana Ritchie. Currey's charge that Franklin was careless about his official papers, letting them lie around openly in the Hôtel de Valentinois does carry some weight. However, if Franklin allowed a heap of unguarded papers to accumulate, the cause was not his negligence but rather the sheer volume of the materials. Congress failed to give him an official secretary. Temple Franklin and Franklin's French clerk were overwhelmed by their jobs. The number of letters and other items from Franklin's eight and a half years in Paris amounts to twice the amount of all materials from the other seventy-five years of his life.

Currey is correct in noting that Franklin tried to avoid Arthur Lee as much as possible, but that was because of Lee's bilious temperament, not because Lee was interfering in Franklin's espionage and profiteering. It is likewise true that Franklin was guilty of nepotism. However, that same charge could be brought against most of the Founding Fathers, including Arthur Lee and John Adams. Moreover, nepotism is not the same thing as espionage. Currey accurately states that Franklin maintained his share in the Vandalia land company. However, Currey errs when he says that Vandalia consumed Franklin's attention. What is more, Currey is absolutely wrong when he states—ad nauseum—that Franklin committed little time to diplomacy, because his private business interests were his primary focus. As noted above, Franklin engaged in no private trade of any kind in France. Indeed, once Franklin retired from his Philadelphia print shop in 1748, he devoted himself primarily to public service and spent hardly any time on private business for the remainder of his life. Arthur Lee and the British government assumed that Franklin was working actively for private gain, and Currey has made the mistake of accepting their conjectures as true.

Given the lack of proof for his conclusions, one might wonder how Currey manages to concoct an entire book on the subject. Beyond the fact that virtually every page of his book contains at least one large or small factual error, there are four other ways in which his argument is constructed. The first is guilt by association. Repeatedly he notes that Franklin consorted with British agents like Bancroft, George Lupton, Joseph Hynson, and John Thornton. But so did John Adams, Arthur Lee, John Paul Jones, and many others. Yet Currey does not accuse them of being traitors. If Franklin had dealings with British agents, this does not mean he knew they were spies. When he did find out about the treachery of persons like Hynson and Thornton, he had nothing further to do with them. Currey also states that Franklin knew all about Silas Deane's treachery. This will be dealt with further below.

Currey pads his theory of guilt by association by overestimating the number of spies who were close to Franklin. He is one of those historians who exaggerate the size and efficiency of the nonexistent British "Secret Service." He says that Wentworth controlled the bureau in Paris and that Bancroft ran the cell in the Passy household. They ensnared Franklin into their web as soon as he set foot in France. In addition to Bancroft and other British agents whom historians have long known about, Currey states that Jonathan Williams Jr., William Carmichael, and Samuel Wharton also were spies. In other words, Franklin could hardly have taken a step without tripping over a British agent. Given Franklin's astuteness, Currey says, he must have known what was going on around him. Currey offers no evidence for the supposed treason of Williams, Wharton, or Carmichael.

Currey's second method comes into play when he has no documentation to support an assertion. In cases like this, he resorts scores of times to phrases like "must have," "may be supposed," "allows for the possibility," "may have," and "could only be."[12] All historians have to speculate occasionally and employ such phrases. But a perusal of Currey's book reveals that he relies on this sleight of hand again and again.

A third method he uses is to declare that key pieces of evidence were intentionally destroyed. Repeatedly when speaking of Franklin, Deane, Jonathan Williams Jr., and others he states that they must have burned or hidden all documents that would be incriminating.[13] In this way Currey provides an excuse for why he has no concrete proof for his thesis.

Finally, when faced with documents showing that Franklin was a loyal American, Currey boldly proclaims that the evidence actually means the opposite of what it says. This is an astounding feat, given that a veritable mountain of documents indicates overwhelmingly that Franklin was a staunch American patriot. After he was attacked viciously by Solicitor General Wedderburn in the Cockpit in 1774, Franklin's resentment against the British government knew no limits. When he signed the treaty of alliance with France on 6 February 1778, he wore the same blue Manchester velvet suit that he had worn on that day in Whitehall four years earlier. By 1778 the suit was faded and worn, but he insisted on wearing it for "a little revenge." Throughout the Revolution he bitterly complained of the British burning of towns, destruction of crops, and other depredations against Americans. During the peace negotiations he argued vehemently for compensation to those Americans who had suffered from these atrocities. In these same peace negotiations Franklin held out against any but the vaguest sorts of compensation for Loyalists who had lost property. His enmity toward Loyalists extended even to members of his family. When his son William, the last royal governor of New Jersey, opted to stay loyal to Britain, Benjamin vowed that he would never again have anything to do with him. To the end of his life Benjamin refused to consider any reconciliation. The old man might have been deficient as a father, but surely he was an ardent American.[14]

So how does Currey deal with these and so many other examples of Franklin's steadfast loyalty to the United States? Again and again, he argues that Franklin was merely camouflaging his true sentiments. In order to hide his perfidy, he wrote letters and essays that were designed to persuade everyone that he loved America and hated Britain. In short, Currey would have us believe that Franklin managed to fool all his contemporaries as well as the vast majority of historians. According to Currey, the thousands of private and public items that Franklin wrote from 1776 to his death were all lies, concealing his greed and treason.[15]

If Currey were correct, and Franklin was indeed a secret agent and friend of Britain, one might suppose that the British government would have been aware of this. Nowhere is there any indication in British archives that George III, Lord North, Lord Suffolk, William Eden, or any other British official viewed Franklin as "one of ours." A cursory reading of George III's letters reveals that he detested Franklin. Apparently Currey would have us believe that the king slyly injected these anti-Franklin barbs into his letters in order to prevent future historians from discovering the truth. Moreover, if one looks at the correspondence of Richard Oswald, Alleyne Fitzherbert, and other British negotiators in Paris in 1782–83, what one sees again and again is that Franklin was a dogged negotiator, one who wanted revenge for British atrocities in America, a man who would stop at nothing short of immediate and full independence. An excellent example of this can be found in Alleyne Fitzherbert's letter of 9 February 1783 to Lord Grantham, the secretary of state for foreign affairs. The preliminary articles of peace had been signed on 30 November 1782, but Fitzherbert was still in Paris, haggling with Franklin and the other American commissioners about possible revisions.

Fitzherbert complained to Grantham of Franklin's "chicanery" and said that some of Franklin's new demands were "ludicrous." Fitzherbert regretfully concluded that "Dr Franklin seems anxious to return to America, which I am sorry for, being persuaded that he will do his utmost, when there, to prevent all Revival of Goodwill & Cordiality with the Mother Country, his Rancour & Inveteracy against which are as violent as ever."[16] This is the person whom Currey would have us believe was actually working secretly for the British.

Unfortunately, Currey's work has won a small contingent of adherents. In a review published shortly after the book appeared, Forrest McDonald, one of the most respected American historians of the past half century, called Currey a "cautious, tough-minded scholar," and claimed that the book presents a case against Franklin so strong that "any jury in the land would vote to convict." McDonald judged that "sentimental attachment to cherished myths will . . . protect Franklin among historians awhile longer, although in the end his removal from the roster of saints is assured."[17] Down to the present day a small number of historians have continued to repeat Currey's charges, though none has been able to go any further than he did in providing hard evidence.[18] Currey's ideas have had an even greater life on the Internet. His thesis appeals to many conspiracy theorists, who seek to find evil where none exists and who refuse to believe what "establishment" authors tell them. An article on Bancroft in Wikipedia repeats Currey's charges. Another Internet site has anonymous contributors who have speculated not only that Franklin was a traitor but that he was a serial killer, a member of the Knights Templar, the inventor of the black helicopter, and the person who started adding fluoride to water in order to control people's minds![19]

Fortunately, the vast majority of historians have rejected Currey's thesis and refused to dignify it by discussing it. They have agreed with *Time* magazine and Columbia University's Richard M. Morris, both of whom reviewed the book when it first appeared. *Time* bluntly said, "There is no evidence any where of disloyalty on Franklin's part."[20] Morris concluded, "Now that Franklin has been indicted by Mr. Currey, let us hope that he will receive a fair trial at the hands of a more impartial jury."[21]

In short, the worst that can be said of Franklin is that, like so many others, he was completely fooled by Bancroft.

Bancroft and Silas Deane

In a well-researched, three-part article published in the *William and Mary Quarterly* in 1959, Julian P. Boyd added murder to the list of charges against Edward Bancroft. Boyd was a respected professor of history at Princeton University and editor of *The Papers of Thomas Jefferson*. The title of the essay reveals Boyd's thesis: "Silas Deane: Death by a Kindly Teacher of Treason?" The vast majority of scholars who have written about Deane and Bancroft in recent decades have accepted Boyd's thesis as either absolutely, probably, or at least plausibly true.

Boyd maintains that Deane knew all about Bancroft's espionage from the start. Indeed, Bancroft, who had the stronger personality, soon made a traitor of Deane. The two became "partners in duplicity." With their "monumental venality," the two men used all of their insider information to their advantage in stock speculations and trading ventures. In 1781, a dispirited Deane accepted bribes from the British government in return for writing letters that expressed pessimism about the benefits of American independence; he advocated a continuing connection with the mother country. From that point on, nearly all of America's political leaders shunned him, viewing him as a traitor. Deane's last years, spent mostly in Ghent and London, were filled with poverty and despondency. Finally, in September 1789, he determined to return to the United States. Just hours after he boarded a ship in the Downs, he took sick and expired. Deane's death, Boyd surmises, was probably not produced by natural causes. Nor was it suicide. In all probability, Bancroft, an expert on drugs and poisons, murdered him. He feared that Deane would return to America and reveal all he knew about Bancroft's treachery.

Boyd's research is impressive. The problem lies with the use he makes of his findings. He begins by maintaining that Deane not only knew about Bancroft but that early on he became Bancroft's partner in crime. A handful of earlier historians had asserted this about Deane, while offering no evidence. Like those writers, Boyd constructs his case on the theory of guilt by association. Boyd assumes that Deane "must" have known about Bancroft. He correctly describes the close friendship that developed between the two men; Deane trusted Bancroft with every detail of his diplomatic work. Boyd claims that Bancroft became Deane's "instructor in duplicity." Bancroft "had an American agent in his pocket." The two men formed an "indissoluble partnership in infamy," and their lives were "welded together in deceit and distrust."[22]

How did Boyd reach this conclusion? He says, "There is no doubt in my mind that Deane was in full concert with Bancroft and knew him to be an intelligence agent from the very beginning of their association together in 1776." Furthermore, "It is incredible to suppose that the two men did not come to a prompt understanding." Deane "evidently" had come to some sort of agreement with British agents. "It is straining credulity too much to suppose that Deane would not have known" about Bancroft.[23] In short, Boyd offers suppositions, not proof. Using his logic, one would have to assume that Franklin, Adams, John Paul Jones, Leray de Chaumont, Lafayette, and several other close friends of Bancroft also knew of his espionage. Moreover, Boyd ignores the fact that not a single document in any British archive indicates that Deane was "one of ours." Boyd proclaims that Bancroft was a "master of deceit." That is true. Why is it then so difficult to believe that he really did fool Deane and all the others? There have been many examples from the past half-century of enemy agents working in America's CIA and Britain's MI6 and going undetected for years or even decades. Therefore Bancroft was far from alone in accomplishing such a feat.

Boyd does offer one piece of evidence that supposedly links Deane directly to espionage. However, this "proof" is based on an error. The source of this "evidence" was British agent George Lupton. In May 1777 Lupton sneaked into the Paris hotel room where Deane was staying. In a closet Lupton found several letters addressed to someone named Benson. Lupton assumed that Benson was Deane, and he reported this to William Eden. Over the following year London postal inspectors intercepted numerous letters from Benson to Samuel Wharton and other business partners in London. George III was shown many of these letters. A perusal of the correspondence of George III, Eden, Paul Wentworth, and others reveals that Benson was a British agent; that agent used the name Benson in his personal business correspondence with partners in England. However, Lupton made one huge error. Benson was not Deane; Benson was Edward Bancroft. Bancroft at that time had a room adjacent to Deane's, and he was spending nearly all his time with Deane. Some of his letters regarding trade got mixed up with Deane's. The two men were jointly involved in numerous speculations and commercial affairs. The alias that Deane himself used when corresponding with Wharton and others was "J. Jones." Correspondence among British ministers makes it clear that Benson was the same person as Edward Edwards—that is, Bancroft. Moreover, if Boyd had carefully read the several letters that Samuel Wharton wrote to Benson, he would have seen that in some of them Wharton refers to Deane in the third person. Thus it is obvious that Wharton was not writing to Deane. Finally, Benjamin Franklin was well aware that Bancroft used the name Benson in his business correspondence with London. Whenever Bancroft was away from Passy or Paris for more than a few days, Franklin instructed the French post office to deliver letters for Benson to the Hôtel de Valentinois.[24]

One reason why it was so easy for Boyd to assume that Deane was on the British payroll is that Deane has had a rather unsavory reputation among historians. Boyd is far from alone in portraying Deane as more interested in stock speculations and war profiteering than in diplomacy.[25] To a large extent, this image of Deane is founded on charges made by Arthur Lee. Starting in 1777, Lee and his allies charged Deane with embezzling public funds and overcharging Congress for defective or shoddy goods. In particular, Lee argued that Deane had colluded with Beaumarchais to sell old, rusty muskets and cannons to America for inflated prices. Even worse, Lee charged that the materials coming from Beaumarchais should have been given to America free of charge. The reason for this, according to Lee, was that the French and Spanish crowns had given Beaumarchais 2 million livres in 1776 so that he could provide secret aid to the American colonies.

There are numerous ways to rebut Lee's allegations. First, it is true that, by today's standards, Deane's private business activities would not be tolerated. But what Deane did was not extraordinary by the standards of his age. If the Continental Congress had demanded that officials give up all private commercial activities, the government would have lost most of its servants. Lee's charges were also off the mark in other ways. Some of the arms that French arsenals provided to Deane were old and of little use, but that was the fault of French officials, not Deane. The vast majority of all the arms and other supplies that he sent to America in 1776 and 1777 were of good quality. It is true that the French and Spanish governments had given Beaumarchais money, but this was start-up capital that the merchant-adventurer needed to purchase ships and supplies. The French and Spanish governments fully expected Congress to pay for the cargoes Beaumarchais dispatched. A large portion of the arms and uniforms that helped the Americans win the Battle of Saratoga, for example, came from the shipments of Deane and Beaumarchais.[26]

In March 1778 Deane received word that Congress wanted him to return to Philadelphia as quickly as possible. Those writers who are disposed to think the worst of Deane have assumed that the reason was that Congress had found out about his financial misdeeds. That is wrong. The letter Deane received from Congress gave no reason for his recall. Deane assumed that Congress simply wanted him to report on the general progress toward increased French aid and an alliance. When Deane left Paris, he fully expected to return there within a few months. Because Congress said nothing about his financial records, he took none of his voluminous account books with him.[27]

The reason for his recall had nothing to do with suspicions of corruption. Congress was upset with him because he had been sending to America dozens of French and other European military officers who, desirous of fame and fortune, wanted to serve in the Continental Army. Most of these volunteers did not speak English. What was worse, some of them expected to replace George Washington as commander in chief.[28] By the time that Deane arrived in Philadelphia, that issue had been replaced by another. Unfortunately for Deane, Arthur Lee's charges against him and Beaumarchais had reached America about the same time he did. Not having any of his account books with him, Deane had difficulty defending himself. For months the delegates got bogged down in a heated debate on this issue. One of Deane's strongest supporters was John Jay. The two sides were about evenly matched in size and vituperation. Deane pleaded for vindication, but in the end Congress came to no resolution. Congress likewise refused to pay Beaumarchais the money he claimed. An outraged Deane responded in December 1778 by publishing a bitter attack on his foes and a stout defense of his own actions in France. With the appointment that September of Franklin as minister plenipotentiary to France, Deane was now out of work. Dispirited, Deane returned to France in the summer of 1780, hoping to salvage his good name and resume his commercial affairs.

Boyd and others critical of Deane generally neglect to report that on numerous occasions throughout the late 1770s and early 1780s, Benjamin Franklin, John Adams, and Thomas Barclay (appointed by Congress in 1781 as American consul in France) reviewed Deane's accounts and found some small irregularities—for example, sundry minor expenses for which there were no vouchers. But they saw no evidence of wrongdoing, and Deane's accounts were no more confusing or incomplete than those of any other agent sent abroad by Congress. After Arthur Lee returned to the United States, a congressional committee found discrepancies even in his records. Franklin and Adams willingly testified to the good work that Deane had performed from mid-1776 to early 1778. Deane's critics also usually fail to mention that many years later the United States government reexamined the cases of Deane and Beaumarchais and decided that the allegations against them had no merit. Regarding Deane, Congress proclaimed that the earlier charges against him had been "ex-parte, erroneous, and a gross injustice." In 1835 and 1841 the government made financial settlements with the descendants of the two men.[29]

When Deane arrived back in Paris in August 1780, he discovered that his profits from earlier investments had all but evaporated. Bancroft had been handling Deane's affairs, and he told Deane that their stock speculations had turned sour. Moreover, some of the ships carrying their merchandise to America had been captured by the British. For the next several months Deane divided his time between a Paris hotel and Bancroft's residence adjacent to the Hôtel de Valentinois. On several occasions Deane visited Franklin, who treated him cordially. But Deane was restless and dispirited. He was able to support himself thanks to a small amount of personal funds plus some handouts from Vergennes. He remained bitter about the hostile reception that had greeted him in Philadelphia. Early in December 1780 he wrote to John Paul Jones that he still wished America well but with less fervor than he had earlier.[30]

His despondency led him to commit the serious blunder that has convinced Boyd and others that all along he must have been a British agent working with Bancroft. In the spring and summer of 1781 Deane wrote numerous letters to members of Congress and various friends in America. By that time his bitterness had turned to defeatism. In these letters he railed against France, claiming that its aid for America was only half-hearted and asserting that France hoped to dominate the fledgling United States. He said he knew American government was weak. He lamented that Congress was riven with factional disputes and the thirteen states were far from united. The spectacular depreciation of the congressional dollar, he judged, was but one sign of the hopelessness and anarchy that prevailed. Furthermore, the war in America was not going well. Britain controlled much of New York and the South. America, he concluded, would be better off if it stopped short of independence and remained in some sort of imperial union with Britain.

Deane was wrong about France, but he was correct about the situation in America in the months before the victory at Yorktown. Many Americans shared his gloomy sentiments. But what made Deane different is that his private communications were made public. In November and December 1781 James Rivington published some of Deane's letters in a New York Loyalist newspaper, the *Royal Gazette*. Upon their appearance, Deane's name immediately became synonymous with that of Benedict Arnold in the eyes of most Americans. Virtually all of his friends and associates rushed to condemn him.[31]

When Franklin learned of the letters, he likewise refused ever to meet with Deane or have anything to do with him. He castigated the letters as "indiscreet and mischievous." He said Deane's career and reputation would be ruined in both America and France. Franklin therefore assumed that Deane would soon move to England, to join up with his fellow traitor, Benedict Arnold.[32] Because Franklin would not answer his letters, Deane was forced to use Bancroft as an intermediary.[33] Deane still clung desperately to the hope that Congress would vote to approve his accounts and pay him the commissions he was owed for the cargoes he shipped to America. Eventually Bancroft was able to get a reluctant Franklin to write to Congress, acknowledging Deane's earlier good work and asking that his accounts be settled.

Boyd and most other writers have cited as proof of Deane's treachery the fact that the British government bribed him to write those letters. As evidence they note a letter of 3 March 1781 from George III to Lord North. The king asserted that Deane could be useful in persuading some of the colonies to end the rebellion. Deane's troubles with Congress, his current penury, and his utter despondency were well known to the British. The monarch said that Deane could be offered £3,000 worth of goods that he could trade in America. In mid-July George III read some of the letters that Deane had written; the British post office had intercepted the letters before they reached America. Upon reading them, however, the king was disappointed. He told North that they had "too much appearance of being concerted with this country, and therefore not likely to have the effect as if they bore another aspect." North agreed with him. In other words, Deane's letters went overboard in their defeatism. They were so anti-French, so pro-British, and so negative about the American government that they would have little effect on the rebels. Nonetheless, George III agreed that the letters should be forwarded to the British commander in America, for his possible use. When they reached General Clinton, he gave them to Rivington.[34]

All of the above is true. However, Boyd and others have misinterpreted some key facts and missed other pieces of evidence. Most of the information reaching London concerning Deane's bitter state of mind was coming from Paul Wentworth. In late 1780 or early 1781 Wentworth recommenced his trips to Paris. There he picked up intelligence from Bancroft, which he then transmitted to North. Wentworth also took it upon himself to cultivate the friendship of Deane. It was Wentworth who suggested to the British government that £3,000 might be advanced to Deane for the purchase of goods that could be sold in New York—which at the time was mostly under British control. There is no evidence anywhere to show that this money was a bribe, in return for which Deane was supposed to write his defeatist letters. Certainly Wentworth hoped that this investment in Deane's commercial projects would help to win Deane's sympathies, which could at some point then be put to use for the British. But nowhere is there any mention of there being a quid pro quo—the money in return for writing the letters. Even more to the point, there is no indication that North's government ever paid Deane anything. Deane's voluminous surviving letters and personal accounts contain no references to his coming into a large sum of money at that time. Neither in 1781 nor in any later year did Deane's financial status improve; nor did he succeed in sending any cargoes to America. He lived in abject poverty until his death in 1789.

In short, via Wentworth, the government was considering ways of winning Deane's favor. But before George III and North gave the final go-ahead to provide any money to Deane, their agents intercepted Deane's letters and got what they wanted for free. When George III perused the stolen letters, he was amazed to find that Deane actually believed the pro-English sentiments contained in them. Boyd states that Deane sent the letters directly to London for prior approval; from there the government sent them to Henry Clinton. However, no letter by North, George III, or anyone else mentions receiving the letters directly from Deane. Rather, George III explicitly refers to them as the "intercepted letters." If Deane had actually written the letters in return for a bribe and then sent them to London for approval, George III's government would have sent them back to Deane and instructed him to tone down his strident defeatism. But the government did not do that. Moreover, early in 1782 Deane was trying to find out which of his letters had been stolen and published. If he himself had sent the letters straight to London, he would have known already which letters had come into British hands.[35] Boyd also misses the fact that in conversation and in letters Deane was expressing his pessimistic ideas months before Wentworth, George III, or North discussed the possibility of giving him money. There was thus no need to bribe him or make any investments in his trading schemes.

In the years after 1781 Deane repeatedly defended his letters and argued that he was not a traitor. After all, numerous patriotic Americans shared his views. The weak and divided condition of the young republic even after it won formal independence led many leading citizens to wonder whether they might not have been better off remaining under the protective apron of the mother country.

For present purposes, the question of whether Deane finally did become a traitor in 1781 is secondary. The main concern is whether this proves that Deane had been a British agent all along, working in tandem with fellow spy Edward Bancroft. Deane's correspondence with Bancroft from late 1781 on provides conclusive evidence in this regard. In October 1781 a dejected and penurious Deane moved to Ghent, where he could live more cheaply than in Paris and where he hoped to interest some Flemish merchants in his trading schemes. His friend Bancroft took charge of Deane's affairs in France, paying his debts, forwarding letters to him, and arranging to ship Deane's household furnishings to Ghent. In his initial letters after moving north, Deane admitted he was pessimistic about the chances of America winning the war or surviving as a strong nation. However, he referred to British soldiers as "the enemy." One of his most extraordinary letters to Bancroft was composed on 23 November. Referring to the news of Cornwallis's surrender at Yorktown, Deane exclaimed, "I congratulate you on the success in America, and hope it may bring us peace." Alluding to the 1778 controversy over his accounts, Deane admitted that he had been "very far from approving the proceedings of Congress . . . and . . . too free and open in expressing of my disapprobation." He conceded that he was gloomy about the chances for survival of a weak and divided new nation, but he stressed that he voiced these opinions "from conviction of the truth." He was dismayed to learn of rumors that he wrote his intercepted letters "in expectation of favors or rewards" from the British government. Deane proclaimed that he wanted what was best for America, and he was upset that his enemies now portrayed him as a traitor and "a partisan for British tyranny." On 20 December Deane penned another poignant letter to his old friend. He suspected that Bancroft's delays in answering his letters resulted from Bancroft's disapproval of Deane's pessimistic views about America. Deane also thought that Bancroft might fear continuing their friendship; most Americans had turned against Deane, and thus Bancroft might not want to be known as a friend of this supposed traitor. The irony in these letters is overwhelming. Deane was trying to justify himself in the eyes of Bancroft, whom he assumed to be a patriotic American. The letters demonstrate not only that Deane had never been a British agent but also that he never knew of Bancroft's espionage.[36]

Bancroft and the Dark Arts

In March 1783 Silas Deane moved from Ghent to London. He had old friends there and hoped to find financial backers for his business plans. Boyd alleges that during the next several years Bancroft worked to control what Deane did, where he lived, and whom he saw.[37] The reason was obvious: Bancroft did not want Deane to reveal all their earlier treasonous activities. Like a clever Svengali, the stronger Bancroft was able to keep the weaker Deane under his sway.

Such assertions have little in the way of factual support. Bancroft never visited Deane during Deane's year and a half in Ghent, and Deane's decision to move to London was his alone. Bancroft and his family did not move from France back to London until three months following Deane's arrival there. After just two weeks in England, Bancroft decamped for the United States. He remained there for nearly a year and did not arrive back in London until August 1784. (More on that trip in the next chapter.) In the years after that, Bancroft made several trips to France concerning his textile dyeing enterprises.

On other occasions, when Bancroft himself was in London, it was Deane who left town. Deane had developed numerous plans for trade and manufactures. In March 1784, he met with Charles James Fox and Lord North to discuss his ideas for American trade with the British West Indies.[38] Through the mid-1780s Deane worked to develop plans for steam engines that could operate tobacco, saw, and grist mills. He also hoped to establish foundries that employed an innovative method for smelting iron. The industrial experts who advised him included James Watt, who had built the first efficient and profitable steam engines, and William Wilkinson, a renowned ironmaster. Deane hoped to put his schemes into practice in the United States. He spent the last five months of 1783 touring Birmingham, Manchester, Leeds, Halifax, Sheffield, Preston, and other manufacturing towns. He revisited many of these places again at various times over the next three years.[39] Deane also devised plans for a canal that would connect the St. Lawrence River with Lake Champlain. This project seemed so potentially lucrative that he was able to win the support of several prominent nobles and government officials. These included Lords Sheffield, Dorchester, and Sydney—Sydney served from 1783 to 1789 under William Pitt as home and colonial secretary and leader of the House of Lords. On several occasions Deane was a houseguest at Sheffield's estate in Sussex.[40] In short, Bancroft and Deane were separated most of the time between 1783 and 1789, which would have made it impossible for Bancroft to "control" his friend.

Deane had little money during these years. He lived as simply as possible on his meager personal funds plus handouts from friends—including free meals and, occasionally, free lodging. He clung vainly to the dream that his earlier European investments would still bring some profits, and he hoped that Samuel Wharton would remit him some money from the sale of his shares in land companies.[41] Moreover, he steadfastly hoped that Congress would settle his accounts and pay him the money he was due. He counted on a friendly welcome in America from his brothers Barnabas and Simeon plus several other loyal friends, once the memories of the 1781 letters had sufficiently dimmed. He was obviously a very intelligent man, and he could be very impressive when meeting with wealthy or powerful supporters of his projects.

It was late in 1787 that Deane's situation began to unravel. From the fall of that year to the spring of 1789 he suffered from an unidentified illness that kept him confined to his room most of the time. Since his arrival in England in 1783 he had been subject to sudden bouts of poor health that laid him low for up to several weeks at a stretch. In March 1784 he reported to Bancroft (then in America) that for weeks he had been confined to his room, with both his sight and hearing impaired.[42] One can only speculate about the precise nature of his ailments on these and numerous other occasions.

The sickness that descended on him sometime in the fall of 1787 was different. It did not dissipate after a few weeks. Throughout all of 1788 he had just a few short periods of partial recovery. Only in April 1789 could Deane report that his health had been restored. Those eighteen months of physical debility were made worse by the virtual collapse of his prospects for financial gain. His personal funds had evaporated, and he came to depend heavily on a trio of friends—Bancroft, William Wilkinson, and a Dr. Jeffries.[43] The three of them looked in on him frequently and supplied him with food and clothing. They also paid his rent and found him lodging in various rooming houses. Jeffries and Bancroft also tended to him medically. Deane's physical appearance deteriorated, and he could no longer put on an impressive show for his putative financial investors. By the spring of 1789 his contacts with Lords Sydney, Dorchester, and Sheffield had become infrequent and tenuous.[44]

In 1789 Bancroft exchanged several letters regarding Deane with Thomas Jefferson, then the United States minister in France. Late in 1788 a Frenchman named Foulloy had approached Jefferson and offered to sell him two account and letterbooks that had belonged to Deane. Foulloy had stolen them. Believing that these official records belonged most properly to the U.S. government rather than to Foulloy or to the British government (to which Foulloy said he would sell them if Jefferson refused), the American minister finally agreed to purchase them. After the initial meetings with Foulloy, Jefferson wrote to Bancroft, asking him to find out whether Deane possessed any other books dating from his time as an American commissioner in Paris. In a letter of March 1789, Bancroft summarized the previous three years of Deane's pitiable existence. Some two or three years earlier "the unhappy man" became "much attached to a woman here in the line of Prostitution." She persuaded him to take a lease on a house in Rathbone Place. Deane gave her control of the house and even borrowed money so that she could furnish it. In addition, Deane stood as security for additional furniture that the woman bought. Deane himself took up lodging on the second floor and paid the woman rent. Eventually Deane had used up all his money and was arrested for nonpayment for the furniture. Under the sway of this woman, Deane gave her his watch and other possessions, so that she could pawn them to pay overdue rent for the house. Bancroft said that "Being thus Stript of almost everything, his distress of mind, and the inebriety, into which he Plunged to escape reflection, brought on him a disorder, which soon produced a total loss of the Powers of his body and mind, insomuch that he could not remember any thing a single minute, nor use either his hands or feet." In January 1788 the wretched woman told Deane that her former husband, the above-named Foulloy, was going to evict him from the house. To keep him from being thrown out into the street, Bancroft found Deane a room elsewhere. Bancroft told Jefferson that Foulloy had stolen Deane's account books and virtually all of his clothing. In the spring of 1789 Deane was recovering from "Complicated Disorders, of Dropsey, Palsey, and Idiotism."[45]

In several undated, scribbled notes to Bancroft from this period, Deane detailed his steady decline in mind and body. In one, he complained that someone has just picked his pocket; he beseeched Bancroft to send him a few shillings. In another he gave a list of the shirts, stockings, and other articles of clothing he desperately needed. In yet another he wrote that twice that day he had tried to walk to Bancroft's home but found himself too weak to make it all the way; he begged Bancroft to come to see him immediately. Sometime in 1788, probably in the summer, Bancroft found Deane lodging in the countryside near London. There Deane would be free from the clutches of the unnamed woman and Foulloy. To pay for Deane's expenses, Bancroft, Wilkinson, and Jeffries contributed to "a Charitable subscription," each of them regularly depositing small amounts into a bank account from which Deane could draw.[46]

With no basis for his suspicions, Boyd states that one cannot entirely believe the above stories. This is extraordinary, given the fact that Deane's own letters plus numerous reports by various American businessmen who happened to see Deane also attest to his recurring illnesses and his reliance on the charity of Bancroft and other friends. Boyd claims to detect a "sense of deviousness" in all that Bancroft did during this period. He asserts that Bancroft was extremely nervous about the whereabouts of Deane's papers. With absolutely no evidence, Boyd speculates that Bancroft might have been "in league" with Foulloy to destroy or hide all of Deane's papers. Even more outrageously, Boyd surmises that Bancroft might have caused Deane's continuing illness, in order to prevent Deane from returning to America. Bancroft, says Boyd, was content to let Jefferson purchase two of Deane's books, because Jefferson would send them to Congress. Hence, the British government would never be able to see them.[47]

In effect, Boyd argues that Bancroft had two rather contradictory fears. First, he did not want Deane to return to America, where he might reveal that Bancroft had been a traitor. In the pages above it should be clear that Boyd's theory in that regard is groundless. Deane himself was not a British agent; nor did he have any knowledge or suspicions of Bancroft's covert activities. Second, Boyd claims that Bancroft was terrified of the British government's gaining access to Deane's papers. Some pages in the letterbooks concerned the John the Painter affair of 1776–77. Boyd maintains that Bancroft's "worst fright" was that the British cabinet would take "hostile acts" against him once "his complicity" in John the Painter's incendiarism was discovered.[48] This argument is nonsense for numerous reasons. The John the Painter episode was old news, and there is no reason to believe that the British government had any further interest in it. The Revolution was long over by 1789, and Britain was discovering that America was an increasingly valuable trading partner. John Adams was welcomed as the first American minister in London in 1785, whereas ten years earlier George III's government had branded him public enemy number one. Silas Deane had given tacit approval to John the Painter's plans in 1776, and yet Deane had no fears about moving to London in 1783. Beyond that, Boyd is utterly wrong to assert that Bancroft had any complicity in the fires set by John the Painter. As noted in an earlier chapter, Bancroft had no prior knowledge of what the deranged Scotsman had been planning. Moreover, the British government knew that Bancroft was innocent. Boyd mistakenly claims that Bancroft feared he might lose his lifetime annual pension of £1,000 if there should be anything incriminating in the Deane papers. Not only was there nothing incriminating (for Deane's letters state unequivocally that Bancroft had no part in the incendiarism), but Bancroft had no fears about losing his pension. The British government had already stopped funding it in 1783. (More on that in the next chapter.) In sum, Bancroft had no reasons for wanting to prevent Deane from leaving England or for wanting to hide Deane's papers.

Even in mid-1788, when Deane's health was at its worst, Bancroft was encouraging him to return to his home in America as soon as he could.[49] On 21 August 1789, less than a month before Deane left London to return to America, Bancroft wrote the following to Jefferson: "He has nearly recovered the use of his bodily faculties and in a considerable degree of his mental also. But having no means of subsistence in this Country, nor any connection which could enable him to obtain it, he goes to receive food raiment, and Lodging for the remnant of his Life, from the affection or Humanity of his Brother [Barnabas] in Connecticut, who is already charged with the support of his son [Jesse]."[50]

This letter shows that Deane still was not completely healthy. Even more important, it demonstrates that Bancroft knew that returning to friends and family in Connecticut was Deane's best option. Bancroft was not standing in his way.

Nonetheless, because Boyd has influenced so many subsequent writers on this topic, one must follow his argument to the end. Boyd does an excellent job of tracing the events leading up to Deane's death. In mid-September Deane left London and traveled by coach to Gravesend, where he boarded the *Boston Packet*. Bancroft and other friends had contributed £70 to cover his travel expenses. A fierce gale caused the vessel to lose both its anchors. The ship's commander, Captain Davis, thereupon brought it back into the Downs for repairs. On 23 September, while the vessel was still stationed in the Downs, Deane was walking on the quarterdeck with Captain Davis, when suddenly, according to later published reports, he "complain'd of a dizziness in his head, and an oppression at his stomach." He was taken to his cabin and put in bed. Twice he attempted to speak, but none of those present could comprehend his mumblings. A "drowsiness and insensibility continually encroached upon his faculties." Four hours after the illness set in, he was dead. His body was taken ashore and buried in the parish cemetery at Deal.[51]

Captain Davis wrote a firsthand account of the event, but no copy of it has ever been found. Boyd is probably correct in surmising that Davis or someone else who had been on board the *Boston Packet* traveled to London to give Bancroft, known to be Deane's closest friend, a full report on the events. Within a week of Deane's death, a long obituary appeared in *Gentleman's Magazine* along with shorter notices in some London newspapers. All of these pieces lauded Deane as an intelligent and hard-working servant of the

United States. The obituaries summarized the manner of Deane's death and agreed that it resulted from natural causes. Furthermore, these death notices appear to have been written by someone who knew Deane well. Boyd is almost certainly correct in conjecturing that Bancroft wrote them or advised the persons who wrote them. After copies of the London obituaries had crossed the Atlantic, numerous American newspapers reprinted them.[52]

Boyd goes on to note that within a week after Deane expired, a different version of his death had begun to circulate. On 30 September John Browne Cutting, an American then residing in London, wrote to Thomas Jefferson that perhaps Deane "had predetermin'd to take a sufficient quantity of Laudanum to ensure his dissolution before the vessel cou'd quit the Downs." In other words, Deane might have committed suicide by taking an overdose of this derivative of opium. Cutting said it was Bancroft who had mentioned this possibility.[53] Boyd hypothesizes that Bancroft began to circulate the theory of suicide in order to cover up the real cause of Deane's death: that he had been poisoned by Bancroft himself.

There are plentiful reasons to doubt this hypothesis. First of all, there is no evidence to show that when Deane died Captain Davis or any other eyewitnesses considered anything other than natural causes. No one suspected murder, and thus there was no need to concoct a story to cover it up. The only time when Bancroft ever mentioned the possibility of suicide was in that one private conversation with Cutting. If Bancroft had really wanted or needed to plant the idea of suicide in order to conceal a murder, he would have mentioned this in the published obituaries.

During the months following Deane's death, several persons approached Bancroft seeking further information about the demise of his friend. One of these was the famous scientist and Unitarian clergyman Joseph Priestley, who wrote to Bancroft in late April or early May 1790. Priestley had never met Deane, but over the years he had formed an acquaintanceship with Bancroft. The reason for Priestley's letter was the publication early in 1790 of a scurrilous pamphlet entitled *Theodosius*. The anonymous author was Philip Withers, an unsavory clergyman who in the spring of 1790 was serving a prison sentence in Newgate for libeling another person. *Theodosius* describes Silas Deane's death, but Withers's real target was Priestley. Withers knew very little about how Deane passed away, and what he did know he twisted for his own purposes. The pamphlet claims that while on his deathbed Deane uttered all sorts of blasphemous, atheistic sentiments and exclaimed that he got all these ideas from Priestley, who was "my instructor, my saviour, and my God." Priestley's freethinking ideas about politics and religion had already made him a target for conservatives, and this new pamphlet brought him even more public animosity. He pleaded with Bancroft to set the record straight. Bancroft obliged by writing a letter that was published in London and Birmingham newspapers. The letter repeated the details of Deane's death, which Bancroft said were based on Captain Davis's written account. Bancroft reaffirmed that Deane suddenly was taken ill and uttered no comprehensible words about Priestley or anyone else in the four hours before his final breath.[54]

In replying to Priestley and others, months after the event, Bancroft had some inconsistencies. He occasionally got dates or the time of day slightly wrong. Once again, Boyd assumes that there was something sinister behind these slight lapses in Bancroft's memory. What Boyd glosses over is the fact that all of Bancroft's later descriptions of Deane's death were consistent in their important points—that is, regarding Deane's sudden collapse, his four-hour state of semiconsciousness, and the natural causes of the death. If Bancroft was intent on spreading the rumor of suicide, surely he would have interjected it into these letters.

To "prove" that the amoral, traitorous Bancroft was a murderer, Boyd asserts that the doctor possessed all the skills needed to kill someone in a way not easily detected. Bancroft, after all, was a world expert on the use of poisons. Boyd builds his case on Bancroft's 1769 *Natural History of Guiana*. Therein Bancroft devoted approximately thirty pages to the topic of arrow poison.[55] But Bancroft could hardly have avoided the topic if he wanted to give a thorough description of Indian culture. When native tribes went to war, they shot poisoned arrows at each other—either by using bows or by blowing them through long, hollow reeds. Bancroft wrote that the Accaww people in particular were feared by other tribes and by the Dutch "on account of their art in the preparation of Poisons of the most deleterious kind." Bancroft noted that the most lethal poison was called "woorara." He altered the name to "curare," and this is how it is generally spelled today. From the Indian holy men, Bancroft obtained the recipe for this poison, and he printed that recipe in his book. The chief ingredients consisted of the barks of five different trees found in the Guiana forests. The smallest quantity of this poison could kill a large animal or a human being in less than a minute. He mentioned that he had performed some experiments to try to find an antidote but that he had not yet found an effective one.

Boyd and numerous other historians following in his wake have focused special attention on a footnote that appears on page 300 of the book. It reads, "As the author has brought a considerable quantity of this Poison to England, any Gentleman, whose genius many incline him to prosecute these experiments, and whose character will warrant us to confide in his hands a preparation, capable of perpetrating the most secret and fatal villainy, may be supplied with a sufficient quantity of the Woorara, by applying to Mr. Becket [Bancroft's publisher], in the Strand."

Boyd used this passage to demonstrate Bancroft's inordinate, morbid fascination with poisons. However, the passage can also lead to a different interpretation. We do not know how much the "considerable quantity" was, but Bancroft told the reader that a minute amount could kill a person. It is probably safe to guess that Bancroft brought to London perhaps one or two jars of the concoction. His interest in the poison was twofold: it was a noticeable feature of the Indian culture he was studying, and as a physician, he wanted to find a cure. Finally, if Bancroft's character was such that he might be inclined to kill someone with the poison, would he announce to the public that he possessed the stuff?

There is even more evidence to rebut Boyd's interpretation. In his book Bancroft mentioned five prominent Spanish, French, and British naturalists or physicians who had preceded him in writing about Indian poisons found throughout South America. The most famous of these was Charles-Marie de La Condamine (1701–74), a member of the French Académie des Sciences. La Condamine had traveled widely throughout South America in the 1730s and 1740s. Early in the sixteenth century, Spanish conquistadors likewise brought back to Europe stories of curare. Later in that century, Sir Walter Raleigh wrote of it in his book *Discovery of the Large, Rich and Beautiful Empire of Guiana*. Yet neither Boyd nor other historians have accused these scholars and explorers of using the mysterious concoction to murder their enemies.

Moreover, Bancroft was not the only traveler who brought poison home with him. After his return to Paris in the 1740s, La Condamine shared samples of curare with members of the Académie des Sciences as well as with scientists in other parts of Europe.[56] Bancroft himself brought to England not just poisons but also other items. In particular, he brought a large collection of snakes, preserved in a liquid solution that he had devised. His explanation of how he preserved the dead snakes is more detailed than the poison recipe, and yet no historians have accused him of harboring a dangerous fascination with serpents.[57]

It was common practice before the twentieth century for scientific travelers to bring back large numbers of plant and animal specimens they had found in exotic locales. They brought them home not only for their own studies but in order to share them with other scholars who were not themselves able to traverse the world. At least one British scientist, Sir Benjamin Brodie, obtained some samples of Bancroft's curare and injected them in small animals to study the effects it had on the neuromuscular system.[58]

More broadly, one can say that the subject of poison has fascinated scholars and the general public since ancient times. Because of the omnipresence and the mystery of poisons, it is no wonder that Bancroft and thousands of others have written about them. Anyone who wishes to judge personally is invited to do a search for "poison" in Google or Amazon.com. Amid the tens of thousands of books and articles that one will find, there is one by Edward Bancroft, entitled *Arrow Poison*. At first glance, one might assume that this book gives added proof that Bancroft was inordinately interested in the topic. If one looks at this "book," however, one sees that it was first published in 1972 and is a mere four pages long. It reprints the pages of the 1769 book wherein Bancroft gives the recipe for curare poison. Bancroft's motives for giving the recipe were to enable scientists to find an antidote. The 1972 editor concludes his brief introduction, however, with a somewhat ghoulish suggestion: "There is probably just one way to find out how good his recipe was, and we wish you success."[59]

Medical researchers and pharmaceutical companies during the past century have imported many shipments of curare to the United States and Europe. Curare has become one of the most significant muscular relaxants of the modern world, important in the development of anesthetics and in the treatment of muscular dystrophy and other ailments.[60] Bancroft's role in analyzing and publicizing curare should thus be applauded, not condemned.

Boyd fails to mention that Bancroft never again studied poisons after 1769. The papers that he delivered in scientific societies were on other topics.

In no book, pamphlet, or letter written in the remainder of his life did Bancroft ever discuss poisons. Nor did any of the hundreds of people who knew him during the last fifty years of his life ever mention that he was an expert on poisons.

The criminal indictment of Bancroft is unconvincing for a host of other reasons also. If Bancroft had wanted to destroy or conceal Deane's papers, he could have done so at any time after 1783; why would he wait until 1789? If he was afraid that Deane would tell people about his espionage, he could have silenced his friend long before Deane boarded a ship bound for America. Deane left London around 15 September and died a week later. Bancroft remained in London. So how, one might ask, did he poison Deane, who was more than a hundred miles away?

Boyd offers as one last "proof" the fact that after 1790 Bancroft never seems to have spoken or written about Deane.[61] This surely indicates that he could not have cared much about his deceased friend. Or does it? The plain fact is that very little is known about Bancroft's activities for the last thirty years of his life. The things that he did write consisted mostly of letters or books regarding his family or about textile dyes. Only a handful of letters to or from Bancroft exist for the entire period from 1790 to his death in 1821. Just as none of his surviving documents from these decades refers to Deane, so also none refers to Benjamin Franklin or a host of other Americans, Britons, and Frenchmen whom he had known well in earlier years.

Finally, a close reading of Boyd reveals a couple of key, often overlooked sentences. He admits that the surviving details about Deane's death are "too fragmentary to permit a definite medical diagnosis." Boyd consulted with one medical expert, who informed him that the available details "include some of the elements of a cerebral hemorrhage" but that they also "conceivably . . . describe some of the toxic effects of opium in the form of laudanum."[62] Laudanum was a legal and widely used painkiller in Europe and the United States in the eighteenth and nineteenth centuries. Perhaps hundreds of thousands of people became addicted to it. There is some indication that Deane used laudanum to relieve his pain. He also was subject to seasickness, and therefore he might have purchased a small supply of that drug in anticipation of his upcoming voyage.[63] However, we do not know whether he obtained it from Bancroft, Dr. Jeffries, or someone else. With no basis for his surmises, Boyd chooses laudanum rather than a cerebral hemorrhage as the cause of death. Going beyond that, he infers that Deane did not accidentally or intentionally take an overdose. Somehow, even though he had not seen Deane for at least a week, Bancroft must have administered that overdose. Boyd concludes that "until further evidence confirms or alters what is known, we are justified in allowing the burden of suspicion to remain fixed upon" Bancroft.[64]

In the years since Boyd's lengthy article appeared, a small number of writers have noticed its ungrounded conjectures and dismissed its thesis as "flimsy" or "crank." There is evidence to show that Deane had not completely recovered from the illness that had plagued him through all of 1788. For example, in June 1789, Deane wrote to George Washington that he was in "an infirm and precarious state of health." In addition, he was worried about a number of other problems. Among these was the fact that he was bankrupt. Lord Sheffield and his other potential business partners had not, in the end, elected to invest any money in his plans for factories and a canal in the United States. Deane had become entirely dependent on the charity of his friends. Even the clothes that he wore when he boarded the *Boston Packet* had recently been purchased for him by Bancroft and others.[65] In other words, Deane was not a well man, physically or emotionally, when he boarded the ship.

In the 1980s various medical researchers cast further doubt on the murder thesis. They examined the ample records of Deane's ill health from 1781 to 1789. The unanimous verdict of several leading experts in neurology, toxicology, and pulmonary disease is that Deane suffered from a chronic lung disease, probably pulmonary tuberculosis. This chronic illness can also explain the sudden attack that he suffered on 23 September 1789. Researchers have confirmed that "longstanding tuberculosis not uncommonly has been found to cause weakened areas in the blood vessels of the central nervous system. These aneurysms can rupture and cause intracranial hemorrhage." In other words, a cerebral hemorrhage or stroke was most probably the cause of Deane's death. What is more, Deane's symptoms during his final hours "are totally inconsistent with the symptoms produced by any poison available in 1789." The suddenness of Deane's death also eliminates laudanum, which would have acted more slowly. Curare can also be rejected as a possible cause. That poison must be injected directly into the bloodstream—via needle or arrowhead. Even Boyd admits that Bancroft was nowhere near Deane at the time of death and thus quite incapable of injecting him with the South American poison. Moreover, curare acts within a few seconds, and so Deane could not have lingered four hours if that poison had been used.[66]

To conclude, Edward Bancroft had no motive to kill Silas Deane, and all the available evidence points to natural causes. Bancroft was many things, but he was no murderer.

10 *In America, 1783–1784*

After the signing of the preliminary articles of peace on 30 November 1782, Bancroft's job as a British agent was finished. He would also no longer be needed as an informal adviser and assistant to Franklin and the other Americans. Writing on 4 February 1783 from Madrid, where he was serving as unofficial American chargé d'affaires, William Carmichael asked Temple Franklin what several others must have been wondering: "What does Bancroft propose to do?"[1]

Returning to England

It was not surprising that he moved back to London, where he had already established himself in business, science, and medicine. Before leaving France, he gave Temple Franklin his power of attorney to handle any small debts or other affairs that were yet pending there.[2] With his wife and children in tow, Bancroft arrived back in London on 23 June 1783. The next few weeks witnessed a flurry of activity. Writing to Temple on 11 July, Bancroft reported, "I have done nothing but eat & Drink since I came here & yet have not seen a fourth part of my former acquaintance—however my Boys go tomorrow to School at Dr. Rose's at Chiswick, & the rest of us take Possession of a small ready furnished House which I have secured at a very moderate Price for my family . . . No. 6 in Duke Street St. James's very near the Parks where my younger ones may Catch a little fresh air. . . . I shall write by the next Post to your Grandfather & Mrs. Jay to whom & to Mr Jay, I beg my most respectful Compliments."[3]

Dr. William Rose was a noted classicist, famous for his translation of Sallust, and a good friend of Samuel Johnson. The boys who were sent to his academy at Chiswick in West London were Edward Nathaniel and Samuel (aged eleven and eight). The third son, John, was just three years old and stayed home with his sisters Maria, Julia, and Catherine (six, four, and two). There was also soon to be a new baby in the family, named Sophia. She was born sometime in the final months of 1783.

One of the tasks that kept Bancroft busy was seeing about his government pension. Due to Edmund Burke's cost-cutting bill of 1782, that pension had been eliminated and then later, at Shelburne's order, reinstated. Bancroft had been receiving £1,000 per year, paid in quarterly installments. According to earlier agreements, £500 of that was to be a lifetime pension, with the additional £500 being paid as long as he resided in France. However, there had been some vague promises that the lifetime pension might be raised to as high as £1,000. Moreover, in the fall of 1782, Lord Shelburne promised Bancroft a one-time gift of "something considerable" for his extraordinary services. Bancroft never received this extra reward. Moreover, by the summer of 1783, the government was in arrears on his regular pension, owing him his most recent payment of £250. Sometime in late June and again in July, Bancroft went to see Lord North on at least two separate occasions. North agreed that, at least for the time being, Bancroft could continue to receive £1,000 yearly. However, due to provisions in Burke's bill, that money would have to come from one of the budgets controlled by Charles James Fox. (The tenuous Fox-North ministry lasted just a few months, from March to December 1783.) Bancroft met with Fox, who gave him reason for hope but said he needed to look into the matter. The issue dragged on for over a month. Again in August, Bancroft pleaded to North, in the name of "justice and humanity," for the resumption of his payments. The situation was urgent, for Bancroft was about to sail to America. He needed the money to pay for his family's expenses during his absence. On 12 August 1783 he left London. Shortly after that the government gave £250 to his wife, Penelope. As far as can be determined, that was the last payment Bancroft ever received.[4]

To America

The journey to the United States was not a sentimental return to see his old home and remaining relatives. The purpose was business. Bancroft had a long list of affairs to oversee. To help him in his work, he brought letters of introduction from Franklin, Jay, Lafayette, and numerous other influential persons. He also carried with him various documents and packages that friends in France asked him to deliver to persons in America. Sundry individuals, including the renowned legal scholar and former royal minister Lamoignon de Malesherbes, also asked him to make small purchases or perform various errands. On behalf of Benjamin Franklin, he was to deliver to Robert R. Livingston, secretary of foreign affairs, copies of proposed commercial treaties with Denmark and Portugal. Silas Deane asked him to explore the market for the import of goods from the Netherlands. John Paul Jones wanted him to get Congress to put pressure on the court of Denmark regarding prize money that Jones claimed for the prizes that had been taken there in 1779.[5] Bancroft's main objectives, however, were three in number: to revive his quercitron dye operation; to collect money owed by Samuel Wharton; and to uphold the financial claims of the Chevalier de Luxembourg against the state of South Carolina.

Bancroft arrived in Philadelphia on 24 September 1783. Over the next couple of months he made two trips to New York City and various spots in New Jersey. From early February to late April 1784 he was in Charleston. On 24 June 1784 he took ship in Philadelphia for his return to Europe.[6] During his numerous forays to various cities, he made good use of the letters of introduction that he carried with him. On 28 September he sent Elias Boudinot, then president of Congress, a long letter giving his reflections on the current state of Anglo-American relations. From Princeton, where Congress was then residing, Boudinot responded cordially that he had laid Bancroft's letter before Congress and that he was "much obliged for the circumstantial state of our public affairs contained therein. The ample accommodation of so high a character as Mr. Jay [who had written to Boudinot in praise of Bancroft] as well as your own reputation will give you the most agreeable welcome in this village whenever it should suit you to visit here."[7] A few weeks later Bancroft met with Superintendent of Finances Robert Morris, who thereupon wrote to John Jay, "I think Doctor Bancroft has merited rewards from this Country which he will never get. I esteem him much. I like his manners and understanding. It seems to me that both will wear well and grow better upon use and acquaintance."[8] Around the first of December, Bancroft met George Washington at Rocky Hill, near Princeton. After remaining several days in the general's entourage, Bancroft spent a week in the home of William Livingston, the governor of New Jersey. He charmed Mrs. Livingston, who said "a more agreeable visitor we could not have entertained." She hoped that he might return to see them again. During this same excursion he paid a visit to New York's governor, George Clinton. He also had several meetings with the French consul general, Jean Holker, and the French ambassador, the Chevalier de La Luzerne. When Bancroft returned to Europe in June 1784, he received free passage on a ship that La Luzerne had chartered for his own return home.[9]

Although visits with such luminaries undoubtedly were flattering and enjoyable, Bancroft hoped that they would also prove useful to his business interests. Those affairs would need all the help they could get. His dyeing enterprise had come to a virtual standstill after 1775. The monopoly he had been granted in 1775 for the import of black oak bark from America to Britain had proved useless, given the termination of Anglo-American trade at the start of the Revolution. Furthermore, his brother, Daniel, had been his chief agent in charge of purchasing and shipping the bark. Daniel, however, had sided with the Crown in the Revolution, and after 1778 the two brothers lost contact with each other.

Several weeks after his arrival in Philadelphia, Bancroft managed to discover the whereabouts of his brother. Daniel had served as a surgeon for a regiment of Loyalist troops during the war. Fearing reprisals after Britain's loss in the war, Daniel recently had moved with his wife and family from Long Island to Nova Scotia. Along with thousands of other displaced Loyalists, Daniel was hoping for grants of land in Canada. On 24 November Bancroft wrote to him, gently chiding Daniel for his "unkind neglect" and asking him to meet him in Philadelphia the following spring. Daniel responded that the British government had promised him seven hundred acres, but Edward persisted in urging him to return to the United States. Daniel finally accepted the invitation. Along with his family, Daniel settled in Wilmington, Delaware. There he established a medical practice while also starting to ship black oak bark to England.[10]

While Edward appeared to have success in getting his quercitron business back on its feet, his efforts to obtain money from Samuel Wharton failed. In part this was not Wharton's fault. Vandalia and the other land companies turned out to be money losers. The companies could never get their territorial domains recognized by the states or Congress. Bancroft and several others (including Thomas Walpole and Silas Deane) also had been Wharton's partners in sundry business ventures involving trade and real estate. Bancroft found that Wharton was a clever, formidable adversary. It was difficult to prove that Wharton had defrauded anyone. Moreover, Bancroft exclaimed that Wharton was so powerful and well connected that few dared to take public action against him. Bancroft appears to have won nothing from his former friend and partner.[11]

Bancroft's third major objective in going to America was to act as agent for one of the most prominent nobles in France. This was Anne-Paul-Emmanuel-Sigismond, Chevalier de Montmorency-Luxembourg. Bancroft's work for Luxembourg forms but a small part in one of the most bizarre stories of the entire Revolutionary period. It involves the frigate *Indien*, which Benjamin Franklin and the other American commissioners ordered to be built in Amsterdam in 1777. This was the same vessel that John Paul Jones hoped to command when he first arrived in France. By the time that the *Indien* was nearing completion, it was clear that it would be one of the most powerful and impressive frigates in all of Europe. It was also clear that Dutch authorities were not about to let it be turned over to the Americans, fearing this would jeopardize Dutch neutrality. The Americans therefore relinquished ownership of the vessel to France. The French also had problems deciding what to do with it. The British ambassador in Holland knew all about the ship and told the Dutch authorities that London would not be pleased if a powerful French warship emerged from a supposedly neutral harbor.

The impasse was finally broken early in 1780. The French government lent the frigate to the Chevalier de Luxembourg for a term of three years. The chevalier was a sort of mercenary commander, using his own private army of legionnaires to fight the British. It would be up to the chevalier to find a way to spirit the huge ship out to the open sea, escaping British cruisers. A few weeks after taking control of the vessel, Luxembourg turned it over to yet someone else. In May 1780 in Paris, he signed a contract with Alexander Gillon, commodore of the navy of the state of South Carolina. Gillon was one of the most colorful, charismatic, and controversial characters of the era. Born in Rotterdam to Scottish parents, by the mid-1760s he had settled in Charleston and become a prosperous shipowner, entrepreneur, and plantation owner.[12] Like several other states, South Carolina maintained its own navy—small and insignificant though it was. In 1778 the South Carolina legislature sent Gillon to Europe to obtain ships and supplies. One historian has characterized Gillon as "a disastrous combination of romantic adventurer and main-chance opportunist, of dreamer and gambler."[13] He got little help from Benjamin Franklin, who resented individual states competing with the national government for money and supplies, or from the French government, which needed all available ships for its own navy.

Just as Gillon was about to return home to report his failure, he was put in contact with Luxembourg, who seemingly had nothing to lose in letting Gillon have the ship. According to their contract, Gillon, as agent for South Carolina, would lease the ship for three years. Gillon changed its name from *Indien* to *South Carolina*. He gave Luxembourg an initial payment of 100,000 livres. In addition, Gillon would owe Luxembourg one-fourth of any profits from the sale of prizes. If Gillon used the ship for any purpose except capturing British vessels, Luxembourg was to be reimbursed accordingly for the time spent away from prize hunting. If the vessel were to be lost at sea or captured by the enemy, Gillon and South Carolina would owe Luxembourg an additional 300,000 livres.

After numerous delays, Gillon finally managed to get the frigate out to the open sea in August 1780. The ship crossed the Atlantic but found Charleston still occupied by the British. Gillon eventually put in at Havana. While sailing from one place to another, the frigate managed to take about a dozen prize vessels. In Havana, Gillon contracted to help the Spanish invade the British island of New Providence, in the Bahamas. The Spanish succeeded in taking the Bahamas, though the British regained them in the final peace settlement. In May 1782 the *South Carolina* headed north and dropped anchor at Philadelphia. After months of legal wrangling over various issues, in December the ship sailed from Philadelphia into Delaware Bay, where it was captured by three British frigates. (News of the recent signing of peace preliminaries had not yet reached America.) Thus ended the frigate's service in the American cause, but the story of litigation was just beginning.

Within a few months, the state of South Carolina was deluged by thousands of claims from persons who had rendered services to or on the frigate. These included about a thousand American and French sailors and legionnaires who had sailed on the ship for varying lengths of time. They demanded back wages plus a share of the prize money. Dozens of French, Dutch, and Spanish merchants and bankers also posted claims for supplies and funds that had been furnished to the *South Carolina*. The biggest single lawsuit came from the Prince de Luxembourg (as the chevalier now styled himself).

Sometime in the early spring of 1783, the Paris banker Ferdinand Grand informed Luxembourg that Edward Bancroft was planning a trip to America. In April Luxembourg assigned to Bancroft full power of attorney to obtain whatever money he could from South Carolina or, failing that, from the private estate of Gillon. Bancroft would receive a 6 percent commission on any funds that he obtained. Soon after arriving in Charleston on 6 February 1784, Bancroft presented memorials to both houses of the legislature. He maintained that Luxembourg was owed 300,000 livres for the loss of the ship plus one-fourth of the prize money.

Luxembourg also demanded indemnification because of Gillon's delays in sailing from Holland and because of Gillon's participation in the Bahamas expedition. He charged that those delays and distractions had taken time away from prize hunting. The legislature initially offered a total payment of £8,381, whereas Bancroft argued for £25,000 (or approximately 587,500 livres). The legislature agreed that Luxembourg was owed for the loss of the frigate. However, Gillon and the legislature disagreed vehemently with Bancroft on two other issues: prize money and the question of delays. Bancroft maintained that the value of the prize vessels and their cargoes was far higher than what Gillon reported. On the other hand, Gillon and the legislature argued that most of the delays in departing from Holland, as well as delays in leaving Philadelphia, had been caused by Luxembourg himself.[14]

After weeks of haggling over these issues, Bancroft asked that an arbitration panel be appointed. The panel was headed by former governor John Rutledge. After Bancroft learned of the panel's preliminary findings, on 9

April he wrote bluntly to Rutledge that he could not "think the proposed award conformable either to the Evidence delivered to the Arbitrators, or to any Principle of Reason or Justice."[15] Rutledge thereupon informed him that, under the circumstances, the panel could not reach a decision. With no end to the squabble in sight, and eager to return to his family and business affairs in Europe, Bancroft left Charleston shortly thereafter.

Twentieth-century American historians who have written of this affair have not treated Bancroft kindly. One has commented on his "curious insolence."[16] Another, calling Bancroft a "habitual spy," has accused him of arrogance.[17] However, the sources used by these historians—primarily the papers of Gillon and the South Carolina legislature—were slanted against Bancroft. Gillon called Bancroft a "quack."[18] Moreover, even before Bancroft had arrived in Charleston, his erstwhile enemies Arthur Lee and Ralph Izard had poisoned the waters there against him.

All of the various claims against Gillon and South Carolina took years to settle. After his return to Europe, Bancroft continued to correspond with the Prince de Luxembourg and others on this matter. As he probably had not earned a penny (or a sou) for all his efforts, he agreed in 1787 to turn over his power of attorney to John Browne Cutting. Eventually Cutting was replaced by a string of other agents. The case was not fully settled until the 1850s, and it is doubtful that the Luxembourg heirs received any money. As with the heirs in the case of Jarndyce vs. Jarndyce in Charles Dickens's *Bleak House,* by the time a final agreement was achieved, virtually all of the expected funds had been taken by attorneys and agents.[19]

Bancroft's hopes for earning substantial sums of money in his trip to America thus proved illusory. Only his quercitron business gave any promise of future profits. While in America, he did engage in a few small business transactions. For example, he had arranged for trunks containing books and other merchandise and three bales of linens to be shipped to him from England. The meager profits from the sale of such items enabled him in March 1784 to send Penelope two bills of exchange worth £75 each.[20] He also purchased part of a share in the first American merchant vessel to trade with China. This was the appropriately named *Empress of China,* which set out from New York in February 1784. More than a year later that ship returned triumphantly from its mission. Investors in that expedition averaged a 25 percent profit, and one can assume that Bancroft's earnings were sent to him in England.[21]

Anglo-American Relations

While in the United States, Bancroft had time to pursue one line of activity that was not business related. Before his departure from England in the summer of 1783, he had informed Lord North that in America he would do whatever he could to improve Anglo-American relations. Those relations had just received a rude jolt from a British order in council dated 2 July. This decree forbade imports into the British West Indies of ships stores, timber, livestock, and all types of grain by any except British subjects in British ships manned by British crews. This order would, in effect, terminate American trade with Jamaica, the Bahamas, and all the other British possessions. Now that the United States was no longer part of the empire, it would be treated like any other foreign country. American merchants in the Middle Atlantic states and New England were sure to protest against this termination of what, before the Revolution, had been a lucrative commerce. Bancroft told North that he would do whatever he could "to promote the views and interests of the British Government."[22] This appealed to North, and that is why the minister agreed to have Bancroft's pension continued, at least for the time being.

By the time Bancroft reached America, Congress was already in an uproar about this apparently hostile British action. In letters to Elias Boudinot and others, Bancroft explained that in taking this step Britain was simply reverting to traditional mercantilist principles, which reserved colonial trade almost exclusively for the mother country. Writing to William Fraser in November 1783, Bancroft reported on the general situation in the new country.[23] Fraser was undersecretary to Lord Carmarthen, who became foreign secretary in the William Pitt ministry that replaced the Fox-North coalition in December 1783. Bancroft informed Fraser that the United Sates lacked the strength for a commercial war. Americans depended too much on their trade with Britain. Bancroft noted that Superintendent of Finances Robert Morris was "heartily tired of his situation" and wished to resign. Congress had no authority to regulate foreign trade, and the thirteen states opposed granting more power to the central government. In addition, Bancroft said that the states did not want to raise more taxes to support Congress and were resisting efforts to pay off the debts accumulated during the war. Indeed, many Americans expected the Confederation to split apart, with the thirteen states either going their individual ways or regrouping into three separate entities—New England, Middle Atlantic, and South.

It should be noted that neither Franklin nor any of the other Americans in France nor the persons Bancroft met in the United States thought it the least bit unusual that he had moved back to England after the war. In their eyes this did not mean he had ceased to be an American. Numerous prominent Americans continued to live or spend extended amounts of time in England. In general, Americans harbored no hostility toward the British people themselves. Indeed, despite the flap over the order in council, the United States and Britain would continue to be each other's most important trading partner. On the other hand, despite the alliance with Versailles, most Americans persisted in their suspicions about the Catholic French.

While in America, Bancroft also contributed several articles to various newspapers. He wrote under the pseudonym "Cincinatus." The several pieces he wrote were directed against articles written by an author calling himself "Common Sense." As virtually all readers knew, the latter was none other than Thomas Paine, who was being paid by the Office of Foreign Affairs as well as by the French to write articles favorable to their interests. In 1783 Paine took up the trade issue and began publishing tirades against the British order in council and calling for Congress and the states to launch a trade war against Britain. Writing for New York's *Independent Journal* in February 1784, Bancroft argued that Common Sense's articles were based on misinformation that could lead to "groundless resentments" against Britain. He pointed out that in 1783 one of the British peace commissioners in Paris, David Hartley, had offered generous terms in a proposed commercial treaty with the United States. According to Hartley, Britain was prepared to let American ships trade freely with British islands, provided that such ships traveled only between the West Indies and ports in the United States. The American commissioners, however, insisted that American ships be allowed to transport West Indies produce to Britain. Hartley rejected such a proposal, as it violated the principles of the English navigation laws. The result was that no commercial treaty was signed. Bancroft noted that neither France nor any other European country would have permitted what the Americans had requested. Trade between a mother country and its colonies had to take place in ships belonging to the mother country. In short, the Americans had no one to blame but themselves for the order in council. Moreover, Bancroft stated that ongoing plans by Maryland and other states to retaliate against Britain by placing high tariffs on British goods would hurt Americans more than the British. Americans imported ten times more from Britain than they exported. In short, the United States needed Britain more than Britain needed the United States. According to Bancroft, Americans had fallen into "idleness, dissipation, and luxury" and would have to return to "industry, economy, probity."[24]

Late in May 1784 Bancroft wrote to Fraser that the political scene in America was one of anarchy and confusion. He reported that Congress was preparing to send Thomas Jefferson to Europe to work with Franklin and John Adams for commercial agreements with Britain and other countries. Bancroft informed Fraser that the Americans now would be more pliable in what they asked for from Britain, and he boasted that his own writings and conversations had contributed to this change of sentiments.[25] Bancroft's gloomy picture of the economic and political disarray in the newly independent United States was similar to what many prominent and ordinary citizens thought at that time. Few Americans would have predicted that within a few years all the states would ratify a new constitution granting more power to the central government.

After he returned to London in August 1784, Bancroft continued to correspond and meet with government officials. He gave additional information on what was happening in America regarding the development of western lands and many other topics. Primarily, however, he dealt with commerce. He advised Prime Minister William Pitt and Foreign Secretary Carmarthen to maintain their hard stance regarding trade with the West Indies. Perhaps, he said, Britain could offer the Americans a few small concessions of some sort, to show them the benefits to be gained by a closer association with Britain. Many Americans, Bancroft asserted, had been better off when they were a part of the British Empire. He predicted that within a few years many would be clamoring to rejoin that empire.[26]

Strange as this prediction might seem to today's reader, it was not so outlandish at that time. Many Americans did indeed have misgivings about the political results of the Revolution. Moreover, thousands of American Loyalists in England as well as ordinary Britons hoped that the United States would come to its senses and rejoin the empire.[27] In clinging to this dream, Bancroft was, at the very least, being consistent. Since 1776 he had maintained that the primary reason why he became a British agent was that he thought it would be in the best interests of both America and Britain if they remained together.

British ministers listened to Bancroft in 1784 but apparently paid no heed to his advice. The war was over, and they had little desire to crush the American economy and force the Americans back into the imperial fold. Besides, as noted above, the newly independent United States remained Britain's best trading partner. By the end of the year Bancroft seems to have realized that his advice was falling on deaf ears, and so he stopped offering it.

The Bancroft Family

While he was in America, Bancroft occasionally received letters from his family, and the news was not good. In early December 1783 he learned that most of the children had come down with smallpox but that they seemed to be recovering. Penelope herself also was not feeling well, a result of giving birth to their new daughter, Sophia.[28] Writing to his wife shortly before Christmas, Bancroft affectionately ended with the words, "May it prove a happy [new] year to us both and to the 6 children. Kiss them for me, and believe me always, My Dear Penelope, your very affectionate husband."[29] (Bancroft had not yet learned of the arrival of the seventh child.)

That his family reciprocated his love is shown in a charming letter written to him in January 1784 jointly by Edward Nathaniel and Samuel Forrester. Addressing their "Dear and Honoured Papa," the boys declared that "it filled our hearts with gratitude and joy" to learn of his safe arrival in America. They sadly reported that their mother was still "indifferent in health." The children had recovered from smallpox, though sister Julia was still in a weakened condition. Their letter closed sweetly as follows: "thank God and his Goodness for all his favours which are many, particularly for being blessed with such a dear and good Papa, le meilleur de tout les Papas qu'il y a au monde and to whom we owe many obligations for all the things you have done for us, and hope we shall be ever sensible of the duty and love we owe as long as we live."[30]

In early April 1784 Edward Nathaniel relayed the sad news that Penelope's health was still weak and that baby Sophia had died from smallpox. As soon as this news reached him in Philadelphia, Bancroft hurriedly wrote to

Penelope, advising her to go to the countryside for fresh air and to eat some of the bark from cayenne pepper. Penelope died on 10 May, just as Bancroft's letter was starting its journey across the Atlantic. Still unaware of his wife's death, Bancroft wrote to her again on 22 June. He told her he was sending her three trunks of clothes, one trunk containing hams, plus a bill of exchange worth 5,000 livres and another worth 100 guineas (that is, £105). He asked her, however, to cash in those bills only if it was absolutely necessary. This was another indication of the precarious condition of his finances. He was sending these items to her rather than bringing them along himself because he was not going straight home to London. On 23 June 1784 he took ship in Philadelphia for France. He spent about two weeks in Paris dealing with his quercitron dyeing business and other affairs.[31] In mid-August he arrived in London. Only then did he learn of Penelope's death. Now that he was the sole parent of six children, his life would have to become more sedentary.

11 *Return to Normalcy*

Family and Finances

When he was reunited with his motherless children in August 1784, Bancroft was thirty-nine years old. He had another thirty-seven years to live. Realizing that he could not pursue his sundry business and scientific pursuits while also caring for small children, he soon arranged to have Maria, Julia, Catherine, and John placed in boarding schools just outside London.[1] The older two boys, Edward Nathaniel and Samuel, continued their studies in Dr. Rose's academy, where they had been sent a year earlier. As far as the scanty evidence permits one to speculate, he remained close to his children. They visited him during school holidays, and he maintained a keen interest in their academic advancement and personal happiness. The few family letters that have survived overflow with obvious affection.

With so many mouths to feed and schooling to provide for, money weighed heavily on Bancroft's mind. When he arrived back in London, his first order of business was his pension, which had not been paid since the summer of 1783. Bancroft was owed £1,000. Sometime in September he managed to see chief minister William Pitt, who had risen to that post after the dissolution of the Fox-North coalition in December 1783. Bancroft explained everything to Pitt, who "appeared very favourably disposed." The minister told him to see the foreign secretary, Lord Carmarthen, who then was to confer with Pitt and all the other ministers to reach a decision. This led to Bancroft's famous letter and memoir of September 1784 to Carmarthen. These were two of the shocking documents that were discovered late in the nineteenth century, revealing to the world Bancroft's "treachery." Bancroft summarized for Carmarthen his entire story. He had not chosen to become a secret agent, for that "kind of Business . . . [was] repugnant to my feelings." But upon the urging of Paul Wentworth and Lords Suffolk and Weymouth, he had agreed to do it. He said his main motive had been his devotion to the empire. When he was offered a pension, he accepted it, "as my situation indeed required." He had given eight years of his life to the British cause, abandoning his business and scientific pursuits. His yearly pension eventually had reached £1,000, of which at least £500 had been guaranteed for life. All that he asked for now was the bare minimum of a yearly £500, "for which the Faith of Government has been often pledged; and for which, I have sacrificed near eight years of my Life, and my pursuits in it; always avoiding any Kind of appointment, or emolument from, as well as any sort of Engagement to, any Government in the United States; in the full determination, of remaining to the end of my Life, a faithful Subject to my natural, and most Gracious Sovereign."[2]

There is no record of Carmarthen's response. Numerous authors have stated that Bancroft continued to receive his life pension, but there is no evidence for this assumption.[3] A guaranteed annual pension of £500 (about $117,500 in today's dollars) would have enabled him and his young children to live comfortably, if not ostentatiously. Yet, as will be seen below, Bancroft's financial condition was perilous in his final years. In short, it appears that Pitt's government felt no obligation to fulfill promises made by predecessors. To support himself and his children, Bancroft would need to revive his quercitron dyeing enterprise and pursue other speculations.

For most of the remainder of his life, Bancroft lived alone in a series of rented lodgings in different London neighborhoods.[4] In addition to the deaths of his wife and youngest daughter in 1784, tragedy struck his family once more in that decade. His youngest son, John, died in August 1786 at the age of six. Little is known about his three daughters during these years.

The outlook for the oldest boy, Edward Nathaniel, seemed extremely bright. In 1789 he matriculated at St. John's College, Cambridge. In 1792 he interrupted his studies to spend several months on the Continent. He accepted a position as private secretary to the new British minister in Munich, Thomas Walpole (son and namesake of Edward Bancroft's former business partner and friend). After returning to England, he obtained his bachelor of medicine degree at Cambridge and then matriculated in the medical school at the University of Edinburgh. In 1795, without waiting to complete his M.D. work, he accepted a position as physician with the army in the West Indies.[5]

The prospects for Edward Nathaniel's younger brother, Samuel, showed equal promise. In 1791, when just sixteen years old, he attended chemical and medical lectures at the University of Montpellier. In 1793 he succeeded his brother as Walpole's secretary in Munich. Later he graduated from Trinity College, Cambridge.[6]

After several years as a widower, in the early 1790s Edward Bancroft found female companionship with a lady simply referred to as Mrs. Rose. She was probably a widow and possibly a daughter-in-law of Dr. William Rose, whose school has been attended by Bancroft's two oldest sons. On several occasions in 1791 she and Bancroft dined with Gouverneur Morris, who was then staying in London for business affairs. Morris maintained a diary that is one of the most candid ever kept by a person of some political prominence. In an entry for August 1791, Morris notes that Bancroft and Mrs. Rose dined with him. Following that he accompanied them to the opera and then escorted them home. Morris mentions that his own mistress currently was out of town. This led him to write, "En route I convinced myself that I may, if I please, receive the Kindness of the Doctor's friend."[7] Morris does not reveal whether he ever made any advances to Mrs. Rose, but if he did he was probably rebuffed. She does not appear to have been "that sort of woman." In letters to his children, Bancroft told them that Mrs. Rose sent them her love.[8] After 1792 there were no further surviving references to the lady.

By the mid-1790s Bancroft began to have difficulties with his younger son, Samuel. Whereas Edward Nathaniel was a prim and proper sort, Samuel was showing signs of recklessness. The two brothers exchanged "quarrelsome correspondence" full of "snapping and snarling" as the older tried to improve the behavior of his sibling.[9] In 1795 Samuel committed some unnamed transgressions that made it imperative for his father to send him from England. Bancroft's old friend John Jay, by then governor of New York, arranged a clerkship for Samuel in a Connecticut law office. However, Jay unhappily informed Bancroft that he found the young man to be totally lacking in circumspection and discretion. It is not known whether Samuel ever took up the clerkship. In December 1796 there came the shocking news that Samuel was being hunted by the police in several states. He had been accused of raping an eight-year-old girl in Pennsylvania. John Jay himself signed a warrant for Samuel's arrest, should he be apprehended anywhere in New York. Samuel managed to escape, making his way to the West Indies and then to Guiana. He returned to England sometime in 1797. Two London newspapers eventually printed short accounts of the affair and mentioned only that the perpetrator had been named Bancroft. There is no indication that Edward Bancroft or any of his friends noticed these pieces, and one can surmise that Samuel never informed his father of his outrageous act. In 1798 Samuel married a woman who brought with her a dowry of 30,000 pounds. It is safe to assume that the lady's family would not have approved the match if it was known that the groom was a pedophile and rapist. In December 1799 Samuel died suddenly of unknown causes.[10]

Benjamin Franklin and Other Americans

While Bancroft himself had been in America in 1783–84, his oldest son, Edward Nathaniel, corresponded with Benjamin Franklin. The twelve-year-old boy had spent half of his life in France. In November 1783 he wrote in French to the American sage in Passy. He reported that he was getting used to English food, especially the meat and *pudding en gateau*. By January the boy's English was good enough for him to write to Franklin in English. He mentioned "the great friendship that has subsisted for many years between my dear Papa and you, who loves you as much as if you was his father." The boy apologized for rambling on with "worthy praise of my dear Papa . . . who is one of the best Fathers."[11] In March Franklin answered, complimenting Edward Nathaniel for his improvements in English. Sounding very much like the frugal, industrious man who appears in *Poor Richard's Almanack* and the *Autobiography,* Franklin advised him: "Pursue your Studies diligently: they may qualify you to act in some honourable Station hereafter, and distinguish you from the ignorant Vulgar. Strive to be one of the best Boys among your Acquaintance; 'tis the Road that leads to the Character of a Good Man. Be dutiful and affectionate to your good Mother, particularly now in the Absence of your Father. . . . [My] Family join in respectful Compliments to Mrs Bancroft."[12]

Bancroft himself likewise stayed in contact with Franklin. While in America, he met Franklin's daughter, Sarah ("Sally") Bache, who found him "agreeable and sensible" and entrusted him with letters to give to her father upon his return to Europe.[13] Soon after his arrival back in London in August 1784, Bancroft met Temple Franklin, who had come to England for a reunion with his father, William. The former Loyalist governor of New Jersey was now living in the British capital. After Temple returned to France in the fall, he kept up a correspondence with Bancroft. Among other things, Temple entrusted Bancroft with letters for the mistress that the young man had managed to acquire during his weeks in London.[14]

After he arrived home from America, Bancroft made three trips to Paris before Franklin's departure from Passy in July 1785. Bancroft's trips primarily concerned his quercitron enterprise and other business affairs. He and Franklin held long, sociable conversations in Passy. Among other things, Bancroft offered medical advice about the kidney stones that again were plaguing the old man. It was Bancroft who recommended to Franklin the ship on which the statesman and his two grandsons eventually returned to Philadelphia.[15] Just before the Franklins sailed from Rouen, Bancroft hurriedly sent them a note, asking them to deliver a letter to his brother, Daniel. Still feigning total allegiance to America, Bancroft admitted that his Loyalist brother "was not on our side in the late contest." He closed by exclaiming to Franklin that "were I a Bishop I would say God bless you all."[16]

Bancroft never met Franklin again, but the two men kept in touch over the next couple of years. In September 1786 Bancroft reported that the London publisher Charles Dilly was planning a new edition of Franklin's works. Bancroft was editing the project and wanted to know if Franklin wished to add any pieces not included in an earlier collection of his writings. He also asked Franklin to send him biographical information for the introduction. In closing, Bancroft said he hoped to visit Franklin in America but that he was too busy with other affairs just then.[17] On 26 November Franklin cordially responded. He liked the idea of the new edition of his works. He promised to send some biographical details, and he said he hoped that Bancroft would indeed visit him in America. As things turned out, the aging, easily exhausted

Franklin never sent the requested information, and Bancroft never made the trip.[18]

Nonetheless, Bancroft persevered with the project and in 1787 issued *Philosophical and Miscellaneous Papers, Lately written by B. Franklin, LL.D*. It was supposed to be the first of two volumes, but the second never appeared. The six pieces in it concerned European emigration to America, Indians, smoky chimneys, maritime conditions, privateering, and the economic health of the new United States. The 186-page book was the largest collection of Franklin's writings published up to that time and enjoyed wide circulation.

Franklin's letter of November 1786 is the last surviving bit of correspondence between the two men. In all probability they had a few more contacts. Certainly, for example, Bancroft would have sent Franklin a copy of the 1787 book.

Bancroft's association with Franklin was so well known that in later years various persons writing about Franklin beseeched Bancroft for any useful information he might provide.[19] Sometime in the early 1800s, when Temple Franklin began to assemble his multivolume edition of Franklin's papers, he likewise contacted Bancroft, who provided him with a firsthand account of the notorious Cockpit incident of 1774.

In the years after the Revolution, Bancroft also stayed in touch with John and Abigail Adams. The couple was back in France from the summer of 1784 until the spring of 1785; John was serving as one of the American commissioners charged with obtaining commercial treaties with European nations. In December 1784 Abigail wrote to a friend describing Bancroft, who had just attended a dinner party at her home in Auteuil: "Dr. Bancroft is a Native of America; he may be thirty or forty years old. His first appearance is not agreeable, but he has a smile which is of vast advantage to his features enlightening them and dispelling the Scowl which appears upon his Brow. He is pleasant and entertaining in conversation; a Man of literature and good Sense; you know he is said to be the author of Charles Wentworth."[20] Abigail obviously had not forgotten Bancroft's "naughty" novel that she had purchased and read in America more than a dozen years earlier.

In May 1785 John and Abigail moved to London, where John would serve until 1788 as America's minister. Over the next several years Bancroft frequently attended the weekly dinners held in the ministerial residence.[21] It was in this period that Bancroft gave Adams an inscribed copy of his *Natural*

History of Guiana, which the minister declared to be a "handsome Volume . . . of great merit."[22] But, as in earlier years, Adams's attitude toward Bancroft continued to run hot and cold. In August 1785 Adams agreed with Thomas Jefferson that Bancroft would make a good American agent in Algiers, dealing with the Barbary pirates. Writing to Jefferson, Adams praised Bancroft as "the greatest Master of the French Language."[23] (Bancroft turned down the appointment, stating that he had too many other obligations.) But in 1787 Adams's wrath again was directed toward Bancroft. That year's May issue of the *Monthly Review* contained a bitterly hostile review of Adams's recently published *Defence of the Constitutions of Government of the United States of America.* Adams leaped to the conclusion that the review must have been the work of Benjamin Franklin, Silas Deane, and Edward Bancroft. We now know that the anonymous reviewer certainly was not any of that trio. Bancroft's last contribution to that magazine had come in October 1786. When, nearly two decades later, the *Monthly Review* printed an unfavorable review of John Quincy Adams's *Letters on Silesia,* the dyspeptic senior Adams again wrongly suspected Bancroft of authorship.[24]

Bancroft remained a close friend and business partner of John Paul Jones for several years, until they had a falling out. The two men met in America in the fall of 1783, and again in London late in 1784. Bancroft got Jones to invest substantial amounts in the quercitron business that was, he hoped, about to become profitable. In a hopeless effort to obtain the prize money owed since 1779, Jones authorized Bancroft to intercede on his behalf with the Danish minister in London. Jones also entrusted Bancroft with some of his personal funds, so that Bancroft could pay Jones's debts in Britain and France and make purchases for him. For his part, Bancroft appears to have invested money in Jones's plans to open a fur-trading enterprise in the northwest coast of North America. By late 1789, however, things had soured between the two men. Jones claimed that Bancroft owed him money and was refusing to pay. From late 1789 through 1791 Gouverneur Morris acted as an intermediary between the two. Bancroft acknowledged that he owed Jones money, but he disputed the amount and pleaded innocent of any fraud. Via Morris, Bancroft made some small payments to Jones. However, at the time of Jones's death in Paris in July 1792, his papers indicated that Bancroft still owed him about £1,800. It is impossible to say whether that figure is accurate, but one thing certain: the joint business speculations of the two men profited neither of them.[25]

Bancroft's association with Thomas Jefferson began in the spring of 1784, when the two men first met in Philadelphia.[26] Their friendship blossomed after the two reached Europe a few months later. In Paris Jefferson served with Adams and Franklin as a congressional trade commissioner; later he became American minister upon Franklin's retirement. Over the next several years they corresponded often. Occasionally Jefferson asked Bancroft to perform various errands for him in London. For example, Bancroft bought a copying machine and sent it to Paris, and he arranged to have maps engraved for a French edition of Jefferson's *Notes on the State of Virginia.* Jefferson owed "an infinitude of thanks" for these and other favors. When Jefferson made an extended trip to England in the spring of 1786, Bancroft was one of the persons he made a special point to see. Likewise, Bancroft met Jefferson in Paris during his business trips there. As noted above, throughout 1785 and 1786 Jefferson pushed for Bancroft's appointment as American envoy to Algiers, which Bancroft declined on "account of his own affairs."[27]

One topic in particular brought Jefferson and Bancroft together. This was the pathetic, complex case of John Paradise and his wife, Lucy Ludwell Paradise. From 1785 through 1789 Bancroft and Jefferson wrote dozens of letters to each other and spent countless hours dealing with the Paradise family's affairs. The Paradises were the kind of minor figures in history who are remembered today only because of their association with famous personages. John was born in Greece of a Greek mother and an English father. He spent most of his life in London. In 1769 he married Lucy Ludwell, daughter of one of the wealthiest men in Virginia and a cousin to the Lee brothers. John was an engaging savant who spoke several languages. Unfortunately, he was also weak, indecisive, too fond of drink, and horrible at overseeing the family's finances. Lucy tended to be an ambitious, intemperate shrew. In their fashionable home on Cavendish Square they welcomed Joseph Priestley, Samuel Johnson, Joseph Banks, Benjamin Franklin, and other such luminaries. Their income derived mostly from Lucy's inheritance of half of the large estate of her father. Her sister, Hannah, married to William Lee, owned the other half.

John and Lucy's problems began with the Revolution. Lucy and her sister quarreled over how the estate was divided and managed. But the biggest issue was that virtually all revenues from the estate stopped coming to the "English" Paradises. Throughout the war, the state of Virginia repeatedly threatened to confiscate the "Loyalist" estate, even though Lucy and John had always professed allegiance to the United States. In 1786 their elder daughter eloped with an Italian count of dubious fortune and character. To make matters worse, Lucy continued her extravagant spending habits. By the end of the Revolution the family was constantly besieged by creditors.

John Paradise and Edward Bancroft had known each other for several years, as both were members of the Royal Society. Bancroft took pity on them and in November 1785 wrote to Jefferson. He asked Jefferson, as a former governor of Virginia, to intercede with the current governor and have the steward of the estate send the Paradises an immediate payment of £1,000. The following February Jefferson wrote to his close friend James Madison, sending him all the materials provided by Bancroft and asking Madison to do whatever he could for the Paradises. For the next several years, Jefferson and Bancroft worked in tandem to help John and Lucy. For their part, the Paradises were exceedingly grateful. Writing to Jefferson in May 1786, Lucy declared, "I cannot say enough in the praise of Dr. Bancroft who seems to interest himself heartily in mine and my familys welfare."[28] Over and over John and Lucy lauded Bancroft as their "truly good friend" whose "kindness must always be remembered." It was Bancroft who in 1787 persuaded John to reconcile himself with the daughter who had eloped and to move back in with his wife after one of their many quarrels. By that time both Jefferson and Bancroft were also lending money to the couple so that they would not be entirely destitute. One of Bancroft's biggest headaches involved protecting John from creditors who wanted him arrested. In 1788 Jefferson approved a plan that eventually would rescue the Paradises from the worst of their miseries. Affairs at the Virginia estate finally had been put in order. Tobacco from the estate would once again be shipped to London. Profits from sales would go to Bancroft, who was appointed chief trustee of the family's finances. Bancroft managed to persuade most of the creditors to accept a schedule of payments that would, over several years, reimburse them for much of what they were owed. After giving each creditor an agreed amount each year, Bancroft would then give the Paradises a yearly allowance of £400. When John Paradise died in 1795 his will left Bancroft a bequest of £300 over and above the debt still owed to his "worthy and constant friend." Given the still shaky state of Paradise's finances, it is unlikely that Bancroft received any of the money.[29]

The Paradise story in itself is a decidedly trivial affair in history. For present purposes, however, it is important because of the light it sheds on Bancroft's character. He worked untiringly for John and Lucy Paradise, even though there was absolutely no chance that he would profit in any way from such involvement. In other words, he could be a true, caring friend. There are several other examples from his life that could also be cited in which he gave much-needed help to friends as well as strangers.[30] Such stories contradict what so many historians have asserted about his "true character" being one of unadulterated treason, dishonesty, avarice, and self-advancement.

One final topic in the Jefferson-Bancroft relationship deserves attention—slavery. Many years earlier in his *Natural History of Guiana* and *History of Charles Wentworth*, Bancroft had expressed deep misgivings about that institution. Sometime around mid-1788 Jefferson and Bancroft dined in Paris with Lamoignon de Malesherbes and the Chevalier de La Luzerne. The foursome had an extended conversation about emancipation. Bancroft followed this up with letters asking Jefferson to respond to inquiries from a new society for the abolition of slavery.[31] These proddings induced Jefferson to compose one of his most candid and revealing letters about it. In January 1789 he told Bancroft about the experiments of some other Virginia planters who had freed their slaves. None of these episodes had turned out well, for "to abandon persons whose habits have been formed in slavery is like abandoning children." The ex-slaves had no concept of private property and thus turned to theft and became "public nuisances, and in most instances were reduced to slavery again." Jefferson planned to leave Paris to visit Virginia later that spring; he would make some firsthand observations on the situation there and report back to Bancroft. In the meantime, Jefferson outlined for Bancroft a plan of action that he proposed to take:

> I shall endeavour to import as many Germans as I have grown slaves. I will settle them and my slaves, on farms of 50. acres each, intermingled, and place all on the footing of the Metayers [sharecroppers] of Europe. Their children shall be brought up, as others are, in habits of property and foresight, and I have no doubt but that they will be good citizens. Some of their fathers will be so: others I suppose will need government. With these, all that can be done is to oblige them to labour as the labouring poor of Europe do, and to apply to their comfortable subsistence the pro-

duce of their labour, retaining such a moderate portion of it as may be a just equivalent for the use of the lands they labour and the stocks and other necessary advances.[32]

Thus, in private Jefferson trusted Bancroft enough to tell him that he was considering freeing his slaves. However, Jefferson wanted to do it in the form of a social experiment—putting ex-slaves alongside German immigrants, to see which group did best. As things turned out, Jefferson never tried his experiment. He imported no Germans and freed no field slaves. But the topic continued to haunt him for the remainder of his life.

In the mid- to late 1780s Bancroft also kept in touch with several other friends from the war years. On occasion he met with Lafayette, who continued to think highly of him.[33] In October 1789 John Jay recommended to George Washington that Bancroft be appointed American envoy to negotiate with the British government over the issues of commerce and the British troops still garrisoned in western outposts. Jay praised Bancroft as "a man in whom entire confidence might be placed." Alexander Hamilton, however, preferred his friend Gouverneur Morris for the job, and Washington therefore appointed him. As things turned out, Morris was not able to achieve any results. It would be left to Jay himself to travel to London in 1794 and arrange for what later became known as the Jay Treaty.[34]

Science and Business Affairs

After his return from America to London in August 1784, Bancroft resumed his career as a physician, scientist, and general man of letters. He continued to attend meetings of the Royal Society and the Medical Society of London. In 19 December 1787 he was elected to London's Society for the Encouragement of Manufactures and Commerce. (This body today is generally called the Royal Society of Arts.) That organization was best known for annual competitions and awards for achievements in agriculture, chemistry, trade, manufactures, and the polite arts (painting and sculpture). From 1791 to 1804 and again from 1809 to 1813 he chaired the society's committee on correspondence.[35] Until old age and poverty put severe limits on his activities, he met socially in London and Paris with high government officials, leading intellectuals, and even prominent artists like Benjamin West and John Trumbull.[36]

In 1788 he joined with John Adams, Thomas Paine, and several dozen other prominent persons in London in contributing to a fund for the ransom of Englishmen captured by Barbary pirates.[37] In 1797 Bancroft was named a foreign honorary member of the American Academy of Arts and Sciences. It is not known who recommended him for the position. John Adams had first pushed to establish the organization in 1780, and it might very well have been he who nominated Bancroft. Although Bancroft never traveled from England to attend any meetings, he sent the academy a copy of his 1794 book on dyes.[38] Bancroft's writings continued to be cited often in newspapers and in literary anthologies of the era.[39]

But those scholarly activities did not put food on the table or pay for the education of his children. Bancroft therefore had to keep his hand in business. The remainder of the 1780s found him involved in numerous lawsuits and vexatious quarrels with former friends and business partners. He continued in his futile endeavors to obtain some money from his investments in American land companies.[40]

Given the failures of his sundry speculations, Bancroft needed desperately to get his quercitron dyeing business up and going. In 1775 Parliament had granted him fourteen-year patents for the importation and use of the barks of the black oak, red mangrove, and American hickory trees. Of the three monopolies, the one for black oak bark, which produced the quercitron yellow dye, was by far the most potentially lucrative. However, the Revolution had totally interrupted that trade and rendered the monopolies useless. Now that Bancroft had been reunited with his brother, Daniel, he had a trusted agent in America who would oversee the purchase and shipment of bark to England. One problem, however, was that some calico printers and textile dyers in England were infringing on his monopolies. They were importing their own bark to make the yellows and other desired colors. To protect his investments, Bancroft therefore petitioned Parliament for a renewal of his patents, which were due to expire in 1789.

In June 1785 Parliament acceded to his request and renewed his three patents for fourteen years—that is, to 1799. This was done partly because the war had prevented Bancroft from using the original patents. Another reason was that Bancroft had promised to sell his dyes at a reasonable rate to all textiles dyers who wished to purchase them. Finally, there is some indication that the government, via William Eden, spirited the renewals through the

Edward Bancroft. Artist Unknown. *Courtesy of the Royal Society*

Commons and Lords as a way to compensate Bancroft for his services as a secret agent.[41]

It seemed that Bancroft's hopes for commercial success might finally come true. The next couple of years included additional positive indicators. Within weeks of his obtaining a renewal of his quercitron monopoly in Britain, he traveled to Paris to lobby the French government for a similar privilege.

A year later Louis XVI's government acceded to his request. Undoubtedly, the fact that Vergennes and other prominent royal officials thought so highly of him was an important factor in granting an American (or so he was considered) such a privilege in France. In 1786 it was estimated that the French and British monopolies would earn him nearly £900 per year. Bancroft also busied himself with all manner of experiments in which he mixed materials to produce a panoply of new colors and improve the production of old ones. In 1787 he was granted an audience with a committee of the Privy Council. There he outlined his plans for a cost-effective method of producing cochineal scarlet, the most expensive of all dyes. This new, cheaper technique would use black oak bark and save English dyers about £200,000 per year. The committee approved his ideas. It is not clear whether the government provided any funding for the expensive equipment and workshops that Bancroft would need for the work.[42]

As things turned out, Bancroft's business luck held out. That is, his bad luck. Some shipments of quercitron bark did reach Britain and France. But brother Daniel reported difficulties in purchasing the desired black oak trees. Many of the trees were being cut and used for tanning and other purposes before he had a chance to buy them. By late 1791 he was recommending to Edward that they purchase land in America so that they could grow their own trees. There were two obvious problems with this idea. First, they would need money to buy large tracts of land. Second, if the trees on it were not already mature, the brothers would have to wait years or decades before they could be cut. Neither of the Bancrofts had such money or the luxury to wait years until the business could turn a profit. What was worse, Bancroft's experiments with scarlet in 1787 and 1788 proved to be ruinously expensive and unsuccessful. He lost about £2,500 of his own money, and this was one of the unprofitable schemes in which his friend John Paul Jones also suffered. Despite his government monopolies in Britain and France, calico printers and textile dyers continued to import black oak bark without going through Bancroft.[43]

Further proof of Bancroft's penury comes from a legal suit he brought in 1788 against Paul Wentworth, his erstwhile espionage handler and business partner. Little is known of Wentworth once the Revolution ended. In 1784 he donated some scientific equipment and an atlas to Dartmouth College in New Hampshire. In 1789 the college returned the favor and bestowed on him, in absentia, the honorary degree of Doctor of Laws.[44] The college knew, of course, that Wentworth had been living in England for many years. What the college obviously did not know was that he had actively sided with Britain during the Revolution. After the war Wentworth took a leading role in the London-based Board of Agents of American Loyalists. Along with others, he sent petitions to Parliament, demanding compensation for property confiscated in America.[45] Given the fact that the American state governments were not honoring the vague promises made to Loyalists in the peace treaty that ended the war, Wentworth and thousands of others hoped that Parliament would offer help. Eventually the British government did make some modest payments to many of the Loyalists, but it is not known how much, if anything, Wentworth himself received. In other ways as well, the 1780s were not kind to him. He never received the baronetcy or government sinecure that he had hoped for as a reward for his work as a secret agent. He invested undisclosed sums in various commercial ventures, including Bancroft's quercitron business. Like Bancroft, he appears to have lost more than he gained in those pursuits.

As so often happens when financial affairs go bad, the former friends turned against each other. In May 1788 Bancroft took the first shot, lodging a formal complaint against Wentworth in the Court of Chancery. In a rambling, repetitive statement, Bancroft recounted a multitude of financial dealings with Wentworth extending back to 1776. He claimed that Wentworth had not complied with his "reasonable requests" and still owed him the considerable sum of £2,200. Bancroft admitted, however, that he had no documents to prove many of his assertions. He said he had trusted Wentworth so completely that he did not bother to retain vouchers for all their transactions. Bancroft expostulated that, during his years in France, Wentworth speculated on the London stock market using Bancroft's money without authorization.[46]

In a sworn statement of June 1789, Wentworth rebutted the charges. He agreed that he and Bancroft jointly speculated in public funds both in London and Amsterdam, using advance intelligence that Bancroft sent from France. But this was done with Bancroft's full "knowledge and approbation." Like Bancroft, Wentworth admitted that he did not keep good records. Given the government's disdain for stockjobbers, the two men kept their transactions "very private and secret." Wentworth asserted that Bancroft had "delusive hopes" of making huge killings in the stock market and insisted on investing more money than was prudent. In his defense, Wentworth provided his own list of large and small transactions, including £56 that he gave to Penelope Bancroft in the spring of 1777 so that she and her children could afford to join her husband in France. Because of Bancroft's financial "embarrassments," on numerous occasions Wentworth had lent him money over the years. In short, Wentworth not only denied Bancroft's allegations but claimed that Bancroft owed him £2,904.[47]

It is not known how the court dealt with these countercharges. Because neither Bancroft nor Wentworth could produce much documentary evidence, it is probably safe to assume that the court took no action at all.

Bancroft might have been unwise or unlucky in most of his business investments, but there is no evidence of dishonesty. If there was a rogue in the 1788–89 dispute, it was Wentworth. Even Wentworth's relatives were turning against him by that time, charging him with theft of funds that they had entrusted to his care. When they threatened him with legal action in 1789, he fled London and sailed to his plantation in Surinam. He died there sometime in December 1793 or January 1794.[48]

Despite Bancroft's many (mostly unsuccessful) forays in the world of business affairs, it would be wrong to conclude that his interest in dyes was solely mercenary. He had a genuinely scientific curiosity about the scores of different vegetable and animal coloring agents then used throughout America and Europe—the raw materials, the extraction processes, the combinations of different dyes, the methods for making the dyes stay fast to cloths, and so on. Since his first observations in Guiana in the 1760s, he had taken voluminous notes and performed hundreds of laboratory tests over the years. In the late 1780s he commenced to organize his vast range of data. The result was a book published in 1794 and entitled *Experimental Researches Concerning the Philosophy of Permanent Colours; and the Best Means of Producing Them, by Dyeing, Calico Printing, etc.* The volume had chapters with titles like "Of the composition and structure of the fibres of wool, silk, cotton, and linen" and "Of substantive animal colours, and principally of the Tyrian Purple." The book was not aimed at a general readership. But for persons involved in the dyeing industry and for chemists, it was immensely important. Bancroft's erudition and his familiarity with the research of all the renowned Continental experts in the field were clearly displayed. He generously acknowledged the work of others—including, for example, the celebrated Claude-Louis Berthollet, with whom he was well acquainted personally.[49] In his preface he stated that the current volume plus a future one "will contain the results of many thousands of experiments and of much observation and reflection during the space of twenty-five years, in which this subject has been my principal occupation; and as it will probably continue to occupy a greater part of my time, whilst life and health are prolonged to me, I may be allowed to hope, that future discoveries will hereafter enable me to publish at least one other volume as supplementary to these, which are intended to convey all the knowledge I have hitherto acquired on this subject."

Even though Bancroft no longer had any formal connection with the British government, he sent copies of the book to his old espionage overseer, William Eden (now Lord Auckland), and other prominent officials. Auckland thanked him by writing, "I shall value it much both as a mark of your friendly recollection, and because I am sure that I shall study it with pleasure, as soon as the troubles which at present affect all Europe shall have so far subsided as to leave the mind at liberty." Auckland conveniently used the ongoing war against revolutionary France as an excuse for not immediately reading Bancroft's dense chemical treatise.[50] Within the scholarly community, the book was well received. The *Monthly Review* praised it floridly: "The Doctor appears to possess no common portion of ingenuity, and he everywhere discovers accuracy, sagacity, and judgment. Not dazzled by the glitter of false theory, he stops to ponder and discuss; and his work is replete with extensive information and curious historical learning. Its composition is easy and perspicuous; the descriptions of the processes are full, without being tedious; and the perusal of the whole is fitted to instruct and entertain the artist and the man of science."[51] The one thousand copies that had been printed sold out within a couple of years. Thereafter, persons wanting to buy second-hand copies were sometimes paying up to six times the original price for them.[52]

In 1798 Bancroft applied for a renewal of his patents on black oak, hickory, and red mangrove bark. They were set to expire the following year. In a twenty-three-page pamphlet submitted to Parliament, he presented a long summary of his activities since the 1770s. He repeated many of the complaints that he had made when applying for renewal in 1785. Despite his best efforts, his monopolies still had not gained him much financially. He had not yet found a way to extract much usable material from the hickory. He had trouble finding sufficient quantities of red mangroves. Regarding black oaks, the main problem was that various interlopers were violating his monopoly. Bancroft had brought suit against these persons but had not yet achieved any results. In the years before 1798, he had submitted written testimony from several printers and dyers in the south of England, who verified that he had always provided them with quercitron at a reasonable price. In his pamphlet he cited several examples of other persons to whom Parliament granted extensions on their monopolies when, due to unforeseen obstacles, the original privileges had not proved profitable. One of these extensions had been for James Watt's steam engine. He also reported that some of his cargoes of black oak bark coming from America had been captured by the French, resulting in significant financial losses. Bancroft claimed that in recent years his quercitron business had run a deficit of £7,000. He was hopeful that once peace returned he could reestablish his business on a sound footing. All that he requested was a six-year extension of his patents. (With hindsight one can say that six years would not have sufficed. The wars against revolutionary and Napoleonic France continued, almost unabated, to 1815.)[53]

In 1799 the House of Commons voted in favor of renewing his monopolies. The House of Lords, however, declined to approve the measure. The official reason was "the Principle that Patents were injurious to the community." In other words, they hampered free trade. But a concerted lobbying effort by special interests also played an important role in swaying the vote against Bancroft. The interlopers who had been violating his monopoly encouraged numerous calico printers from the north to petition Parliament against the renewal. According to Bancroft, his opponents deceived Parliament by claiming that he made a profit of 500 percent in his sale of quercitron throughout the country. Their "extravagant misrepresentation," as Bancroft called it, won the day.[54] Given that his dyeing business had always been a money loser, Bancroft was perhaps better off without his monopolies.

Years later, Bancroft declared that he had "long since forgiven my opponents." He derived some consolation from the fact that after the expiration of his patent the price of quercitron rose dramatically, thereby demonstrating that, despite his monopoly, he had worked hard to keep prices down.[55]

By 1799 Bancroft was virtually bankrupt. Sometime in 1800 he left for the Continent, returning from Portugal to England in December of that year.[56] It is possible that this trip had been a temporary escape from his creditors. In April 1801 he wrote to his daughter-in-law, wife of his deceased son Samuel, that his creditors were hounding him so mercilessly that it was imperative that he go abroad. After several delays, he finally departed in September 1802. He sailed to South Carolina, where he spent several weeks in a vain effort to make good on some of the Luxembourg claims. The trip was a failure, and by the end of December he was back in London. The passage of time brought him no relief. In July 1804 Thomas Walpole, son of Bancroft's deceased friend and business partner, brought suit against Bancroft. Walpole provided evidence that in 1780 his father and Bancroft had "engaged in a joint speculation to a very considerable amount." Evidently, Walpole put up most of the money and accepted a promissory note for an amount equal to Bancroft's share in the enterprise. The speculation proved a failure, and Bancroft was never able fully to repay the loan. As a result, the court found him to owe £6,400 to Walpole's estate.[57] In November 1804 Bancroft abruptly left London again, this time for South America and the Caribbean. He spent several months in Guiana, continuing the studies of local flora and fauna that he had commenced in the 1760s. He also performed field research on yellow fever to help his son Edward Nathaniel, who was deeply engaged in studying that disease. In April 1805 he visited Barbados, where he was welcomed by "the gentlemen of the island." By July he was back in London.[58]

Final Years

Extremely little is known about the last fifteen years of Bancroft's life. In fact, for some years there is hardly a scrap of information. He appears to have attended occasional meetings of the Medical Society of London and the Society for the Encouragement of Manufactures and Commerce. But he virtually disappeared from high society; there are no references to his dining with leading politicians or intellectuals. There were two reasons for this. One was his poverty. He simply could not afford the lifestyle he had enjoyed earlier. The second was his age and his health. He turned sixty in 1805, and his letters started to contain more references to severe headaches and other ailments.

Despite these problems, he continued his scientific research. Part of this work was done on behalf of his son Edward Nathaniel. From 1795 to 1799 Edward Nathaniel had served the army in the West Indies, where he had achieved the position of inspector of hospitals. Following this, he directed the British hospital staff in Portugal, in the Mediterranean, and then in Egypt. In 1802 he returned to London and took up private practice, while remaining on half-pay in the army. Two years later he obtained his M.D. degree. In 1805 he was admitted to the Medical Society of London and a year later was named a fellow in the Royal College of Physicians. In 1806–7 he gave the prestigious Goulstonian Lectures, choosing as his topic yellow fever. He joined the staff of St. George's Hospital in 1808, and in that position he obtained a large part of the lucrative medical practice in the city's west end. The Royal College appointed him censor in 1808, largely because of his successful defense of the prerogatives of physicians against the pretensions of army surgeons. He published some studies on typhus, but his principal research focus was on yellow fever, which he had witnessed often during his army service.[59]

Edward Nathaniel had long suffered from a pulmonary affliction, and in 1811 ill health forced him to give up all his positions in London and move to the more salubrious climate of Jamaica. There he resumed his army career as chief of the army medical staff. Just before his departure from England, Edward Nathaniel had completed most of the work for what would become his magnum opus. His father edited it, wrote a foreword, and had it published late in 1811. Entitled *Essay on the Disease Called Yellow Fever, with Observations concerning Febrile Contagion, Typhus Fever, Dysentery, and the Plague*, it ran to more than five hundred pages. One mid-nineteenth-century medical expert wrote of it, "Never has any work effected a greater revolution in professional opinion in this country." The tome was both scholarly and polemical. Edward Nathaniel cleverly skewered the theories of those scholars whose ideas he rejected. In some important ways, this was unfortunate, for his own theories were flawed. In particular, he was grievously wrong in maintaining that yellow fever was not contagious and that it was identical to malaria. On his behalf, however, it should be noted that he was not the only researcher of that era to make these mistakes.[60]

With the possible exception of a brief return to England in 1817, Edward Nathaniel never lived in his homeland again.[61] Within a year or so of his arrival in Jamaica, he found the demands of his army position too strenuous. Therefore he returned to half-pay and took up a private medical practice in Kingston. In 1812 he married Ursula Hill Hoseason.

When not aiding his son, Bancroft senior remained busy with his own researches. In 1813 he published his long-overdue second volume of the *Experimental Researches Concerning the Philosophy of Permanent Colours* along with an expanded version of the first volume. Together, the two stout volumes ran to more than eleven hundred pages. Some of his theories eventually were proved erroneous, but in general his work was well received by dyers and scientists. A twelve-page review published in the *Quarterly Review* in 1814 closed with these words: "Dr. Bancroft has investigated the whole subject . . . with great attention, and has made many elaborate experiments. . . . We sincerely wish that he may be enabled long to continue his favourite pursuits . . . contingent on 'the prolongation of a life, of which the sixty-ninth year is now passing away.'"[62]

In the twentieth century, vegetable dyes were largely replaced by synthetic varieties. Nonetheless, one twentieth-century expert has written that Bancroft's "classical works on dye pigments are veritable mines of information," while another has concluded that Bancroft "must always be referred to by those who are studying the history of dyes."[63]

By the time that his two-volume compendium appeared, Bancroft was clearly slowing down. In order to meet his expenses, he sold his private library. His final publication came in 1816. Written in French, it was an article on lac dye published in the journal *Annales de Chimie.*[64] After around 1811 Bancroft rented rooms in the Chelsea area of London, but he started spending much of his time in Margate, Kent. There he stayed with one or perhaps both of his unmarried daughters, Maria and Catherine. His other daughter, Julia, had married the Reverend George Augustus Lamb in 1806. Lamb was the rector of the parish church in Iden, Sussex, not far from Margate.[65]

Bancroft had always been subject to severe headaches. These were now compounded by the infirmities of old age and financial destitution. In May 1819 he wrote to his son Edward Nathaniel to report on his health and finances. He complained of stomach spasms, vomiting, jaundice, reddish orange urine, and loss of appetite. He then beseeched his son for some financial support. In closing, he wrote, "If you do not soon relieve me, my struggles must end."[66] We do not know how or if the son responded to this plea.

Just as there has been some confusion about the date of Bancroft's birth, the same is true for his death. Several authors have been off by a year, putting it in 1820, while others have erred by just a day, giving it as 8 September 1821.

The end actually came on 7 September 1821.[67] He died at Addington Place in Margate, where he was living with Maria. His will was presented before probate court later that month. It had been drawn up in 1802. In it Bancroft had named his son as executor, but because Edward Nathaniel was in Jamaica, Maria performed that role. The terms were simple. Bancroft stipulated that all of his worldly possessions be divided equally among his four surviving children. In probate court Maria swore that her father's estate was worth less than £200. A few months later she raised the value to £300. However, when all of Bancroft's debts were taken into account, it was realized that his net worth was at or below zero. A final marginal note in the court record simply states, "insolvent."[68]

Though Bancroft had been living in obscurity for several years, he was still well enough known to receive obituaries in the *Gentleman's Magazine* and the *Annual Register*. His body was interred in the Lamb burial plot in the churchyard in Iden. His gravestone was still there a century later, but no trace of it remains today.

Epilogue

Edward Bancroft was dead but not forgotten in the nineteenth century. His novel, political commentaries, and *Natural History of Guiana* were known to specialists in those areas. In the field of textile dyes, his *Experimental Researches* continued to be one of the most often cited reference works. Both Britain and America claimed him as their own. In the United States he was best remembered as a friend of Benjamin Franklin and other Revolutionary leaders. His scientific accomplishments merited him an entry in Britain's prestigious *Dictionary of National Biography* in the 1880s.

His son Edward Nathaniel lived in Kingston, Jamaica, almost continually from 1811 to his death in 1842. He remained on half-pay in the army and maintained a private medical practice. Gradually he switched his research from medicine to botany. One type of hibiscus that he was the first to identify is now known as *Hibiscus bancroftianus*. He contributed numerous articles to botanical journals in Jamaica and Britain and served for several years as president of the Horticultural and Agricultural Society in Kingston. Moreover, he was named a corresponding member of the London Horticultural Society in 1826 and France's Académie Royale de Médecine in 1835. Slave registers from the 1820s record that he owned at least four slaves. Given his father's open objections to slavery, one might surmise that the son never let the father know about this. His wife, Ursula, died in 1830 while giving birth to the couple's seventh child. In 1840 Edward Nathaniel returned to full-time service as an army physician in order to help his son William gain admittance to the Royal Military Academy Sandhurst. Upon Edward Nathaniel's death, the physicians and surgeons of Jamaica placed a mural tablet in his memory in the Cathedral Church of Kingston.[1]

Extremely little is known of the later lives of Edward Bancroft's three daughters. Julia Lamb died at the parsonage in Iden in 1851 and was buried near the spot where her father had been interred thirty years earlier. Her two sisters, Maria and Catherine, never married. It is not known how they supported themselves for the remainder of their lives, though it is clear that they had to live frugally. Maria was living in Coblentz, Germany, when she died in 1853. Catherine expired in 1866 at age eighty-four in Southsea, Portsmouth.[2]

One of the few letters by Edward Bancroft's children that have survived happens to be a long and extremely fascinating one. It was written in February 1852 by Catherine to her nephew William. The young man had graduated from Sandhurst and was serving as an officer in the Sixteenth Bedfordshire Regiment, in which he would remain for the rest of his career. William was traveling in the United States at the time. By 1852 he had become interested in his family's history. One reason for his trip to the United States was to find some of his long-lost relatives and see the places where his grandfather Edward had lived. He succeeded in meeting some of his distant cousins, including George Bancroft, a former secretary of the navy and U.S. ambassador to Britain. By 1852 George was also on his way to becoming perhaps the most famous and influential American historian of that century. Cousin George had a particular interest in the Revolutionary period and knew about Edward Bancroft's connections with Franklin, Adams, and other Founding Fathers. He beseeched William to find out whatever he could about his grandfather. William thereupon wrote to his Aunt Catherine and asked her to tell him all she remembered about his grandfather.

Her chatty, rambling, affectionate response to her "dear nephew" touched on many subjects. She also endeavored to help him "toward satisfying Mr. Bancroft's demands . . . and also whether we have any important Papers of our Father's to confide to you." She regretfully reported that few personal papers of Edward Bancroft remained. At some point in the 1840s she and her sister Maria had been visiting their niece Nancy Mackenzie (daughter of their deceased brother Samuel). Until that time Nancy and her husband had been storing a trunk in one of their closets. The trunk contained all manner of papers that had belonged to Edward Bancroft. The Mackenzies did not have room to keep the trunk and requested that Catherine and Maria remove it. Therefore "during some of the hottest days of July we spent our time in looking over all these papers & finally after selecting a very few that could be at all interesting the rest were consigned to the flames—for what else were we to do." Catherine assured William "that not one of the papers burnt would have been of the smallest value to you—they chiefly related to private business and commissions for English dog houses," among other such affairs. She explained that the issue of dog houses concerned the Marquis de Lafayette. At some point in the early 1800s, Lafayette "was setting up an English farm" on one of his estates in France and sought advice from his old friend Bancroft. Catherine noted that she and her sister did not burn the couple of Lafayette letters that had been in the trunk. They sold them to collectors for "perhaps half a crown a piece." The only papers "that we have kept are of no value to any body but ourselves & you shall have them when we die."

The papers that were not consigned to the flames survive today in the possession of Bancroft's descendants in England. They consist of a handful of family or business letters plus thousands of pages of research notes on an extremely wide range of topics—plants and animals, human anatomy, the morbid effects of meat in Guiana, moral perceptions, crimes, punishments, funeral rites, the vocabulary of native American languages, bees and wasps, the treatment of prisoners, the religions of ancient nations, paper making, cannibalism, liver disease, snakes, and many other subjects too numerous to mention. In addition, there is a small collection of baptismal records and other such documents. Today these papers are stored in two stout metal boxes.[3]

In her letter of 1852 to William, Catherine went on to discuss what little she knew of her family's history, tracing it back to the seventeenth century in England. Of her own father, Edward Bancroft, she rhapsodized that he had been "the most unostentatious person in the world . . . he had merit & worth of his own and therefore never bragged." He had "made many valuable discoveries in natural history . . . [and] of the properties of various dyeing shrubs, & plants, greatly to the benefit of North America & England." The patent that the English government had given him would have made "Princes of us all," but wars led to the capture of "a great number of his vessels," such that "he sustained great pecuniary losses." Despite this, he "gave his children the best education he could afford." She concluded by apologizing for not knowing more about her family's history. Her father "spoke very little on such subjects, his mind was chiefly given to deep scientific research & he always thought Virtue the best hereditary rank to be proud of."

Starting in the 1860s, various Bancroft relatives in Massachusetts and New York commenced to take an interest in their distant cousin. The American Bancrofts somehow learned of the Luxembourg claims dating from the 1780s and became convinced that Edward had won large sums of money for his work in that cause. They came to believe that Edward had deposited $7 million in a Massachusetts bank and that any person who could demonstrate a blood connection to him was entitled to it. These hopes were delusional. No such treasure existed. Bancroft's British descendants sometimes were equally gullible. Two of his granddaughters believed that he had been a close friend of King Louis XVI of France. According to this legend, Bancroft accompanied the king to the scaffold in January 1793. Before being placed on the guillotine, the king gave Bancroft the lace ruffles from his shirt.[4]

The historian George Bancroft raised further interest in Edward. In 1866 he published his ten-volume *History of the United States of America*. In volume 9 he wrote that Edward Bancroft had "accepted the post of a paid American spy to prepare himself for the more lucrative office of a double spy for the British ministers."[5] This brief statement was the extent of what George had to say about his distant cousin. It was the first time that any scholar had conjectured that Edward Bancroft had been a spy. And conjecture it was. George Bancroft cited no documentary evidence of any kind. Moreover, his clever guess was wrong in postulating that Edward had been a paid agent of the Americans. Following in George Bancroft's wake, a handful of other historians in the 1860s and 1870s briefly repeated his supposition but added no new information or documentation. The vast majority of authors, however, continued to write of Edward Bancroft as a loyal American patriot.

George Bancroft's charge against Edward set off a firestorm among the Bancroft clan. Relatives both in England and America inveighed against Cousin George's "cruel" treatment of Edward.[6] There the matter lay until the late 1880s, when an American researcher obtained permission to read and make photographic copies of thousands of British diplomatic documents heretofore closed to the public. This researcher was Benjamin Franklin Stevens (no relation to *the* Benjamin Franklin). Born in 1833 in Vermont, Stevens moved to London in 1860. There he became a bookseller and purchasing agent for numerous American libraries. From 1866 to his death in 1902 he also served as United States dispatch agent, which put him in charge of receiving and sending American diplomatic, consular, and naval correspondence. Eventually he would publish several books reprinting documents relating to the American Revolution.

When Stevens started to work in the British Museum and the Public Record Office in the late 1880s, he made particular use of the papers of William Eden. It did not take him long to conclude that the many letters by or about Dr. Edwards and Dr. Bancroft pointed to the very same person. Most of these letters would be reproduced in his twenty-five-volume *Facsimiles of Manuscripts in European Archives Relating to America, 1773–1783*, which was published in installments from 1889 to 1898. But even before the first volume appeared, the American Bancroft clan had gotten wind of it. They enlisted Francis Wharton in their cause. Wharton was an employee in the U.S. Department of State, and he was just about to publish his six-volume edition of *The Revolutionary Diplomatic Correspondence of the United States*. In 1888 Wharton and Stevens exchanged several heated letters.[7] Stevens refused to back down and was confident that, once his facsimiles of the relevant documents were published, the scholarly community would agree that Bancroft and Edwards were indeed the same person. In contrast, Wharton argued that "Edwards" must have been one of the many aliases used by Paul Wentworth or one of the other British agents in France. To buttress his case, Wharton composed a twenty-page defense of Bancroft and included it in the first volume of his *Revolutionary Diplomatic Correspondence*. He cited the absolute trust that people like Benjamin Franklin, Silas Deane, the Marquis de Lafayette, the Comte de Vergennes, and John Paul Jones had placed in Bancroft. Wharton confidently concluded:

> To believe him guilty of such atrocious and yet exquisitely subtle perfidy we must believe that, ingenuous, simple-hearted, and credulous as he appeared to the general observer, occupying to Franklin and to America a position not unlike what Boswell did to Johnson . . . , he was, nevertheless, a dissembler so artful as to defy the scrutiny of Franklin, with whom he was in

constant intercourse; an intriguer so skillful as, without money or power, to deceive Vergennes and the multitudinous police with which Vergennes encircled him; a villain so profoundly wary as to win the confidence of Paul Jones, professedly aiding him in desperate secret raids on the British coast, and yet, by an art almost unfathomable, reserving the disclosure of these secrets to British officials until a future day which never came; a double traitor, whose duplicity was so masterly as to be unsuspected by the British court, which held him to be a rebel; and by such men as La Fayette, as John Adams, as Jefferson, who regarded him as a true friend. This amusing combination of apparently absolutely inconsistent characteristics may exist in bewildering harmony in the character of Edward Bancroft; but such a phenomenon should not be believed to exist without strong proof.[8]

Francis Wharton was an otherwise astute and conscientious historian, but he must have felt some embarrassment soon after he composed those words. In the same year he wrote them, 1889, Benjamin Franklin Stevens published the first volumes of his monumental collection. There, in plain sight, one could find all the proof needed to demonstrate that George III and Lord North knew that Bancroft worked for them. There also one could see samples of handwriting revealing that Dr. Edwards and Dr. Bancroft were one and the same. In addition to the many documents reprinted by Stevens, other historians soon published yet other items—most famously, Bancroft's 1784 letter and memoir to Lord Carmarthen.

It took several decades for the American and British members of the Bancroft clan to accept this verdict. In the 1930s, while doing research for his book *Divided Loyalties,* Lewis Einstein spoke with one of Bancroft's distant American relations. She told him that in the 1890s, when the news had broken about Bancroft's espionage, one of his British descendants was so outraged and embarrassed that he burned all of Bancroft's surviving papers, lest they contain incriminating evidence. That story has been repeated by several other authors. The person who supposedly consigned the documents to the flames was William Bancroft, who by the 1890s was a retired lieutenant-general.[9]

In actuality, the American relative who spoke with Lewis Einstein was totally mistaken. It is true that some of Edward Bancroft's papers had been burned. These were the various business letters and other odds and ends that Catherine and Maria destroyed in the mid-nineteenth century, because they had no room to store them. There is no reason to believe that there was anything incriminating in the documents they consigned to flames. Given how careful Bancroft had been to conceal his espionage, he would have been a poor spy to have left such evidence in his personal belongings. The papers that his daughters retained were duly bequeathed to their nephew William in the 1860s. He retained them until his death in 1903, and today they belong to two of his great grandchildren.

What, finally, can one conclude about Edward Bancroft? One of the three portraits of him that survive is a small, black silhouette. The image has an air of mystery. This befits a man who, after all, had been a spy. Yet, though he worked as a British secret agent, he was not a traitor to the United States. He had been born a subject of Great Britain and its empire, and he chose to remain so when the American colonists rebelled. He was not a murderer. He was no more greedy for fame or fortune than most of the prominent British and American figures with whom he dealt throughout his life. He was a good family man and a kind and generous friend to many people. Both before and after the Revolution he devoted most of his energies to science, though he also took a keen interest in a wide range of other topics. He provided thorough, accurate intelligence to the British government throughout the Revolution, though his superiors, for a variety of reasons, often did not or could not act on that information. In that regard, Bancroft was no different from many other spies in history. As one recent historian of espionage has written, "Good intelligence has often been badly used."[10]

Despite all that is now known about Bancroft, one still might ask: Why did this scientist and man of letters become a spy? It would be easier to answer this if, many years later, he had written his memoirs. But rare is the spy who does that. If his espionage had been discovered at the time by Franklin or by French police, he might have been put on trial. Then he would have had to discuss his motives. Two times in his life, however, he did explain why he had agreed to become a secret agent. The first came in 1776, when he wrote a summary of his initial dealings with Silas Deane. The second came in 1784, with his letter and memoir to Lord Carmarthen. On both occasions, he stressed that it had been the British government that had first approached him. He asserted that he had agreed to do the work primarily because he hoped in some fashion to prevent a breakup of a union that he considered beneficial for both Britain and America. Despite such personal testimony, most historians until now have painted him as an

Edward Bancroft. Artist Unknown. *Courtesy of the Franklin Collection,
Yale University Library*

avaricious intriguer who betrayed his country and did it grievous harm by
helping to prolong the war. In doing so, they have ignored his obvious sympathy for American grievances, voiced most famously in his *Remarks on the
Controversy* of 1769. During the Revolution, he hoped that by letting each
side know what the other wanted and what the other was doing each would

come to its senses and find some suitable compromise. With the benefit of hindsight, we can view this line of thought as hopelessly naive. But until France and Britain openly went to war against each other in the spring of 1778, many persons in Britain clung to the hope that the colonies could be kept in the fold.

Throughout the Revolution and for at least a year after the Treaty of Paris was signed, Bancroft continued to believe that both Britain and the new American republic would be better off if they reunited. Though no American political leaders of the 1780s regretted gaining independence from Britain, many did have severe doubts about the shaky political and economic condition of the new country that they had patched together. It was only in 1785 that Bancroft abandoned his hope that the Americans would rejoin the empire.

All of the available evidence about Bancroft is consistent with this interpretation. Admittedly, the above thesis about his motives cannot be proved beyond a reasonable doubt. However, when a historian attempts to discern the motives of any individual from the past, he or she stands on slippery ground. Can one person ever truly get inside the mind of another? Historians have had similar challenges in getting to the true inner feelings about many of America's Founding Fathers—to cite just one famous group of individuals. One biographer has referred to George Washington's character as "famously elusive." The many mysteries and inconsistencies surrounding Thomas Jefferson have led authors to write books about him with titles like *American Sphinx, Paradoxical Patriot,* and *Grieving Optimist.* Benjamin Franklin's biographers have wondered "who can do more than guess" about a "maddening" figure who was a "man of many masks." It was Franklin himself, in the guise of Poor Richard, who counseled, "Let all men know thee, but no man know thee well."[11]

Bancroft would be surprised to learn that nowadays he is best remembered as a spy. He certainly would have hoped that, within his family and descendants, he was remembered as a loving husband and father. To the outside world, he would have expected his chief claim to fame to be his *Natural History of Guiana* and, even more, his various discoveries and writings about vegetable dyes. He was probably not ashamed of his work as a secret agent, because he considered that he was doing it in a just cause. But he would have considered it a brief hiatus from his much longer career in research and writing.

No figure in history can command posterity to think of him as he would have wished. At the very least, however, we should acknowledge that Bancroft was a man of many talents and good qualities. He was a first-rate scientist who also happened to be a first-rate spy.

Abbreviations

AL	Arthur Lee
APS	American Philosophical Society
BF	Benjamin Franklin
BL	British Library
EB	Edward Bancroft
ENB	Edward Nathaniel Bancroft
JA	John Adams
JCC	*Journals of the Continental Congress*
JPJ	John Paul Jones
JWJ	Jonathan Williams Jr.
PBF	Leonard Labaree et al., eds., *The Papers of Benjamin Franklin,* 39 vols. to date (New Haven: Yale University Press, 1959–)
PCC	*Papers of the Continental Congress*
PJPJ	James C. Bradford, ed., *The Papers of John Paul Jones, 1747–1792,* 10 reels of microfilm plus a printed *Guide* (Alexandria, VA: Chadwyck-Healey, 1986)
PW	Paul Wentworth
SD	Silas Deane
SW	Samuel Wharton
TJ	Thomas Jefferson
TNA	The National Archives, United Kingdom
WTF	William Temple Franklin

Notes

CHAPTER ONE. *Early Life*

1. Other old style (i.e., Julian) dates below will also be changed to the new, Gregorian style.

2. Genealogical information comes chiefly from these sources: John Green's Family Data; Bancroft, "Bancroft Family"; Westfield Athenaeum, Birth and Death Records.

3. Historical Society of Pennsylvania, Edith Bancroft Ashmore Collection (hereinafter cited as Ashmore Collection), copy of probate records, 27 April–20 May 1747.

4. Ibid., EB memorandum.

5. Butterfield, *Diary and Autobiography of John Adams,* 4:71.

6. Isham, *Deane Papers,* 5:534.

7. In most places throughout this book the words "England" and "Britain" are used interchangeably.

8. Anderson and Anderson, "Edward Bancroft." The authors of this otherwise fine article go too far in stating as a certain fact that Bancroft was apprenticed to Williams.

9. Ashmore Collection, EB memorandum; Bancroft, "Bancroft Family"; John Green's Family Data.

10. Ashmore Collection, EB to Thomas Williams, 4, 21 December 1763.

11. Ibid., 4 December 1763.

12. Ibid., 21 December 1763.

13. Ibid., EB memorandum and other papers.

14. Ibid., EB diary fragment.

15. In later years Gale wrote approvingly of EB. See *PBF,* 33:500–501.

16. Ashmore Collection, copy of deed dated 18 November 1766 (old style).

17. EB, *Natural History of Guiana*, i. Here and elsewhere I use EB's punctuation, spelling, and capitalization. However, I do not follow his unsystematic, confusing habit of italicizing various words.

18. Ibid., 34–35, 108–9.

19. Ibid., 130–31, 214–15.

20. Ibid., 198.

21. Delbourgo, *Most Amazing Scene*, 182–83.

22. *PBF*, 19:160–62; Piccolino and Bresadola, "Drawing a Spark," 51–57.

23. Delbourgo, *Most Amazing Scene*, 182. Also see Delbourgo and Dew, *Science and Empire*, 269–71.

24. Delbourgo, *Most Amazing Scene*, 199. Also see Keesey, "Electric Fish," 149–64.

25. EB, *Natural History of Guiana*, 260–61.

26. Ibid., 334.

27. Ibid., 257–58.

28. Ibid., 343–48.

29. Ibid., 366–75, 397–98. For a discussion of EB's attitudes toward modern capitalism, see London, "Novel and Natural History," 101–16.

30. Excellent discussions of this topic can be found in Chaplin, *Subject Matter;* and Drayton, *Nature's Government.*

31. EB, *Natural History of Guiana*, 301.

32. Ibid., 400.

33. Henry F. May offers an excellent overview of the shared values of many European and American political and intellectual leaders in *Enlightenment in America.*

34. See Bailyn, *Atlantic History;* Bailyn and Denault, *Soundings in Atlantic History;* and Greene and Morgan, *Atlantic History.*

35. *Annual Register*, 1769.

36. *JCC*, 24:92. None of the books seems to have been purchased, probably for financial reasons.

37. Available in a modern reprint. New York: Arno, 1971.

CHAPTER TWO. *On the Rise in London*

1. Historical Society of Pennsylvania, Edith Bancroft Ashmore Collection (hereinafter cited as Ashmore Collection), EB memorandum. In the hand of Julia Louisa Allen, who copied it from the original, which she had found in the bedroom wardrobe of her mother, Julia Louisa Lamb (daughter of EB). Numerous historians who have written, in passing, about EB, have jumbled the dates and sequence of his travels during these years. Some, for example, have written that he first arrived in Britain only in 1769. Thanks to this memorandum, composed by EB around 1805, these errors can be corrected in the pages below.

2. For excellent analyses of British-colonial relations through the century, see essays by Keith Mason, John Derry, H. T. Dickinson, and Frank O'Gorman in Dickinson, *Britain and the American Revolution.* Also see Egnal, *Mighty Empire.* Two very different but extremely influential works on the growing colonial resentment of British policies are

Bailyn, *Ideological Origins;* and Breen, *Market Place of Revolution.* Perceptive analyses of the differing ways in which "empire" was interpreted in that era can be found in Marshall, *Oxford History of the British Empire,* vol. 2: *The Eighteenth Century.*

3. EB, *Remarks,* 7.

4. Ibid., 47.

5. Ibid., 95.

6. Ibid., 99–103.

7. Ibid., 101.

8. Ibid., 117.

9. Ibid., 39–41.

10. Ibid., 4–63.

11. Ibid., 81–83.

12. Ibid., 52–54, 66–67.

13. Syrett, *Papers of Alexander Hamilton,* 26:353.

14. For example, Morgan, "Postponement of the Stamp Act," 379–80; and Van Alstyne, *Empire and Independence,* 41.

15. One author who suggests PW as a collaborator is Bemis, "British Secret Service," 475. Bemis cites a letter of 17 December 1777 from PW to William Eden. But a reading of that letter indicates only that PW had read EB's *Remarks;* there is no mention of PW helping to write it.

16. EB, *Remarks,* 109.

17. Isaacson, *Benjamin Franklin,* 229, 249.

18. Boyd, "Silas Deane,"181; Pearl, "New Perspectives," 48. This is one of the few instances where I disagree with Pearl. Otherwise, his MA thesis is extraordinarily well researched and perceptive.

19. Edinburgh University Library, Special Collections, Matriculation Records for medical students. I thank Jo Currie for locating the information regarding Daniel Bancroft.

20. *PBF,* 16:224.

21. Ashmore Collection, EB memorandum; Bancroft, "Bancroft Family," 49.

22. Information on PW and the Kleinhoop estate can be gleaned from Internet sites maintained by the Nationaal Archief Suriname and by descendants of plantation owners there, e.g., http://nationaalarchief.sr/geschiedenis/plantages/commewijnerivier/appecappe. Also see Wentworth, *Wentworth Genealogy,* 3:7–13, plus additional pages 8A–8D included in some copies of the book.

23. Sheffield Archives, WWM/R/1/766, PW to Rockingham, 25 March 1767; WWM/R/1/959, PW to Rockingham, 29 January 1768. Letter to author from Robin Wiltshire (of Sheffield Archives), 14 July 2006.

24. Wilderson, *Governor John Wentworth,* 14, 146–48, 153, 166, 171, 192, 208–10; Stevens, *Facsimiles,* no. 1781, Beaumarchais to Vergennes, 17 December 1777.

25. Numerous authors have erroneously stated that EB worked on PW's plantations in 1763–66. In the earlier years, EB was in the western Dutch districts, whereas PW's plantations were further east, in the district of Surinam. For evidence of their initial meeting in London in 1769, see TNA, C 12/160/29, statement of PW, 27 June 1789.

26. Published in London by T. Becket.

27. Delbourgo, "Fugitive Colours."

28. London, "Novel and Natural History," 101–16. A slightly revised version is printed in her *Women and Property,* 86–96. The *Charles Wentworth* reprint was published in New York by Garland in 1975.

29. EB, *Charles Wentworth,* 1:29–30.

30. Ibid., 3:209.

31. Ibid., 3:217.

32. EB and Voltaire were alike in yet another way. Most intellectuals and explorers in early modern Europe viewed the scientific investigation of South America and other parts of the world as merely an arm of imperial expansion. The new findings were important mostly because of the ways in which they could benefit the mother countries. EB and Voltaire were among the few who rejected this imperialistic incentive for scientific discoveries. On this general topic see, among other works, Drayton, *Nature's Government.*

33. EB, *Charles Wentworth,* 2:231.

34. Ibid., 3:106–7.

35. Ibid., 106–7, 117–24.

36. MacNalty, "Edward Bancroft," 9.

37. Butterfield, *Diary and Autobiography of John Adams,* 4:72–73.

38. Butterfield, *Adams Family Correspondence,* 1:138, 3:156–57.

39. Bancroft, "Bancroft Family," 49; Ashmore Collection, EB memorandum; John Green's Family Data. Genealogical records among family descendants state that the wedding to Penelope Fellows took place sometime in 1770 or 1771. I have narrowed that to the period from April to September 1771. EB arrived in England from America in April 1771 and the following September left his wife for a one-year stay in Ireland. Their first child was born in May 1772, which further indicates a mid-1771 wedding date.

40. Bancroft, "Bancroft Family," 49; Ashmore Collection, EB memorandum.

41. These notes are part of the Bancroft Family Papers currently in the possession of EB's descendants Anthony Bancroft Cooke and Alicia Salter.

42. APS, BF Papers, EB to BF, undated.

43. *Boston Evening Post,* 15 June 1772; *PBF,* 19:175.

44. John Green's Family Data.

45. *PBF,* 19:341.

46. Bancroft Cooke/Salter Collection, Joseph Banks to EB, 1 June 1772.

47. MacNalty, "Edward Bancroft," 9.

48. See University of Illinois, Historical Survey Collection, SW Papers.

49. For the tortuous story of Vandalia and other land companies, see Abernethy, *Western Lands,* esp. chap. 3; Alvord, *Mississippi Valley;* Onuf, *Origins,* chap. 4; Royster, *Fabulous History;* and *PBF,* 17:8–11, 22:19–21.

50. Bancroft Cooke/Salter Collection, BF to EB, 21 May 1773.

51. Trengrove, "Chemistry at the Royal Society," 347–48; Ashmore Collection, copy of EB's Certificate of Election, 20 May 1773; Anderson and Anderson, "Edward Bancroft," 364; MacNalty, "Edward Bancroft," 9.

52. Hunt, *Medical Society of London,* 15–47; Hunting, "Medical Society of London," 350–54; Penelope Hunting to author, 3 January 2006. The most recent and complete gen-

eral history of the organization is Hunting, *Medical Society of London*. Several authors have stated that EB was also a member of the Royal College of Physicians. That society was open only to Oxford and Cambridge graduates, and thus EB was not eligible. His son, Edward Nathaniel, however, did attend Cambridge and later joined the Royal College of Physicians.

53. Colonel R. D. Kinsella-Bevan (registrar of the Medical Society of London) to author, 23 August 2006. Microfiche copies of the society's records are housed at the Wellcome Institute for the History of Medicine.

54. Colin A. McLaran (head of Special Collections, University of Aberdeen) to author, 7 January 1993; Anderson and Anderson, "Edward Bancroft," 360–62.

55. Ashmore Collection, EB memorandum.

56. WTF, *Memoirs of the Life and Writings of Benjamin Franklin*, 1:358–59. For an excellent discussion of the Hutchinson Affair, see *PBF*, 19:399–413, 21:37–70.

57. There were three petitions in March (to the king, the House of Lords, and the House of Commons) and another three in May. BF signed all of them. EB signed the March and May petitions to the House of Lords and perhaps some of the others. The lists of signers for some of the petitions have disappeared. *PBF*, 21:155–57, 214–16.

58. Ibid., 21:345n.

59. For example, O'Toole, *Honorable Treachery*, 30.

60. For a list of EB's contributions, see Nangle, *Monthly Review, First Series*, 3.

61. *Monthly Review* 52 (1775): 310–14.

62. Ibid., 51 (November 1774): 393; Boyd, *Papers of Thomas Jefferson*, 1:676.

63. Butterfield, *Diary and Autobiography of John Adams*, 4:73.

64. *PBF*, 23:424–25.

65. Bancroft, "Bancroft Family," 78; Ashmore Collection, genealogical notes.

66. [EB and SW], *Facts and Observations; PBF*, 22:149–54; Abernethy, *Western Lands*, 121–22, 142–43.

67. Stevens, *Facsimiles*, 211, EB to Mr. Bearda, 31 October 1777; EB, *Facts and Observations* (1798), 2–4; Boyd, "Silas Deane," 183.

CHAPTER THREE. *Initiation in Covert Activity*

1. *PBF*, 22:149–54, 305–7.

2. Ibid., 22:373–74.

3. Isham, *Deane Papers*, 1:127, 143, 161, 195–218; *PBF*, 22:489, 25:23; EB, *Narrative*, 23. Some historians have suggested that he faked illness to cover up his skullduggery. For corroboration of his illness in June and July 1776, see Thomas Walpole's letter of 27 July 1776 to EB in the Bancroft Cooke/Salter Collection.

4. EB, *Narrative*, 28.

5. Ibid., 28, 31, 35; Isham, *Deane Papers*, 3:151–52; Wharton, *Revolutionary Diplomatic Correspondence*, 2:106; Morton and Spinelli, *Beaumarchais Correspondance*, 3:13, 15.

6. On the roots of French involvement in the Revolution, see Dull, *French Navy and American Independence*; Dull, *Diplomatic History of the American Revolution*, 33–81;

and Dull, *French Navy and the Seven Years' War,* 245–54. Also see Schaeper, *France and America,* 38–62, 73–91.

7. Crout, "Diplomacy of Trade," 47.

8. Kammen, *Rope of Sand,* 282–83, 300–301.

9. Ibid., 283, 286.

10. Wilderson, *Governor John Wentworth,* 153.

11. Stevens, *Facsimiles,* 315, PW to William Eden, undated (on or after 12 December 1777); Bemis, "British Secret Service,"474–75.

12. A photographic copy can be found in Stevens, *Facsimiles,* no. 890. The full document was published by Paul Leicester Ford in 1891 (EB, *Narrative*). The elongated title of the document in Ford's edition is Ford's own creation. It is also reprinted in Isham, *Deane Papers,* 1:177–84.

13. Bemis, "British Secret Service," 475, 477, 478.

14. Bemis, "Secret Intelligence," 233–49.

15. Einstein, *Divided Loyalties,* 8, 45.

16. Hendrick, "Worse Than Arnold," 390; Hendrick, "Arch-Traitor of the Revolution," 46–48; Hendrick, *Lees of Virginia,* 263–65, 273–91, 321–22.

17. Three of the longer treatments of Bancroft are: Miller, "Spy Activities," 70–77, 157–70; Jones, "Dr. Edward Bancroft," in Janes and Scott, *Westfield,* 120–33; and O'Toole, "Intrigue in Paris," in Thompson, *Secret New England,* 65–81. These three pieces add nothing new and lack documentation. Miller's article is especially unreliable. Here is just one example of the influence of Bemis et al. on popular historians today: McCullough, *John Adams,* 201, 234, 344. In the second half of the twentieth century, the most influential author to write on Bancroft was Julian P. Boyd. Because Boyd wrote mostly about the late 1780s, he is discussed in a later chapter.

18. Reprinted in Bemis, "British Secret Service," 493. Bemis made some slight alterations or errors in transcription. I have remained faithful to the original manuscript, located in TNA, FO, 4/3.

19. Two examples: Stevens, *Facsimiles,* 316 (Joseph Hynson to Edward Smith, 17 December 1777), 321 (PW to Eden, 25 December 1777).

20. Wilson, *History of the American People,* 2:226, 237, 256, 277, 311–13, 327.

21. Norton, *British-Americans,* 4–8, 43–47.

22. On the transatlantic empire and what it meant to be "American" or "British," see Armitage, *Ideological Origins;* Armitage and Braddick, *British Atlantic World;* Brooks, "Controlling the Metaphor," 233–54; Christie, "British Politics and the American Revolution," 205–26; and Colley, *Britons.*

23. Quoted in Kaye, *Thomas Paine,* 16.

24. Quoted in Morgan, *Benjamin Franklin,* 86.

25. Quoted in Einstein, *Divided Loyalties,* 406–7.

26. Boyd, *Papers of Thomas Jefferson,* 1:269.

27. For an excellent treatment of this topic, see Phillips, *Cousins' Wars,* chap. 5.

28. Historical Society of Pennsylvania, Edith Bancroft Ashmore Collection, Daniel Bancroft to EB, 3 November 1775.

CHAPTER FOUR. *First Steps*

1. Legg, *British Diplomatic Instructions*, 151–52; Stevens, *Facsimiles*, 1371.

2. The voluminous information that British agents collected can be found in numerous sources. Some examples: Legg, *British Diplomatic Instructions*, 153–62; Stevens, *Facsimiles*, 1367–72, 1450; Butler, *Colonel St. Paul of Ewart*, esp. 2:420, 427; Fortescue, *Correspondence of King George*, 3:380–81; Van Alstyne, "Great Britain," 311–46; Pearl, "New Perspectives," 68–70; and Tracy, *Navies*, esp. 119, 126, 138–41, 181.

3. Bates, "Diplomacy of Lord Stormont," ii.

4. Isham, *Deane Papers*, 1:290, 326.

5. Stevens, *Facsimiles*, 7 (PW to Suffolk, 25 January 1777), 891 (Garnier to Vergennes, 16 August 1776), 1397 (Robert Morris to SD, 20 December 1776–29 January 1777, a copy in EB's hand, showing EB's work as a copyist and informal secretary); Isham, *Deane Papers*, 1:243–44, EB to SD, 16 September 1776; *PBF*, 23:202–5, 235; Historical Society of Pennsylvania, Edith Bancroft Ashmore Collection (hereinafter cited as Ashmore Collection), EB memorandum.

6. Stevens, *Facsimiles*, 1368, Stormont to Weymouth, 9–10 October 1776.

7. Ibid., 7 (PW to Suffolk, 25 January 1777), 1368, 1372, 1413 (Stormont to Weymouth, 9–10 October, 6 November 1776, 15 January 1777).

8. *PBF*, 16:225n.

9. Some examples: Browne, "Sketch," 104; Brown, *Empire or Independence*, 132; Patton, *Patriot Pirates*, 63–65.

10. Einstein, *Divided Loyalties*, 9–10, 13.

11. Pearl, "New Perspectives," 78. Other examples of this line of thought: Augur, *Secret War*, 137; Isaacson, *Benjamin Franklin*, 335. In an earlier book I voiced this same opinion. See my *France and America*, 75. Bancroft appears in several places in that book, as a minor character. I relied on what earlier historians had written about him, and I repeated some of their errors.

12. For example, see Isham, *Deane Papers*, 209–10.

13. Ibid., 1:250; *PBF*, 25:23–24.

14. Isham, *Deane Papers*, 1:237–43. Other surviving letters to Deane from this period in this collection are found at: 1:243–44, 249–52, 345–50, 364–65, 414–15, 479–81, 482–86, 489–91, 494–96, 2:3–6, 15–17.

15. Stevens, *Facsimiles*, 467, AL to SD, 28 July 1776.

16. Ibid., 1368, Stormont to Weymouth, 9–10 October 1776; *PBF*, 10:266n, 23:55n.

17. Isham, *Deane Papers*, 1:210.

18. Ibid., 1:290 (1 October 1776), 398 (3 December 1776).

19. Ibid., 1:479–81; *PBF*, 23:296.

20. Isham, *Deane Papers*, 1:487.

21. *Monthly Review* 56 (1776): 145–49. Also see *PBF*, 23:69–79, 156–59, 424–25, 431.

22. The most detailed study of this affair is Warner, *John the Painter*. Though she correctly notes the very limited contacts that Bancroft had with Aitken, she falls into the same old stereotypes regarding Bancroft's duplicity, treason, amorality, and so on. Also see York, *Burning the Dockyard*.

23. Warner, *John the Painter*, 135–36.

24. Ibid., 164–66; Pearl, "New Perspectives," 83–86; Stevens, *Facsimiles*, 635, EB to SD, 7 February 1777.

25. Fortescue, *Correspondence of King George*, 3:423–27; Isham, *Deane Papers*, 2:3–6, 15–17; *Gazetteer and New Daily Advertiser* (London), 18 March 1777; *Morning Chronicle and London Advertiser*, 18 March 1777.

26. Warner, *John the Painter*, 232; Pearl, "New Perspectives," 86.

27. Isham, *Deane Papers*, 2:24–25.

28. Einstein, *Divided Loyalties*, 14; Wharton, *Revolutionary Diplomatic Correspondence*, 1:624; Pearl, "New Perspectives," 84; Stevens, *Facsimiles*, 145, PW to Suffolk, 26 March 1777.

29. BL, Add. Mss., 34413, fol. 422, [John Vardill?] to Eden, [April 1777]; PCC, M247, r91, i78, v2, p 447, EB to Committee for Foreign Affairs, 31 March 1778; Stevens, *Facsimiles*, 145; TNA, c/12/160/29, EB complaint vs. PW, 24 May 1788.

30. Boyd is the chief proponent of a strong Bancroft-Aitken connection. See his "Silas Deane," 337–42. Pearl effectively refutes Boyd's suppositions in "New Perspectives," 83n.

31. Hutchinson, *Diary and Letters*, 2:141, 144.

32. Private collection, EB to PW, Friday morning, __ February 1777; Stevens, *Facsimiles*, 477, Suffolk to Eden, 21 July 1777; Bemis, "British Secret Service," 493–94. It would be tedious to mention all the historians who have erred in discussing how much money Bancroft received and when he received it.

33. EB complaint vs. PW, 24 May 1788.

CHAPTER FIVE. *Our Man in Paris*

1. Butterfield, *Diary and Autobiography of John Adams*, 4:74.

2. For example, Einstein, *Divided Loyalties*, 11; MacNalty, "Edward Bancroft," 10.

3. Bancroft Cooke/Salter Collection, extract from parish registers of Saint-Pierre de Chaillot; John Green's Family Data.

4. Lopez and Herbert, *Private Franklin*, 220.

5. On Chaumont's involvement in the Revolution, see my *France and America*.

6. Stevens, *Facsimiles*, 474 (William Carmichael to Joseph Hynson, 18 June 1777), 225 (PW to Eden, 11 December 1777), 489 (PW to Eden, 7 January 1778); BL, Add. Mss., 34414, PW to Suffolk, 16 November 1777; Bemis, "British Secret Service," 491.

7. Potts, *Arthur Lee*, esp. 126.

8. Schaeper, *France and America*, 137–44.

9. Ibid., 161–67.

10. Ibid., 148; Dull, *Diplomatic History*, 83–84; *PBF*, 25:565–68.

11. Stevens, *Facsimiles*, 474, Carmichael to Hynson, 18 June 1777.

12. For example, Stevens, *Facsimiles*, 1801, American commissioners to Vergennes, 26 December 1777, in EB's hand.

13. BL, Add. Mss., 34413, EB to PW, 24 April 1777.

14. Stevens, *Facsimiles*, 200, PW to Suffolk, 24 September 1777.

15. *PBF*, 25:272–73.

16. Ibid., 25:665.

17. Isham, *Deane Papers*, 5:307.

18. For example, Bemis, "British Secret Service," 476; Isaacson, *Benjamin Franklin*, 333–34; Potts, *Arthur Lee*, 172; Morton and Spinelli, *Beaumarchais and American Revolution*, 54, 59.

19. *PBF*, 25:22–25.

20. Ibid., 25:96; Stevens, *Facsimiles*, 204 (Lupton/Van Zandt to Eden, 15 October 1777), 210 (J. Waters to Edward Brown, 30 October 1777).

21. Butterfield, *Diary and Autobiography of John Adams*, 4:73. Also see *PBF*, 24:177–91.

22. Stevens, *Facsimiles*, 696 (Lupton/Van Zandt to Eden, 22 May 1777), 251 and 254 (EB to PW, 27 May 1777).

23. Ibid., 152, 156, 180, 195, 200, 218, 224, 228, 270, 273, 277, 305, 321, 322, 335, 484, 704, 769; BL, Add. Mss., 34415, PW to Eden, 4 February 1778; *PBF*, 25:22–25.

24. Stevens, *Facsimiles*, 62, 65, 151, 190, 196, 200, 254, 473, 492.

25. Ibid., 62 (EB to PW, 10 April 1777), 250 (PW to Suffolk, 14 April 1777).

26. For EB's letter and enclosures, see ibid., 4, 251, 254.

27. Ibid., 151. Although the words *code* and *cipher* are often used interchangeably, there is a slight difference between them. Typically, a cipher involves substituting numbers or letters for the actual letters in a word. For example, the letter *a* might be replaced by the letter *t,* and the letter *n* by the number 17. Thus in a ciphered letter the word *an* would appear as "t 17." In a code, there might be a list of thousands of words that are replaced entirely by a string of letters or numbers. For example, the word *France* might appear in code as 7984. Most of the systems used by governments and individuals in the eighteenth century were a combination of these two methods. See Kahn, *Codebreakers*, xv–xviii; and Morris, *John Jay: Revolutionary*, 660–64.

28. If one reads *PBF* vols. 23–26 and compares them to EB's reports, one can confirm that EB gave full and accurate summaries and analyses of virtually everything of importance regarding Franco-American relations.

29. Johnston, "American Privateers," 352–74; Morgan, "American Privateering," 79–87.

30. Stevens, *Facsimiles*, 1540–41; *PBF*, 24:73–77.

31. Stevens, *Facsimiles*, 180, 182, 274, 704 (PW to Suffolk, 15, 17 July, 5 August, ca. 17 October 1777); *PBF*, 25:55n.

CHAPTER SIX. *The Franco-American Alliance*

1. Mackesy offers an excellent analysis of Saratoga, though he upholds the older view in *War for America*, 102–61. For a different interpretation, see Dull, *Diplomatic History*, 89–92; *PBF*, 25:246n; and Tudda, "'Messiah That Will Never Come,'" 780n, 781, 802, 810.

2. Stevens, *Facsimiles*, 1791, F. Grand to Vergennes, 23 December 1777; Bemis, "British Secret Service," 487.

3. BL, Add. Mss., 46490, PW to Eden, 10 December 1777; Stevens, *Facsimiles*, 225, 717, PW to Eden, 11 December 1777.

4. *PBF,* 25:260–61.

5. BL, Add. Mss., 34414, [PW] to SD and SD to "ABC," 12 December 1777; Add. Mss., 61861B, "Account of the Agreement in favour of Mr. Wentworth." In subsequent letters to Eden, PW gives slightly different summaries of his long conversations with Deane. He also jumbles the dates, citing the 12th–13th and in another place 15th–16th. For present purposes it does not matter which dates one accepts.

6. Stevens, *Facsimiles,* 231, 233–34, 317, 333, 489, 769, PW to Eden, 17, 18, 22 December 1777, 4, 6, 7 January 1778.

7. PW's activities in Paris during these weeks are amply documented in Stevens, *Facsimiles,* esp. 231, 233–34, 315, 317, 1781, 1786; Isham, *Deane Papers,* 2:271ff.; and Schiff, *Great Improvisation,* 115–18.

8. Stevens, *Facsimiles,* 321, PW to Eden, 25 December 1777.

9. Ibid., 322, PW to Eden, 28 December 1777.

10. Ibid., 327, 769, PW to Eden, 1, 4 January 1778. As so often happens with PW's long-winded, hastily scribbled letters, he sometimes confuses or is unclear about dates. His initial meeting with Franklin occurred either on 31 December or 1 January.

11. Ibid., 489, PW to Eden, 7 January 1778; Dull, *Diplomatic History,* 91–92; Schiff, *Great Improvisation,* 119–23.

12. Stevens, *Facsimiles,* 315, 322, PW to Eden, shortly after 12 December 1777, 28 December 1777.

13. Fortescue, *Correspondence of King George,* 4:33–34; *PBF,* 26:652n.

14. Stevens, *Facsimiles,* 492, EB to PW, 22–28 January 1778.

15. *PBF,* 25:565.

16. Bemis, "British Secret Service," 494.

17. For example, MacNalty, "Edward Bancroft," 11; Currey, *Code Number 72,* 6, 196.

18. For example, Bemis, "British Secret Service," 491; O'Toole, *Honorable Treachery,* 35; Schiff, *Great Improvisation,* 133.

19. BL, Add. Mss., 34414, PW to Suffolk, 16 November 1777.

20. Fortescue, *Correspondence of King George,* 4:36.

21. Stevens, *Facsimiles,* 1857, 1858, Stormont to Weymouth, 6 February 1778.

22. O'Toole, *Honorable Treachery,* 33; Boyd, "Silas Deane," 330; *Pennsylvania Packet or the General Advertiser,* 9 March 1780.

23. Stevens, *Facsimiles,* 234, PW to Eden, 22 December 1777; Wharton, *Revolutionary Diplomatic Correspondence,* 1:630–34.

24. New York Public Library, Manuscripts Division, Thomas Addis Emmet Collection, Carmichael to [SD?, JWJ?], 27 July 1777.

25. Stevens, *Facsimiles,* 1372, 1413 (Stormont to Weymouth, 6 November 1776, 15 January 1777), 289 [EB to (Walpole), 3(?) November 1777]; *PBF,* 23:424–25. On SW, see Wharton, *Revolutionary Diplomatic Correspondence,* 1:608–10; *Dictionary of American Biography,* s.v. "Wharton, Samuel"; and Marshall, "Lord Hillsborough," 717–39.

26. Stevens, *Facsimiles,* SW to St. Pierre [EB], 15 November 1777. Also see Clark, *Naval Documents,* 6:412–13; *Gentleman's Magazine* (1823): 574; Bemis, "British Secret Service," 492n; and Einstein, *Divided Loyalties,* 421–23.

27. BL, Add. Mss., 24321, 34413–14. In 34414, see esp. Todd to Eden, 27 October, 3 November 1777, "Friday night" [December 1777?]. On the post office, see Ellis: "British Communications"; and Ellis, *Post Office*.

28. For examples of EB using white (i.e., invisible) ink, see Stevens, *Facsimiles*, 289 [EB to T. Walpole, 1? November 1777], 290 [EB to SW, 1? November 1777].

29. Ibid., 211, EB to Mr. Bearda, 31 October 1777.

30. Ibid., 300, J. Wharton to EB, 8 November 1777.

31. See Paltsits, "Use of Invisible Ink," 361–64; Pennypacker, *General Washington's Spies*, 1:51–52; and Kahn, *Codebreakers*, esp. 522. An excellent overview of this topic, with reproductions of archival documents, can be found on the Web site "Spy Letters of the American Revolution," http://www.si.umich.edu/spies/.

32. See Stevens, *Facsimiles*, 301 [unsigned, either J. or S. Wharton to EB], 10 November 1777.

33. See Ver Steeg, *Robert Morris*; Nuxoll, *Congress and the Munitions Merchants*; and Ferguson, *Papers of Robert Morris*.

34. Boyd, "Silas Deane," 326, 327, 330. William Pearl effectively rebuts Boyd in "New Perspectives," 80n.

35. Stevens, *Facsimiles*, 717, PW to Eden, 11 December 1777.

36. Fortescue, *Correspondence of King George*, 3:511, North to George III, 13 December 1777.

37. Stevens, *Facsimiles*, 324, PW to Eden, undated [end of 1777].

38. Ibid., 1791, 1795 (F. Grand to Vergennes, 23, 24 December 1777), 1794 (Aranda to Vergennes, 24 December 1777); Bemis, "British Secret Service," 484; Isham, *Deane Papers*, 2:270.

39. Stevens, *Facsimiles*, 226, Vardill to Eden, 12 December 1777.

40. Ford, *Letters of William Lee*, 1:284–86.

41. The issue of private business carried on by public servants was one that divided Congress. See Morgan, "Puritan Ethic," 3–43; Henderson, *Party Politics*, 5, 171–72, 187–96, 226–28; and Rakove, *Beginnings of National Politics*, 244–64.

42. Fortescue, *Correspondence of King George*, 3:511, North to George III, 13 December 1777.

43. BL, Add. Mss., 24321, SW to [Benson], 24 February 1778.

44. Ibid., [SW] to Benson, 13 Mar 1778.

45. *PBF*, 27:229.

46. Stevens, *Facsimiles*, 224, PW to Eden, 7 December 1777; BL, Add. Mss., 34415, Mary to PW, 19 March 1778.

47. Stevens, *Facsimiles*, 342, PW to Eden, 27 March 1778.

48. APS, Franklin Papers, [SW] to St. Pierre, 22 May 1778; BL, Add. Mss., 24321, [SW] to Benson, 21 April 1778, [SW] to St. Pierre, 27 November, 8 December 1778; *PBF*, 26:299n, 472, 28:271, 29:276.

49. There were, confusingly, two men named Joseph Wharton. One was Samuel's brother and the other Samuel's son. Both of these Josephs moved to Paris. On the Whartons, see Wharton, "Wharton Family," 326, 455–58; *PBF*, 27:229, 463–64, 28:508, 29:589; APS, Franklin Papers, draft of a passport for Joseph Wharton Jr., October 1779.

50. See BL, Add. Mss., 34413, fols. 107–8. In 1789 Eden was raised to the peerage as Baron Auckland, and his papers in the British Library are called the Auckland Papers. They can be found in Add. Mss., 34412–71, 37689–37718, 45728–30, 46490–91, 46519, 54238, 59704. In Stevens, *Facsimiles,* see 235.

51. See Stevens, *Facsimiles,* 332, 489, 769 (PW to Eden, 4, 6, 7 January 1778); and Fortescue, *Correspondence of King George,* 4:13.

52. For example, Bemis, "British Secret Service," 477; Isaacson, *Benjamin Franklin,* 550n; Currey, *Code Number 72,* 298n.

53. Legg, *British Diplomatic Instructions,* 156.

54. TNA, SP, 78/301, Stormont to Weymouth, 15 February 1777; Stevens, *Facsimiles,* 1505, Stormont to Weymouth, 2 April 1777.

55. Stevens, *Facsimiles,* 1779, Stormont to Weymouth, 15 December 1777.

56. BL, Add. Mss., 34414, PW to Suffolk, 16 November 1777.

57. BL, Add. Mss., 46490, Thomas Jeans to Lt. Col. Edward Smith, 27 March 1777; PW to Eden, 10 December 1777; Stevens, *Facsimiles,* 250 (PW to Suffolk, 14 April 1777), 204 (Van Zandt/Lupton to Eden, 15 October 1777); Dull, *Franklin the Diplomat,* 37–40. With no supporting evidence, numerous writers have assumed that Carmichael was a British spy. For example, Potts, *Arthur Lee,* 173.

58. BL, Add. Mss., 34414, PW to Suffolk, 16 November 1777. On Francy, see Morton, "Beaumarchais, Francy," 943–59.

59. Stevens, *Facsimiles,* 327, PW to Eden, 1 January 1778.

60. Ibid., 489, PW to Eden, 7 January 1778.

61. Boyd, "Silas Deane," 324.

62. Stevens, *Facsimiles,* 492, EB to PW, 22–28 January 1778.

63. Relying on what earlier historians had written, I myself also committed that error: Schaeper, *France and America,* 75.

64. The current Earl of Mansfield owns the Stormont papers. Upon application, they can be viewed at the National Register House in Edinburgh. For the relevant materials, see National Register of Archives for Scotland, Murray Family, Earls of Mansfield Survey, NRAS776/Box16. I am much indebted to Alison Rosie, registrar of the NRAS, for help in this matter.

65. Stevens, *Facsimiles,* 1881, PW's summary of intelligence from Edwards, 4 March 1778; *PBF,* 25:710–11; Dull, *French Navy,* 103–5.

66. Fortescue, *Correspondence of King George,* 4:53.

67. *PBF,* 26:138–41; Schiff, *Great Improvisation,* 139–44.

68. Stevens, *Facsimiles,* 1881, PW's summary of intelligence from Edwards, 4 March 1778.

69. Ibid., 411, Eden to North, 30 March 1778; *PBF,* 26:299.

70. BL, Add. Mss., 34413, abstracts of EB reports, 2, 16 April 1778; 34415, PW to Eden, 3 April 1778, [EB] to [PW], 9–16 April 1778; Stevens, *Facsimiles,* 448, PW to Eden, 24 April 1778.

71. Einstein says that PW happened to meet JA in Paris on 2 May 1778. However, the man JA encountered was not PW but rather his relative, John Wentworth, the last royal governor of New Hampshire. Einstein, *Divided Loyalties,* 15; Butterfield, *Diary and Autobiography of John Adams,* 2:308.

CHAPTER SEVEN. *Gauging Bancroft's Role*

1. A sampling: Bemis, "British Secret Service," 478; MacNalty, "Edward Bancroft," 7; Van Doren, *Benjamin Franklin*, 583; Currey, *Code Number 72*, 146; Morton, *Americans in London*, 217; Shepperson, *John Paradise*, 355; and Burke, *Twin Tracks*, 168.

2. Einstein, *Divided Loyalties*, 27–28. See also Boyd, "Silas Deane," 327.

3. Dull, *Diplomatic History*, 64.

4. Weintraub, *Iron Tears*, 209.

5. Thomas, *John Paul Jones*, 163–64.

6. Van Alstyne, "Great Britain," 312–13.

7. See Stevens, *Facsimiles*, esp. 154, 162, 173, 179, 204, 221, 226, 228. There are also numerous unpublished Lupton letters to Eden in BL, Add. Mss., 34414–15. In the latter, see esp. those of 15, 21 January 1778.

8. Stevens, *Facsimiles*, 275, Eden to George III, 20 October 1777.

9. BL, Add. Mss., 34413–14, numerous documents on Hynson; Stevens, *Facsimiles*, esp. 154, 205, 208, 279, 280; *PBF*, 24:514–15, 518n, 25:45n, 48–50. Also see Bemis, "British Secret Service," 478–82; and Einstein, *Divided Loyalties*, 51–71, 411–17.

10. Tracy, *Navies*, 184, 195–96; Prelinger, "Benjamin Franklin," 266; Taylor, *Papers of John Adams*, 6:264–65; *PBF*, 25:414–19; Stevens, *Facsimiles*, 329; Fortescue, *Correspondence of King George*, 4:45–51, 111–12, 133–36.

11. Wharton, *Revolutionary Diplomatic Correspondence*, 1:539–40, 3:32; Smith, *Letters of Delegates*, esp. 11:516n, 12:295; *JCC*, 13:116.

12. Schiff, *Great Improvisation*, 98.

13. Ibid.

14. Ward, *Forth*, 10.

15. Ibid., 14–15, 94.

16. For example: BL, Add. Mss., 34414, North to Eden, 29 September 1777; Fortescue, *Correspondence of King George*, 3:410–11, North to George III, 31 December 1777 (misdated 1776).

17. Stevens, *Facsimiles*, 696, 702, Lupton to Eden, 22 May, 27 June 1777.

18. Fortescue, *Correspondence of King George*, 4:46–47.

19. Isham, *Deane Papers*, 1:489–91.

20. Ward, *Forth*, 16–18, 24.

21. Stevens, *Facsimiles*, 145, PW to Suffolk, 26 March 1777.

22. Ward, *Forth*, 23; Dull, *French Navy and American Independence*, 81, 377.

23. Ward, *Forth*, 25.

24. Ibid., 71–75; Scott, *British Foreign Policy*, 249–50, 256–57.

25. A later chapter deals with Arthur Lee's supposed uncovering of Bancroft's espionage.

26. Stevens, *Facsimiles*, 477.

27. Barnes and Owen, *Private Papers Earl of Sandwich*, 1:231–32, 245–47, 254.

28. BL, Add. Mss., 46490, Elliot to Eden, 28 June 1777, plus related materials in the same folder.

29. BL, Add. Mss., 34414, North to Eden, 29 September 1777.

30. Fortescue, *Correspondence of King George*, 3:483.

31. Bemis, "Secret Intelligence," 233–49.

32. Fortescue, *Correspondence of King George*, 3:410–11, 4:13, 18–19.

33. Ibid., 3:481–82.

34. Ibid., 3:532.

35. Einstein, *Divided Loyalties*, 28.

36. Stevens, *Facsimiles*, 249. Also see Fortescue, *Correspondence of King George*, 3:510.

37. Fortescue, *Correspondence of King George*, 3:496.

38. Christie, *Myth and Reality*, 12–13. Also see 84–92.

39. Mackesy, *War for America*, 23. Also see Carl B. Cone, "George III: America's Unknown King," in Kaplan, *American Revolution*, 1–14.

40. Morton, "Beaumarchais, Francy," 944–47.

41. Bemis, "Secret Intelligence," 235n.

42. Grant, *John Adams*, 229; Dickinson, *Britain and the American Revolution*, 57 (essay by John Derry), 156 (essay by Stephen Conway); Rodger, *Command of the Ocean*, 329–30. Two excellent biographies of North are Thomas, *Lord North;* and Whiteley, *Lord North.*

43. Fortescue, *Correspondence of King George*, 4:27–29.

44. Ibid., 4:133–35.

45. BL, Add. Mss., 24321, SW to [Benson/EB], 24 February 1778; Van Alstyne, "Great Britain," 344–45; Fortescue, *Correspondence of King George*, 4:46.

46. Thomson, *Secretaries of State*, esp. 18–32, 86–87; Cobban, *Ambassadors and Secret Agents*, 17–18; Wickwire, *British Subministers*, 22–24; Porter, *Plots and Paranoia*, 16–23; Scott, *British Foreign Policy*, esp. 10–11, 114, 126, 161–64, 245, 290.

47. Dull, *Diplomatic History*, 45.

48. Rodger, *Command of the Ocean*, 331–32.

49. BL, Add. Mss., 34415, unsigned memo of EB, 9–16 April 1778 ; Bemis, "British Secret Service," 494.

50. *PBF*, 26:220–23.

51. Brown, *American Secretary*, 160; Fortescue, *Correspondence of King George*, 4:133–36.

52. Thomson, *Secretaries of State*, 134.

53. Brown, *Empire or Independence*, 245–46.

54. On Eden and his supposedly vaunted Secret Service: Augur, *Secret War*, 133–37; Bates, "Diplomacy of Lord Stormont," 10–12; Bemis, "British Secret Service," 474; Currey, *Code Number 72*, 6, 78–79; Cuthbertson, *Loyalist Governor*, 24; Deacon, *History of British Secret Service*, 109–14; Einstein, *Divided Loyalties*, 13, 18, 59; Isaacson, *Benjamin Franklin*, 333; O'Toole, *Honorable Treachery*, 29–31, 497n; Schiff, *Great Improvisation*, 73–76; Van Doren, *Benjamin Franklin*, 580; Wickwire, *British Subministers*, 169; Wood, *Americanization of Benjamin Franklin*, 185–86.

55. See Pennypacker, *General Washington's Spies;* Bakeless, "Washington's Spy System," 28–37; Thompson, "George Washington," 3–8; and Rose, *Washington's Spies.*

56. Van Alstyne, "Great Britain," 324. Also see York, *Burning the Dockyard*, 20n; Porter, *Plots and Paranoia*, 16–23; Andrew, *Her Majesty's Secret Service*, 1–4; Cobban, "British Secret Service," 237–38.

57. Stevens, *Facsimiles*, 1946, 2024; Bates, "Diplomacy of Lord Stormont," 11–12; Cobban, "British Secret Service," 233.

58. Most historians believe that the idea for the commission was Eden's and that he wanted a position in it as a step up the career ladder. For example, Whiteley, *Lord North*, 175. On the other hand, in a private letter to his brother Morton, the British minister in Munich, Eden expressed some reluctance in accepting the assignment: BL, Add. Mss., 34415, 6 March 1778.

59. Brown, "William Eden," 100–101.

60. Stevens, *Facsimiles*, 447.

61. Ibid., 448.

62. See his correspondence in BL, Add. Mss., 34414–16.

63. Auckland, *Journal and Correspondence*.

64. Dickinson, *Britain and the American Revolution*, 14. In that same collection of essays, see the pieces by Stephen Conway (155–79) and H. M. Scott (180–204). Also consult Rodger, *Command of the Ocean*, 329, 607–8; Baugh, "Politics of British Naval Failure," 221–46. Not every author agrees with Dickinson regarding the virtual impossibility of Britain winning the war. See Dull, *French Navy and American Independence*, 187–94, 213–14.

CHAPTER EIGHT. *In for the Long Haul, 1778–1783*

1. Stevens, *Facsimiles*, 448, PW to Eden, 24 April 1778, which summarizes several letters from EB.

2. References to intelligence from PW, EB, or from Paris in general are scattered through Fortescue, *Correspondence of King George*. Examples: 4:152, 172, 178–80, 189, 193, 228, 306, 348, 378, 382, 414, 5:123, 178, 204, 216, 223, 268.

3. See Cornwall Record Office, Rogers of Penrose, RP/3/64, RP/3/65, RP/3/82.

4. Among other works, see Bemis, *Diplomacy of the American Revolution*; Dull, *Franklin the Diplomat*; Schiff, *Great Improvisation*; and Isaacson, *Benjamin Franklin*.

5. Fortescue, *Correspondence of King George*, 4:414.

6. Ibid., 4: 152–53, 178, 193, 387, 518, 5:216.

7. Isaacson, *Benjamin Franklin*, 386–87; Thomas, *John Paul Jones*, 148–50.

8. Bemis, "British Secret Service," 494.

9. For different perspectives on the peace negotiations, see Bemis, *Diplomacy of the American Revolution*; Dull, *Franklin the Diplomat*; Hutson, *John Adams and the Diplomacy of the American Revolution*; Morris, *Peacemakers*; Hoffman and Albert, *Peace and the Peacemakers*; Harlow, *Founding of the Second British Empire*, 1:223–447; Scott, *British Foreign Policy*, 310–38; and Stockley, *Britain and France at the Birth of America*.

10. Morris, *Peacemakers*, 374; Morris, *John Jay: Winning*, 429n.

11. Admittedly, this concession was not as great as it sounded. Spain controlled both banks of the river in New Orleans and could stop or regulate any navigation passing through there.

12. Keir, "Economical Reform," 368–85; Fortescue, *Correspondence of King George*, 5:499, 502; Bemis, "British Secret Service," 494.

13. Yale University, Sterling Memorial Library, BF Papers, no. 25219, Vaughan to Shelburne, 6 August 1782 (copy); *PBF*, 38:43n.

14. Morris, *Peacemakers*, 528n.

15. TNA, CO, 5/8, E. Edwards [EB] to Strachey, 4 December 1782. Also see *PBF*, 38:378, 461n, 462n, 464–65.

16. Because EB usually conferred privately with the British representatives, he left no paper trail for historians to use. Hence, there is virtually nothing about EB in Oswald's papers from this period: TNA, FO 27/2, 97/157. However, the two men knew each other before the peace negotiations commenced. A letter (in a private collection) of 29 November 1781 from Oswald to EB concerns private business affairs. Upon EB's return to England in the summer of 1783, he occasionally saw Vaughan and Oswald, whom he called his "friends." See APS, WTF Papers, EB to WTF, 11 July 1783.

17. University of Michigan, William L. Clements Library, Shelburne Papers, box 71, Fitzherbert to Shelburne, 5 January 1783.

18. Ibid., Fitzherbert letters, 4, 15, 26 December 1782, 5, 15, 25 January, 9 February 1783. Also see Bemis, "British Secret Service," 491.

19. *PBF*, 38:433–34n, 444n; Bemis, *Diplomacy of the American Revolution*, 249–51.

20. Giunta, *Emerging Nation*, 1:725–27.

21. Shelburne Papers, box 71, Fitzherbert to Shelburne, 15 December 1782.

22. *PBF*, 30:lix–l, 33:li, 38:164–67.

23. Most of the surviving letters that EB sent to BF or WTF came from Chaillot. Examples: Ibid., 29:175, 35:418–19, 38:460.

24. Archives nationales, Minutier central, Étude 83, five documents dated 30 August 1779.

25. *JCC*, 11:686; Einstein, *Divided Loyalties*, 399–402.

26. *JCC*, 15:1115, 1128; *PBF*, 30:543–44; Butterfield, *Diary and Autobiography of John Adams*, 2:397; Smith, *Letters of Delegates*, 14:55–56.

27. Examples: *PBF*, 26:338, 27:665, 31:503, 36:407.

28. Ibid., 29:567, 644, 731.

29. Ibid., 28:87–88, 29:175, 223, 434. APS, WTF Papers, EB to WTF, 20 March 1779, Mrs. Bousie to EB, [21 March 1779], Joshua Johnson to EB, 13 July 1779.

30. For example, *PBF*, 31:164.

31. Ibid., 31:345–47, 407, 450, 460, 32:19–21. Bancroft Cooke/Salter Collection, William Carmichael to EB, 25 January 1780.

32. *PBF*, 28:587. Also see 28:588n, 29:4, 23–24, 68, 119; and *PJPJ*, EB to JPJ, 23 February 1779.

33. *PBF*, 30:197–98.

34. Ibid., 32:10, 36, 67–69, 100, 168–69, 185, 532; *PJPJ*, JWJ to JPJ, 17 March 1780; *PCC*, M332, BF-JWJ account dated 31 March 1781 (listing payment to EB from March 1780).

35. Butterfield, *Diary and Autobiography of John Adams*, 4:68; Taylor, *Papers of John Adams*, 8:144.

36. Sundry undated BF-EB-WTF notes can be found in APS, BF and WTF Papers. These include, EB to WTF, ca. 11 November 1782, regarding the visit of Walpole. Also see Butterfield, *Diary and Autobiography of John Adams*, 2:308, 364–65, 4:90.

37. *PBF*, 36:72–73. The passage as quoted by the editors of *PBF* is to be preferred over the altered version published by Elkanah Watson's son: Watson, *Men and Times*, 155. In 1781 Watson was new to the scene and mistakenly assumed that EB was an unofficial British agent who had been sent to sound out Franklin on the possibility of peace.

38. *PBF,* 37:100n; APS, BF Papers, John Coakley Lettsom to BF, 28 January 1784.

39. Hans, "UNESCO of the Eighteenth Century," 516, 518, 520; *PBF,* 32:331n; Bancroft Cooke/Salter Collection, "Tableau des frères de la R ∴ L ∴ des Neuf Soeurs," 1782; *PJPJ,* JPJ to EB, 28 February 1783.

40. Taylor, *Papers of John Adams,* 8:79.

41. Bates, "Diplomacy of Lord Stormont," 19.

42. For example, *PJPJ,* JPJ to SD, 25 March 1778, and JPJ to WTF, 19 October 1778.

43. Stevens, *Facsimiles,* 1881, EB to PW, 4 March 1778; Thomas, *John Paul Jones,* 148–49.

44. Butterfield, *Diary and Autobiography of John Adams,* 4:166.

45. Ibid.; *PJPJ,* JPJ to EB, 27 May 1778, JPJ to William Carmichael, 27 May 1778, JPJ to JWJ, 29 May 1778; *PBF,* 26:535, 558, 578–79, 595–96; Thomas, *John Paul Jones,* 141–47.

46. *PBF,* 27:254n, 479n, 572n, 573n; *PJPJ,* JPJ to EB, 14, 21, 24 August, 9, 14, 23, 30 September, 4, 7, 16 October, 11 November, 18 December 1778. In *PJPJ,* see EB to JPJ, 23, 28 September, 10 October 1778, JWJ to JPJ, 30 August 1778, and JPJ to JWJ, 20 October 1778. Regarding the sword, see APS, WTF Papers, undated letter of EB to WTF.

47. The *Bonhomme Richard* was a much better ship than many historians have judged. See Schaeper, *France and America,* 227–38.

48. *PJPJ,* JPJ to EB, 9 March 1779.

49. Idzerda, *Lafayette,* 2:258.

50. See Patterson, *Other Armada.*

51. *PJPJ,* JPJ to EB, 13 August 1778, EB to JPJ, 14 October 1778.

52. *PBF,* 31:105–12. Although nearly all historians have taken Jones's side in this issue, there is much evidence to support Landais. See Schaeper, *John Paul Jones.* Neither the court nor Congress ever investigated or made a judgment about Jones's charges concerning the encounter off Flamborough Head.

53. The complex story of the Jones-Chaumont dispute is covered in Schaeper, *France and America,* chaps. 8–9. Also see *PBF,* 32:168–69, 189n, 199–200, 214n. In *PJPJ,* see JPJ to Garnier, 28 March 1780, and JPJ to Duc de La Rochefoucauld, 28 March 1780.

54. *PBF,* 32:260–61.

55. Bancroft Cooke/Salter Collection, "Couplets chantés à M. Commodore Paul Jones dans un souper." Author's translation.

56. *PJPJ,* JPJ to EB, 27 June 1780; *PBF,* 33:28, 64.

57. *PJPJ,* JWJ to JPJ, 15, 23 July, 27 August, 21 October 1780, JPJ to EB, 17 July, 7 August, 23 September, 17 October, 9 November 1780, JPJ to Baudouin, 19 July 1780, Baudouin to JPJ, 27 July 1780, JPJ to William Carmichael, 9, 22 August 1780, JPJ to Edme-Jacques Genet, 13 November 1780, JPJ to Leray de Chaumont, 24 November 1780. Yale University, Sterling Memorial Library, BF Papers, JWJ Letterbooks (hereinafter cited as JWJ Letterbooks), JWJ to EB, 29 August, 4 September 1780.

58. Thomas, *John Paul Jones,* 99. Thomas also states that occasionally EB withheld from his British superiors information about ship sailings if he happened to own a share in the cargoes. Moreover, Thomas speculates that EB might have had a "sentimental streak," leading him to omit mentioning in his messages in bottles in the Tuileries Gardens any reference to the Jones squadron that sailed for British waters in August 1779. There is no evidence to support these conjectures.

59. Details on EB's children can be found in John Green's Family Data and in Bancroft, "Bancroft Family."

60. Butterfield, *Diary and Autobiography of John Adams*, 2:299; 4:86, 99. Taylor, *Papers of John Adams*, 6:10–14.

61. Ferling and Braverman, "John Adams's Health Reconsidered," 83–104. Also see Hutson, *John Adams*, 77.

62. Butterfield, *Diary and Autobiography of John Adams*, 4:67.

63. Ibid., 2:304.

64. Grant, *John Adams*, 3–4.

65. Butterfield, *Diary and Autobiography of John Adams*, 4:74.

66. Ibid.

67. Historical Society of Pennsylvania, Edith Bancroft Ashmore Collection (hereinafter cited as Ashmore Collection), Lafayette to EB, 28 May 1783.

68. Taylor, *Papers of John Adams*, 7:395, 8:143, 223; Butterfield, *Diary and Autobiography of John Adams*, 2:396–97; *PBF*, 28:479.

69. Butterfield, *Diary and Autobiography of John Adams*, 3:46, 69–71, 75; Morris, *Peacemakers*, 374; *PBF*, 38:174n; Klingelhofer, "Matthew Ridley's Diary," 129.

70. Idzerda, *Lafayette*, 2:268–69. Also see Kelly, *Sir Edward Newenham MP*, 147–48.

71. *PBF*, 29:580.

72. EB's report to Vergennes, 25 June 1779, can be found in Archives du Ministère des Affaires étrangères, Mémoires et documents, Angleterre, vol. 55, fols. 124–29. Also see Idzerda, *Lafayette*, 2:284–87; Elliott, *Catholics of Ulster*, 219; York, "The Impact of the American Revolution on Ireland," in Dickinson, *Britain and the American Revolution*, 224–32; and Morris, *Peacemakers*, 35.

73. For example, the case of Caleb Whitefoord, Richard Oswald's secretary in Paris. See Hewins, *Whitefoord Papers*, 192–97.

74. Roberts and Roberts, *Thomas Barclay*, 316n9; *Histoire de la Société Royale de Médecine* (1779): 30. I thank Kate Ohno for the latter reference.

75. Butterfield, *Diary and Autobiography of John Adams*, 2:304; *PJPJ*, JPJ to William Carmichael, 27 May 1778.

76. TNA, C/12/160/29, case of EB vs. PW, 24 May 1788; Ashmore Collection, Joseph Wharton to EB, 25 December 1778. JWJ Letterbooks, JWJ to EB, 10 March, 26 April, 11 May, 24 June, 11, 23 November, 16 December 1779, 8, 26, 30 March, 6 May, 18 August 1780.

77. JWJ Letterbooks, JWJ to EB, 16 December 1779, 30 March 1780; *PBF*, 35:418–19; Schaeper, *France and America*, 295–302; APS, BF Papers, EB receipt for 1,500 livres, 29 August 1781.

78. JWJ Letterbooks, JWJ to EB, 11 May 1779, 6 May, 29 August, 26 September 1780.

79. MacNalty, "Edward Bancroft," 11–12.

80. Abernethy, *Western Lands*, 230; Schaeper, *France and America*, 292, 313n; Boyd, "Silas Deane," 534–35.

81. Bancroft Cooke/Salter Collection, SW to EB, 17 October 1780, 29 May 1783; APS, WTF Papers, EB to WTF, 21 October 1782; *PBF*, 34:163, 521–22, 35:52, 424, 36:221, 37:212, 468, 38:178, 364–66, 378–79, 39:220, 531–32. On SW's earlier record of unreliability, see Marshall, "Lord Hillsborough," 717–39.

82. Bancroft Cooke/Salter Collection, certificate dated 26 March 1783.

83. Smyth, *Writings of Benjamin Franklin*, 9:50, BF to Livingston, 12 June 1783 (also to appear in vol. 40 of *PBF*). By "employed" Franklin meant that EB labored for the American cause, not that he held any official, paid position.

84. Morris, *John Jay: Winning*, 526, also 541, 631. Jay to Livingston, 10 June 1783, can be found in the digital edition of Jay's papers. Morris's two-volume edition of Jay's papers will soon be eclipsed by *The Selected Papers of John Jay*, edited by Elizabeth M. Nuxoll.

85. Ferguson, *Papers of Robert Morris*, 7:786.

86. Idzerda, *Lafayette*, 5:132–33.

87. Ashmore Collection, EB memorandum, various entries.

CHAPTER NINE. *Arthur Lee: Spy Catcher? Benjamin Franklin: Traitor? Edward Bancroft: Murderer?*

1. Augur, *Secret War*, 133.

2. Butterfield, *Diary and Autobiography of John Adams*, 2:346. Potts offers a decidedly pro-Lee interpretation in *Arthur Lee*, esp. 159–60, 166–67, 172–73, 177, 179–81, 202–3.

3. Stevens, *Facsimiles*, 266 (report of conversation between Joseph Wharton and Dr. Ruston, 23 September 1777), 300 (Wharton to EB, 8 November 1777). Pearl, "New Perspectives," 8n.

4. A copy of Livingston's report of 11 April 1778 can be found in *PCC*, M247, roll 132, 476. Also see Isham, *Deane Papers*, 4:63–65; *PBF*, 26:652n, 27:229; and *Pennsylvania Packet or the General Advertiser*, 14 March 1780.

5. *PCC*, M247, roll 110, 2:232–34, AL to Samuel Petrie, 8, 9 April 1779, Petrie to AL, 9 April 1779; Doniol, *Histoire de la participation*, 3:169.

6. *PBF*, 26:256, 652n, 27:229–33. Isham, *Deane Papers*, 4:63–65; Wharton, *Diplomatic Correspondence*, 1:630–35; *PJPJ*, JPJ to M. Livingston, 13 March, 25 April 1779, Livingston to JPJ, 13 March 1779; *PCC*, M247, roll 110, 1:251, Livingston to AL, 15 July 1778; Bancroft Cooke/Salter Collection, Joseph Wharton to EB, 13, 15 March 1779.

7. *PBF*, 23:162.

8. Ibid., 211.

9. Deacon, *History of the British Secret Service*, 112–13.

10. See Williams, *Police of Paris*.

11. Stevens, *Facsimiles*, 312, 327, 489, 769, PW to Eden, 25 December 1777, 1, 4, 7 January 1778.

12. Currey, *Code Number 72*, esp. 126, 136, 138, 145, 146, 149, 151, 173.

13. Ibid., 14, 15, 203.

14. Among many other sources attesting to Franklin's steadfast loyalty to the United States, see Dull, *Franklin the Diplomat*, 41, 53, 55–57, 71; Dull, *Benjamin Franklin and the American Revolution*, chap. 5; and Isaacson, *Benjamin Franklin*, 296, 298, 304, 308–9, 317, 347, 412–13.

15. Currey, *Code Number 72*, 17, 59–60, 162, 184.

16. University of Michigan, William L. Clements Library, Shelburne Papers, box 71, Fitzherbert to Grantham, 9 February 1783.

17. Review of Currey in *William and Mary Quarterly,* 3rd ser., 31 (1974): 151. Alan S. Brown criticized McDonald's review, prompting McDonald and Currey to respond: ibid., 32 (1975): 179–85.

18. Lloyd, *Guinness Book of Espionage,* 27; Poteat, "Benjamin Franklin," 21–24. Also see Craig, "Benjamin Franklin in France"; and Craig, "Benjamin Franklin: Secret Service."

19. It is possible that the Wikipedia article might have been altered in the time since this writing. Also see www.museumofhoaxes.com/hoax/forum. In the search box provided, type the following: Benjamin Franklin, British Spy?

20. *Time,* 18 December 1972.

21. Review of Currey in *American Historical Review* 79 (1974): 574.

22. Boyd, "Silas Deane," esp. 322, 336.

23. Ibid., 168n, 187, 332, 337. The handful of historians before Boyd who assumed that Deane must have been a traitor include Augur, *Secret War,* 316; Abernethy, *Western Lands,* 206–9, 277; and Samuel Eliot Morison, review of Fortescue, *Correspondence of King George,* in *New England Quarterly* 2 (1929): 156–62. The number of historians assuming this in the aftermath of Boyd's article has grown exponentially. Examples: Haussmann, "Doctor of Duplicity"; Royster, *Fabulous History,* 234; Nelson, *Thomas Paine,* 140; Taylor, *Papers of John Adams,* 6:14; James, *Silas Deane;* Patton, *Patriot Pirates,* 221–26. Boyd's thesis has received its widest publicity in a textbook used in universities throughout the United States: Davidson and Lytle, *After the Fact,* xv–xxxi. While defending Deane against the charge of treason, Joel Richard Paul accepts all that Boyd says about Bancroft: *Unlikely Allies,* esp. chap. 36.

24. BL, Add. Mss., 24321, SW to Benson, 13 March, 21 April 1778; Stevens, *Facsimiles,* 162, 792; *PBF,* 23:202n, 28:271; APS, Benjamin Franklin Bache Papers, SW to Benson, 19, 22 May 1778; Dull, *Franklin the Diplomat,* 34–35. Boyd is not the only writer to err in assuming that Benson was Silas Deane. See Currey, *Code Number 72,* 102–3, 138, 179; Augur, *Secret War,* 179–80; and Morris, *John Jay: Winning,* 49.

25. For example, see Goldstein, "Silas Deane," 75–97; and Grant, *John Adams,* 201.

26. Schaeper, *France and America,* esp. 51–52, 73–85.

27. Morton and Spinelli, *Beaumarchais Correspondance,* 4:96–97; Isham, *Deane Papers,* 2:443–44; Taylor, *Papers of John Adams,* 6:10–14.

28. Prelinger, "Less Lucky Than Lafayette," 263–71.

29. See Schaeper, *France and America,* 82–83, 208–9, and sources cited therein; *JCC,* 18:951–53; and *PBF,* 36:648, 37:42–44, 74, 38:468–69. For a thorough, persuasive defense of SD see Paul, *Unlikely Allies,* esp. chaps. 13, 18, 21, 23, 32, 33-35.

30. Connecticut Historical Society, SD Papers, box 9, various accounts of SD and EB; Isham, *Deane Papers,* 4:152; *PBF,* 36:522n; Ford, *Letters of William Lee,* 3:817; *PJPJ,* SD to JPJ, 2 December 1780.

31. Isham, *Deane Papers,* esp. 4:347–84, 500–505.

32. *PBF,* 36:453, 37:74. Despite BF's numerous condemnations of SD, Currey stubbornly insists—albeit with no evidence—that BF remained on friendly terms with him. See *Code Number 72,* 240–41.

33. *PBF,* 36:507–25; Isham, *Deane Papers,* 5:63–64.

34. Fortescue, *Correspondence of King George*, 4:29–30, 5:200, 204, 216, 223, 224.

35. Ibid., 5:20–21, 59–60, 71–72, 123, 200, 204, 216, 237, 268, 329; Isham, *Deane Papers,* 5:59–60.

36. Isham, *Deane Papers,* 4:530–31, 533, 536–41, 551, 5:17–18. In her *Secret War* (333), Helen Augur cites two letters that Deane wrote "E. Edwards" in March 1782. She says they demonstrate Deane's awareness that "Edward Edwards" was the chief alias Bancroft used with the British government. However, the "E. Edwards" here was Ezekiel Edwards, a Philadelphia merchant who spent most of 1782 in Europe on business affairs. See Isham, *Deane Papers,* 5:77–79; and *PBF,* 38:252.

37. Boyd, "Silas Deane," esp. 527–29.

38. Bancroft Cooke/Salter Collection, SD to EB, 9 March 1784.

39. Ibid., SD to EB, 23 December 1783, 2 February, 13 April, 2 May, 15 July 1785, 21 May 1786. William Wilkinson's brother John was even more famous as an ironmaster. On William see *PBF,* 23:480n, 29:260n, 34:175–76n.

40. Bancroft Cooke/Salter Collection, SD to EB, __ October 1784, 7 December 1785, plus several undated letters; Isham, *Deane Papers,* 5:465–70, 482–85; Boyd, "Silas Deane," 524–25.

41. Isham, *Deane Papers,* 5:451, 470.

42. Bancroft Cooke/Salter Collection, SD to EB, 24 September 1783, 9 March, 24 December 1784. Also see Isham, *Deane Papers,* esp. 5:219, 234.

43. This was probably John Jeffries, a noted physician and scientist.

44. Bancroft Cooke/Salter Collection, Sheffield to EB, 29 October 1789; Isham, *Deane Papers,* 5:489.

45. Boyd, *Papers of Thomas Jefferson,* 14:629–32.

46. Ibid., 14:605–6, 657–58, 15:3–4, 39; Bancroft Cooke/Salter Collection, undated letters from SD.

47. Boyd, "Silas Deane," 525–27.

48. Ibid., 516.

49. Bancroft Cooke/Salter Collection, William Wilkinson to EB, 25 June 1788.

50. Boyd, *Papers of Thomas Jefferson,* 15:353.

51. Boyd, "Silas Deane," 172–73.

52. *Gentleman's Magazine* 59 (September 1789): 866; *American Mercury* (Hartford), 28 December 1789; *Gazette of the United States* (Philadelphia), 12 December 1789; Boyd, "Silas Deane," 174.

53. Boyd, *Papers of Thomas Jefferson,* 15:500.

54. *Gentleman's Magazine* 60 (May–June 1790): 383–86, 518–20; Historical Society of Pennsylvania, Edith Bancroft Ashmore Collection, J. Priestley to EB, undated; Isham, *Deane Papers,* 5:533–34; Schofield, *Enlightened Joseph Priestley,* 275n.

55. EB, *Natural History of Guiana,* 257, 267–68, 281–307.

56. Ibid., 299.

57. Ibid., 218–20.

58. Raghavendra, "Neuromuscular Blocking Drugs," 363–65.

59. EB, *Arrow Poison,* intro. by John Parker (Menomonie, WI: Vagabond, 1972).

60. See Raghavendra, "Neuromuscular Blocking Drugs," 363–67.

61. Boyd, "Silas Deane," 540.

62. Ibid., 175.

63. Boyd, *Papers of Thomas Jefferson*, 15:500; Isham, *Deane Papers*, 5:483.

64. Boyd, "Silas Deane," 550.

65. *Isham, Deane Papers*, 5:526; Alsop, *Yankees at the Court*, 164–65; Warner, *John the Painter*, 251; Pearl, "New Perspectives,"14–15; Stinchcombe, "Note on Silas Deane's Death," 619–24.

66. Anderson and Anderson, "Death of Silas Deane," 104–5; Dennis Kent Anderson to author, 26 March 2006; Davidson and Lytle, *After the Fact*, xxx–xxxi. (Unfortunately, the 6th edition of this work has shortened the discussion regarding poisons.)

CHAPTER TEN. *In America, 1783–1784*

1. APS, WTF Papers, Carmichael to WTF, 4 February 1783.

2. Ibid., EB to WTF, 14 June 1783.

3. Ibid., EB to WTF, 11 July 1783.

4. BL, Add. Mss., 61863, EB to North, 22 July 1783, PW to North, 5 August 1783; Bemis, "British Secret Service," 494–95; Butterfield, *Diary and Autobiography of John Adams*, 4:72n; *Connecticut Journal*, 8 October 1783.

5. *PBF*, 39:594; Bancroft Cooke/Salter Collection, T. Walpole to EB, 6 July 1783; Hamer, *Papers of Henry Laurens*, 16:337–39.

6. The best source on all his movements during his months in America is Historical Society of Pennsylvania, Edith Bancroft Ashmore Collection (hereinafter cited as Ashmore Collection), EB diary fragment.

7. Bancroft Cooke/Salter Collection, Boudinot to EB, 1 October 1783.

8. Ferguson, *Papers of Robert Morris*, 8:707.

9. Ashmore Collection, EB to Daniel Bancroft, 24 November–8 December 1783, EB to Penelope Bancroft, 9 December 1783; Morris, *John Jay: Winning*, 671.

10. Ashmore Collection, EB to Daniel Bancroft, 24 November–8 December 1783, plus a note entitled "Dr. Daniel Bancroft." Also Wickes, *History of Medicine*, 133. Some writers have asserted that Daniel served in the Continental Army during the Revolution. The cause for this error is a brief note in "The Complete Service Records of Soldiers Who Served in the American Army during the Revolutionary War," housed in the National Archives (see microfilm version, National Archives and Records Service, M881). There one can find a small card with the name Daniel Bancroft, stating that he served in the Sixth Regiment of Massachusetts. No dates or other information are on the card. This entry is either a complete error or, more likely, refers to a different Daniel Bancroft.

11. Bancroft Cooke/Salter Collection, SW to EB, 29 May 1783, SW to Robert Ellison, 19 June 1784; APS, BF Papers, BF to Ingenhousz, 29 April 1785, Ingenhousz to BF, 11 June 1785; Boyd, "Silas Deane," 535–36; Isham, *Deane Papers*, 5:211–12, 451.

12. The South Carolina port was "Charles Town" until changed to Charleston in 1783.

13. Stone, "*South Carolina* We've Lost," 159–72.

14. Bancroft Cooke/Salter Collection, Benjamin Guerand to EB, 17 April 1784; Ashmore Collection, EB memorandum, diary fragment, EB to Daniel Bancroft, 24

November–8 December 1783; Bancroft, "Bancroft Family," 68; Ferguson, *Papers of Robert Morris*, 8:318; Isham, *Deane Papers*, 5:211–12; EB, *Facts and Observations Justifying the Claims of the Prince of Luxembourg.*

15. Smith, "Luxembourg Claims," 95; Smith, "Commodore Alexander Gillon," 189–219.

16. Smith, "Luxembourg Claims," 96.

17. Lewis, *Neptune's Militia*, 113.

18. Ibid., 207n.

19. Lewis states that Bancroft received an administrator's fee as well as a hoped-for commission. Ibid., 113. However, Bancroft's own letters indicate that the only money he might have obtained would have been the 6 percent commission. Also on the Luxembourg claims, see Marcus, *Documentary History of the Supreme Court*, 5:450–94.

20. Bancroft Cooke/Salter Collection, EB to Penelope Bancroft, 26 March 1784, Francis Coffyn to Penelope Bancroft, 6 April 1784.

21. Ibid., [Joseph Wharton?] to EB, 25 January 1785; Smith, *Empress of China*, 118–19.

22. BL, Add. Mss., 61863, EB to North, 22 July 1783.

23. George Bancroft, *History of the Formation of the Constitution*, 331–33, 367–70; Wharton, *Revolutionary Diplomatic Correspondence*, 1:626–27; Ferguson, *Papers of Robert Morris*, 8:543–45. Depending on the source one uses, the man's name was "Fraser" or "Frazer."

24. "To the Writer of Common Sense," *Independent Journal*, 28 January 1784 (reprinted in the same paper on 4 February 1784). This article and copies of it from other newspapers can be found in the Bancroft Cooke/Salter Collection. For Anglo-American trade relations, see Ferguson, *Papers of Robert Morris*, vols. 8–9; Harlow, *Founding*, 1:448–92; and Giunta, *Emerging Nation*, 2:91–104.

25. Giunta, *Emerging Nation*, 2:382–84.

26. Ibid., 2:506–8; Abernethy, *Western Lands*, 310n; Bancroft, *History of the Formation of the Constitution*, 380–81, 403–4; Einstein, *Divided Loyalties*, 49.

27. Norton, *British-Americans*, 250–55.

28. Bancroft Cooke/Salter Collection, EB to Penelope Bancroft, 9 December 1783.

29. Ibid., EB to Penelope Bancroft, [December 1783].

30. Ashmore Collection, ENB and Samuel Forrester Bancroft to EB, 19 January 1784.

31. Bancroft Cooke/Salter Collection, ENB to EB, 10 April 1784, EB to Penelope Bancroft, 3 May, 22 June 1784, Daniel Bancroft to Penelope Bancroft, 27 June 1784.

CHAPTER ELEVEN. *Return to Normalcy*

1. Historical Society of Pennsylvania, Edith Bancroft Ashmore Collection (hereinafter cited as Ashmore Collection), EB diary fragment.

2. Original in TNA, FO, 4/3. Reprinted in Bemis, "British Secret Service," 492–95.

3. Some examples: Van Doren, *Secret History*, 431; Boyd, "Silas Deane," 547; Currey, *Code Number 72*, 263; Morton, *Americans in London*, 217; Patton, *Patriot Pirates*, 63.

4. Numerous letters in various collections give his addresses: 6 Duke Street, near St. James's, from July 1783 to late 1784 or early 1785; 12 Villiers Street, York Buildings, Westminster, to September 1786; 21 Charlotte Street, Rathbone Place, to August 1789; Francis Street, Bedford Square, to April 1803; Margaret Street, for several years; by 1811 in an unidentified location in Chelsea.

5. Bancroft, "Bancroft Family," 80–84; file on ENB in the Edinburgh University Library, provided by archivist Jo Currie; John Green's Family Data.

6. Ashmore Collection, Samuel Bancroft to EB, 15 September 1791, Samuel Bancroft to ENB, 22 August 1793, Samuel Bancroft to Diana Dixon, 1796; Bancroft, "Bancroft Family," esp. 72, 78, 80; Bancroft Cooke/Salter Collection, Thomas Walpole to EB, 5 July 1792, EB to Maria Frances Bancroft, 12 October 1792; MacNalty, "Edward Bancroft," 14; John Green's Family Data.

7. Morris, *Diary of the French Revolution,* 2:246. Also see 2:241, 369–70.

8. EB to Maria Frances Bancroft, 12 October 1792.

9. Ashmore Collection, Samuel Bancroft to ENB, 23 August 1793.

10. Columbia University, Papers of John Jay, EB to John Vaughan, 15 August 1795, John Jay to EB, 22 April 1796, Jay to Samuel Bancroft, 16 October 1795; Vaughan to Jay, 7 November 1795, Jay to Vaughan, 21 January 1796. Articles on the rape are scattered through many newspapers. Some examples: *Argus* (New York), 12 December 1796; *Greenleaf's New Daily Advertiser* (New York), 16 December 1796; *Herald* (New York), 17 December 1796; *Centinel of Freedom* (Newark, NJ), 21 December 1796; *Whitehall Evening Post* (London), 18 March 1797; *Telegraph* (London), 18 March 1797. On Samuel's marriage and death, see these London papers: *Whitehall Evening Post,* 27 December 1798; *Morning Post and Gazetteer,* 17 December 1798; *Lloyd's Evening Post,* 20 December 1799; *Morning Herald,* 7 April 1800; and *Oracle and Daily Advertiser,* 10, 12 April 1800.

11. APS, BF Papers, ENB to BF, 18 November 1783, 10 January 1784 (both forthcoming in *PBF*).

12. Yale University, Sterling Memorial Library, BF Papers, BF to ENB, 26 March 1784. The boy's final letter to BF was written on 17 April 1784 (APS, BF Papers, and forthcoming in *PBF*).

13. APS, BF Papers, Sarah Bache to BF, 20 June 1784 (forthcoming in *PBF*).

14. APS, WTF Papers, EB to WTF: several undated letters from the period September 1784 to early 1785, plus letters dated 24 February and 24 March 1785.

15. Bancroft Cooke/Salter Collection, undated notes regarding BF's health plus BF to EB, 2 July 1785; APS, BF Papers, EB to BF, 2 July 1785 (forthcoming in *PBF*).

16. APS, WTF Papers, EB to WTF, 18 July 1785.

17. APS, BF Papers, EB to BF, 5 September 1786 (forthcoming in *PBF*).

18. Library of Congress, BF Papers, BF to EB, 26 November 1786 (forthcoming in *PBF*).

19. For example: Bancroft Cooke/Salter Collection, William Saling (sp?) to EB, [undated, probably late 1790s], requesting anecdotes about BF.

20. Ryerson, *Adams Family Correspondence,* 6:5.

21. Ibid., 6:305, 433, 482, 7:20, 153, 187; Butterfield, *Diary and Autobiography of John Adams,* 3:184.

22. Butterfield, *Diary and Autobiography of John Adams,* 4:72. Adams's copy of the book today is in the Boston Public Library.

23. Boyd, *Papers of Thomas Jefferson*, 8:347, 400.

24. Butterfield, *Diary and Autobiography of John Adams*, 4:73–74n; Nangle, *Monthly Review*, 3.

25. *PJPJ*, EB to JPJ, 27 October 1783, JPJ to EB, 11 October 1785, 30 April 1792, JPJ to JA, 7 January, 10 July 1786, JA to JPJ, 21 January 1786, JPJ to Amoureux, 25 July 1786, JPJ to Mrs. Townshend, 4 September 1787, JPJ to John Ross, 27 December 1789, G. Morris to JPJ, 9 July 1790, "Schedule of the Property of John Paul Jones" (drawn up by G. Morris, 18 July 1792); Ryerson, *Adams Family Correspondence*, 6:5, 384, 389; Boyd, *Papers of Thomas Jefferson*, 8:597, 9:10–11, 10:209, 13:585, 14:605–6, 629–32, 692; Morris, *Diary of the French Revolution*, 1:467, 475, 504, 514, 515, 526, 558.

26. Ashmore Collection, EB diary fragment; Boyd, "Silas Deane," 537.

27. Bancroft Cooke/Salter Collection, Elizabeth Walpole to EB, 10 April 1786; APS, WTF Papers, EB to WTF, 24 February 1785; Boyd, *Papers of Thomas Jefferson*, 8:347, 522, 544, 9:299–300, 557, 10:393, 649; Butterfield, *Diary and Autobiography of John Adams*, 3:184.

28. Boyd, *Papers of Thomas Jefferson*, 9:454.

29. Shepperson, *John Paradise*, esp. 184, 265, 271, 325, 343, 353–56, 364, 389, 396–97, 438; Ryerson, *Adams Family Correspondence*, 8:367. EB and the Paradises can be found throughout vols. 9 to 15 of Boyd, *Papers of Thomas Jefferson*. As late as 1815 EB was still aiding that family. See Ashmore Collection, EB diary fragment, entry for 1 January 1803; Library of Congress, TJ Papers, EB to TJ, 5 September 1815.

30. One example: the case of Samuel Andrews, an American merchant captain who died in France in November 1782. In his will, Andrews named his friends EB and JWJ as his executors. EB and JWJ worked for the next three years in settling the estate. Indiana University, Lilly Library, JWJ Manuscripts, EB to JWJ, 2 December 1782, de Neufville and Co. to EB, 17 January 1785; Yale University, Sterling Memorial Library, JWJ Letterbooks, JWJ to EB, 20 December 1782, 6 February 1783; *PBF*, 36:596n.

31. Boyd, *Papers of Thomas Jefferson*, 13:285–86, 606–8.

32. Ibid., 14:492–93.

33. Idzerda, *Lafayette*, 5:329, 333.

34. Jackson and Twohig, *Diaries of George Washington*, 5:454–55; Morris, *Diary of the French Revolution*, 1:195–96; Bancroft Cooke/Salter Collection, Jay to EB, 2 March 1790.

35. Sophie Cathorne (RSA archives) to author, 30 January 2008; Allan and Abbott, *Virtuoso Tribe*, 360; *Morning Chronicle and London Advertiser*, 10 March 1788; *The Times*, 7 June 1788; *Diary or Woodfall's Register*, 8 March 1791, 10 March 1792; *Star* (London), 22 March 1793; Bancroft Cooke/Salter Collection, General Melville to EB, 18 April, 3 May 1796.

36. Bancroft Cooke/Salter Collection, La Luzerne to EB, 9 July 1790, Marquis de Barthélemy to EB, 11, 15 June, 11 October, undated 1791, Sir George Staunton to EB, 28 July 1797; Boyd, *Papers of Thomas Jefferson*, 15:292, 18:xl.

37. *World* (London), 22 April 1791.

38. For this information I thank Elizabeth Carroll-Horrocks, director of Archives of the American Academy of Arts and Sciences.

39. For example, in David Rivers, *Literary Memoirs of Living Authors of Great Britain, Arranged According to an Alphabetical Catalogue . . . and Including a List of Their Works*, 2 vols. (London, 1798). Volume 1 mentions EB's *Charles Wentworth* and *Experimental*

Researches. Also see *Morning Post and Fashionable World* (London), 12 January 1796; and *E. Johnson's British Gazette and Sunday Monitor* (London), 20 November 1803.

40. Bancroft Cooke/Salter Collection, Thomas Walpole to EB, 22 September 1785, 16 March 1794, Jean Holker to EB, 16 March 1792; Isham, *Deane Papers,* 5:470.

41. House of Lords Record Office, HL/PO/PU/1/1785/25G3n88, "An Act for vesting in Edward Bancroft . . ."; EB, *Facts and Observations* (1798), 1–7; APS, EB to WTF, 24 March 1785; Browne, "Sketch," 104; Boyd, "Silas Deane," 519; MacNalty, "Edward Bancroft," 11; *Statutes at Large,* 9:519; *London Gazette,* 18 December 1798, 1206.

42. Some sources state that EB obtained the French monopoly in the summer of 1785, while others give 1786. My own reading of the vague references to it is that he first applied for it in 1785 and finally received it a year later. He spent several weeks in Paris during the summer of both years. Ashmore Collection, scattered biographical notes on EB's life; Bancroft, "Bancroft Family," 70; Pearl, "New Perspectives," 39n; Boyd, "Silas Deane," 519n.

43. Ashmore Collection: Daniel Bancroft to EB, __ June, 26 November 1791, "Short Life of Edward Bancroft"; Bancroft Cooke/Salter Collection, Thomas Walpole to EB, 14 October 1792.

44. I wish to thank Barbara L. Krieger for supplying me with several documents of the period 1784–89 from the Dartmouth College Archives.

45. Board of American Loyalists, *Case and Claim of the American Loyalists;* Board of Agents for the American Loyalists, *Summary Case;* Norton, *British-Americans,* 305n. Another Loyalist signer of parliamentary petitions was William Franklin.

46. TNA, C/12/160/29, complaint of EB, 24 May 1788.

47. Ibid., response of PW, 27 June 1789.

48. Cuthbertson, *Loyalist Governor,* 28, 48–50, 94. Genealogical and other records vary in the date given for PW's death. Regarding his final years and death, see http://nationaalarchief.sr/geschiedenis/plantages/commewijnerivier/appecappe/; *Gentleman's Magazine,* 1794, 480; Wentworth, *Wentworth Genealogy,* 3:7–13.

49. MacNalty, "Edward Bancroft," 11; Bancroft Cooke/Salter Collection, Berthollet to EB, 31 October 1814.

50. Bancroft Cooke/Salter Collection, Auckland to EB, 18 November 1794. In the same collection, also see Lord Hawke to EB, 13 March 1795.

51. Reprinted in Keen, *Revolutions in Romantic Literature,* 132–33.

52. EB, *Experimental Researches* (1813), 1:i–ii; *Whitehall Evening Post,* 29 July 1800.

53. EB, *Facts and Observations Briefly Stated* (1798), 8–20.

54. *Courier and Evening Gazette* (London), 23 February 1799; *Whitehall Evening Post,* 23 May 1799; *Observer* (London), 26 May 1799; EB, *Experimental Researches* (1813), 2:85–86.

55. Ibid.

56. *St. James's Chronicle or the British Evening Post,* 18 December 1800; *Lloyd's Evening Post,* 19 December 1800.

57. *The Times,* 16 July 1804.

58. Some of the genealogical and biographical notes kept by EB's descendants give the dates of his trip to South America as 1803–4, but most state 1804–5. For present purposes it does not matter which time period one accepts. See Bancroft, "Bancroft Family," 74; Ashmore Collection, EB to Mrs. Samuel Bancroft, 2 January 1802, plus various anonymous, undated notes.

59. Colonel R. D. Kinsella-Bevan, registrar of the Medical Society of London to author, 23 August 2006; Bancroft, "Bancroft Family," 80–84; *Dictionary of National Biography*, s.v. "Edward Nathaniel Bancroft."

60. In 1817 ENB published a second edition, in which he lashed out at some of his critics. Also see Mullett, "Politics, Economics and Medicine," 247.

61. ENB probably returned to England for an extended stay in 1817. Family records indicate that in April of that year his oldest child, Ursula, was baptized in Margate Church. This was a second baptism, as the girl had already been baptized in Jamaica. In October of the same year, his wife gave birth to their second child, Edward James, in London. It is likely that ENB accompanied his daughter and pregnant wife in this voyage to England. See John Green's Family Data.

62. *Quarterly Review* (April–July 1814): 203–15.

63. Cannon, *Dye Plants and Dyeing*, 10; Browne, "Sketch," 107. Also see MacNalty, "Edward Bancroft," 12–13; and Edelstein, "Historical Notes," 735.

64. EB, "Instruction concernant les preparations nommées 'lac-lake' et 'lac-dye.'"

65. Bancroft, "Bancroft Family," 74–76; sundry letters in Ashmore Collection and Bancroft Cooke/Salter Collection.

66. Ashmore Collection, EB to ENB, 31 May 1819.

67. Those citing 1820 include Ford in EB's *Narrative*, 17; Morton, *Americans in London*, 217; Church of Jesus Christ of the Latter-Day Saints, International Genealogical Index. EB's obituary in *Gentleman's Magazine* (1821), p. 379, gave the date 8 September 1821 and thus misled some later writers. For information on the gravestone and the correct date, see John Green's Family Data.

68. TNA, Probate 11/1647, 28 September 1821. Also see John Green's Family Data. EB had drawn up an earlier will just before his voyage to America in 1783. He gave it for safekeeping to his friend Benjamin Vaughan. The terms of this earlier will are not known. See Vaughan's acknowledgment of receipt of the will in Bancroft Cooke/Salter Collection.

Epilogue

1. Slave Registers of Former British Colonial Dependencies, 1812–34, online database; John Green's Family Data; Bancroft, "Bancroft Family," 81–85; Mabberley, "Edward Nathaniel Bancroft's Obscure Botanical Publications," 7–17.

2. Bancroft, "Bancroft Family," 78–79.

3. These papers, which include the 1852 letter of Catherine Penelope, are in the possession of Anthony Bancroft Cooke and Alicia Salter.

4. Historical Society of Pennsylvania, Edith Bancroft Ashmore Collection (hereinafter cited as Ashmore Collection), Statement Referring to the Claims of the Descendants of Edward Bancroft, undated; John Bancroft to William Charles Bancroft, 9 October 1869. Bancroft, "Bancroft Family," 73.

5. Bancroft, *History of the United States*, 9:62–63.

6. Bancroft, "Bancroft Family," 56; Ashmore Collection, John Bancroft to William Charles Bancroft, 9 October 1869.

7. Some copies of the Wharton/Stevens correspondence can be found in the Ashmore Collection. Therein one can also find letters between Stevens's son and Bancroft family members dating from the early 1900s.

8. Wharton, *Revolutionary Diplomatic Correspondence,* 1:640–41.

9. Einstein, *Divided Loyalties,* 102, 430; Jones, "Dr. Edward Bancroft," 130; MacNalty, "Edward Bancroft," 13; Pearl, "New Perspectives," 2n.

10. Andrew, *Codebreakers,* 1.

11. By Ellis see *His Excellency: George Washington,* 6, and *American Sphinx;* Mapp, *Thomas Jefferson: America's Paradoxical Patriot;* Burstein, *Inner Jefferson;* Morgan, *Benjamin Franklin,* 146, 306, 313; Dull, *Franklin the Diplomat,* 67; Wood, *Americanization of Benjamin Franklin,* 13–15; *PBF,* 24:3, 26:3.

Bibliography

Unpublished Manuscripts

American Philosophical Society. Papers of Benjamin Franklin, William Temple Franklin, and Benjamin Franklin Bache.

Archives du Ministère des Affaires étrangères (France)

   Correspondance politique. États-Unis. Vols. 1–35; supplément, vols. 1–4.

   Mémoires et documents. Angleterre. Vol. 55.

Archives nationales (France). Minutier central. Étude 83.

Bancroft, Edith. "The Bancroft Family." Unpublished manuscript, ca. 1939. Private collection of John Green.

Bancroft Cooke/Salter Collection. Bancroft Family Papers in the possession of Anthony Bancroft Cooke and Alicia Salter.

British Library. Additional Manuscripts. 24321, 34413, 34414, 34415, 34416, 41064, 46490, 61861B, 61863.

Columbia University. Papers of John Jay.

Connecticut Historical Society. Silas Deane Papers.

Cornwall Record Office (United Kingdom). Rogers of Penrose. RP/3/64, RP/3/65, RP/3/82.

Edinburgh University Library. Special Collections. Matriculation Records.

Historical Society of Pennsylvania. Edith Bancroft Ashmore Collection; Benjamin Franklin Papers.

Indiana University. Lilly Library. Jonathan Williams Jr. Manuscripts.

Library of Congress. Manuscripts Department. Papers of Benjamin Franklin, John Holker, and Thomas Jefferson.

London Metropolitan Archives. Papers of Parker, Garrett and Company.

The National Archives (United Kingdom). SP 78/285–306; CO 5/8; C/12/160/29; AO 13/53 Claims New Hampshire C-W; FO 4/3, 27/2, 97/157; Probate 11/1647.

National Archives and Records Administration (United States)

Papers of the Continental Congress, Microfilm Edition, M247, rolls 52, 67,117, 132, 155; M332.

The Complete Service Records of Soldiers Who Served in the American Army during the Revolutionary War, Microfilm Edition, M881.

National Register of Archives for Scotland. Murray Family. Earls of Mansfield Survey (NRAS776/Box16).

New York Public Library. Manuscripts Division. Thomas Addis Emmet Collection.

Sheffield Archives (United Kingdom).Wentworth Woodhouse Muniments.

United Kingdom. Records of the Parliament Office. House of Lords.

Public Bill Office: Original Acts.

Record Office. HL/PO/PU/1/1785/25G3n88.

University of Illinois. Historical Survey Collection. Samuel Wharton Papers.

University of Michigan. William L. Clements Library. Shelburne Papers. Vols. 68–71.

Wellcome Institute for the History of Medicine. Records of the Medical Society of London.

Westfield (Massachusetts) Athenaeum. Birth and Death Records.

Yale University. Sterling Memorial Library. Benjamin Franklin Office. Papers of Benjamin Franklin; Jonathan Williams Jr. Letterbooks.

Newspapers

London: *Courier and Evening Gazette, Diary or Woodfall's Register, E. Johnson's British Gazette and Sunday Monitor, Gazetteer and New Daily Advertiser, Morning Chronicle and London Advertiser, London Gazette, Lloyd's Evening Post, Morning Herald, Morning Post and Fashionable World, Morning Post and Gazetteer, Observer, Oracle and Daily Advertiser, St. James's Chronicle or the British Evening Post, Star, Telegraph, The Times, Whitehall Evening Post, World*

American: *American Mercury* (Hartford, CT), *Argus* (New York), *Boston Evening Post, Centinel of Freedom* (Newark, NJ), *Connecticut Journal, Daily Advertiser* (New York), *Gazette of the United States* (Philadelphia), *Greenleaf's New Daily Advertiser* (New York), *Herald* (New York), *Independent Journal* (New York), *Norwich Packet, Pennsylvania Packet or the General Advertiser, Philadelphia Gazette and Universal Daily Advertiser, Weekly Museum* (New York)

Web sites

Adams Family Papers: An Electronic Archive. www.masshist.org/digitaladams

The Adams Papers, The Papers of George Washington, and The Papers of Thomas Jefferson. http://rotunda.upress.virginia.edu

John Green's Family Data. www.green.gen.name

Journals of the Continental Congress. http://memory.loc.gov/ammem/amlaw/lwjc.html

Letters of Delegates to Congress, 1774–1789. http://memory.loc.gov/ammem/amlaw/lwdg.html

Papers of Benjamin Franklin. www.franklinpapers.org

Papers of John Jay. www.columbia.edu/cu/lweb/digital/jay/

Papers of the Continental Congress. Available at www.footnote.com

Spy Letters of the American Revolution. www.si.umich.edu/spies/index-timeline.html

Printed Primary Sources

Abbot, W. W., and Dorothy Twohig et al., eds. *The Papers of George Washington: Confederation Series.* 6 vols. Charlottesville: University Press of Virginia, 1992–97.

The Annual Register; or, A View of the History, Politics, and Literature for the Year of 1769. London: J. Dodsley in Pall-Mall, 1769. (Plus volumes for subsequent years.)

Aspinall, A., ed. *The Later Correspondence of George III.* 5 vols. Cambridge: Cambridge University Press, 1962–70.

Auckland, William Eden, Baron. *The Journal and Correspondence of William, Lord Auckland.* Edited by Robert John Eden, Baron Auckland, his son the Bishop of Bath and Wells. 2 vols. London: R. Bentley, 1861.

Bancroft, Edward. *Arrow Poison.* Introduction by John Parker. Menomonie, WI: Vagabond, 1972.

———. *An Essay on the Natural History of Guiana. Containing a Description of many Curious Productions in the Animal and Vegetable Systems of that Country. Together with an Account of the Religion, Manners, and Customs of several Tribes of its Indian Inhabitants. Interspersed with a Variety of Literary and Medical Observations, in Several Letters.* London: T. Becket and P. A. De Hondt, in the Strand, 1769; repr., New York: Arno Press and New York Times, 1971.

———. *Experimental Researches Concerning the Philosophy of Permanent Colours; and the Best Means of Producing Them, by Dyeing, Calico Printing, etc.* 2 vols. London: T. Cadell and W. Davies, 1813. (The first volume was originally published by T. Cadell in 1794 and was expanded and revised for the 1813 reissue. The two-volume edition was reprinted in Philadelphia by Thomas Dobson in 1814.)

———. *Facts and Observations, Briefly Stated, in Support of an Intended Application to Parliament.* London: Frances Street, Bedford Square, 1775.

———. *Facts and Observations Briefly Stated, in Support of an Intended Application to Parliament.* London: Private printing, 1798.

———. *Facts and Observations Justifying the Claims of the Prince of Luxembourg against the State of South Carolina and against Alexander Gillon, Esq., Late Commodore of the Navy of the Said State.* Charleston, SC: Private printing, 1784.

———. *The History of Charles Wentworth, Esq., in a Series of Letters. Interspersed with a Variety of Important Reflections, Calculated to Improve Morality, and Promote the Œconomy of Human Life.* 3 vols. London: Becket, 1770; repr., New York: Garland, 1975.

———. "Instruction concernant les preparations nommées 'lac-lake' et 'lac-dye.'" *Annales de Chimie* 3 (1816): 225–37.

——. *A Narrative of the Objects and Proceedings of Silas Deane, as Commissioner of the United Colonies to France; Made to the British Government in 1776.* Edited by Paul Leicester Ford. Brooklyn, NY: Historical Printing, 1891.

——. *Remarks on the review of* The Controversy Between Great Britain and Her Colonies. *In which the errors of its author are exposed, and the claims of the colonies vindicated, upon the evidence of historical facts and authentic records. To Which is subjoined, a proposal for terminating the present unhappy dispute with the colonies; recovering their commerce; reconciling their affection; securing their rights; and establishing their independence on a just and permanent basis. Humbly submitted to the consideration of the British legislature.* London: Printed for T. Becket and P. A. Hondt, 1769.

——, ed. *Philosophical and Miscellaneous Papers. Lately Written by Benjamin Franklin LL. D.* London: C. Dilly, 1787.

Bancroft, Edward, and Samuel Wharton. *View of the Title of Indiana.* London: Private printing, 1775; repr., Philadelphia, 1776.

Bancroft, Edward Nathaniel. *An Essay on the Disease Called Yellow Fever, with Observations concerning Febrile Contagion, Typhus Fever, Dysentery, and the Plague.* London: T. Cadell and W. Davies, 1811; repr. with additional notes by John B. Davidge, Baltimore: Cushing and Jewett, 1820.

——. *A Letter to the Commissioners of Military Enquiry Containing Animadversions on Some Parts of Their Fifth Report; and an Examination of the Principles on Which the Medical Department of Armies Ought to Be Formed.* London: T. Cadell and W. Davies, 1808.

Barnes, G. R., and J. H. Owen, eds. *The Private Papers of John, Earl of Sandwich, First Lord of the Admiralty, 1771–1782.* 4 vols. London: Navy Records Society, 1932–38.

Bates, Albert, ed. *The Deane Papers: Correspondence between Silas Deane, His Brothers and Their Business and Political Associates, 1771–1795.* Hartford: Connecticut Historical Society, 1930.

Board of Agents for the American Loyalists. *The Summary Case of the American Loyalists.* London: Private printing, 1785.

Board of American Loyalists. *Case and Claim of the American Loyalists Impartially Stated and Considered.* London: Printed by order of their agents, 1783.

Boyd, Julian P., et al., eds. *The Papers of Thomas Jefferson.* 34 vols. to date. Princeton, NJ: Princeton University Press, 1950– .

Bradford, James C., ed. *The Papers of John Paul Jones, 1747–1792.* 10 reels of microfilm plus a printed *Guide.* Alexandria, VA: Chadwyck-Healey, 1986.

Burnett, Edmund G., ed. *Letters of Members of the Continental Congress.* 8 vols. Washington, DC: Carnegie Institution, 1921–36.

Butterfield, Lyman H., ed. *Diary and Autobiography of John Adams.* 4 vols. Cambridge, MA: Harvard University Press, 1962.

Butterfield, Lyman, et al., eds. *Adams Family Correspondence.* 8 vols. to date. Cambridge, MA: Harvard University Press, 1963– .

Clark, William Bell, William James Morgan, and Michael J. Crawford, eds. *Naval Documents of the American Revolution.* 11 vols. to date. Washington, DC: Department of the Navy, 1964– .

Copeland, Thomas W., et al., eds. *The Correspondence of Edmund Burke.* 10 vols. Chicago: University of Chicago Press, 1958–78.

Davies, K. G., ed. *Documents of the American Revolution, 1770–1783.* 21 vols. Dublin: Irish University Press, 1972–81.

Doniol, Henri. *Histoire de la participation de la France à l'établissement des États-Unis d'Amérique.* 6 vols. Paris: Imprimerie nationale, 1885–99.

Donne, W. B., ed. *The Correspondence of King George III from 1760 to December 1783.* 2 vols. London: J. Murray, 1867.

Edwards, Adele Stanton, ed. *Journals of the Privy Council, 1783–1789.* Columbia: University of South Carolina Press, 1971.

Elias, Robert H., and Eugene D. Finch, eds. *Letters of Thomas Attwood Digges (1742–1821).* Columbia: University of South Carolina Press, 1982.

Ferguson, E. James, et al., eds. *The Papers of Robert Morris: 1781–1784.* 9 vols. Pittsburgh: University of Pittsburgh Press, 1973–95.

Fitzpatrick, John C., ed. *The Diaries of George Washington, 1748–1799.* 4 vols. Boston: Houghton Mifflin, 1925.

Ford, Worthington Chauncey, ed. *Journals of the Continental Congress.* 34 vols. Washington, DC: National Archives and Records Service, 1904–37.

———. *Letters of William Lee, Sheriff and Alderman of London; Commercial Agent of the Continental Congress in France; and Minister to the Courts of Vienna and Berlin, 1766–1783.* 3 vols. Brooklyn, NY: Historical Printing Club, 1891.

Fortescue, Sir John, ed. *The Correspondence of King George the Third, from 1760 to December 1783,* 6 vols. London: Macmillan, 1928.

Franklin, William Temple, ed. *Memoirs of the Life and Writings of Benjamin Franklin.* 2nd ed. 6 vols. London: Henry Colburn, 1818–19.

Gentleman's Magazine. Volumes for 1789, 1790, 1821.

Giunta, Mary A., et al., eds. *The Emerging Nation: A Documentary History of the Foreign Relations of the United States under the Articles of Confederation, 1780–1789.* 3 vols. Washington, DC: National Historical Publications and Records Commission, 1996.

Great Britain. *Royal Commission on Historical Manuscripts.* Eleventh Report. *Dartmouth Papers.* Teaneck, NJ: Chadwyck-Healey, 1985.

———. *Royal Commission on Historical Manuscripts. Reports on Manuscripts in Various Collections.* 6 vols. London: Historical Manuscripts Commission, 1901–9.

Hamer, Philip M., et al., eds. *The Papers of Henry Laurens.* 16 vols. Columbia: University of South Carolina Press, 1968–2003.

Hardman, John, and Munro Price, eds. *Louis XVI and the Comte de Vergennes: Correspondence, 1774–1787.* Oxford: Voltaire Foundation, 1998.

Hewins, W. A. S., ed. *The Whitefoord Papers: Being the Correspondence and Other Manuscripts of Colonel Charles Whitefoord and Caleb Whitefoord, from 1739 to 1810.* Oxford: Clarendon Press, 1898.

Hoffman, Paul P., ed. *The Lee Family Papers, 1742–1795.* 8 rolls of microfilm. Charlottesville: University of Virginia Library, 1966.

Hutchinson, Peter Orlando, ed. *The Diary and Letters of His Excellency Thomas Hutchinson, Captain-General and Governor-in-Chief of His Late Majesty's Province of Massachusetts Bay in North America.* 2 vols. London: S. Low, Marston, Searle and Rivington, 1883.

Idzerda, Stanley J., et al., eds. *Lafayette in the Age of the American Revolution: Selected Letters and Papers, 1776–1790.* 5 vols. Ithaca, NY: Cornell University Press, 1977–83.

Ingraham, Edward D., ed. *Papers in Relation to the Case of Silas Deane*. Philadelphia: Seventy-Six Society, 1855.

Isham, Charles, ed. *The Deane Papers*. 5 vols. New York: New-York Historical Society, 1887–91.

Jackson, Donald, and Dorothy Twohig, eds. *The Diaries of George Washington*. 6 vols. Charlottesville: University Press of Virginia, 1976–79.

Klingelhofer, Herbert F. "Matthew Ridley's Diary during the Peace Negotiations of 1782." *William and Mary Quarterly*, 3rd ser., 20 (1963): 95–133.

Labaree, Leonard W., et al., eds. *The Papers of Benjamin Franklin*. 39 vols. to date. New Haven: Yale University Press, 1959– .

Legg, L. G. Wickham, ed. *British Diplomatic Instructions, 1689–1789*. Vol. 7: *France, Part IV, 1745–1789*. Camden Society Publications, 3rd ser., vol. 49. London: Royal Historical Society, 1934.

Lincoln, Charles Henry, comp. *Naval Records of the American Revolution, 1775–1788*. Washington, DC, 1906.

Marcus, Maeva, ed. *The Documentary History of the Supreme Court of the United States, 1789–1800*. Vol. 5: *Suits against States*. New York: Columbia University Press, 1995.

Materials Relating to the American Revolution from the Auckland Papers. Yorkshire, UK: EP Microform, 1974.

Meng, John L., ed. *Despatches and Instructions of Conrad Alexandre Gérard, 1778–1780*. Baltimore: Johns Hopkins University Press, 1939.

Morris, Gouverneur. *A Diary of the French Revolution*. Ed. Beatrix Cary Davenport. 2 vols. Boston: Houghton Mifflin, 1939.

Morris, Richard B., ed. *John Jay: The Making of a Revolutionary: Unpublished Papers, 1745–1780*. New York: Harper and Row, 1975.

———. *John Jay: The Winning of the Peace: Unpublished Papers, 1780–1784*. New York: Harper and Row, 1980.

Morton, Brian N., and Donald C. Spinelli, eds. *Beaumarchais Correspondance*. 4 vols. Paris: Éditions A.-G. Nizer, 1969–78.

Neeser, Robert Wilden, ed. *Letters and Papers Relating to the Cruises of Gustavus Conyngham, a Captain of the Continental Navy, 1777–1779*. New York: Naval Historical Society, 1915.

Nuxoll, Elizabeth M., ed. *The Selected Papers of John Jay*. 1 vol. to date. Charlottesville: University of Virginia Press, 2010– .

Rumsey, James. "Letters of James Rumsey, Inventor of the Steamboat (Concluded)." *William and Mary Quarterly* 25 (1916): 21–34.

Russell, Lord John, ed. *Memorials and Correspondence of Charles James Fox*. 4 vols. London: Richard Bentley, 1853–57.

Rutt, John Towill, ed. *Life and Correspondence of Joseph Priestley*. 2 vols. London: R. Hunter, 1832; repr., Bristol, UK: Thoemmes, 2003.

Slave Registers of Former British Colonial Dependencies, 1812–1834. Online database.

Smith, Paul H., et al., eds. *Letters of Delegates to Congress, 1774–1789*. 26 vols. Washington, DC: Library of Congress, 1976–2000.

Smyth, Albert H., ed. *The Writings of Benjamin Franklin*. 10 vols. New York: Macmillan, 1905–7.

The Statutes at Large, from the Nineteenth Year of the Reign of King George the Third, to the Twenty-Fifth Year of the Reign of King George the Third, Inclusive. Vol. 9. London: Charles Eyre and Andrew Strahan, 1786.

Stevens, Benjamin Franklin, ed. *Facsimiles of Manuscripts in European Archives Relating to America, 1773–1783.* 25 vols. London: Privately printed, 1889–98; repr., Wilmington, DE: Mellifont, 1970.

Syrett, Harold C., et al., eds. *The Papers of Alexander Hamilton.* 27 vols. New York: Columbia University Press, 1961–81.

Taylor, Robert J., et al., eds. *The Papers of John Adams.* 14 vols. to date. Cambridge, MA: Harvard University Press, 1977– .

Watson, Winslow C., ed. *Men and Times of the Revolution; or, Memoirs of Elkanah Watson.* New York: Dana, 1855.

Wharton, Francis, ed. *The Revolutionary Diplomatic Correspondence of the United States.* 6 vols. Washington, DC: Government Printing Office, 1889.

Withers, Philip. *Theodosius; or, A Solemn Admonition to Protestant Dissenters, on the Proposed Repeal of the Protestant Test and Corporation Acts.* London, 1790.

Secondary Sources

Abernethy, Thomas Perkins. "Commercial Activities of Silas Deane in France." *American Historical Review* 39 (1934): 477–85.

———. *Western Lands and the American Revolution.* 1937; repr., New York: Russell and Russell, 1959.

Abraham, J. Johnston. *Lettsom: His Life, Times, Friends and Descendants.* London: Heinemann, 1933.

Adrosko, Rita J. *Natural Dyes and Home Dyeing.* Mineola, NY: Dover, 1971.

Allan, D. G. C. "'Dear and Serviceable to Each Other': Benjamin Franklin and the Royal Society of Arts." *Proceedings of the American Philosophical Society* 144 (2000): 245–66.

Allan, D. G. C., and J. L. Abbott, eds. *"The Virtuoso Tribe of Arts and Sciences": Studies in the Eighteenth-Century Work and Membership of the London Society of Arts.* Athens: University of Georgia Press, 1992.

Alsop, Susan Mary. *Yankees at the Court: The First Americans in Paris.* New York: Doubleday, 1982.

Alvord, Clarence W. *The Mississippi Valley in British Politics: A Study of the Trade, Land Speculation, and Experiments in Imperialism Culminating in the American Revolution.* 2 vols. New York: Russell and Russell, 1916.

Anderson, Dennis Kent, and Godfrey Tryggve Anderson. "The Death of Silas Deane: Another Opinion." *New England Quarterly* 57 (1984): 98–105.

Anderson, Godfrey Tryggve, and Dennis Kent Anderson. "Edward Bancroft, M.D., F.R.S, Aberrant 'Practitioner of Physick.'" *Medical History* 17 (1973): 356–67.

Andrew, Christopher M. *Codebreakers and Foreign Offices: The French, British, and American Experiences.* Washington, DC: Wilson Center, 1984.

———. *Her Majesty's Secret Service: The Making of the British Intelligence Community.* New York: Viking, 1986.

Armitage, David. *The Ideological Origins of the British Empire.* New York: Cambridge University Press, 2000.

Armitage, David, and Michael J. Braddick, eds. *The British Atlantic World, 1500–1800.* New York: Palgrave Macmillan, 2002.

Aston, George Grey, Sir. *Secret Service.* London: Faber and Faber, 1930.

Augur, Helen. *The Secret War of Independence.* New York: Duell, 1955.

Bailyn, Bernard. *Atlantic History: Concept and Contours.* Cambridge, MA: Harvard University Press, 2005.

———. *The Ideological Origins of the American Revolution.* Cambridge, MA: Harvard University Press, 1967.

———. *The Ordeal of Thomas Hutchinson.* Cambridge, MA: Harvard University Press, 1974.

Bailyn, Bernard, and Patricia L. Denault, eds. *Soundings in Atlantic History: Latent Structures and Intellectual Currents, 1500–1830.* Cambridge, MA: Harvard University Press, 2009.

Bakeless, John. "General Washington's Spy System." *Manuscripts* 12 (1960): 28–37.

———. "Spies in the Revolution." *American History Illustrated* 6 (June 1971): 36–45.

———. *Turncoats, Traitors and Heroes.* 1959; repr., New York: Da Capo, 1998.

Bancroft, George. *History of the Formation of the Constitution of the United States of America.* Boston: D. Appleton, 1882.

———. *History of the United States, from the Discovery of the American Continent.* 10 vols. Boston: Little, Brown, 1866.

Basye, Arthur Herbert. "The Secretary of State for the Colonies, 1768–1782." *American Historical Review* 27 (1922): 13–23.

Bates, Helen B. "The Diplomacy of Lord Stormont in Relation to American Affairs, 1775–1778." PhD diss., University of Michigan, 1933.

Baugh, Daniel A. "The Politics of British Naval Failure, 1775–1778." *American Neptune* 52 (1992): 221–46.

Bemis, Samuel Flagg. "British Secret Service and the French-American Alliance." *American Historical Review* 29 (1924): 474–95.

———. *The Diplomacy of the American Revolution.* New York: D. Appleton Century, 1935.

———. "Secret Intelligence, 1777: Two Documents." *Huntington Library Quarterly* 24 (1961): 233–49.

Bendikson, L. "The Restoration of Obliterated Passages and of Secret Writing in Diplomatic Missives." *Franco-American Review* 1 (1936–37): 240–56.

Bizardel, Yvon. *Les Américains à Paris sous Louis XVI et pendant la Révolution: Notices biographiques.* Paris: Librairie historique Clavreuil, 1978.

Black, Jeremy. *George II: Puppet of the Politicians?* Exeter, UK: University of Exeter Press, 2007.

———. *George III: America's Last King.* New Haven: Yale University Press, 2006.

Blouet, O. M. "Bryan Edwards, F.R.S., 1743–1800." *Notes and Records of the Royal Society* 54 (2000): 215–22.

Boies, Bessie. "Edward Bancroft: A British Spy." MA thesis, University of Chicago, 1908.

Bossy, John. *Under the Molehill: An Elizabethan Spy Story.* New Haven: Yale University Press, 2001.

Boston Public Library. *Catalogue of the John Adams Library in the Public Library of the City of Boston.* Boston: Trustees of the Boston Public Library, 1917.

Boyd, Julian P. "Silas Deane: Death by a Kindly Teacher of Treason?" *William and Mary Quarterly,* 3rd ser., 16 (1959): 165–87, 319–42, 515–50.

Brecher, Frank. *Securing American Independence: John Jay and the French Alliance.* Westport, CT: Praeger, 2003.

Breen, T. H. *The Market Place of Revolution: How Consumer Politics Shaped American Independence.* Oxford: Oxford University Press, 2004.

Brooks, Christopher K. "Controlling the Metaphor: Language and Self-Definition in Revolutionary America." *Clio* 25 (1996): 233–54.

Brown, Alan S. "William Eden and the American Revolution." PhD diss., University of Michigan, 1953.

Brown, G. I. *Scientist, Soldier, Statesman, Spy: Count Rumford: The Extraordinary Life of a Scientific Genius.* Phoenix Mill, UK: Sutton, 1999.

Brown, Gerald S. *The American Secretary: The Colonial Policy of Lord George Germain, 1775–1778.* Ann Arbor: University of Michigan Press, 1963.

———. "The Policy of Lord George Germain toward America, 1775–78." PhD diss., University of Minnesota, 1948.

Brown, Weldon A. *Empire or Independence: A Study in the Failure of Reconciliation, 1774–1783.* 1941; repr. with new introduction, Port Washington, NY: Kennikat, 1966.

Browne, C. A. "A Sketch of the Life and Chemical Theories of Dr. Edward Bancroft." *Journal of Chemical Education* 14 (1937): 103–7.

Buel, Richard, Jr. *In Irons: Britain's Naval Supremacy and the American Revolutionary Economy.* New Haven: Yale University Press, 1998.

Burke, James. *Twin Tracks: The Unexpected Origins of the Modern World.* New York: Simon and Schuster, 2003.

Burnett, Edmund C. "Ciphers of the Revolutionary Period." *American Historical Review* 22 (1917): 329–34.

Burstein, Andrew. *The Inner Jefferson: Portrait of a Grieving Optimist.* Charlottesville: University Press of Virginia, 1995.

Butler, George Grey, ed. *Colonel St. Paul of Ewart, Soldier and Diplomat.* 2 vols. London: St. Catherine Press, 1911.

Butterfield, Herbert. *George III, Lord North, and the People, 1779–1780.* London: G. Bell and Sons, 1949.

Cannon, John, and Margaret Cannon. *Dye Plants and Dyeing.* Portland, OR: Timber, 2003.

Chaplin, Joyce E. *Subject Matter: Technology, the Body, and Science on the Anglo-American Frontier, 1500–1676.* Cambridge, MA: Harvard University Press, 2001.

Chernow, Ron. *Alexander Hamilton.* New York: Penguin, 2004.

Christie, Ian R. "British Politics and the American Revolution." *Albion* 9 (1977): 205–26.

———. *The End of North's Ministry, 1780–1782.* New York: St. Martin's, 1958.

———. *Myth and Reality in Late-Eighteenth Century British Politics: And Other Papers.* London: Macmillan, 1970.

Clark, William Bell. "In Defense of Thomas Digges." *Pennsylvania Magazine of History and Biography* 77 (1953): 381–438.

———. "John the Painter." *Pennsylvania Magazine of History and Biography* 63 (1939): 1–23.

———. *Lambert Wickes, Sea Raider and Diplomat: The Story of a Naval Captain of the Revolution.* New Haven: Yale University Press, 1932.

Cobban, Alfred. *Ambassadors and Secret Agents: The Diplomacy of the First Earl of Malmesbury at the Hague.* London: Jonathan Cape, 1954.

———. "British Secret Service in France: 1784–1792." *English Historical Review* 69 (1954): 226–61.

Colley, Linda. *Britons: Forging the Nation, 1707–1837.* New Haven: Yale University Press, 1992.

Craig, Robert B. "Benjamin Franklin in France: Espionage, Intrigue, and the Darker Side of Poor Richard." Paper delivered at the annual meeting of the Northeast American Society for Eighteenth-Century Studies, Providence, RI, 7 November 2003.

———. "Benjamin Franklin: In His Majesty's Secret Service?" Paper delivered at the annual meeting of the British Society for Eighteenth-Century Studies, University of Oxford, 6–8 January 2005.

Crane, Verner W. "Franklin's 'The Internal State of America' (1786)." *William and Mary Quarterly,* 3rd ser., 15 (1958): 214–27.

Crout, Robert Rhodes. "The Diplomacy of Trade: The Influence of Commercial Considerations on French Involvement in the Angloamerican War of Independence, 1775–1778." PhD diss., University of Georgia, 1977.

Crowhurst, Patrick. *The Defence of British Trade, 1689–1815.* Folkestone, UK: Dawson, 1977.

Currey, Cecil B. *Code Number 72/Ben Franklin: Patriot or Spy?* Englewood Cliffs, NJ: Prentice-Hall, 1972.

———. *Road to Revolution: Benjamin Franklin in England, 1765–1775.* Garden City, NY: Anchor Books, 1968.

Cuthbertson, Brian C. *The Loyalist Governor: Biography of Sir John Wentworth.* Halifax, NS: Petheric, 1983.

Darnton, Robert. "The Memoirs of Lenoir, Lieutenant de Police de Paris." *English Historical Review* 8 (1970): 52–59.

Davidson, James West, and Mark Hamilton Lytle. *After the Fact: The Art of Historical Detection.* 5th ed. Boston: McGraw-Hill, 2005.

Deacon, Richard. *A History of the British Secret Service.* Rev. ed. London: Granada, 1980.

Delbourgo, James. "Fugitive Colours: Shamans' Knowledge, Chemical Empire, and Atlantic Revolutions." In *The Brokered World: Go-Betweens and Global Intelligence, 1770–1820,* ed. Simon Schaffer et al., 271-320. Sagamore Beach, MA: Science History Publications, 2009.

———. *A Most Amazing Scene of Wonders: Electricity and Enlightenment in Early America.* Cambridge, MA: Harvard University Press, 2006.

———. "Natural Knowledge as an Atlantic Process: Edward Bancroft and the *Natural History of Guiana*." Paper delivered at the Columbia University Early American History Seminar, 10 February 2004.

Delbourgo, James, and Nicholas Dew, eds. *Science and Empire in the Atlantic World.* New York: Routledge, 2008.

De Noya, Mary. "Washington's Secret Army." *Daughters of the American Revolution Magazine* 116 (1982): 102–5.

Dickinson, Harry T. *The Politics of the People in Eighteenth-Century Britain.* New York: St. Martin's, 1994.

———, ed. *Britain and the American Revolution.* London: Addison Wesley Longman, 1998.

Drayton, Richard. *Nature's Government: Science, Imperial Britain, and "Improvement" of the World.* New Haven: Yale University Press, 2000.

Dukes, Cuthbert E. "London Medical Societies in the Eighteenth Century." *Proceedings of the Royal Society of Medicine* 53 (1960): 699–706.

Dull, Jonathan R. *The Age of the Ship of the Line: The British and French Navies, 1650–1815.* Lincoln: University of Nebraska Press, 2009.

———. *Benjamin Franklin and the American Revolution.* Lincoln: University of Nebraska Press, 2010.

———. "Benjamin Franklin and the Nature of American Diplomacy." *International History Review* 5 (1983): 346–63.

———. *A Diplomatic History of the American Revolution.* New Haven: Yale University Press, 1985.

———. *Franklin the Diplomat: The French Mission.* Philadelphia: American Philosophical Society, 1982.

———. *The French Navy and American Independence: A Study of Arms and Diplomacy, 1774–1787.* Princeton, NJ: Princeton University Press, 1975.

———. *The French Navy and the Seven Years' War.* Lincoln: University of Nebraska Press, 2005.

Dulles, Allen. "American Mission in Paris." In *Spies, Spies, Spies,* ed. Barbara Nolen. New York: Franklin Watts, 1965.

———. *The Craft of Intelligence.* New York: Harper and Row, 1963.

———, ed. *Great True Spy Stories.* Secaucus, NJ: Castle, 1968.

Edelstein, Sidney M. "Historical Notes on the Wet-Processing Industry. VI: The Dual Life of Edward Bancroft." *American Dyestuff Reporter,* 25 October 1954, 711–12, 735.

"Edward Bancroft @ Edw. Edwards, Estimable Spy." *Studies in Intelligence* 5 (1961): 53–67.

Egnal, Marc. *A Mighty Empire: The Origins of the American Revolution.* Ithaca, NY: Cornell University Press, 1988.

Einstein, Lewis. *Divided Loyalties: Americans in England during the War of Independence.* Boston: Houghton Mifflin, 1933.

Elliott, Charlene. "Color Codification: Law, Culture and the Hue of Communication." *Journal for Cultural Research* 7 (2003): 297–319.

Elliott, Marianne. *The Catholics of Ulster: A History.* New York: Basic Books, 2001.

Ellis, Joseph J. *American Sphinx: The Character of Thomas Jefferson.* New York: Knopf, 1997.

———. *His Excellency: George Washington.* New York: Knopf, 2004.

Ellis, K. L. "British Communications and Diplomacy in the Eighteenth Century." *Bulletin of the Institute of Historical Research* 31 (1958): 159–67.

———. *The Post Office in the Eighteenth Century: A Study in Administrative History.* London: Oxford University Press, 1958.

Ferguson, E. James. "Business, Government, and Congressional Investigation in the Revolution." *William and Mary Quarterly,* 3rd ser., 16 (1959): 293–318.

———. *The Power of the Purse: A History of American Public Finance, 1776–1790.* Chapel Hill: University of North Carolina Press, 1961.

Ferling, John, and Lewis E. Braverman. "John Adams's Health Reconsidered." *William and Mary Quarterly*, 3rd ser., 55 (1998): 83–104.

Fitzmaurice, Lord Edmond. *Life of William, Earl of Shelburne, Afterwards First Marquess of Lansdowne, with Extracts from His Papers and Correspondence.* Rev. ed. 2 vols. London: Macmillan, 1912.

Flavell, Julie, and Stephen Conway, eds. *Britain and America Go to War: The Impact of War and Warfare in Anglo-America, 1754–1815.* Gainesville: University Press of Florida, 2005.

Gardiner, Robert, ed. *Navies and the American Revolution, 1775–1783.* London: Chatham, 1996.

Garfield, Simon. *Mauve: How One Man Invented a Color That Changed the World.* New York: W. W. Norton, 2001.

Goldstein, Kalman. "Silas Deane: Preparation for Rascality." *Historian* 43 (1980–81): 75–97.

Grant, James. *John Adams: Party of One.* New York: Farrar, Straus and Giroux, 2005.

Greene, Jack P., and Philip D. Morgan, eds. *Atlantic History: A Critical Appraisal.* New York: Oxford University Press, 2008.

Griffiths, Trevor, Philip A. Hunt, and Patrick K. O'Brien. "Inventive Activity in the British Textile Industry, 1700-1800." *Journal of Economic History* 52 (1992): 881–906.

Guttridge, G. H. *David Hartley, M.P., an Advocate of Conciliation, 1774–1783.* Berkeley: University of California Press, 1926.

Haefele, Walter R. "General George Washington: Espionage Chief." *American History Illustrated* 24 (1989): 22–27, 69.

Halsted, Janet G. "Silas Deane: Intelligence Agent and Ambassador from the Continental Congress." MA thesis, Southern Connecticut State University, 1999.

Hans, Nicholas. "UNESCO of the Eighteenth Century: La Loge des Neuf Soeurs and Its Venerable Master, Benjamin Franklin." *Proceedings of the American Philosophical Society* 97 (1953): 513–24.

Harlow, Vincent T. *The Founding of the Second British Empire, 1763–1793.* 2 vols. London: Longmans, Green, 1952–64.

Haussmann, Albert. "Doctor of Duplicity." *Yankee Magazine* (July 1975): 78–87.

Henderson, Herbert James. *Party Politics in the Continental Congress.* New York: McGraw-Hill, 1974.

Hendrick, Burton J. "Arch-Traitor of the Revolution." *Reader's Digest*, January 1936, 46–48.

———. *The Lees of Virginia: Biography of a Family.* Boston: Little, Brown, 1935.

———. "Worse Than Arnold." *Atlantic Monthly*, October 1935, 385–95.

Himmelfarb, Gertrude. *The Roads to Modernity: The British, French, and American Enlightenments.* New York: Knopf, 2004.

Hoffman, Ronald, and Peter J. Albert, eds. *Peace and the Peacemakers: The Treaty of 1783.* Charlottesville: University Press of Virginia, 1986.

Horn, David B. *British Diplomatic Representatives, 1689–1789.* London: Royal Historical Society, 1932.

———. *The British Diplomatic Service, 1689–1799.* Oxford: Clarendon Press, 1961.

———. "The Machinery for the Conduct of British Foreign Policy in the Eighteenth Century." *Journal of the Society of Archivists* 3 (1966): 229–40.

Hunt, Thomas, ed. *The Medical Society of London, 1773–1973.* London: William Heinemann Medical Books, 1973.

Hunting, Penelope. *The Medical Society of London, 1773–2003.* London: Medical Society of London, 2003.

———. "The Medical Society of London." *Postgraduate Medical Journal* 80 (2004): 350–54.

Hutson, James H. *John Adams and the Diplomacy of the American Revolution.* Lexington: University Press of Kentucky, 1980.

Isaacson, Walter. *Benjamin Franklin: An American Life.* New York: Simon and Schuster, 2003.

Jacob, Margaret C. *The Origins of Freemasonry.* Philadelphia: University of Pennsylvania Press, 2006.

James, Coy H. *Silas Deane: Patriot or Traitor?* East Lansing: Michigan State University Press, 1975.

James, William M. *The British Navy in Adversity: A Study of the War of American Independence.* London: Longmans, Green, 1926.

Jeffreys-Jones, Rhodri. *Cloak and Dollar: A History of American Secret Intelligence.* 2nd ed. New Haven: Yale University Press, 2003.

Johnston, Ruth Y. "American Privateers in French Ports, 1776–1778." *Pennsylvania Magazine of History and Biography* 53 (1929): 352–74.

Jones, Edward Alfred. *The Loyalists of New Jersey.* Newark: New Jersey Historical Society, 1927; repr., Boston: Gregg Press, 1972.

Jones, Harold N. "Dr. Edward Bancroft." In Edward C. Janes and Roscoe S. Scott, eds. *Westfield, Massachusetts, 1669–1969: The First Three Hundred Years,* 120–33. Westfield, MA: Westfield Tri-Centennial Association, 1968.

Jones, R. V. "Benjamin Franklin." *Notes and Records of the Royal Society of London* 31 (1977): 201–23.

Kahn, David. *The Codebreakers: The Story of Secret Writing.* Rev. ed. New York: Scribner, 1996.

Kammen, Michael G. *A Rope of Sand: The Colonial Agents, British Politics, and the American Revolution.* Ithaca, NY: Cornell University Press, 1968.

Kaplan, Lawrence S., ed. *The American Revolution and "A Candid World."* Kent, OH: Kent State University Press, 1977.

Kaye, Harvey J., *Thomas Paine and the Promise of America.* New York: Hill and Wang, 2005.

Keegan, John. *Intelligence in War: Knowledge of the Enemy from Napoleon to Al-Qaeda.* New York: Knopf, 2003.

Keen, Paul, ed. *Revolutions in Romantic Literature: An Anthology of Print Culture, 1780–1832.* Peterborough, ON: Broadview, 2004.

Keesey, John. "How Electric Fish Became Sources for Acetylcholine Receptor." *Journal of the History of the Neurosciences* 14 (2005): 149–64.

Keir, David Lindsay. "Economical Reform, 1779–1787." *Law Quarterly Review* 50 (1934): 368–85.

Kelly, James. *Sir Edward Newenham MP, 1734–1814: Defender of the Protestant Constitu-tion.* Dublin: Four Courts, 2004.

Kennett, Lee. *The French Forces in America, 1780–1783.* Westport, CT: Greenwood, 1977.

Kidd, Colin. *British Identities before Nationalism: Ethnicity and Nationhood in the Atlantic World, 1600–1800.* Cambridge: Cambridge University Press, 1999.

Kite, Elizabeth S. "Silas Deane: Diplomatist and Patriot Scapegoat of the Revolution." *Daughters of the American Revolution Magazine* 60 (September 1926): 537–46.

Lee, Richard Henry. *Life of Arthur Lee, LL.D., Joint Commissioner of the United States to the Court of France, and Sole Commissioner to the Courts of Spain and Prussia, during the Revolutionary War.* 2 vols. Boston: Wells and Lilly, 1820.

Lewis, George E. *The Indiana Company, 1763–1798: A Study in Eighteenth Century Frontier Land Speculation and Business Venture.* Glendale, CA: Arthur H. Clark, 1941.

Lewis, James A. *Neptune's Militia: The Frigate* South Carolina *during the American Revo-lution.* Kent, OH: Kent State University Press, 1999.

Lewis, Lesley. *Connoisseurs and Secret Agents in Eighteenth Century Rome.* London: Chatto and Windus, 1961.

Lloyd, Mark. *The Guinness Book of Espionage.* New York: Da Capo, 1994.

London, April. "Novel and Natural History: Edward Bancroft in Guiana." *Genre* 31 (1998): 101–16.

———. *Women and Property in the Eighteenth-Century English Novel.* New York: Cam-bridge University Press, 1999.

Lopez, Claude-Anne. "Benjamin Franklin and William Dodd: A New Look at an Old Issue." *Proceedings of the American Philosophical Society* 129 (1985): 260–67.

———. "The Man Who Frightened Franklin." *Pennsylvania Magazine of History and Biography* 106 (1982): 515–26.

———. *Mon Cher Papa: Franklin and the Ladies of Paris.* New Haven: Yale University Press, 1966.

Lopez, Claude-Anne, and Eugenia W. Herbert. *The Private Franklin: The Man and His Family.* New York: W. W. Norton, 1975.

Lysing, H. *Secret Writing: An Introduction to Cryptograms, Ciphers, and Codes.* New York: D. Kemp, 1936.

Mabberley, D. J. "Edward Nathaniel Bancroft's Obscure Botanical Publications and His Father's Plant Names." *Taxon* 30 (1981): 7–17.

Mackesy, Piers. *The War for America, 1775–1783.* Cambridge, MA: Harvard University Press, 1965.

MacNalty, Arthur S., Sir. "Edward Bancroft, M.D., F.R.S., and the War of American Independence." *Proceedings of the Royal Society of Medicine* 38 (November 1944): 7–15.

Mahoney, Harry Thayer. *Gallantry in Action: A Biographic Dictionary of Espionage in the American Revolutionary War.* Lanham, MD: University Press of America, 1999.

Maier, Pauline. *From Resistance to Revolution: Colonial Radicals and the Development of American Opposition to Britain, 1765–1776.* New York: Knopf, 1972.

Mapp, Alf J. *Thomas Jefferson: America's Paradoxical Patriot.* Lanham, MD: Rowman and Littlefield, 2007.

Marshall, P. J. *The Making and Unmaking of Empires: Britain, India, and America, c. 1750–1783.* Oxford: Oxford University Press, 2005.

———, ed. *The Oxford History of the British Empire*. Vol. 2: *The Eighteenth Century*. Oxford: Oxford University Press, 1998.

Marshall, Peter. "Lord Hillsborough, Samuel Wharton, and the Ohio Grant, 1769–1775." *English Historical Review* 80 (1965): 717–39.

Massey, Gregory D. *John Laurens and the American Revolution*. Columbia: University of South Carolina Press, 2000.

Mathews, Hazel C. *Frontier Spies: The British Secret Service, Northern Department, during the Revolutionary War*. Fort Meyers, FL: Ace [private printing], 1971.

Matthew, H. C. G., and Brian Harrison, eds. *Oxford Dictionary of National Biography*. 60 vols. Oxford: Oxford University Press, 2004.

May, Henry F. *The Enlightenment in America*. Oxford: Oxford University Press, 1976.

McClellan, James E., III. *Science Reorganized: Scientific Societies in the Eighteenth Century*. New York: Columbia University Press, 1985.

McCullough, David. *John Adams*. New York: Simon and Schuster, 2001.

McCusker, John J. *How Much Is That in Real Money?* New Castle, DE: Oak Knoll, 2001.

Middelkauff, Robert. *Benjamin Franklin and His Enemies*. Berkeley: University of California Press, 1996.

Miller, Daniel A. *Sir Joseph Yorke and Anglo-Dutch Relations, 1774–1780*. The Hague: Mouton, 1970.

Miller, Margaret A. "The Spy Activities of Doctor Edward Bancroft." *Journal of American History* 22 (1928): 70–77, 157–70.

Moore, Norman. *The History of St. Bartholomew's Hospital*. London: C. A. Pearson, 1918.

Morgan, David T. *The Devious Dr. Franklin, Colonial Agent: Benjamin Franklin's Years in London*. Macon, GA: Mercer University Press, 1996.

Morgan, Edmund S. *Benjamin Franklin*. New Haven: Yale University Press, 2002.

———. "The Postponement of the Stamp Act." *William and Mary Quarterly*, 3rd ser., 7 (1950): 353–92.

———. "The Puritan Ethic and the American Revolution." *William and Mary Quarterly*, 3rd ser., 24 (1967): 3–43.

Morgan, William James. "American Privateering in America's War for Independence, 1775–1783." *American Neptune* 36 (1976): 79–87.

Morris, Richard B. *The Peacemakers: The Great Powers and American Independence*. New York: Harper and Row, 1965.

Morton, Brian N. *Americans in London*. New York: William Morrow, 1986.

———. "Beaumarchais, Francy, Steuben, and Lafayette: An Unpublished Correspondence or 'Feux de joye' at Valley Forge." *French Review* 49 (1976): 943–59.

Morton, Brian N., and Donald C. Spinelli. *Beaumarchais and the American Revolution*. Lanham, MD: Lexington Books, 2003.

Mowat, R. B. "British Spies in the American Revolution." *Discovery*, August 1934, 225–27.

Mullett, Charles F. "Politics, Economics and Medicine: Charles Maclean and Anticontagion in England." *Osiris* 10 (1952): 224–51.

Mullin, Arthur. *Spy: America's First Double Agent, Dr. Edward Bancroft*. Santa Barbara, CA: Capra, 1987.

Murrin, John M. "The French and Indian War, the American Revolution, and the Counterfactual Hypothesis: Reflections on Lawrence Henry Gipson and John Shy." *Reviews in American History* 1 (1973): 307–18.

Nangle, Benjamin Christie. *The Monthly Review, First Series, 1749–1789: Index of Contributors and Articles.* Oxford: Clarendon Press, 1934.

———. *The Monthly Review, Second Series, 1790–1815: Index of Contributors and Articles.* Oxford: Clarendon Press, 1955.

Norton, Mary Beth. *The British-Americans: The Loyalist Exiles in England, 1774–1789.* Boston: Little, Brown, 1972.

Noyes, Robert Gale. *The Neglected Muse: Restoration and Eighteenth-Century Tragedy in the Novel (1740–1780).* Providence, RI: Brown University Press, 1958.

Nuxoll, Elizabeth M. "Congress and the Munitions Merchants: The Secret Committee of Trade during the American Revolution, 1775–1777." PhD diss., City University of New York, 1979.

Onuf, Peter S. *The Origins of the Federal Republic: Jurisdictional Controversies in the United States, 1775–1787.* Philadelphia: University of Pennsylvania Press, 1983.

O'Toole, George J. A. "Benjamin Franklin: American Spymaster or Mole." *International Journal of Intelligence and Counterintelligence* 3 (1989): 45–53.

———. *Honorable Treachery: A History of U.S. Intelligence, Espionage, and Covert Action from the American Revolution to the CIA.* New York: Atlantic Monthly, 1991.

Owen, David. *Hidden Secrets: The Complete History of Espionage and the Technology Used to Support It.* Buffalo, NY: Firefly Books, 2002.

Pacheco, Josephine F. "French Secret Agents in America, 1763–1778." PhD diss., University of Chicago, 1951.

Palmer, Gregory. *Biographical Sketches of Loyalists of the American Revolution.* Westport, CT: Meckler, 1984.

Paltsits, Victor H. "The Use of Invisible Ink for Secret Writing during the American Revolution." *New York Public Library, Bulletin* 39 (May 1935): 361–64.

Patterson, A. Temple. *The Other Armada: The Franco-Spanish Attempt to Invade Britain in 1779.* Manchester, UK: Manchester University Press, 1960.

Patton, Robert H. *Patriot Pirates: The Privateer War for Freedom and Fortune in the American Revolution.* New York: Pantheon, 2008.

Paul, Joel Richard. *Unlikely Allies: How a Merchant, a Playwright, and a Spy Saved the American Revolution.* New York: Penguin, 2009.

Pearl, William D. "New Perspectives on Dr. Edward Bancroft." MA thesis, George Washington University, 1973.

Pennypacker, Morton. *General Washington's Spies on Long Island and in New York.* 2 vols. Brooklyn, NY: Long Island Historical Society, 1939–48.

Phillips, Kevin P. *The Cousins' Wars: Religion, Politics, and the Triumph of Anglo-America.* New York: Basic Books, 1999.

Piccolino, Marco, and Marco Bresadola. "Drawing a Spark from Darkness: John Walsh and Electric Fish." *Trends in Neurosciences* 25 (2002): 51–57.

Pocock, J. G. A. *Virtue, Commerce, and History: Essays on Political Thought and History, Chiefly in the Eighteenth Century.* Cambridge: Cambridge University Press, 1985.

Porter, Bernard. *Plots and Paranoia: A History of Political Espionage in Britain, 1790–1988.* London: Unwin Hyman, 1989.

Potent, S. Eugene. "Benjamin Franklin: The Spy No One Knew, for Sure." *Intelligencer* 10 (1999): 21–24.

Potts, Louis W. *Arthur Lee: A Virtuous Revolutionary.* Baton Rouge: Louisiana State University Press, 1981.

Prelinger, Catherine M. "Benjamin Franklin and the American Prisoners of War in England during the American Revolution." *William and Mary Quarterly,* 3rd ser., 32 (1975): 261–74.

———. "Less Lucky Than Lafayette: A Note on the French Applicants to Benjamin Franklin for Commissions in the American Army, 1776–1785." *Proceedings of the Western Society for French History* 4 (1976): 263–71.

Raghavendra, Thandla. "Neuromuscular Blocking Drugs: Discovery and Development." *Journal of the Royal Society of Medicine* 95 (2002): 363–67.

Rakove, Jack N. *The Beginnings of National Politics: An Interpretive History of the Continental Congress.* New York: Knopf, 1979.

Randall, Willard Sterne. *Benedict Arnold: Patriot and Traitor.* New York: William Morrow, 1990.

———. *A Little Revenge: Benjamin Franklin and His Son.* Boston: Little, Brown, 1984.

Renaut, Francis P. *Le secret service de l'Amirauté britannique au temps de la guerre d'Amérique, 1776–1783, d'après les documents retrouvés dans les archives britanniques.* Paris: Éditions du Graouli, 1936.

Ritcheson, Charles R. *Aftermath of the Revolution: British Policy toward the United States, 1783–1795.* Dallas: Southern Methodist University Press, 1969.

———. *British Politics and the American Revolution.* Norman: University of Oklahoma Press, 1954.

Roberts, Pricilla H., and Richard S. Roberts. *Thomas Barclay (1728–1793): Consul in France, Diplomat in Barbary.* Bethlehem, PA: Lehigh University Press, 2008.

Rodger, N. A. M. *The Command of the Ocean: A Naval History of Britain, 1649–1815.* New York: W. W. Norton, 2005.

Rose, Alexander. *Washington's Spies: The Story of America's First Spy Ring.* New York: Bantam, 2006.

Royster, Charles. *The Fabulous History of the Dismal Swamp Company: A Story of George Washington's Time.* New York: Knopf, 1999.

Rule, John C. "Gathering Intelligence in the Age of Louis XIV." *International History Review* 14 (1992): 732–52.

Sabine, Lorenzo. *Biographical Sketches of Loyalists of the American Revolution.* 2 vols. Boston: Little, Brown, 1864.

Schaeper, Thomas J. *France and America in the Revolutionary Era: The Life of Jacques-Donatien Leray de Chaumont, 1725–1803.* New York: Berghahn, 1995.

———. *John Paul Jones and the Battle off Flamborough Head: A Reconsideration.* New York: Peter Lang, 1989.

Schiebinger, Londa. *Plants and Empire: Colonial Bioprospecting in the Atlantic World.* Cambridge, MA: Harvard University Press, 2004.

Schiff, Stacy. *A Great Improvisation: Franklin, France, and the Birth of America.* New York: Henry Holt, 2005.

Schofield, Robert E. *The Enlightened Joseph Priestley: A Study of His Life and Work from 1773 to 1804.* University Park: Pennsylvania State University Press, 2004.

Schulte Nordholt, Jan Willem. *The Dutch Republic and American Independence.* Translated by Herbert H. Rowen. Chapel Hill: University of North Carolina Press, 1982.

Scott, H. M. *British Foreign Policy in the Age of the American Revolution.* Oxford: Oxford University Press, 1990.

———. "British Foreign Policy in the Age of the American Revolution." *International History Review* 6 (1984): 113–25.

Sellers, Charles C. *Patience Wright, American Artist and Spy in George III's London.* Middletown, CT: Wesleyan University Press, 1976.

Shepperson, Archibald B. *John Paradise and Lucy Ludwell of London and Williamsburg.* Richmond, VA: Dietz, 1942.

Simms, Brendan. *Three Victories and a Defeat: The Rise and Fall of the First British Empire.* London: Allen Lane, 2007.

Skemp, Sheila. *Benjamin and William Franklin.* New York: St. Martin's, 1994.

Smith, D. E. Huger. "Commodore Alexander Gillon and the Frigate South Carolina." *South Carolina Genealogical and Historical Magazine* 9 (1908): 189–219.

———. "The Luxembourg Claims." *South Carolina Genealogical and Historical Magazine* 10 (1909): 92–115.

Smith, Philip Chadwick Foster. *The Empress of China.* Philadelphia: Philadelphia Maritime Museum, 1984.

Stahr, Walter. *John Jay: Founding Father.* New York: Hambledon, 2005.

Stinchcombe, William. *The American Revolution and the French Alliance.* Syracuse, NY: Syracuse University Press, 1969.

———. "A Note on Silas Deane's Death." *William and Mary Quarterly,* 3rd ser., 32 (1975): 619–24.

Stockley, Andrew. *Britain and France at the Birth of America: The European Powers and the Peace Negotiations of 1782–1783.* Exeter, UK: University of Exeter Press, 2001.

Stone, Richard G., Jr. "The *South Carolina* We've Lost: The Bizarre Story of Alexander Gillon and His Frigate." *American Neptune* 39 (1979): 159–72.

Syrett, David. *The Royal Navy in European Waters during the American Revolutionary War.* Columbia: University of South Carolina Press, 1998.

Thomas, Evan. *John Paul Jones: Sailor, Hero, Father of the American Navy.* New York: Simon and Schuster, 2003.

Thomas, Peter D. G. *Lord North.* London: Allen Lane, 1976.

Thompson, Edmund R. "George Washington: Master Intelligence Officer." *American Intelligence Journal* 5 (July 1984): 3–8.

———, ed. *Secret New England: Spies of the American Revolution.* Portland, ME: Provincial Press, 2001.

Thompson, James Westfall, and Saul K. Padover. *Secret Diplomacy: Espionage and Cryptography, 1500–1815.* Rev. ed. New York: Frederick Ungar, 1963.

Thomson, Mark A. *The Secretaries of State, 1681–1782.* Oxford: Clarendon Press, 1932.

Tilley, John A. *The British Navy and the American Revolution*. Columbia: University of South Carolina Press, 1987.

Tracy, Nicholas. *Navies, Deterrence and American Independence: Britain and Seapower in the 1760s and 1770s*. Vancouver: University of British Columbia Press, 1988.

Trees, Andrew S. *The Founding Fathers and the Politics of Character*. Princeton, NJ: Princeton University Press, 2004.

Trengrove, Leonard. "Chemistry at the Royal Society of London in the Eighteenth Century. IV: Dyes." *Annals of Science* 26 (1970): 331–53.

Tudda, Chris. "'A Messiah that Will Never Come': A New Look at Saratoga, Independence, and Revolutionary War Diplomacy." *Diplomatic History* 32 (2008): 779–810.

United States Central Intelligence Agency. *Intelligence in the War of Independence*. Washington, DC: CIA, 1976.

Valentine, Alan. *Lord North*. 2 vols. Norman: University of Oklahoma Press, 1967.

Van Alstyne, Richard W. *Empire and Independence: The International History of the American Revolution*. New York: J. Wiley, 1965.

———. "Europe, the Rockingham Whigs, and the War for American Independence: Some Documents." *Huntington Library Quarterly* 25 (1961): 1–28.

———. "Great Britain, the War for Independence, and the 'Gathering Storm' in Europe, 1775–1778." *Huntington Library Quarterly* 27 (1964): 311–46.

———. "Parliamentary Supremacy versus Independence: Notes and Documents." *Huntington Library Quarterly* 26 (1963): 201–33.

Van Doren, Carl. *Benjamin Franklin*. Garden City, NY: Garden City Publishing, 1938.

———. *Secret History of the American Revolution*. New York: Viking, 1941.

Ver Steeg, Clarence L. *Robert Morris: Revolutionary Financier. With an Analysis of His Earlier Career*. Philadelphia: University of Pennsylvania Press, 1954.

Waddington, Keir. *Medical Education at St. Bartholomew's Hospital, 1123–1995*. Rochester, NY: Boydell, 2003.

Ward, Marion. *Forth*. London: Phillimore, 1982.

Warner, Jessica. *John the Painter: Terrorist of the American Revolution*. New York: Thunder's Mouth, 2004.

Weber, Ralph E. *Masked Dispatches: Cryptograms and Cryptology in American History, 1775–1900*. Fort George G. Meade, MD: Center for Cryptologic History, National Security Agency, 2002.

———. *United States Diplomatic Codes and Ciphers, 1775–1938*. Chicago: Precedent, 1979.

Wecter, Dixon. "Benjamin Franklin and an Irish 'Enthusiast.'" *Huntington Library Quarterly* 4 (1941): 205–34.

Weintraub, Stanley. *Iron Tears: America's Battle for Freedom, Britain's Quagmire, 1775–1783*. New York: Free Press, 2005.

Wentworth, John. *The Wentworth Genealogy: English and American*. 3 vols. Boston: Little, Brown, 1878.

Wharton, Anne H. "The Wharton Family." *Pennsylvania Magazine of History and Biography* 1 (1877): 324–29, 455–59, 468.

Whiteley, Peter. *Lord North: The Prime Minister Who Lost America*. London: Hambledon, 1996.

Wickes, Stephen. *History of Medicine in New Jersey and of Its Medical Men, from the Settlement of the Province to A.D. 1800*. Newark, NJ: M. R. Dennis, 1879.

Wickwire, Franklin B. *British Subministers and Colonial America, 1763–1783*. Princeton, NJ: Princeton University Press, 1966.

Wilderson, Paul W. *Governor John Wentworth and the American Revolution: The English Connection*. Hanover, NH: University Press of New England, 1994.

Williams, Alan. *The Police of Paris, 1718–1789*. Baton Rouge: Louisiana State University Press, 1979.

Wood, Gordon S. *The Americanization of Benjamin Franklin*. New York: Penguin, 2004.

York, Neil Longley. *Burning the Dockyard: John the Painter and the American Revolution*. Portsmouth, UK: Portsmouth City Council, 2001.

Index

Franklin, Benjamin (continued)
letters, 38–40; and Continental Congress, 46–47; as colonial agent, 54; affection for Britain, 63; and son, 63; arrival in Paris, 68–69, 126; trusts Bancroft's information, 75; his two grandsons, 84–85; moves to Passy, 85; relations with Arthur Lee, 86–87; range of duties, 89–90; Bancroft's work for him, 89–92, 115; correspondence with Congress, 103–4; privateers, 105; and treaty with France, 109, 114; meets Wentworth, 112–13; and spies, 128; meets Louis XVI and Vergennes, 131; and Hynson, 137–38; appointed minister, 160–61; as peace commissioner, 164–66; close relationship with Bancroft, 170–75, 189, 192, 193, 230; and Jones, 177–81, 183; and Adams, 185–86; supposed awareness of spies, 198–206, 211; and Gillon, 233; final contacts with Bancroft, 244–46

Franklin, William, 33, 63, 84, 238

Franklin, William Temple: editor of Franklin papers, 40; accompanies Franklin to France, 84; his work for Franklin, 90, 109, 170; friend of Bancroft, 174, 179, 194, 228, 245–46

Fraser, William, 55, 236

Gale, Benjamin, 3, 5

Garnier, Charles-Jean, 47, 71, 174

Gates, Horatio, 63, 107

George III: proclamation of 1763, 15; receives Bancroft's information, 114, 115; distrust of Bancroft and Wentworth, 110, 144–45, 161; pays North's debts, 155; and Deane, 212–13

Gérard, Conrad-Alexandre, 48, 49; treaty with Americans, 109, 110, 113–14; to America, 132

Germain, Lord George, 14, 65, 151, 152–53

Gillon, Alexander, 233–35

Goldsmith, Oliver, 42

Grafton, Augustus, Duke of, 72

Grand, Ferdinand, 85, 87, 104

Grand, Georges, 100

Grantham, Thomas Robinson, Baron, 165, 205–6

Grenville, George, 14, 15, 16, 22, 33

Grenville, Thomas, 164–65

Griffiths, Ralph, 42, 47, 48

Guiana, 3, 5–12

Hamilton, Alexander, 21, 33

Hartley, David, 166, 173, 237

Hendrick, Burton J., 57–58

Hertford, Francis Seymour Conway, Earl of, 33

Hillsborough, Wills Hill, Earl of, 151

History of Charles Wentworth, 25–29

Holker, Jean/John, 100, 231

Hopkinson, Francis, 62

Hoseason, Ursula Hill, 260

Howe, Richard, Lord, 42, 72, 143, 148–49

Howe, William, 72, 156

Hutchinson letters, 38–40

Hynson, Joseph, 89, 137–38, 145

Indiana Company, 33–34, 43

Indians: Guiana, 8–10; North America, 15, 33, 43

Ingenhousz, Jan, 192–93

Inks and dyes: Bancroft's research on, 24, 32, 34–35, 231–32, 256–58, 261; commerce in, 30–31, 44, 231–32, 252–54

Invisible ink, 96, 118, 124

Ireland, 31, 37, 188–89

Izard, Ralph, 41; congressional appointment, 87; business affairs, 114, 122; returns to America, 161; on Bancroft, 184–85, 195–97

Jay, James, 74

Jay, John: as peace commissioner, 164–65, 168; and Bancroft, 193, 230, 243–44, 251

Jeans, Thomas, 125, 126

Jefferson, Thomas, 33, 62; as peace commissioner, 164; and Bancroft, 217–18, 220, 247, 248–51

Americans, 109, 110, 113–14; meets
Wentworth, 111; suspects a spy, 128;
Jay's distrust of, 165; and peace
negotiations, 169; and Bancroft, 188–89;
distrust of Lee, 198

Voltaire, 9, 27–28

Walpole, Thomas, 33–34, 43, 48; friend
and partner of Bancroft, 75, 90, 117, 174
Walpole, Thomas (son), 243, 259
Walsh, John, 8
Washington, George, 33, 34, 62; spy
network, 154; and Bancroft, 193–94, 231,
251
Watson, Elkanah, 174
Wedderburn, Alexander, 39–40, 153
Wentworth, John, 25, 53
Wentworth, Paul, early career, 22, 24–25,
53–54; and Bancroft's entry into
espionage, 54–55, 58–59; receives
Bancroft's information, 69, 90, 93–106,
114–15; and Arthur Lee, 74; on Bancroft
and John the Painter, 79; lends money
to Penelope, 81; confers with Bancroft,
92, 94, 103–4, 105, 111–12, 113, 115; confers
with Deane, 109–10; meets Franklin,
112–13; and Stormont, 113, 126–28; on
Bancroft's private investments, 120;
private business, 122–23, 190; tree in
Tuileries Gardens, 123–31; new methods

to communicate with Bancroft, 132–33,
156–57, 159–60; gauging his importance,
135, 140, 142–43; George III's distrust of,
144–45; and Eden's secret service, 154,
156, 202; in Parliament, 160; rift with
Bancroft, 169, 254–56; and possible
bribe to Deane, 213; death of, 256
Weymouth, Thomas Thynne, Viscount, 55,
59, 66; use of Bancroft's information,
66, 69, 70, 127, 142; aware of Bancroft's
activities, 74; information from
Stormont, 113, 115, 127; leaves office, 151;
poor performance of, 151
Wharton, Francis, 267–68
Wharton, Joseph: business with Bancroft,
117, 118, 190–91; other business, 122; to
America, 123; Lee's charges against
Bancroft, 196–97
Wharton, Samuel: land companies, 33, 43,
216; friend and partner of Bancroft,
90–91, 114, 117–19, 122, 135, 192–93,
208–9, 232; business affairs, 123;
Franklin's trust in, 173
Wilkinson, William, 216, 217, 218
Wilkes, John, 63, 87
Williams, Jonathan, Jr., 87–88, 191, 192
Williams, Thomas, 3, 4
Williamson, Hugh, 72, 74
Wilson, Woodrow, 60
Winckelmann, Johann Joachim, 67